Jack and Jaquelyn

An Adventure in
Evolutionary Intimacy

Jack and Jaquelyn

An Adventure in
Evolutionary Intimacy

Jack Zimmerman Ph.D.
Jaquelyn McCandless M.D.

For information please contact:

Jack Zimmerman
jackmzimmerman@gmail.com

Jaquelyn McCandless
docjbmccandless@yahoo.com

ISBN–13: 978-1493752287
ISBN–10: 1493752286

Gratitude

We gratefully acknowledge the loving support of our children and grandchildren—and all the couples that have been on the journey with us. The circle is growing. . . We also want to thank Margaret Ryan for her expert and insightful editing, Sarah Anderson for the front cover photographs, and Larry Bramble for the book and cover design. We also received meaningful comments and guidance about the manuscript from Mark Gerzon, Linda Sussman, Emilie Conrad, Richard Moss and Aaron Kipnis.

Also by the Authors

Children with Starving Brains: A Medical Treatment Guide for Autism Spectrum Disorder—Fourth Edition
Jaquelyn McCandless
Bramble Books 2009

The Way of Council—Second Edition
Jack Zimmerman (with Virginia Coyle)
Bramble Books, 2009

Flesh and Spirit: The Mystery of Intimate Relationship
Jack Zimmerman and Jaquelyn McCandless
Bramble Books, 1998

About the Authors

Jaquelyn McCandless, M.D., is a board-certified psychiatrist, anti-aging specialist and irreverent explorer of sexual alchemy.

Jack Zimmerman, PhD, is an educational consultant, counselor and intrepid survivor of transformational relationship.

For almost forty years they have been offering a variety of relationship workshops and trainings in the US and abroad—all the while loving and inspiring each other as they explore the inseparability of sexuality and spirituality.

Contents

Prologue

We begin our story at a time when the darkness in the world is deep. Fear and despair are running rampant like a frightened herd of antelope. This is also a time when the indescribable light of compassion is preparing to create a new dawn, as we move into the heart of the evolutionary *Great Turning* that Joanna Macy speaks of so eloquently. My story is about a couple—Jaquelyn and Jack—who sense this *Turning* all around them—profoundly so in their relationship and even in their bodies. Increasingly they feel like they're part of a growing evolutionary community in the midst of a civilization not so slowly going crazy. What of our culture will stay on the path and what will fall by the wayside to become the debris of evolution? In fact, is there a definable path to stay on? Can the spiritual forces that have been stirred by human unconsciousness be transformed into a powerful awakening the likes of which evolution has never seen before? Can a critical mass of humanity co-create the desperately needed *Turning* perhaps in collaboration with a new sense of divinity? And how exactly might that new divinity be described? People are talking about evolution all over the world now, but up until recently it has been seen as a still mysterious process that happens *to* life on the planet. Now perhaps for the first time the possibility exists for evolution to be co-created consciously with humans leading the way. Will such a co-creation actually manifest?

Before we begin to live these questions, you need to know a little more about my connection to Jaquelyn and Jack, who they are, and why I am committed to telling their story. You can think of me as the tangible presence of their relationship and also the witness of their forty-year exploration along the path of intimacy. Now in their early eighties, "J&J," as they like to be called, have chosen me to be the tour guide for their journey. My way of responding to the existential questions I have posed—along with many others—will be to thread together a sequence of stories about J&J's intimacy that I trust will convince you that sexuality and love can join together as inseparable partners in the *Great Turning*. Besides being a witness I have also been a mentor and mirror for J&J's relationship, and so I am well-equipped to be their storyteller. To more deeply capture my identity I suggest you think of me as a *'we,'* part of which consists of all the various voices that make up J&J's individual selves. Beyond that, I am the *we* that has developed from their living together so intensely for many years. That *we* is an entity in itself, a relational being with its own heart and mind and soul—and, yes, even its own (very different) kind of body, as you will see. I have embraced J&J with devout attention for many years and, as a consequence, become a third presence in their life together. So it is not surprising that they refer to me familiarly and anthropomorphically as their *"Third."* I am delighted to be telling their story—the story of a man learning to love a woman who is discovering how to embrace the emerging and mysterious divine feminine in herself that has been hidden, suppressed and violated in so many women for millennia.

As they trudged along the path of relationship, the *we* that I embody increasingly felt, sounded and looked to J&J like an essential part of the evolutionary change the world hungers for now. This growing sense of we is evolving radically for an increasing number of people as the boundaries among humans dissolve. Where one person ends and another begins is certainly not what it used to be. No one can doubt the growing tangible existence of interdependence in a world where the forces of nature, economics, the generation of information and energy, pollution, disease and violence have increasingly and irreversibly transcended personal, cultural and national boundaries.

It is time to *talk story* as the people say in the Islands where Jack and Jaquelyn live now full time. As J&J's Third, I am convinced that sharing stories, particularly relationship stories, is a necessary part

3

of this moment in human evolution. The tradition of storytelling is as old as awareness and now the need for new stories is urgent. New stories lead eventually to a new mythology and, from my perspective, the time is ripe for creating a new mythology quite different from that which has shaped the world during the past five thousand years. For eons humans shared their adventures orally before writing them down. Writing led to scripture. With the development of the written word, the fluidity of what gave humans a sense of life's meaning and what they could call truth began to solidify. Recent history has been shaped to a large extent by long-standing forces in the world battling over whose scripture and gods are the true ones. This battle of right and wrong has grown increasingly insane—and violent—to the point where many people are searching for a new, more embracing mythology on which to base a radically new way of understanding reality. For the new mythology to be sustainable, I believe it has to begin with the intimate sharing of stories and build slowly. I am convinced that intimacy is the ground of evolution now.

So can evolution be co-created consciously in this maelstrom of a world? This Third answers with a humble, respectful and yet firm, "yes." There is really no other choice. Since I trust that relationship itself, particularly intimate relationship, is evolving now in remarkable ways, I offer a story of the intimacy between a pair of lovers as a part of what I see and embrace as the evolution of love. I offer it in trust that this evolution will also transform relationships between humans and the earth, parents and children, friends, co-workers, community members—and even those among cultures, religions, races and nations.

In marriage the traditional vows often end with "... until death do you part." My story is one of a mature marriage in which the vows also include the challenging transition *between* life and death. In this story marriage leads to a consummation of intimacy that takes the couple into a consciousness not often experienced or at least described before the present moment in history. The tales I want to thread together will explore the challenges and untapped possibilities of such a marriage, including a deepening of sexual union, healing through the transformation of erotic energy, living sustainably with nature and other adventures that arise when a couple embrace relationship as a *spiritual* path.

A few years ago Jack had a dream that speaks to this current evolution. Let me pass the story-teller's wand to him for a moment so he can share his night-story, just as he did with Jaquelyn immediately on awakening...

You and I are part of a large gathering of people of all ages and cultures. The mood is electric with the inspiration of a shared vision. The celebration is about the coming of the new era of Eros—of love—which we are anticipating as a tsunami of consciousness.

As this moment approaches, a man in a dark suit dashes through the crowd and disappears. He is one of those who have been battling the change and trying to maintain the status quo in any way they can. We see him and feel the presence of others like him who have infiltrated our group. We know that a last ditch counter-revolution will soon be launched to battle the forces of life-affirming evolution. We are concerned that there will be a new level of suffering as the end game plays out. Nevertheless, the inescapability of it all is self-evident. Evolution will take place whatever it will be...

Time passes and the scene shifts. The battle is over. As I awake in the new world it appears I am living alone at the edge of the city just as the old shaman used to reside at the edge of their tribal villages. I wonder what has happened to Jaquelyn, until I realize she and I have become one being. 'I' do not exist anymore. There is only *we-consciousness*. At first *we* feel alone, which we know is a test of our courage and perseverance. But before long a small group of men and women appear at our doorway. We are delighted, since they are our old friends and former colleagues in the evolutionary movement. They tell us they had been missing us and wondering where we had gone after the wild transition. They talk as if we had all gone through a nuclear winter.

We discuss how the *Great Turning* couldn't be taking place without experiencing the full power of the shadows that dominated a large part of the old culture. Only with this experience would we be able to deal with these lingering forces in the new era.

"I just had a powerful dream," Jack told the still sleeping Jaquelyn, who stirred and turned over to hear what he had to say.

Jaquelyn was soon wide awake. "It's frightening to think we have to live through a period of chaos even more devastating than what is already going on."

"Yes, and the dream calls for humility and courage in what is to come."

"You mean in our writing or in our life?"

"Both. There's no separating them at this point. We don't know whether we're writing our books or they are writing us. What is clear from the dream is that we will be together as a merged being as evolution progresses. We have to find a compelling way to describe how that merging came to pass. There is a lot at stake."

"Why are we living by ourselves at the edge of the city, wondering what has happened?"

"Apart from the association with the shamanic tradition, I suspect that part of the dream speaks to my lingering doubts about how all of us can work together to bring the needed evolutionary changes. Although the dream is telling us there is to be a period of chaos before we can transition into the era of Eros, we do in fact get through it. I'm reminded how men shy away from chaos, while women seem more at home with it. Yet we know from biological systems that there can't be any meaningful change without a chaotic transitional period."

"But chaos is already happening in the world. Does it have to get worse? I think if women took over the reins now, we could avoid a lot of destruction."

"Time in dreams is often elusive, so we don't know if the dream is describing what has already transpired or what is yet to come—or both. Yes, if women took over the reins now, they would be more able to handle whatever chaos remains, because they would be less likely to fight the transition the way men do. The fact that a bunch of our buddies show up at the end of the dream is encouraging. That does seem to bode well for the future."

"And what does all this have to do with how we tell our story?"

"Our message may be a stretch of the imagination for some, so above all, the story has to be real. That means we share only that which we have lived and are still living, including the dark side of it all. The dream deflates any tendency towards arrogance or thinking we really know what's going to happen. We need to avoid sounding like missionaries. There's little room for any of that in the new era. We're both more respectful of those familiar shadows because we've been tempered in the fire of our relationship."

"So that means we're ready to get on with the writing?"

"That means we're ready to start telling the story, side by side. It's our story, in a way that transcends all our deep imprinting of individuality. We've had to work hard to get to this awareness. As long as we live that truth, the narrator of our story will stay the course and fulfill the mission."

◆

J&J have it right. I am ready now to take the storyteller's staff and embark on the journey.

To begin I have to say that Jaquelyn and Jack becoming a couple could be called an "unlikely event." First of all they come from markedly different family, cultural and religious backgrounds. Jaquelyn is a twin and grew up as one of nine children in a small town in Oklahoma that bordered on a Native American reservation. Her father was a devout member of the Pentecostal Church who believed the Bible was literally the word of god. Her mother worked endlessly to take care of a very full house. As part of the dust bowl migration, the family moved to Marysville, a larger town in Central California, when Jaquelyn was a teenager. Despite her popularity with teachers and classmates, and the good grades she earned, there was no family expectation she would continue her education beyond high school. Meanwhile Jack grew up in Manhattan, has only one sibling, could be described superficially as a cultural Jew and was the recipient of the blessings of high expectations, educationally and in virtually every other respect. It is surprising they got together at all and even more surprising that their relationship has been devoted to exploring the depths of intimacy and consciousness.

There are many choices of where to start the story. I could begin at the beginning when they met in 1973 in Los Angeles in connection with the formation of a center devoted to exploring the art of holistic healing those with life-threatening illness, primarily cancer. The adventure at the "Center for Healing Arts" brought together traditional medicine, so-called alternative medicine (Jaquelyn is well-versed in both), depth psychology (Jack in Jungian and Jaquelyn in Freudian methodology) and a wide variety of spiritual streams that were so much a part of the unique awakening that took place in California in the 1960s and 1970s.

Like many relationships that begin in midlife, J&J each came as a package complete with children, professions and a well-established perspective on reality. They met when Jack was forty-two and Jaquelyn, forty-one, each with children from previous marriages. Jaquelyn's three from her second marriage at nineteen were all in their teens, as were Jack's three from his only previous marriage at twenty-three. (Jaquelyn's marriage at eighteen was annulled after nine months.) The two children from Jaquelyn's third marriage, which was ending when she met Jack, were four (Richard) and seven (Elizabeth). These two appear more frequently in our story, primarily because J&J raised them together. However, it is actually one of their thirteen grandchildren, Chelsey, who affects the story most of all.

Chelsey was born autistic in the mid-1990s when the disorder was becoming endemic in America and in many other parts of the world. The challenges of Chelsey's impairment for her mother (Elizabeth), her father (Jim) and their other children drew Jaquelyn and then Jack into deep healing relationships with their granddaughter that led inevitably to profound changes in J&J's life together. For Jaquelyn the focus on Chelsey drew her out of a psychiatric practice with a specialty in anti-aging, returned her to clinical medicine, and soon established her as a leading expert in the treatment of Autism Spectrum Disorder (ASD). This shift also included an ongoing involvement with an innovative community of autism physicians and researchers who called themselves, 'DAN!'—Defeat Autism Now! Even more profoundly Chelsey's plight and Chelsey herself opened Jaquelyn's heart to a new and deeper love. In Jack's case Chelsey inspired an irresistible curiosity and fascination with relationship as a path of healing, which in turn successfully challenged his self-involvement and opened his heart as well.

Richard, the youngest of the eight children appears from time to time in our story. Richard's gift—and also his burden—is to see and reflect the shadows of others in imaginative, dramatic and challenging ways. He is a sort of Peter Pan through a glass darkly, a man of creative spirit, unusual sense of humor and intelligence—and also a man with substantial wounds. As a consequence, he drew J&J into a form of the Oedipal dance that was persistently challenging.

When J&J met, Jack was the headmaster of a secondary independent school in Southern California, an assignment that soon became incompatible with the devotion and time needed to nourish their expanding life together. He left his post in 1975, the same year J&J were married. But education appeared again in a new and radical form three years later during a tenuous period in their early years when Jack had a vision of a primary, middle and high school in which the traditional Native American practice of council played a central role. The school actually manifested in 1980, was called "Heartlight," and lasted long enough—four years—to start a wave of renewal for the council practice that eventually, with the inspiration and collaboration of many others, found its way into public and private schools, communities, families, and J&J's intimate work with couples. The council work started in California, then spread to other parts of the United States and ultimately led to many programs abroad as well. Council plays a ubiquitous role in our story. The four years of the school's existence were challenging and unstable ones for J&J, so its closure because of the huge demands on Jack's time, energy and their finances was a relief to them both.

Intentional community has also played a major role in shaping J&J's path, principally through their involvement with The Ojai Foundation in Ojai, California. Jack became part of the renewal of the Foundation in 1979 when Joan Halifax was invited to take over its leadership and chart a new vision for the community and its stunning forty acres in the upper Ojai Valley. During the ensuing twenty-five years, Jack filled a variety of leadership roles for the foundation, including taking on the role of president for fifteen years after Joan left. Jaquelyn often thought of the foundation as an "institutional mistress" creating a powerful triangle that acted like a burr in the saddle of their relationship. Then with Jaquelyn's plunge into the autism world in 1996, a second triangle arose because of her involvement with DAN! The two-community based triangles led to several years of living somewhat parallel lives that culminated in Jack moving to Phoenix in 2003 for six months to support Chelsey's healing on a daily basis.

The primary story I want to share begins several months after his return from Phoenix, since those recent years of relative maturity reveal the potential of the path of relationship when a couple has been devotedly doing the work long enough to be blessed by the grace of relational consciousness. I want to focus mainly on this mature part of the story because it embraces and supports the evolutionary vision that is so sorely needed now.

But what of the first twenty-five years and all the struggles to seed, cultivate and prepare for the harvest in maturity?

The shadows during this period were formidable—J&J barely managed to survive on a few occasions. I want to touch on that part of the story first, since it is a more familiar tale of power struggles and boundary issues, sexual awakening, step-parenting, the effects of workaholism, triangles with other people and communities, the endless learning about how to be vulnerable and still survive, the search for integrity and more. Even describing those earlier years briefly will help you get to know J&J and to see that the path they traveled is available to a lot more people than might be imagined. We call this brief journey through the earlier years "Reminiscing."

1 ✍ Reminiscing

J&J are in a mood to reminisce now, in part because they have been preparing to tell their story for a long time. Even during their shaky beginnings they knew intuitively that they were accountable to a presence beyond themselves and their loved ones, a presence that was more personal than the familiar associations with god or spirit, yet still elusive and mysterious. I have to confess that I had been tracking them from afar long before they recognized they had a "Third." It takes a while for that kind of awareness to settle into a couple, as you will discover shortly, sometimes as long as a lifetime—if then.

Currently in their early eighties, J&J's recent dialogues have naturally gone back to earlier years as they try to further illuminate the complexities of their long journey together. Needless to say, I listen in. In fact, they always invite me to join their councils, even putting down a special pillow for me when they sit down to do their practice. Let's tune in to one of these dialogues. I'll weave in a few explanatory comments to round out their discussion. Don't worry about the details at this juncture. The picture will become clearer as the story unfolds.

Jaquelyn is describing an experience she had at the youth center in Honoka'a, the town on the Big Island of Hawaii where J&J live currently. Jack has been involved at the center for years, but this was the first time Jaquelyn participated directly with the youth by being a special guest for one of the monthly "girls' nights."

"When I met with the girls yesterday, a bright nine year-old asked me what I was like when I was young. The story that arose immediately had to do with my four years as the head drum majorette at Marysville High School in California. I had learned how to twirl a baton in Oklahoma—and I was a natural. I could twirl it under my legs and behind my back, and toss it high in the air. Within a few days of starting ninth grade in Marysville, they discovered my talent and had me teaching a bunch of other girls how to twirl—and prance. I loved prancing in front of the band, marching down the football field at half time in my high white boots and very short skirt. Even though I didn't see myself as beautiful, I knew my legs were attractive because of all the attention they got even at fourteen. No one was in front of me! I twirled and I pranced and people cheered."

"You're still a prancer—an erotic prancer! When we make love, you prance and twirl my baton."

The sudden smile that lit up Jaquelyn's face revealed the familiar paradoxical mixture of ageless innocence and a woman who knows sexuality in every cell of her body. "I never thought about a baton as phallic before, but, of course, it's true. I know exactly how to handle your baton."

He laughed. "Yes, in every way."

"I told the girls all the tricks I knew about twirling, like how I twirled between my legs and behind my back. When I tossed it up in the air, I had to bend my head all the way back to reach up and catch the baton again. I have to say I was a great teacher. Everyone was blown away by my skill. A few years later I won second prize in baton twirling at the California state competition in Sacramento."

"Wow—in the whole state? That's incredible. Your body was supple and you had those white boots."

"And I could turn flips and do hand-springs—flip, flip flip!"

"As you still can in your eighties."

"I probably could. I don't know."

"No, I meant sexually," Jack explained. "You take our erotic energy and turn it into a prance—and now I realize that was exactly what you were doing in my dream the night after we sent the book manuscript off to Margaret for editing. In the dream I was watching a celebration of the emerging divine feminine in the world and having a great time."

"Sounds good to me!" Jaquelyn exclaimed.

"Then you suddenly appeared—prancing across the room, lithe as a dancer and lean, as you are now. Your head was thrown back and your body was arched in a beautiful way, as you pranced out of the room—just like you did at Marysville High. Prancing is the only word for it."

"Five boys asked me to the Junior Prom. I picked the one I wanted and told the other four to ask my friends—Rita, Kathleen, Janice and Barbara. Two of them actually did."

"You were running the show," Jack acknowledged.

"I also had some terrific teachers who took an interest in me. One told me something life-changing. He said: *"Jackie* is a chorus girl's name. You're going to be a professional woman. I want you to use *Jaquelyn."* I hardly even knew that my name was Jaquelyn; everyone called me Jackie-Belle. That teacher was one of many blessings. In medical school the dean mentored me personally because I had three little kids and they were wondering how in the hell was I going to do all the work with two-, three- and four- year-olds at home."

"By having a very devoted husband."

"Yes, Herb was great . . ."

Let me explain. Jack is the fourth—and the last—of Jaquelyn's husbands. Herb McCandless, the second, was a successful engineer and the father of her first three children. The fact that she continued to use Herb's name as her professional identity honors his loving devotion to support her through the rigors of medical school.

"By the way," Jaquelyn continued, *"prancing* is not quite *strutting.* Prancing has an artistic quality to it. Strutting is sort of pushy, like showing off, but prancing is an art. You have to know how to do it."

"Looking back, it's clear you were still prancing when we got married," Jack observed. "In those early days you were out in front, guiding me, leading the band. That's also how you were when you plunged into DAN! and the whole autistic community many years later."

Jaquelyn's involvement in DAN!'s core group of autism treatment professionals led to her attending many conferences all over the country and making presentations in front of large audiences.

"Did I really dance with the DAN! group?" Jaquelyn wondered.

"Yes, you pranced in that circle, despite the fear of speaking at large conferences," Jack answered with a smile. "The baton twirler can't show too much vulnerability."

"Not when you're out on the field in front of so many people."

"I didn't prance when I was young," Jack offered in a quiet voice.

"Or strut?"

"Or strut. The way I first learned to prance was by being your lover."

"How about when you were playing football in high school?"

"I was scared shitless, although I played pretty well. I faced my fear of being hurt—there were no nose guards in those days—but the bonding among the team members was worth it all. I discovered erotic prancing with you, starting with the first day of the group."

"The group?"

"The weekly therapy group where we met—the one you and Bill led. Your prancing was totally formidable to me."

"How did I prance?" Jaquelyn wanted to know.

"You said to the men in the group, 'Imagine having a sexual weekend with me in Santa Barbara and then tell us all what comes up for you.'"

"That was kind of nervy of me, wasn't it?" Jaquelyn said in her innocent voice.

"Yes, very prancy—on the edge of strutty." They both laughed.

"I didn't plan it that way," Jaquelyn protested playfully.

"You didn't *plan* anything—and still don't," Jack said with a big smile. "The inspiration just comes. I was so intimidated in the group that I didn't see your vulnerability at all."

"Did you really know how sexual I was in the group?" Jaquelyn asked, again in that innocent voice.

"Are you kidding? Asking the men to imagine being with you sexually was only part of it. We talked about sex a lot and I always knew where you stood, particularly as I became aware that you were interested in me. Then, after the group, when we started our journey together, I suddenly found myself with the prancing goddess. It was like I had died and gone to heaven. I was a loose cannon. We had a lot of mother–son stuff to work on too."

Because Jack's sexual experience was limited, compared with Jaquelyn's, he felt more like a son than a lover in those early years. That mother–son pattern was amplified by Jaquelyn's fierce "mother bear" feelings for her children, particularly the two younger ones whom they ended up raising together.

"What I disliked the most about you in those days," Jaquelyn remembered, "was how you catered to young needy women—what you called your *anima figures*. Believe it or not, even after all these years I still don't get what you mean by that. The idea seems so abstract."

"I'll try again." Jack took a moment to gather his thoughts. "Every man carries an inner image of the feminine that sits in his psyche like a transparent slide that shapes—usually unconsciously—how he relates, particularly to women. This inner image can be projected onto any women who resembles it sufficiently—with a variety of results, including that the man falls head over heels in love. In any event this inner image affects his whole range of feelings about love and sexuality, and usually evolves very slowly over time."

"This image is a picture of what a man desires in a woman," Jaquelyn offered.

"Yes and when he projects her onto someone, the woman becomes bigger than life."

"The real woman reminds him of this inner image and so it stirs him deeply," Jaquelyn wanted to be clear.

"Exactly! He sees something in a woman that stirs him profoundly, because he has discovered a piece of himself *outside his body*. The feelings can be very compelling and lead to all kinds of weird and often obsessive behavior. This deep sense of the feminine is much more than a physical image, although beauty, figure, and hair are certainly a part of it. For me the feminine image had to be different from my mother so I could fall in love without the incest taboo being activated. That's why, when you and I met, my anima was that of a young, beautiful, elusive, and wanting-to-be-cared-for woman—as you noted. That was the opposite of my mother. Rosa fit my inner image extremely well, so the impact of my projection was very real and compelling. I was obsessed with Rosa when you and I met. She was interested in a loving friendship but not intimacy."

"I wanted you to love a *woman*, not a daughter," Jaquelyn remembered.

"You were almost the opposite of my anima— powerful prancer, sexual priestess and mother, all rolled into one. I had to completely overhaul my sense of the inner feminine to be your lover. Putting it mildly, I struggled with integrity in those early years."

"Tell me about it!" Jaquelyn could still feel the pain. "I would have left you when you went to Greece with Rosa if it weren't for the kids. That was four years into our marriage. I got down to 112 pounds because I couldn't eat. I was devastated and depressed and wondered if I should leave. Fortunately, your love for Liz and Richard had grown by then. I would not have stayed if it hadn't been for the kids. It was so painful to feel rejected for a younger woman while I was trying to learn to love you. I hated to see you compromising yourself by wanting to be with a daughter figure."

"I wish I could have seen it that way. My compulsive feelings about Rosa were demeaning for me too. I behaved in absurd ways that I couldn't believe sometimes."

"But you did love the kids and I didn't want to uproot them."

"Trying to connect with Rosa in Greece was a crude way to face my obsession but with her help I finally let go. We parted in Greece after a day, and I went on to visit the birthplace of Gaia in the bowels of a Cretan mountain 200 feet underground! As I began to realize more consciously what had happened, the turnaround started. The love letters I wrote you from Crete were the beginning of a new level of real, objective love for me. My old inner feminine images had to be uprooted and transformed for that to happen."

"Rosa wasn't much of a sister either and took advantage of your projection."

"She wanted company and my affection but not intimacy."

"But she still used you."

"Perhaps, but my projection and behavior were my responsibility." Jack could still feel the anguish of what he had put Jaquelyn through.

"I agree. Looking back, I wonder if you were out to humble me."

"Not consciously, but the drama did help you to discover how much you loved me and also what your limits were. By the way, this is the first time I've heard you say categorically that you would have left if it were not for the kids. That adds a touch of irony to all the trials and tribulations I've had step-parenting Richard. Liz has mostly been a joy."

"You were Liz's true father."

"I was a good father for her. I saw her beauty and even as she grew into an attractive woman, you and I had enough erotic energy between us to keep it all in balance."

"Whether you meant to or not, you humbled me quite a bit in those early years." Jaquelyn had no difficulty recalling the feelings. "I had enjoyed a lifetime of being the star and teacher—and the one who always had lots of boyfriends. You had your strengths too, particularly the power of your mother's love as an only child for seven years until Ann was born. That was the basic inner security that allowed you to love my children. You had learned how to care about people. But before your ego got cleaned up, you did such hurtful things. No man ever gave me a bad time before I met you. They did what I wanted them to do."

"I guess you needed a new experience, as painful as it turned out to be," Jack dared to venture.

"The main thing that kept us together, besides the kids, was the sexual attraction. I felt it from the first. It was uncanny. I didn't know why I was attracted to you. Looking back, I'm grateful that I was smart enough to know how sexual you were, even though that was your greatest insecurity. You're an extremely sexual man."

"After you initiated me sexually, I was like a wild bull in a china shop," Jack recalled. "When I look at it now, it feels like my sense of reality was out of control. I had to create a whole new personality to replace how I had hidden my sexual insecurity—and that changed everything. When a wound is being healed, it's like a previously uninhabited room in one's psychic house has been opened for the first time. There was no cohesive presence in my erotic room, so my thinking there was fuzzy a lot of the time. I had no comfortable place to sit, and there were no curtains on the windows."

In fact the oedipal dynamic had been strong in Jack's family of origin because of the limited sexual connection between his mother and father. Nothing overtly physical actually happened as far as he and his sister knew, but the incestuous energy was there like an underground current. His mother made him feel special, which set up the conditions for an oedipal victory with all its many shadows. Fortunately, she was aware of their mother-son attachment and did her best to keep the triangle with his father in check. But the wound was there, which led to Jack's suffering with premature ejaculation until he met Jaquelyn. His insecurity even affected how he felt about his genitals—they were never large enough for a "real woman." He had a lot to learn.

"Because of my past," Jack continued. "I had to break away from the mother part of you too. That wasn't easy, since you are a rare combination of fierce mother bear and sexual priestess."

"But my older children were like buddies," Jaquelyn recalled. "I was so young when they were born that we sort of grew up together. I took them everywhere, even to the hospitals where I interned. I remember them watching me work in the emergency rooms, wide-eyed, but well behaved. Giving birth to Bruce when I was twenty was a powerful spiritual experience for me. They gave me chloroform and I left my body. In that consciousness I saw him as the Christ child. I was afraid people would think I was crazy so I didn't tell anyone about the experience for many years. My bond with the older kids was strong and they grew up pretty independently. With Elizabeth it was different and beyond anything I had experienced before. There was something about her innocence and need for my support that touched me deeply."

"Yes," Jack agreed. "I remember the challenges when I began to parent Liz. The two of you had a mysterious and profound connection, like you were still tied together umbilically."

"She seemed to live in her own world. I remember we had only been married a year when you asked me to do a ceremony of severing the virtual umbilical cord between Liz and me, so you could be her parent too."

"I had no leverage with her because of how attached you were. She didn't care what I said or did, so we had to change that if I were going to be her step-father. For a long time I tiptoed around your "mother-bearness." All this was going on as you were teaching me how to be your lover. It was confusing and overwhelming at times."

"Obviously there was rebellion in the way you were acting out with several women," Jaquelyn observed, "not to mention that you couldn't turn down a good offer!"

"Ouch—but true," Jack groaned. "I remember you set up a video in our bedroom once and filmed our lovemaking so I could become a better lover. You were the director, literally positioning me and telling me what to do. So I guess I had to rebel. Then, finally, we came to the brink after being married for seven years when I crossed the boundary with Rebecca. That was the closest we've ever come to splitting."

"You never had sex three nights in a row with anyone besides Rebecca. You were on a camping trip with a bunch of kids. Your other excursions were isolated events."

"What I did was extremely hurtful to her—and to you," Jack remembered with a grimace. "I saw my unconsciousness the third night and told Rebecca we had to stop, but the damage was done. Then, two days later, you confronted me in front of Callie, our old psychic friend—"

"—who had seen Rebecca just that morning and heard the whole story. Callie really let you have it," Jaquelyn remembered with some satisfaction.

"Yes, it was very painful. Rebecca was a friend and co-worker. My relationship with her was tangible and real. After realizing the pain I had caused, I knew I couldn't ever do that again. Something burned up in me, sitting there with you and Callie, and I began to embrace a different kind of relationship with you."

"You did help Rebecca leave her limited marriage," Jaquelyn added.

"Yes, but in such a brutal way that she didn't re-enter relationship for several years. She was deeply hurt."

"She flattered you in the way she loved you."

"Yes, my ego was thoroughly involved. She was also unlike you in many ways, just like a few of the men you've been attracted to over the years were very different from me. We both had so much to learn. You also went outside our marriage too."

"There were only two occasions after we were married. If you were going to play around with anima figures, I wasn't going to hang around, so I went off with Morris—a man I knew worshipped me—but he couldn't get it up! Obviously, my sexuality overwhelmed him. The other man—it was about a year later—had an implant and I wanted to experience how that felt. I climaxed but the experience was meaningless. I always thoroughly enjoyed sex, but eventually I realized that I didn't really *know* sexuality until I started loving you. That's the truth of it."

"I was a good student and we learned together," Jack responded. "I was healing my sense of sexual inadequacy by being your lover. As that happened, you began to touch your divine womanhood more deeply."

"Still it was hard for a long time. Several powerful women went after you in the early days. It's terrible how dishonorable women can be with other women."

"That's a painfully dark part of the patriarchy. You weren't too sisterly, yourself, before I met you."

"Yes, I did my share of damage. I would never do that now—out of the question. I love women so much now."

"And you love men too, despite your anti-patriarchal passions. It's quite a paradox. I knew I had a lot to learn from you when we started out, but the prancing goddess doesn't always realize that she has something to learn too."

"True enough. When I blew the whistle marching down the field, everybody had to pay attention and shift the music. But that all got turned around during the Ojai years."

J&J had been married four years in 1979 when Jack became involved with the renewal of the Ojai Foundation's land-based community under Joan Halifax's leadership. He worked closely with Joan in creating the vision for the community's educational program, raised funds for community development, and most of all spearheaded the children's program. The latter included bringing groups of students to the foundation's lovely forty acres in Southern California's upper Ojai Valley. Jack's involvement grew with the community and by the mid-1990s the foundation's rustic facilities (trailers, tipis, yurts, and tents) had matured to include a lovely stucco staff house with three separate apartments, a shared kitchen, and a common living space. In 1995, after living together for twenty years in their adobe home in Calabasas, J&J moved into the staff house at Ojai. It was a challenging time for Jaquelyn.

Jack nodded. "You were a good sport and agreed to live on the land for a while. But community life was not your cup of tea."

"Yes, in part because what was happening for you at the foundation often didn't feel inside our relationship at all. Your deep involvement felt to me like you were with another woman."

"Like many men, I was continually discovering terrain outside my primary relationship that needed to be integrated. Ojai was a good example of that. We struggled and did our best, but when you saw that community living was not for you, you bought a little house in West Hills and that became your base. We both commuted between Ojai and LA—mostly you did."

"It was hard because you had a real role at Ojai—a leadership position," Jaquelyn remembered. "I was more of an outsider. I came up almost every weekend and everyone was nice to me, but I wasn't really part of the community. For a year and a half, while I shuttled back and forth, I participated in the community but I never put down roots. Even though you didn't cross sexual boundaries any longer, you were still quite drawn to several powerful women who were connected with the foundation and they had a strong influence on you. I suppose that was all part of trying to expand your manhood."

"That's a generous way of describing it," Jack responded. "Yes, we had established good sexual boundaries years before that—and our love was growing despite the challenges of living in two places. Then, in 1996, Chelsey was diagnosed with autism and everything changed, particularly for you. You became a medical doctor again and a researcher with a fierce passion to heal all the Chelseys of the world. Before long I was drawn into her healing process too, mostly through relating to her intensely through her autistic veil. By the end of the millennium, you had become part of the leadership of DAN! and identified with the growing community of parents and grandparents of autistic children. As I began to pull away from Ojai at the start of the new millennium, you were moving into a new life of service. You became DAN!'s prancer. You lived a life of healing children and felt empowered in new ways."

"She raised the level of love in both of us." Jaquelyn had a way of speaking the heart of something with only a few words.

"And inspired you to go become a writer. You wrote the autism book in a flurry of passionate research. You knew you had to get it out and you had good support."

"Our love for Chelsey came through the book. That's one reason it sold so well too—over sixty thousand copies in the U.S. alone, plus being translated into four languages."

"You traveled a lot and so we spent weeks and weeks apart every year."

"It's hard for me to believe I could ever have done that," Jaquelyn added, shaking her head.

"It wasn't that long ago," Jack reminded her. "I learned to be alone while you were traveling all over the world. I missed you a lot—and it was also a gift."

"Yes, it helped you become a better writer."

"Looking back I see why our Third calls us an 'unlikely couple.' We had to make it through some tough times to finally show up at the door marked *evolutionary intimacy*. As novitiates we've been very fortunate to be prodded along the path by a guide as patient and understanding as our Third."

2 ❧ More Reminiscing

To complete the introduction to our story, we need to hear a little more from J&J, particularly regarding Jaquelyn's preparations for encountering the vulnerable aspects of the divine feminine that needed to emerge in her. We pick up J&J a few days after the previous conversation and, once again, they're in a reflective mood.

"I got into reading my old journals the other day, including the time when I was pregnant."

"That was another rough time, even though we went through the abortion together."

"Did we ever consider keeping the baby?" Jaquelyn's tone was wistful.

"Not really. We both felt that raising two children and relating to six others was more than enough considering the fullness of our lives. But looking back I wish we had handled it more consciously."

"I remember accusing you of not really trying to help me abort the baby using your skill in working with energy fields. Why couldn't you have done something?"

He could hear the sadness in her voice. "I shudder to think how my self-involvement limited my love in those days, and also gave me the capacity to avoid what I didn't want to see. The shadows were formidable."

"And I was flying high when we met —before your loose boundaries began to strip me of power. You had to knock me off my pedestal to balance our relationship. You did it in the most effective way you could by hitting me where I felt the strongest—in my sexuality."

"You were my sexual mentor and director. When we met I had my kingdom as Headmaster, but you told me I had to choose between that life and our relationship. I made the right choice, but leaving school shifted me from twelve-hour days with a huge list of responsibilities, including teaching three classes, to a suddenly empty work life."

"You became a psychology graduate student," Jaquelyn reminded him.

"Yes, but that was all—and you were running the world."

"Yes, I was used to calling the shots. I had left the three main men in my life before you. No man had ever left me. I felt I outgrew them, or at least intimidated them. It all started with my baton twirling. I was a big fish in a little pond and my emerging sexuality more than compensated for not feeling beautiful. Wendell was the beautiful twin. My uncle, among others, was unconscious enough to actually tell me that."

Jack groaned. "It's amazing how cruel some people can be. Obviously, we both needed to change radically to reach the level of love that has graced us in recent years. Don't forget, you also left me once —and in a most ironic way. We were remembering the other day how in the group you had us fantasize about going to Santa Barbara with you for a sexual weekend. Then two years later you actually left our relationship to go there with Morris. When you left, I descended into purgatory. It was the hardest four days of my life."

"During which—it was 1978—you had the vision of a school where the kids sat in council every morning. That gave birth to "Heartlight," which lasted four years. In turn, that led to the introduction of council sessions in private and then public schools. Now thousands of kids all over the world are sitting in council regularly!" Jaquelyn shook her head in disbelief.

"Yes, it is amazing to think about how that started," Jack agreed. "Our drama became the catalyst for council and eventually to leading relationship intensives too. But first you had to leave your old place of power to face your insecurities and become vulnerable. You had to wake up and discover what the prancing and sexual power had covered over when you were young. The evolving goddess in women is both omnipotent and vulnerable. That paradox is at the core of her nature —and so hard for men to fathom."

"Because men don't understand that there's power in vulnerability," Jaquelyn said, emphasizing the word *power*.

"They feel they're about to be devoured by the fierce, multi-armed Kali and then suddenly the goddess shifts into her vulnerability and is overcome by a river of tears. You cry now about what's happening to women all over the world. I live with an emerging goddess who is possessed viscerally every day by tragic events she reads about on the Internet."

"I feel it in my body, as if it's happening to me."

"I came to understand all that," Jack acknowledged the long process.

"The vulnerability opened my eyes to a larger world. Before that I wasn't paying too much attention to what other people were doing, particularly in distant places."

"Without vulnerability the door to intimacy is at best ajar."

Jaquelyn's smile appreciated his one-liner. "I always made sure that men loved me the most. Every man I was with never stopped loving me, but I couldn't cast that kind of a spell on you. I was disavowed from that kind of power with you right from the beginning—obviously, to keep me from prancing off into the wild blue yonder! I measured men in terms of their overt sexuality in those days. You were an exception, but I'm grateful I saw your potential so clearly. For a woman to be a lover, she has to be sensitive and receptive to the man's sexuality and yet not be overwhelmed by the 'testosteronic' nature of it. Since deep sexuality had yet to be uncovered in you, I could be the initiator and stay in my prancing consciousness. That whetted my appetite. Then you woke up and started relating to all kinds of women. That brought new vulnerability into my life, including an expansion of sensitivity to both love and sexuality. It was a painful expansion of awareness. I even went through a period when I thought the only reason you married me was because I was a doctor."

"Your being a doctor was a delightful bonus that supported our years at the Center for Healing Arts. Having an MD as the medical director gave our healing work authenticity. But from the beginning the magnetic core of our relationship was karmic and erotic. I knew that after the last night of the group you led with Bill when you were so critical of me for all my schmoozing and the way I tried to get everyone to love me. You were right too!"

"Little did I know what was going to happen," Jaquelyn reflected. "I had no idea that I needed to become more sensitive."

"It's clear now how the emerging divine feminine path evolved for you. From the beginning you were empowered in that deeply sexual, inseparable flesh-and-spirit, way we've come to know. You used that power to separate from your father because of his religious fundamentalism. All that gave birth to the prancer. Then, in order for you to become a candidate for embodying the divine feminine, you had to develop new dimensions of sensitivity. That required vulnerability, which in turn meant bringing you down from the prancer pedestal to see if your love was strong enough to transform your ego. I shudder to think how close you came to saying, 'I'm out of here. . . It's too painful' when I was caught in all my shadows with other women."

"Yes, it was my way or the highway until I met you."

"Another thing our relationship taught me is that, as the woman becomes more empowered, one of the man's greatest challenges is to stay awake and not slip into adoration of the emerging goddess in her. Adoration creates a distancing that avoids deeper intimacy and shifts control to the woman. The true goddess-in-relationship cannot be in control; vulnerability is part of her evolution. You ran our life in the beginning, as I went through seven years of boot camp that tested your love. The climax was dramatic. What I put you and Rebecca through created a life-changing need for atonement in me. I can still touch the anguish I felt."

Jaquelyn had a moment of appreciation. "The sensitivity that awoke in me as a result was amazing and gave birth to a whole new level of consciousness . . . and then there's the awakenings that came through our relationships with the children—all eight of them and

Chelsey too. You've spent a lot of energy and time with them all."

"Yes, I've danced deeply with your family—Liz, Richard, and Chelsey, particularly. Until more recently you have been less involved with mine."

"There were fewer of you, so your family doesn't have the feeling of clan like mine does."

"Yes," Jack agreed. "The summer and Christmas Eve parties we had every year were primarily your family's parties. But in recent years it has been balancing out."

"I grew up in a clan—all nine of us kids in a small house. Mom was focused on the more dependent kids, including Wendell. Dad called the dependent ones his 'cross to bear.' He was mean to Wendell. When Wendell wouldn't cry when dad used his belt, he just beat him harder. Finally, Mom would have to say, 'That's enough.' Dad's cruelty came from being jealous of Mom's devotion to the dependent ones. Of course, there were no more beatings after Wendell got polio at fourteen."

"You have a touch of your father's attitude about dependency, although you are drawn to the wounded birds too. Your love is a complex mixture. I'm glad to hear you describe your father so starkly, since you've had a tendency to romanticize him. Each of us has to be entirely realistic about our predominant parent growing up—your father and my mother."

"My father loved my independence—and he loved watching me do flips. He and Mom had such a strong sexual connection that he could enjoy my budding sexuality—until it conflicted with his fundamentalism. Then all hell broke loose, but I was already on the path of prancing."

"Yes, your prancing and independence won out hands down until I showed up. It takes a lot for the prancer —the Amazon queen —to prepare for the divine feminine that's evolving now. After all, what's emerging is a new evolutionary goddess of love!"

"It's been wondrous journey, that's for sure."

Part I

Light and Shadow

3 ❧ Initiation of the Spirit Lovers

Now we turn the clock back ten years from when J&J were reminiscing about the past. Jaquelyn, then 71, and Jack, 72, are still struggling with integrating their busy lives and their intimacy. Jack had recently completed his six month pilgrimage to Phoenix to be with Chelsey. Jaquelyn had been traveling a lot at the time, gathering material for a new edition of her book on the treatment of autism and giving talks at conferences all over the country, as well as abroad. Meanwhile, Jack kept the home fires burning at their condo in the San Fernando Valley, counseling individuals and couples, and continuing a lessening involvement with The Ojai Foundation. During this period, he also spent an increasing amount of time alone at their second home in the northeast part of the Big Island. In those days they shared this simple house with a blue metal roof set in an old macadamia orchard with a few friends who were also lovers of the Islands. The "Blue House" also became a place of healing for Chelsey who gave it that name (because of the blue metal roof) when she began visiting their Big Island retreat during the summers, starting in 1999.

Because of their busyness, being at the Blue House alone or with Chelsey became a special treat for J&J. They struggled with living parallel lives and often acknowledged that, were it not for their consistent capacity for deep and loving sexual communion, the brambles and thorns of their many differences would have been even more of a challenge. Inspired and imaginative sexuality had become their home ground and, as their love deepened, the capacity for creating erotic union blessed them with only rare exceptions. As you have heard, Jaquelyn had a challenging but willing student in Jack. He had a lot to learn, but by that time he was doing whatever he could to further his training as the lover of what they had come to call the emerging goddess in Jaquelyn.

My first story offers a good example. The frustratingly slow pace of Chelsey's healing from her impairment made it clear that she might very well still be unable to lead an independent life by the time it was ready for J&J to make "the crossing," as they had come to call the end of life. This eventuality initiated many councils about how they might continue her healing after they died, an eventuality that was consistent with J&J's ongoing vision that they were in training to be spirit guides as part of their elderhood. They figured, if they could start their training as "spirit lovers" while still in their bodies, they would be able to fulfill the mission of being healers and guides more readily after the crossing.

So how does a couple practice being spirit lovers?

The larger bedroom of the Blue House looks out at the windward side of the Big Island through a set of French doors and a wooden deck. At night the glass doors act like otherworldly mirrors for whatever goes on in the bedroom. J&J had been relishing a few weeks alone on the Island and, as will soon be apparent, the doors' capacity for reflection inspired Jaquelyn in a playful and erotic way. When my story begins, J&J had just worked through a long council and were headed for making love. The time for words had passed.

As he had been learning to do during the past few weeks, Jack began redirecting the stirrings in his loins upward to his heart and throat. This practice was the result of their recent commitment to enter a state of erotic arousal without the familiar rapid plunge into physical contact. The motivation had to do with creating an erotic field for healing at a distance—Chelsey in particular—as well as staying more conscious now that their erotic connection seemed to be intensifying steadily. Within a few seconds his tumescent surge had joined the gratitude that they were together again after his return from Phoenix.

Then, in the silence, Jaquelyn crossed her arms to pull her sweatshirt over her head, accompanied by a hint of a seductive smile and the particular erotic light in her eyes he had known since the beginning. He liked her hair short and how the blond curls reflected the candle light. She looked at least fifteen years younger than seventy-one—-an excellent advertisement for the nutritional and hormonal practices she had been advocating for years. He lingered on the delicate sensitive mouth a while, now slightly open knowing it was being observed. Her mouth never ceased to amaze him. Words of love, groans of passion, confrontations that left him stripped of defenses all passed between those soft tender lips. Kissing them meant setting out on an unknown sensual adventure. Would a teasing appetizer lead to a dance of tongues, like two entranced serpents exploring each other's undulating bodies?

In making the tour of her face, he usually saved her eyes for last. At that moment, their brown seemed lighter and richer than usual, perhaps from the tiny specks of gold that were reflections of the candle light. They were windows to her soul all right, just as the poets said. At different times, when they seemed on fire and he looked deeply, the soul he encountered might be that of the passionate lover or the warrior mother protecting her young or even a goddess like Kali, whose wildness he could not fathom. When that kind of light shown in her eyes, Jack knew he was not looking at Jaquelyn the person. Yes, they were becoming more aware of her empowerment, but even Jaquelyn could not always be sure who was looking at him through those beautiful windows.

Jack wandered past the familiar strong shoulders with just a hint of roundedness, as if embracing the breasts that were usually a little hidden in the clothes she wore. He was always surprised when he saw them unveiled, voluptuous without being large, looking like the sweetest fruit of a divine tree. He knew them intimately and how the lightest touch around the nipples stirred the small circles of devotees to join their already aroused mistress in celebration. How delicate he had to be sometimes! And yet, at other times, the fruit was yearning to be taken boldly, held for another tantalizing moment of appreciation . . . and then devoured. Finally, he scanned the folds of her sweat pants searching for the swell of her hips. For a moment the witness became a ravenous man.

There was no denying the fire but, as far as he knew, the game was still to redirect the energy away from physical expression. At the same time he felt shy—-perhaps it was a touch of fear—-as if he had never seen this wild woman uncovered before. That actually might be true he thought. "Maybe I've never allowed myself to see the full divine woman arising in her until now."

Seeing her breasts in the candlelight left Jack breathless. It had been a while since they had made love. "I've put on a few pounds since we've been here," Jaquelyn said, reading his mind or rather the desire in his eyes. "I want to dance."

"I love your breasts," he managed to say finally.

"I know," she said, "but I have to lose a few pounds or I won't be able to fit into my clothes."

Jaquelyn's practical comment offered a moment to catch his breath. Jack absorbed her beauty and his growing desire slowly, while continuing to shift the focus upward to his heart. Then Jaquelyn stood up and began to take off her sweat pants. Jack arose too, realizing the invitation to dance was literal, not a metaphor.

"I want us to dance," Jaquelyn continued, "and watch our reflections in the doors until they become the dancers and we become the witnesses."

Jack began to take off his clothes, which naturally brought on waves of arousal that threatened his meager capabilities to transmute energy. Jaquelyn looked at the combination of his almost six-foot slender frame and broad shoulders with pleasure. "He brings me a lover's body more and more these days," she thought, appreciating the almost white thinning hair and well-groomed graying beard that for years now had been in her full-time care. The beard created a balanced setting for the prominent nose and soft brown eyes. She had always found it significant that his pubic hair was still a light brown, virtually the same color as the full head of hair he had when they first met. Just the sight of his generous silvery body hair, reflecting the candlelight induced the "warm, fuzzy feeling" she always had when they held each other at night.

When Jack looked up from pulling off his socks, Jaquelyn was standing over him, her long slender legs rising upwards in the candlelight, the perfectly formed thighs disappearing into her gateway to heaven. Her upper body had already begun to move slowly to the strains of silent music. He ran his hands along the outlines of her legs, being careful not to touch them, despite the pull of their powerful magnetism.

By the time Jack matched her slow undulations, they had abandoned their conscious effort to redirect the Eros, trusting that transferring reality to the reflections in the French doors would accomplish the same end. As they began to move, he noticed he was almost fully erect. Jaquelyn felt her nipples grow hard as if he were already caressing them gently.

They danced slowly, looking in their reflections repeatedly, doing their best to shift identity to the images moving in unison only a few feet away, in a different world. Jaquelyn began to stroke the outer energetic boundaries of his phallus, which needed little coaxing to come to full attention. He returned the favor, sensually stroking the field around her breasts until he was sure he could taste the sweetness that filled them.

Their transparent counterparts seemed to be enjoying themselves thoroughly as the human dancers turned up the heat. Jaquelyn moved her pelvis slowly in the field of his erect penis, coming close without touching. Jack responded with undulations and a slow flicking movement.

Jaquelyn groaned. "I'm feeling everything as if we were actually caressing each other with incredible lightness."

Jack's body was aching to be held, so he looked at their images and emptied himself again of expectations and fantasies. The dance began to feel timeless, as reality shifted further to the phantom lovers. Jaquelyn turned her back to him, bent over slightly and moved her buttocks slowly back and forth. He dropped to his knees and imagined his cock elongating until it entered her. She felt her pelvis extending downward to greet him. . . and closed her eyes with an inaudible sigh.

They turned and faced each other. Jaquelyn began to massage her own breasts as if to draw the nectar out. He took hold of his erect phallus and directed it toward her multicolored flower that was now wet and glistening in the flickering light. A final thought passed through his mind. We will surely be making love soon—-and then he realized that "he" was no longer the center of his reality. Their otherworldly partners seemed to be shaping the dance now. No longer the dancers, the physical Jack and Jaquelyn stopped and watched. They were sure that the movement in the glass doors continued—-and gave themselves over to it.

Jack could feel the transformation but he had no sense of where they were headed. So he sat down on the edge of the bed, while Jaquelyn disappeared into the bathroom. When she didn't reappear immediately, he got into bed and waited, no longer showing the previous signs of arousal.

When she returned, Jaquelyn asked, "Shall we make love or just hold each other and sustain the energy?"

The question separated him from their counterparts, which felt like a great loss. They lay in bed a while, side by side, just touching, looking at their now still reflections in the glass doors. After a while, Jaquelyn said in a quiet voice, "What's happening with you?"

"I'm thinking how sweet a piece of chocolate would taste in our mouths right now."

"What a great idea," Jaquelyn purred and he left immediately to fetch the little box of treasures from the freezer. They each ate two passionately. "Here" she said, "Take this third piece and let it dissolve slowly in your mouth. . . while we make love." The last few words were said silently. He never got the message. His passion had shifted into the world of images and spirit lovers. Jack devoured the third chocolate only a little more slowly than the first two.

Jaquelyn felt annoyed. "I told you to let it dissolve slowly, so we could enjoy the sweetness while we kissed and made love. But maybe you're tired of me telling you what to do."

"I'm confused. I thought we were going to bring the energy into the physical when we were dancing, but then we moved it all into the spirit world. You asked whether we should make love or not, as if we were running the show. I don't feel like I have much to say about what's happening."

"Does that upset you?"

"Not really," Jack responded. "But it can be puzzling."

"Why did you wolf down the chocolate? It feels like you lost interest in our experiment."

"The chocolate satisfied me, and I felt a little obsessive about eating it. In any event I'm not as turned on now, for whatever reason."

Jaquelyn sighed. "I guess you displaced your passion into the ghostly lovers—and the chocolate."

"Apparently." They both looked at the glass doors again. The dancers were gone.

"I can handle that," Jaquelyn said softly, without a trace of a smile.

"As we've said, this is all an experiment," Jack reminded her, feeling a little guilty.

"Of course," she replied. "This is all an experiment."

Before they got out of bed the next morning, Jack had an insight about what might have derailed their lovemaking the night before. "We forgot what we came to in our council just before we started dancing. We forgot the teachings we were given."

"You mean about the divine woman and the divine man?"

"Yes. We were told that there would be three steps. You actually brought through the insight after we meditated near the end of the council. The first step is for you to imagine the divine woman while I imagine the divine man."

Jaquelyn remembered. "Then you get initiated by the divine woman and I by the divine man. Then we make love with each other as initiates."

"What happened last night was just the beginning of the first two steps. We were learning to see ourselves as spirit lovers while we were dancing with our images in the glass doors. That initiated a new aspect of the divine woman and divine man. We weren't ready to make love with each other. The third step comes later."

"How much later?"

"That's usually my question!" Jack said with a laugh. "We'll find out when our initiators are ready. In case you forgot, we're not running the show."

"But it's still such an incredible journey!"

By late afternoon of the following day, both of them knew they would make love that evening. Jaquelyn took a long bath, languishing in the large tub and watching the sky turn pink through the large picture window that extended the tub's full length. Nature seemed close, as if she were taking a bath with the clouds that the trade winds were blowing inland from the ocean. Jack wrote most of the afternoon, showered then donned the sleek pajama pants and sweater he wore for their evenings together now.

He found Jaquelyn lying on the bed unclothed, her clean and anointed body reflecting the late afternoon light. Obviously, the council would come after they made love for a change.

"Why did you put clothes on?" she asked with a little smile.

"So I could have the sensual pleasure of taking them off," Jack answered matching her smile and beginning to undress.

They made love in the fading light, as huge banks of clouds flowed pass the house on their way to the crest of Mauna Kea to the west. Like the original couple returning to the Garden, they wandered down every sensual path, gazing at the beauty all around them in a state of almost child-like wonder. There were no thoughts; only images played through their minds that matched the changing beauty outside. Jaquelyn began by massaging the sensitive spot in the small of his back with her feet. That part of Jack's body had always felt especially alive and in that moment it was itching to be touched. He thanked her with a kiss and then another. Each kiss led them to a new part of the Garden more irresistible than the last.

As their minds began to interpenetrate, they spoke of the sense of merging dualities—-Jaquelyn and Jack, male and female, spirit and flesh. When finally she couldn't wait any longer, he entered her—and knew more than ever before what it was to return home. As she felt him slowly filling her, Jaquelyn came into a new knowing of the divine woman that had been visiting her since her youth. When their climax finally arrived, it shattered any illusion that they were separate beings. In that moment, beyond boundaries,

Jaquelyn's song of celebration filled the Garden with new life. The divine pair smiled.

After holding each other for a long time silently, they started talking again, still in bed.

"In the world we just visited, love lives in the flesh of the mind," Jaquelyn began. "What we're being shown brings Eros into the far reaches of the mind."

"Yes, we were divinely embraced," Jack said still smiling. "After these last few years of busyness, we've finally opened enough of a path to find the clearing in the forest."

"Yes, and I have to tell you what I saw while we were making love. What we've been calling the divine woman and the divine man entered us. Perhaps at last the divine pair has chosen us as disciples. It feels like we were just initiated. I saw it clearly. They use our bodies to learn about the physical plane."

"To refine their teachings," Jack interjected playfully. "Deities evolve too!"

"Yes, for almost thirty years this level of spirit has been preparing to enter our flesh and help us with our work. The divine man and woman have touched us before at moments like this, but now they're asking to reside in us."

"We've been through boot camp and now we're being invited to become disciples. A new aspect of our Third was born tonight—a part that somehow shares the flesh of our sexuality. I don't know how else to describe it."

"We've been inseminated—maybe it's the new book," Jaquelyn murmured. "While we were making love, I saw the great mother holding our writings to her breast."

"Tonight was a new kind of mutual initiation," Jack offered. "You envision and initiate, while I recognize you and help you see yourself. But it has to be an initiated man that recognizes the woman for her to believe him. Otherwise she can't see her full divinity and be recognized as the source of life that she embodies. It takes a man who is willing and able to say all that out loud."

Jaquelyn laughed. "You see why I've been pushing so hard to overcome your resistance."

"Yes, you have to keep on being more and more creative to embody the divine woman."

His words yanked her out of their merged state. She turned away from him.

"What's the matter," Jack asked.

"What you just said grounded me hard. You always say I have to be more."

Jack didn't answer for a while. "If you're willing, I think we should look at what just happened head on. It has happened several times recently."

"Haven't I earned your love yet?" Jaquelyn asked.

"I'm just letting you know that you're being met finally. We *both* have to be more creative to entertain the divine pair and keep their attention. You're always challenging me to stretch. But don't misread me. Your artistry is already extraordinary—and, by the way, we're not grounded at all. We're still out there exploring, experimenting."

Jaquelyn smiled. "I love you so much. It's hard to stay mad at you."

"What comes out of my mouth is a mixture of love and unconsciousness. I'm giving it all to you. We're polishing our ability as lovers. You're exquisite and there are times I play hard to get. Having to move away from physical and even energetic sexuality into the further reaches of the spirit world is a challenge for me."

"Is that why you stopped being turned on last night?"

"That's not *why* that happened," Jack responded. "It felt more like I was being asked to slow down and remember the teachings."

"What about the chocolate?"

"The chocolate incident perfectly captures our old sexual dynamic. You give me something tempting and tell me to take it slowly. I gobble it up. It was a brilliant orchestration and a set up. You want me to do what you tell me to do. (*She nodded vigorously, laughing.*) The job of the man—when it is right action for him to obey his goddess—is to do so gracefully with his full power."

"Doesn't that mean having your mind in tune with mine so you'll *know* what I want you to do?" Jaquelyn asked with mock innocence.

"In fact we're both becoming part of a larger integrated mind."

"But we are still going to be distinct. What is really happening is learning how our minds can make love. That's been the tough assignment for a while now."

"Yes and now the ante is up," Jack countered. "The man has to be authentic and playful in the game of minding the woman."

"Why not just surrender?"

"Just? There are always new levels of surrender and always room for more authenticity. Our lovemaking tonight was my first orgasm in a while. I felt like a volcano. Fire poured out of my cock for a long time. I've always wanted to completely surrender my mind and just let whatever is meant to happen, happen. Meanwhile you've been a strong force moving our sexuality away from a primary focus on the physical, all of which seems right. Basically you're the initiator in this transition. You're the muse, I'm just the poet. So you're embodying the goddess and I'm mortal."

"Tonight was an incredible initiation for us," Jaquelyn said, relieved to feel reconnected.

"We're finally in kindergarten. How are we going to live up to our initiation and manifest what we've been given?"

"We've been doing that already in our workshops and with clients. Maybe now we can transmit the message more strongly through the writing."

"You were, in fact, an artist tonight," Jack was glowing now. "The sounds you made and the words you spoke while we made love were incredible. I took them in with the intention they infuse the writing."

"The new book may be at a different level. I inseminate you and you become the mother of the book. We are reversing traditional roles."

"I could feel you preparing in the tub this afternoon."

"Like the Queen of Sheba," Jaquelyn said with a laugh.

"The spot in my back is still hot. It feels like an umbilical cord attaches there that connects with a powerful energy source."

"Could it be the divine feminine?" They both laughed at his inability to escape the still greater surrender that lay ahead.

4 ✎ Descent

Having been together only a few times during the six months Jack spent in Phoenix, J&J took delightful sips of each other's presence in the early summer of 2003—and then spent a whole month with Chelsey at the Blue House. Their willingness to live apart in service to Chelsey's healing had infused their love with a transpersonal quality that would grow in the years to come. Nevertheless, the challenges of living parallel lives persisted and, as with most couples, vestiges of their old unconscious patterns remained like boxes of past life remnants stored in the corners of an overstuffed garage. The feeling that they had conquered a pattern was cause for celebration, which included wondering why it had taken them so long to empty the boxes and recycle their contents. Then, lo and behold, they would find themselves thrown back into the old pattern again, shaking their heads in disbelief.

The next story provides a good example. The time is the fall of 2003 during a month-long separation that followed the summer spent mostly together. Jaquelyn is living in their LA condo, engrossed in her world of treating autistic children, while Jack is snugly ensconced in the Blue House, his much preferred haven when she was busy and traveling. After several weeks of solitary living, Jack felt as if he had been on a personality fast, cleansed of past irritations and judgments of himself and Jaquelyn. New fears and difficulties along the path of relationship were always possible--but not the old ones.

As you will see, that left them vulnerable to discovering yet more unopened boxes in a dark corner of the garage.

They talked on the phone every evening that September after Jack meditated. He prepared carefully for the ritual, showering if he hadn't been swimming that day, and changing into the pajama pants and sweater that lived at the Blue House now. The outfit was almost as old as their relationship.

He arranged the altar carefully as a permanent fixture in their bedroom. The antique music box still housed the whale-ear fossil that they had been using as a talking piece that summer. A Brazilian rain stick lay in front of the powerful koa-wood sculpture of a breaching whale. The pillow representing their Third supported a recent picture of Chelsey. A small decorative bag containing the "healing berries" Jack's daughter, Elissa, had brought back from one of her shamanic trips to the Peruvian jungle and two small bronze statues representing the divine pair completed the altar.

Each night he placed a pillow on the floor at the foot of their bed for himself and another in front of the old rocker, Jaquelyn's usual seat. He always began by winding up the music box that had initiated all their councils with Chelsey that summer, and lighting the candle inside the blue glass dish that made lovely circular shadows on the carpet as the room darkened. He tried to start the meditation promptly at 6:30 in the evening, as discussed with Jaquelyn, so that after its completion forty-five minutes later, there would still be time for a leisurely chat on the phone before she needed to get to bed (it being three hours later in California). Once the candle was lit and the music box lid opened, he took out the whale ear, placed it in front of the music box and settled back on his pillow to meditate.

So it was on a warm evening in early September. The day had been good to him, including an early morning swim in the local pool and several hours of writing. The new brochure from the Ojai Foundation had come in the mail that day with a lovely rose design on the cover. The image touched him because of his long love affair with roses, but what blew him away was the new co-director's letter on the inside cover." It began:

"There are so few places left where one can be a whole human being…"

42

Marlow's words went right to Jack's heart, creating unrestrained admiration for his successor's writing skills that, in turn, led to the pleasure of realizing their final transfer of leadership responsibilities before Jack went to Phoenix was now fully complete. There were no lingering attachments. Marlow's life-partner and his co-director, Leslie, had designed the brochure so imaginatively that he was tempted to call them both that day to express his delight. As he went through the calendar, page by page, looking at the rich offering of programs he found the two couples' intensives he and Jaquelyn were scheduled to lead, one a second level and one a training for experienced couples who wanted to take the work out to others.

Then the annual New Year's retreat caught his eye. The event had become a time of reunion for Jack with his sister, brother-in-law, and nieces and nephews, who lived in and around New York City, as well as in San Diego. Since he saw this part of his clan rarely, celebrating the turning of the year in Ojai had taken on additional importance for him. In years past he and Jaquelyn had co-led the four-day celebration but she had grown weary of the intensity of the ritual and the traditional climactic sweat lodge was definitely not her favorite ceremony. So in the waning years of the old millennium Jaquelyn had opted to stay at their condo in the Valley even if it meant being by herself on New Year's Eve. Although they assured each other it didn't really matter, the implications of being separated at year's end became a painful experience for them both.

These and other shadows around the Foundation receded into the past as the new millennium progressed, although their memory lingered on for Jaquelyn. Yes, he had turned over the directorship to Marlow and Leslie, but he continued to visit the land almost every week to teach or attend meetings, even though for shorter periods of time. A ritual gripe of Jaquelyn's was that their trips to the Island had to be coordinated with his obligations at the foundation.

Jack had just talked with his sister about the New Year's gathering to see if they were planning to come, although what he really wanted to do was to take off for the Island, skip all the craziness of the holidays and be alone with Jaquelyn. That idea had been playing though his mind particularly during the past week because Jaquelyn had also mentioned the possibility of celebrating the holidays alone together at the Blue House — even though that would mean missing the large family gathering on Christmas Eve that meant so much to her, particularly when Chelsey participated.

Jack had told the foundation staff he was open to co-leading the Year-End retreat as usual, but the brochure had listed three other people. His momentary confusion was immediately replaced by a feeling of liberation. He saw the misunderstanding as an omen that meant he was not to be at the foundation for the year's end and in fact was not meant to be in California at all in December. He could hardly wait to tell Jaquelyn that the universe seemed to be supporting their being alone together during the Holidays.

Meanwhile, Jaquelyn's day had not gone well. The news from her daughter, Liz, about Chelsey was bleak, including descriptions of wild behavior, intense orality and tearing pages out of her favorite books. As a result, Liz had dipped into despair and mother and daughter had decided to suspend a lot of the ongoing biomedical treatment program temporarily to see if that had anything to do with the manic streak that had taken over. The more likely cause, however, was Chelsey's adjustment to the new group that she joined at her special school and lingering transition difficulties after her time on the Island. On top of all that Jaquelyn had been battling her computer and felt unprepared for the upcoming talk she was giving at a major conference in Denver. She was not in a good mood when Jack made his call.

"Hi, sweetheart," he began

"Hi darling. How was your day?"

"Good, I got a lot of writing done and even had a swim too."

"Good!" Jaquelyn echoed. "It's very hot here, over a hundred, although I didn't go out at all today."

"It's raining here now, although as usual the day started out lovely. It poured just before I meditated. Did you sit with me this time?"

"I've had too much catching up to do. I just got off the Internet a few minutes before you called. I've been fighting with my computer all day."

"I'm sorry to hear that but it's OK," Jack responded. "I meditated for you. I have some interesting news." He proceeded to tell Jaquelyn about some house improvements he was making. Her response was unenthusiastic —not at all what he had expected. Then he went on to share his excitement about New Year's.

"I got the new foundation brochure in the mail today. Did you get one at the condo? (She had not.) It's beautiful. Marlow's letter is a real gem. I was reading through it and saw that they have three other people listed to do the Year End retreat."

"Did you expect to see your name?"

"Yes, or just as the brochure said last year. I never put my name in officially but I told the office I was open to being there if my family wanted to come. Anyway, my reaction was, hooray! It means we're supposed to come here, like you suggested the other day. We've been talking about being on the Island for the holidays for a long time. Maybe this is the year!"

"Well, I had a long talk with Liz today about all that. I told her we were probably going to Sedona this year at Thanksgiving since we didn't go last year. She said that, if they went to Sedona for the usual family gathering, then they would have to spend Christmas with Jim's side of the family—and that would mean driving to Mission Viejo right after the Christmas Eve party in L.A. 'But Chelsey always gets into trouble down there,' Liz added. So I asked her if we could keep Chelsey here at the condo instead and to my surprise Liz didn't say no."

Jack's body began to contract but he didn't get the signal soon enough to give him proper warning. The vision of avoiding the Christmas frenzy and relishing a long stretch with Jaquelyn alone vanished rapidly. The sense that so much for Jaquelyn revolved around Chelsey rose up in him like an old ghost returning to its long abandoned haunt. He didn't take a breath or wait long enough for his body to tell him what was happening.

"I don't want to plan my life around Liz's difficulties with Chelsey spending time with her in-laws, even though —"

" —No, you just want to plan your life around the Ojai brochure!" Jaquelyn shot back in angry voice. The words and tone caught Jack completely by surprise, stuffing whatever remained of his year-end dream back down his throat. He felt as if he had been hit in the stomach. The intense month with Chelsey that summer and the time alone had left him open and vulnerable. It was only a momentary flash of irritation for Jaquelyn but it took him down. Despair loomed. Their deep devotion to Chelsey's healing was never enough for Jaquelyn. That was all that really mattered to her! The marriage was primarily a vehicle for Chelsey's healing now. In the seconds that he was silent, he tried to break the plunge into petulance. He even knew he was falling and flashed on how that would have seemed impossible just minutes earlier, but even those thoughts were just twigs on the side of the cliff as he plunged downwards.

Frustration told him to hang up. Unfairness told him to blast her inconsistencies. Anger almost brought him to say everything he felt in that moment about her preoccupation with Chelsey. Instead, he put the phone down on the carpet without saying a word. For twenty seconds he was in hell, far more discouraged at the failings of his heart than irritated at Jaquelyn's new arrangement with Liz.

He looked at the phone, now a part of the altar. His heart was pounding. How long would he have to let it lie there before something would break his fall? No voice came out of the phone for what seemed like a long time. Then he heard Jaquelyn start up again, not realizing that she no longer had his ear. He couldn't hear the words, just the muffled voice sounding forlorn from far across the Pacific. He had never hung up on her in more than thirty years. Staying present no matter how angry had always been their commitment. The old shadows laughed diabolically. A dark minute passed slowly.

Then a presence, not really a voice, suggested that he was being a little dramatic. Who was that? Who saw him so clearly on his knees and struggling? Who saw his contracted heart? Asking the questions began to pull him out of the dive. Like a pilot plunging earthward desperately pulling up on the stick, the witness presence slowly gave him some control and finally the strength to counteract the forces of gravity. He picked up the phone after a lifetime of feelings. "I didn't hear a word you said," he began. "I was so upset I put the phone down. I cannot go back into that old place again."

"Does that mean you don't want to listen to what I have to say?" At moments like this Jaquelyn's genius was to be absolutely straightforward. Her anger had subsided. The remark that flew out of her mouth took some of the old bitterness with it. She was mainly tired, very tired and discouraged about Chelsey. She didn't understand why Jack had reacted so strongly. They had been battling about the foundation for years. What was the big deal? "You did say that it was the brochure that gave you permission to go away for Christmas, didn't you?"

"Not exactly."

"Jack Zimmerman, be honest with me. Did you not say that because your name wasn't on the list for New Year's that you were able to miss the program? I heard you distinctly."

"Yes and no. You missed the point and took what I said in an entirely different way. I saw the omission as an omen, not giving me permission. That wasn't the feeling of it at all. I couldn't wait to tell you."

"It will never change. The foundation is your family and that's that. Some things never change. It's better now but it hasn't really changed."

The phrase "take no prisoners" rose in his mind. The familiar sense of unfairness also rose up again but this time he was ready. "Let's take a breath and begin again."

Silence.

"What was your day like?" Jack asked finally. Jaquelyn was ready. "I'm really down about Chelsey. Liz is at her wits end." She told him the details. He listened to the familiar struggles but he was alerted now, bruised but centered. As she went on, he saw how the whole family was welded together by the common desire to heal Chelsey. His heart opened again.

Jack thought of Ignatius of Loyola. The first Jesuit's teaching about desolation and consolation came back to him, as it had many times over the years. "There are natural cycles of desolation and consolation—that is, separation from and connection with the soul or the divine," Ignatius had written more than 450 years ago. The challenge of being enlightened, one could even say mature, is to have the faith that consolation will follow desolation even when one is in the midst of despair. Jack wondered why he couldn't remember that a few minutes earlier, particularly when it had to do with a relatively minor issue. He had shared that teaching with so many people over the years—obviously, because he was still learning it himself, he thought.

They talked for half an hour, about Chelsey's problems and Jaquelyn's stress from treating so many ASD children. They never mentioned holiday plans again but trusted that it would all work out. They ended the phone council as they usually did:

"Good night. I love you.

"Good night sweetheart. I love you too."

Jack ate by himself as he had for so many days, thinking about all three generations of women that he loved so much. He acknowledged how Jaquelyn, Liz and Chelsey were all in a state of overwhelm right now, each in their own way. Somehow his job was to help balance that. He was OK with the assignment, humbled by his fall, but OK now. At least, the recovery period had been shorter. That was a good sign.

5 ❧ The Goddess at the Beach

Another one of J&J's ongoing challenges was their attachment to the powerful sexual bond between them —the tie that was essential to surviving the early unstable times and which continued to be at the frontier of their learning about love, consciousness and "other worlds," to use Jaquelyn's words. She knew in her woman's heart that they had to rely less on that which they both cherished. For years, even as she initiated Jack into deeper erotic intimacy, she often urged him to let go what she saw as his attachment to the physical nature of their passion so they had the choice to move beyond that level of joy into a more "imaginal erotic consciousness"—another favorite phrase of Jaquelyn's.

Not surprisingly, Jack saw their sexual dance in a somewhat different light. From his point of view, it was their lovemaking itself that consistently, powerfully—and paradoxically—moved them into that more spiritual world that she was so keen to explore. Jaquelyn was convinced, however, that no matter how extraordinary the state of consciousness of their lovemaking, it was still rooted in the physical world and, as she said more than once, "we can't take that kind of physicality with us." In fact, Jaquelyn envisioned learning to make love in a way that would survive the passage through the veil, and she sensed that attachment to the physical joys of lovemaking were in the way of accomplishing that.

Furthermore, Jaquelyn's emerging goddess-self knew they could not enter the elusive level of erotized spiritual healing they envisioned, not to mention becoming spirit lovers, until they understood the mysterious nature of their sexual connection more clearly. That required full consciousness in the midst of ecstasy. Although Jack was making slow progress along that path, the level of presence it required felt like trying to control a herd of horses let out of the barn in springtime. Despite the challenges, Jack was game and ready to explore his sexual nature when Jaquelyn called. So the dance continued . . .

This leads me to the next story which also highlights the importance of dream-sharing in illuminating J&J's path of awakening.

On a cloudy and windy evening in late January, 2004, Jack read several "rushes" from his writing out loud to Jaquelyn. One piece they had worked on together particularly delighted her, which left him feeling elated and a little pleased with himself.

Jaquelyn seized the moment to make her point once again. "You see how creative you can be, when we collaborate and let the energy build without falling right into making love?"

Jack got the message and responded playfully: "You have a one-track mind and I know why!"

"Why?" Jaquelyn asked coyly.

"Because you, yourself, are so profoundly attached to making love that you have to counteract that passion with an equally devout desire to transcend physical sexuality."

Jack's teasing tempted her to reward them both for their several days of restraint during which they had been debating their attachment vigorously, but she feared a rush of passion might overwhelm the creative flow he had finally established in his writing. Instead she laughed and invited him to lie down and just hold her. Tiredness replaced temptation and they soon fell asleep in each other's arms fully clothed.

They awoke after midnight, groggy and cold, got ready for bed and slept for several more hours until Jack woke up again, this time from a vivid dream. As was their practice, he shared it immediately.

You and I are at the edge of the ocean, reclining comfortably in beach chairs in our bathing suits when I become aware that a woman is standing just a few feet away, looking down at us. Her hastily tied back blonde hair frames an amazingly beautiful mature face that belongs to a woman in mid-life. Even her few wrinkles are lovely. Equally striking is her voluptuous, well-formed body that looks like that of a woman many years younger. Her ample breasts are hardly covered by a bikini and, as I let my eyes move down her body slowly, I realize, except for the skimpy top, she is completely nude.

The look on the woman's face is a strange mixture of desire, need and other-worldliness. Her large dark-brown eyes plead with us to release her from a profound erotic spell. As I meet her gaze, I feel a mixture of primitive arousal and discomfort. It is clear that she has chosen us to participate in an erotic healing ceremony without concerns for privacy but I am unclear about what to do. I don't want to dishonor the invitation and, in fact, I am strangely drawn to her outrageous lack of inhibition. Still, I am not sure what my role is to be. So I turn to you for guidance. Our eyes meet for a second and I see the goddess shining through you, asking us to fully honor this woman as a manifestation of the divine feminine that needs to be released from the repressions of the patriarchy. She has been searching for a couple on the path to support her liberation. We surrender to the ceremony.

Moving in slow motion, we both let our fingers touch the primary energy centers in her upper body, starting with her Third Eye. Transmitting energy feels like an appropriate way of conducting the healing while maintaining respectful boundaries. Her body shudders with pleasure, as she feels the energy flowing through our hands. Clearly, this wild woman is extremely sensitive. Her eyes open wider as I move down to her throat, while you let your hand rest lightly on her chest in between her breasts. I am beyond ordinary emotion now, performing my part of the ritual, without any sense of being separate from you. I am at one with both forms of the goddess —my beloved beside me and the ecstatic stranger we are helping to heal. Finally, you and I let our hands drop and gently kiss as the dream ends . . . All this happened just a moment ago.

"Your body is still buzzing," was all Jaquelyn could say at first. They both remained silent for a while, still holding each other gently.

"Well, what do you think?" Jack asked finally.

"Did the woman remind you of anyone?"

"Not any person I know, although she is obviously representative of your desire to help heal women from thousands of years of sexual suppression."

"Since she had a few wrinkles, it can't be me!" Jaquelyn quipped.

"Of course!" (laughter)

"I think the dream is a rite of passage," Jaquelyn continued, "mostly to help you support the empowerment of women without any attachment to your personal pleasure. It's what we were talking about just before we fell asleep."

"Yes, in the dream the healing takes place beyond personal patterns —and we do it together. She could have asked me to actually make love with her, but she needed something beyond that from both of us."

"She wanted you to serve the goddess selflessly. It was like a test. Your pleasure is to please the goddess now. That's what men have to learn to do. Women have been seduced, cajoled and forced into serving men and male deities for millennia. Now all women on the path of intimacy need to teach their man to please them as lovers. The dream is right on. You are being asked to help the divine feminine be manifest in all women."

"The dream is clear!" Jack exclaimed.

"Why does the woman come to us rather than another couple at the beach?" Jaquelyn asked.

"It's not explicit in the dream but it seems obvious that she knows you're on the path of manifesting the divine feminine and I'm learning to serve the goddess. Men have so much to learn but also every woman on the path has to learn how to fully accept the loving service of her divine man. That level of devotion may take some getting used to for women."

"Try me!"

"I have, for almost thirty years, although I must admit my skills are only now getting close to meeting the challenge."

"It's not your skills; it's your heart—and your courage—that need improvement," Jaquelyn countered.

"You mean in facing the full power of your emerging goddess-ness?"

"Yes, and to celebrate the physical love we share and serve the awakening of the divine feminine at the same time. That's why we need to go beyond attachment to the physical. Is that too much to ask?" Jaquelyn's tone was both innocent and forceful.

"Whether it is or not, that's what you're asking. In the dream the woman's wildness is the part of the goddess that wants to be embraced now. I know that part of you, sexually and in other ways. So there can be further healing of the divine feminine every time we make love."

"That's why it is so important that you stay conscious no matter what I do."

Jack was ready. "It's a tall order and in this moment I affirm that intention. It may take a while for my body to catch up but—"

"May I remind you that it's not your body that is resisting. It's your mind, your patterned mind that needs transforming."

"Ah, the mind that never forgets."

"Yes, just like an elephant's!"

They both laughed and got up to make the bed.

Part II

Initiation

6 ✲ Gulch Bardo

So what does it take to transform a patterned mind? Jack's initiatory dream made it clear that Jaquelyn and he were being invited to shed old patterns and move along their path more rapidly. A breakthrough was in the wind, one that would likely require access to Jack's wilder parts, perhaps those he didn't even know existed. But for you to fully appreciate what happened next, I need to first describe J&J's relationship to the Islands and how they ended up at the "Blue House" in the first place.

In 1989 Jaquelyn visited the Big Island's south shore to do a solo meditation retreat after the suicide of her twin brother, Wendell. The pain and medical complications of his wheel-chair life due to polio had finally been more than he could bear. Jaquelyn was empathetic, nonjudgmental—and heartbroken. Jack joined her on the Island after a few weeks. They stayed in a rental that was not far from the ongoing lava flows originating from Mauna Loa's new Kilauea fissure, and so became acquainted with the goddess Pele's volcanic nature up close. In fact, the house they stayed in and the black sand beach they visited frequently during the retreat were completely destroyed by a major lava flow a few years later. Jaquelyn identified with this fiery power of the feminine that she knew intuitively but hadn't named yet. For Jack, Pele represented a wild and possibly destructive part of nature that was intriguing but unfamiliar to him. Growing up in New York City, walking its streets to school and celebrating its parks literally as oases of playfulness, created an early longing for such wildness.

Over the next few years, J&J's connection with the Island deepened, and they began searching for a place there where they could spend more time as their life simplified and elderhood approached. Jack soon got over his surprise that they were headed for a Hawaiian sunset and Jaquelyn was delighted with the prospect of slowing down in a tropical environment. After several years of viewing properties beyond their means, a close friend found a bargain parcel in the sparsely populated Hamakua District near the small town of Honoka'a. Andrew invited them to participate in his investment, and J&J plunged into the shared adventure.

Although a part of the land had been host to a macadamia orchard years before, large portions remained in their ancient riparian state, particularly the stretch along the *Honokaia Gulch,* which formed the property's eastern boundary. The land was accessible only by means of an old but paved "Cane Haul Road" that became impassible about a mile beyond the property. The house—with its blue metal roof—was only a few years old at the time of Andrew's purchase, but it had not been lived in for months and was in serious need of tender loving care. The forty-two acres also needed a lot of maintenance because of the lush Hawaiian environment. Since J&J would be off-island most of the time at first, a caretaker family was needed who could do the ongoing work of mowing and fence building to keep out the feral pigs, as well as cutting up the limbs of the large eucalyptus windbreaks that often fell after a storm and blocked the driveway. So Seppe, Mikki, and their three children moved in a month after the purchase and before long had built a simple cabin augmented by an old camper kitchen that became their rustic paradise. They lived an indigenous life, eating out of their garden and riding their horses through the local meadows and forest lands.

J&J saw themselves as stewards more than partial owners of the property because of the raw beauty of the land and their sense from the very beginning that something sacred had or would happen there. The gulch particularly captured their attention. Its steep slopes, varying between fifty and eighty feet apart, formed the drainage channel for hundreds of acres of local meadowlands and native forest. The gulch ran full after heavy rains, creating several pristine swimming holes for nature devotees. Much of the time, however, only a modest stream ran through the boulders, ferns, and wild ginger, eventually flowing through a large culvert under the Cane Haul Road just 150 feet east of their front gate. From there the water ran down towards the ocean, some two miles away.

There is a distinctly primal flavor to the wetter and relatively unpopulated parts of the Big Island that lie along its northeastern shore and then *"mauka"*—inland, towards the majestic slopes of Mauna Kea. The weather is changeable, literally minute to minute some days. Nature is still mostly feral in this portion of the Island where the old cultures were prominent and the *kahuna* practiced their ancient shamanic arts. Feral pigs live in the wide open spaces between a few clusters of simple homes and small farms. The region abounds with dense forests and the undulating meadows that for years supported the large sugar plantations and are now planted in harvestable eucalyptus. Seeing a pair of *i'o* (Hawaiian wild hawks) riding the complex air currents is an occasional treat, while glimpses of white owls and multi-colored tropical birds are more rare. Egrets share the pastures symbiotically with naturally fed cattle enjoying what must be a cow's Garden of Eden.

This kind of natural beauty changes people. One can feel a tangible connection between the land and the residents who have lived in this rural part of the Island for generations. Clusters of banana trees and macadamia orchards abound, and the traditional muddy *lo'i* patches that produce taro for *poi* and other traditional dishes are still tended as they have been for generations. After a while, the rhythms of the land slow down most people, and those in touch with the magic soon surrender to the indigenous needs of human biology, particularly the kind of slowed-down sensuality that is becoming rarer on the mainlands of contemporary culture. For those who allow the land, the winds, the ocean, and Pele's volcanic fires to infuse their lovers' bodies, sexuality takes on a distinctive feral quality. It is perhaps only a gentle exaggeration to say that the languid life of the Island can easily become foreplay for inspired intimacy.

In the early spring of 2004 Jaquelyn was still heavily involved with the world-wide autism community. She had been invited to give several talks, including one at a major conference in Washington, D.C. that had both a medical and political focus. It was a particularly important meeting, so, when Jack suggested she sneak away to the Island for a few weeks to prepare for her trip, she readily agreed. Getting out of Los Angeles for almost a month was appealing to both of them—at least until they found themselves drenched by the Island's rainiest March in decades. It rained a little every day, and some days a lot more. Eventually the Island's porous volcanic soil became soaked, creating large pools of water along the roads and in the meadows.

As the day for Jaquelyn's departure grew closer, there was no let up in the rain. She was eager to leave and get the presentations over with; Jack was ready for some alone time for writing. The plane to L.A. left Kona in the late afternoon, and, with the weather being what it was, they decided to leave the Blue House at noon. The rain increased in intensity through the morning hours. By the time they stuffed her two large suitcases and computer in their small Toyota Tercel and headed down the driveway, it was coming down in buckets.

The first shift in their sense of reality began as Jaquelyn got back into the car, her raincoat soaked through from just opening and closing the gate. Jack failed to notice the specks of blood on her fingernails from scraping away the mud and rocks that had piled up against the metal frame. He looked down the Cane Haul Road in amazement to where the rushing waters of the gulch were now cascading over the low lava rock walls that marked the bridge. The water hit the *mauka* wall like surf on a steep shore, spraying great plumes of water high into the air, sweeping across the short section of road that covered the large culvert, and hitting the wall on the *makai* (ocean) side of the road, creating a second plume. The surges came every four or five seconds in steady pulses. J&J found out later that more than eight inches of rain had fallen in just the two hours before they had left the house. The culvert, large enough to walk through without stooping, was overwhelmed by the deluge, forcing the water to sweep over the road relentlessly on its way to the ocean.

There was only one way out—over the bridge. Jack drove the old Tercel slowly towards the rushing water, as Jaquelyn released her seat belt to take off the wet raincoat. When he stopped and looked at the flooded bridge with wonder, his sense of reality began to shift further. The desire to get Jaquelyn to the airport joined with a reckless urge he didn't recognize.

"Why don't we call Seppe and see if he'd be willing to pull us through with the tractor," Jaquelyn said anxiously, also wanting to get to the airport.

"He'd never bring the new tractor out in this downpour," Jack answered definitively. "That's not a possibility. We'll never make it back up the driveway. Let's go for it!"

There was an eternal pause . . . Even years later, they would replay this moment with wonder. Jaquelyn braced herself, realized that she had never put her seat belt back on and instead grabbed the handle above the passenger door. She let silence be her answer. Jack abandoned what was left of his cautious self, gunned the Tercel, and plowed into the water.

A towering wave hit the front of the car, swept it against the near edge of the *makai* wall, spun them around and carried them down into the gulch rear-first like an insignificant piece of driftwood. Jaquelyn clutched the handle and surrendered to the deafening roar of the water. Jack held on to the wheel absurdly, as if he still had control of the car.

"Oh, sweetheart. I'm so sorry!!" he shouted as they dropped several feet, hit a large boulder and spun around.

"We're together all the way, darling!" Jaquelyn called out over the roar and felt herself shift into a witness state. They hit more boulders below the bridge, bounced up into the powerful current and turned over. The cacophony of metal crunching against the rocks and the relentless power of the water drowned out any further words.

"We're crazy," flashed through Jaquelyn's mind mixed with admiration for Jack's wildness. In that instant she realized—without emotion—that death could happen *just like that*. They were together; that's all that mattered. She had no idea how strong their connection would be at such a moment and now she knew. She felt them as a single entity, a unified being.

Jack had shifted partially out of his body as well, strangely relaxed and out of control at the same time. They stayed aware of each other even in the detached state. The water would have its way; they would have to ride it out. The car careened down the western edge of the gorge, slammed into a huge boulder, rolled over completely again and landed in deep water on its side.

They were motionless for a few seconds until Jaquelyn shouted, "The water's rising. I'm going under. Help me!" She saw Jack above her, hanging from his seat belt as the water level rose above her chin. He realized he had closed his eyes several seconds before, just after they had plunged off the road. Now that they were open, he could see Jaquelyn's face just above the turbulence.

"Keep your head above water until I get out of this seat belt," Jack shouted. "It's jammed!"

"Hurry," Jaquelyn shouted back, feeling fear for the first time. A cold dread clutched her chest at the thought of suffocating. Images of drowning people flooded her—it seemed like all the people who had ever drowned, she said later in telling the story. Drowning was the nightmare way to go, but we are together, she thought. The pulse of fear left and before another could overtake her, a huge wave hit the car and rolled them over twice more. She held on to the handle like a bronco rider. The dread of drowning vanished into a still witness state. She wondered how it would all end. There was another crunch, another wave hit, and then suddenly they slammed up against something that held them against the pulsing waves. The driver's door was face down in the water and the roof of the little hatchback was jammed up against what appeared to be a tree.

The ride from the bridge had taken less than a minute, an eternal minute played out in counterpoint with their amazement at what was happening. They couldn't have just plowed into the water in that suicidal way. It wasn't possible! The bottom of the car now faced the roaring flood, creating rhythmic sprays above them and shielding them from the rocks being swept down the gorge. Apparently the ride was at least temporarily over. The roar was deafening, but their heads were only inches apart. "Are you alright?" Jack asked.

"I think so," Jaquelyn said simply. "Are you?"

"Yes, I think so. I can't believe I did that."

"*We* did it," Jaquelyn reminded him. "We both decided to do it. Now we're here." He felt a surge of love that matched the water. "But you're crushing me," she said a little louder. "Move, if you can."

Jack stirred from his altered state and realized he was still in his seatbelt and pressing a good part of his weight against her left side. "I can't get this seatbelt off," he stammered, jabbing at it with his left hand. His right hand had blood all over it. After what seemed an eternity, Jack managed to get the belt off and shift his body. He was sitting with his feet in water on top of Jaquelyn's huge suitcase that had been tossed into the front of the little hatchback. They rearranged themselves gingerly, so as not to dislodge the car from its perch.

As the waves and rocks continued to hit the car, they took stock. There was water swirling around their feet. Through the top of the driver's window they could see the water slowly eroding the soil around the roots of the tree that was holding the car. They seemed to be on a rocky rise that was covered by a foot of muddy turbulence. Just beyond the tree the gulch dropped away precipitously. The front windshield was completely smashed but amazingly still intact. Beyond it they could see the main part of the gulch, now a fifty-foot-wide hungry water monster gobbling up rocks as it cascaded downward towards the ocean. Out the rear window they saw a narrower torrent adding its voice to the deluge. They were surrounded by wild water. The rain was still coming down at a furious rate. Obviously, the tree was essential to their survival.

In that moment Jaquelyn had never loved a child of nature as much as she loved that tree and the tiny patch of ground that held its roots. "Let's pray that the rain stops and the tree holds," she said returning to the traditions of her childhood. She had a flash of her father's tall frame kneeling by his bedside every night, praying to

Jesus like a child. Jaquelyn prayed, her eyes on the base of the tree and the swirling water. She was at peace being with Jack. If they were at the end of their path, they would at least go together.

Jack's prayer led him quickly to an assessment of Jaquelyn's condition. She was soaked through and through. The hair she fussed over just moments before leaving the house was drenched and plastered to her head. Her eyes were shining with the innocence of a child, as she sat in lotus position amidst the debris and water. Seeing her that way propelled him through a doorway—into a new experience of love. It wasn't that he felt how much he loved this beautiful woman inviting him to pray. She wasn't so much the object of his love as the source of it. He had no thoughts of how this might turn out or whether he should be planning a rapid escape from the car. No manly courage arose in him. There was just love. The roar of the water was love; the car was a beloved; the tree was a savior. The whole scene was love. He reached out his hand and started to caress her face.

"Careful!" Jaquelyn said with sudden concern. "We don't want to move too much and dislodge the car."

"Right," Jack responded and let his arm drop slowly. He still felt dream-like and, at the same time, more real than ever before. "I love you," he said in a voice that was beyond emotion, yet quite audible against the roar of the water.

"And I love you," Jaquelyn said and smiled a goddess smile. He could not believe how much he loved her in that moment. All previous moments paled in comparison.

"We've talked a lot about how we might go out together," Jaquelyn went on, "but I thought it would be in a plane, not like this."

"Yes," Jack said, realizing he wasn't thinking in the usual way. Had he been injured and didn't feel it yet? He touched his head. "Ow. I've got quite a lump here just above my ear."

"Yes, you're bleeding from some lesions, but I don't think they're serious," doctor Jaquelyn reported. She had already assessed his wounds. She was more worried about his right hand. "How's the hand?" she asked. He looked at it for the first time. There were two cuts, one that looked pretty deep, but the wetness kept washing the blood away.

"My hand's OK. I want to tell you how much I love you. That's all I want to say."

"I know," Jaquelyn said softly. Their heads were close enough to hear each other. "We're so blessed to have the love we have. If we cross now, we will have lived a blessed life."

The grace Jack felt in that moment made him feel young and incredibly humble. "I knew some of our end-of-life practices were going to be challenging, but I didn't expect we would be doing this as part of our training." She laughed and wanted to take him in her arms, but was afraid to move and disturb their balance.

"I think we're really stuck on this tree," Jack said, knowing exactly what Jaquelyn was thinking. They both looked at the base of the tree for a few moments, again in prayerful silence. The tree responded, "I'm not going anywhere. Continue with your council until the rain lets up a little." They both got the message. "I should be figuring out how to get us out of here safely," Jack said finally, "but I just want to be with you. You are so beautiful. Your eyes are full of light."

Jaquelyn realized that she was letting herself show her love for him without restraint. There was no holding back now. She let his love in all the way as well and felt completely at peace. "Maybe we've died already and don't know it," she said with her wise and innocent smile.

Jack actually contemplated whether that might be true and then realized he had been uncontrollably shaking since they had "arrived" at the tree. He took a few deep breaths and felt a dull pain shoot across his right rib cage. "How 'ya doing?" (He was slurring his words a little.)

"Pretty good. The cold is the worst part. I don't feel much pain—yet—but I'm cold and wet and shaking."

"I can't stop shaking either," Jack responded. "I guess it's from shock as well as the cold. Strangely, I didn't have much fear during the wild ride."

"I wasn't afraid as we were tumbling but those few seconds in deep water were terrifying. The idea of suffocating by drowning is really frightening for me. The water came up to my nose."

"And I couldn't get out of my damn seat belt to really help you. We were fortunate another wave swept us here up against the tree." "Your seat belt may have saved you from really getting hurt." Jaquelyn suggested. "I wonder what would have happened if I'd had mine on. Thank God for my strong right tennis arm that held on to this handle." She gently touched the arm hold over the passenger door. "That somehow kept me from getting banged up. Or maybe it was our connectedness that actually kept us from getting hurt badly." She paused and smiled. "I always knew I was crazy. Now I know that you're totally crazy too." They laughed in their wounded capsule, water roaring all around them.

They were silent again for a while, letting the gulch dominate the council while they continued to watch the water swirling around the base of the tree. "I guess we weren't ready to cross over just yet," Jaquelyn said finally. "The cold is the worst part of this. I don't care about anything else. All my baggage is wet, my computer is ruined undoubtedly—and I don't care. We're together. I can't imagine what this would have been like alone."

"Totally different—and awful. I can't even imagine it. Maybe being together prevented us from losing it."

"I felt with you all the time, except for those moments under water," Jaquelyn continued above the roar. "Being together kept the fear from taking over. Neither of us shouted or panicked. We tumbled together and survived—so far."

"I think we were slightly out of our bodies. It was almost as if I was watching it all, wondering how it was all going to turn out."

"Maybe we're not back in our bodies yet, except for the shaking. My only thought just now was about Chelsey. There's more healing to do at a distance. I'm glad we're still going to be around."

"Me too," Jack agreed, "although in some ways it doesn't really matter. We know we're going to continue helping her out after the crossing too."

"Yes, but I would miss her dear sweet body. Do you think anyone will see us down here? It's still raining hard and misty."

"There won't be much traffic on the Cane Road in this kind of weather. We could be here a while. Let me see if I can open this back door and look around. It's like the hatch of our little vessel."

"Be careful!" Jaquelyn warned him. "Don't shift your weight too quickly."

"The tree is holding. We're really wedged in here, and the water is a little lower now. I think we'll be OK." Jack moved her huge suitcase carefully and tried opening the rear passenger side door. It took a lot of strength to finally push it open. He poked his head out and looked around. In the direction the car was pointing the main part of the gulch was still a wild water-beast bouncing from boulder to boulder before disappearing in great growls and plumes just past their little island. "There's a big drop just on the other side of the tree," Jack said simply, and once again was overcome with awe at how close they had come to disaster. In the direction of the other shore, the gulch had created an entirely new stream, perhaps only fifteen feet wide but clearly too deep and turbulent to cross. They would have to wait until someone saw them. Maybe Seppe and the kids would come out to watch the downpour and discover their car. They were only 200 feet or so from the road, but the rain was still like a curtain of water, cutting down visibility. He lowered himself slowly back into the car. His right hand was bleeding generously but, as the blood was being washed away continuously, he couldn't see how deep the cuts were. He felt no pain. "It may be awhile before we're found," Jack said simply. Jaquelyn shivered and wrapped her arms more tightly around herself. The pressure on her ribs made her wince a little as the adrenaline began to wear off.

At that moment, not very far away, Seppe donned his boots and raincoat, grabbed his large yellow umbrella, and left the cabin to explore the storm. He was watching the water begin to lift chunks of asphalt along the bridge when he noticed the car. A cold dread crept into his heart, but he pushed it away before heading back to the cabin to get his kids. As Bianca (14), Chris (12), and Hannes (7) pulled on their boots and slickers, an image came to Seppe that was as clear as direct sight. There was Jack driving the car in the rain with Jaquelyn sitting next to him. He shouted to the kids to follow him and rushed out of the cabin, his slender, muscled frame on full alert. The water was still pouring over the bridge, although its intensity had diminished slightly.

The four of them covered the short distance to the bridge quickly, Hannes dancing in the large puddles. Bianca grabbed her younger brother's hand and held on, as they approached the torrent. Seppe asked her if she saw the car just as she noticed something white in the misty, driving rain down in the gulch. "We had better check it out and see who it is," he said and disappeared down the utility road that ran parallel to the gulch about thirty feet to the west.

Bianca knew that Jaquelyn was supposed to leave that day and deduced what had happened. "I'll go back to the house and get the cell phone," she said, her voice even and strong. She ran the short distance back to the cabin, turned around and met Seppe as he was coming back up the utility road.

"It's them," was all Seppe could say. The last time he felt such fear and sadness was when Hannes almost died from a hospital mishap. In that moment he knew that Jack and Jaquelyn had become family. Bianca dialed 911 and gave a complete description of the scene and its location. The emergency rescue dispatcher said they'd be there in less than twenty minutes. Then, phone in hand, she went down the utility road to see the car close up.

Meanwhile Jack began to take stock of the Tercel's contents for the first time. The computer case was damp, but undamaged. The jack and tire tools had somehow ended up in the front seat. He put them back in the rear compartment that was a jumble of mats and debris. They could see the entire base of the tree now as the flood receded a little. "We're going to be OK," Jack repeated simply after a long silence. "Maybe Seppe will find us. He knew we were leaving for the airport around now."

"He called this morning and advised us to leave early," Jaquelyn added. "He doesn't usually express that kind of concern except for his own kids. His voice on the phone was tight. Maybe he had a premonition."

"There's still a part of me that can't believe I actually tried to cross the bridge."

"Don't sweat it, darling," Jaquelyn reassured him. "We both wanted to risk it. We were together and now we're even more together, blessed and lucky to have survived. That's all that matters."

"Yes, and you've been so calm and present. I've never felt this kind of love before. It's not even so much about you or me. It's more like a state of awareness."

"I understand. I feel the same way."

They spoke at some length of needing to pursue their work in the world more vigorously. "We've been given a reprieve," Jack shouted into the roar. "I had better get on with the writing too. Every day is precious."

"Apparently we still have a mission to fulfill," Jaquelyn agreed. "I know we have powerful guides ready to help us." Gratitude and humility graced their council.

When they lapsed into silence again, Jack had an urge to get out of the car and look around. He opened the rear door again and lifted himself out awkwardly with his arms.

The ground under the car was clear of water now and covered with old leaves from the tree, a Christmasberry, he thought. They're like weeds around here, he remembered someone telling him. A "rescue weed," he thought and patted the tree affectionately. Then he put his hand on the car. The old Tercel had taken a much worse beating than its passengers, and he felt a pang of gratitude for how it had served them for so many years, even before they had shipped it to the Island.

At that moment Jack saw Bianca across the smaller torrent, no more than thirty feet away, holding the cell phone to her ear. She was smiling and waving her other hand. Then he looked up towards the road and saw that a large group had gathered near the bridge, now clear of water. He recognized Seppe's yellow umbrella. They had been found!

Jack turned back to the car and pulled opened the door. "I just saw Bianca with a cell phone. Obviously, she's called 911."

"Where is she?"

"On the other side of the smaller stream, on the bank below the utility road."

"Thank God," Jaquelyn said through trembling lips. "This cold is getting to me."

"The rescue team shouldn't take too long. It's not raining anywhere nearly as hard as it was. The water isn't touching the tree now."

"I love that tree. We'll have to come back and thank it. Right now my ribs are beginning to hurt. I must have been banged up more than I realized. I'm not sure I can get out of the car."

"I'll help you out. Don't worry," Jack reassured her.

"How about your hand?"

"It's OK. The rain keeps washing the blood away." He was still shaking.

Ten minutes later a yellow emergency vehicle made its way carefully down the muddy utility road. In addition the three local firemen had called Hilo to request the "Monkey," a rescue specialist, who was on his way. The captain of the rescue crew immediately clambered down the bank to evaluate the scene. The smaller torrent was clearly impassible. He asked Jack if anyone was hurt, shouting over the roar of the water. Jack could barely make out his words but finally shook his head. Good, the captain thought. Then we can use the belaying lines and harnesses, as soon as the Monkey gets here. The younger rescuers stared at the gulch in awe. They didn't get to do a rescue like this very often.

Jack pulled himself out of the intimacy with Jaquelyn a little reluctantly to prepare for the rescue. It took the Monkey another half hour to arrive, collect his ropes and rings, and clamber down the steep bank. His muscular torso was covered only by a blue tank top with HFD imprinted on it. He was wearing shorts and sturdy shoes. A dangle of belay clips was hanging from his belt, which also held a length of nylon rope. A short, dark beard partially covered a good-looking face. He enjoyed his work—and his reputation.

The rain had eased to a normal, steady Hawaiian pace. The Monkey surveyed the scene and decided that climbing the tree and using its branches as a bridge seemed the best route to the car. The man looked like he wasn't badly hurt—elderly, but walking around all right, a little dazed maybe. I'm not sure about the woman. I'll need help to get her out. *Well, they don't call me "Monkey" for nothing*, he thought.

"What's happening?" Jaquelyn shouted and felt a stabbing pain dart across her chest. She realized that she had been taking only shallow breaths since they had slammed up against the tree. She tried a slightly deeper one and was stopped abruptly by the searing pain. "Maybe a rib fracture," she said out loud in her doctor's voice and suddenly felt vulnerable. "When are we going to get out of here?" she shouted to Jack. He pulled open the rear door a few inches and peered inside. She was still sitting on the junction of the driver's door and the floor, in lotus position. Her arms were wrapped around her chest gingerly. He could feel her discomfort viscerally.

"This guy with ropes and belay rings is casing the situation. They should have us out of here soon."

"Good," Jaquelyn said and imagined soaking in a warm tub in the house. It was her first thought of something happening after the wild ride. She kept her breathing shallow to avoid the pain. "I can't stop shaking."

"Me too, although it's better now that I'm walking around." Jack kept circling the small patch of ground around the car, pacing. He was ready to get off their island. The captain and the younger men were securing a line to the large tree on the bank. They gave the other end to the Monkey who tied it around his belt. He climbed the tree easily and moved out on its slender branches over the water slowly. Jack watched in admiration. The branches bent towards the water but held his muscular body, and he quickly dropped onto their little island.

"Quite a ride," the Monkey said with a touch of a smile.

"Yes, we were pretty lucky to get through it."

"Extremely lucky, I would say, and this tree that stopped you sure was a big help. Well, we're going to get you and your wife out of here in comfort. I'm going to jury-rig a harness from these belts I have. The harness equipment wasn't in Hilo, but I didn't want to wait for it. We'll make do with what we have."

"I could probably get across with the help of a rope," Jack said.

"No, all you have to do is relax and we'll pull you across. You can help me get her out of the car. We'll send her across first."

Jack thought about her computer and other baggage for the first time. "Can you get the luggage out too? We were on our way to the airport. One of them is very heavy."

"Don't worry. We'll send the bags across after we get you taken care of," the Monkey said with a smile.

The two men moved towards the car. "Here, this door opens. It's how I've been getting in and out." Jack started to climb into the car to help Jaquelyn.

"You hold the door open and I'll see to your wife," the Monkey said, not wanting to test the strength of this geezer. He lifted himself up on the car's side and slipped easily through the opened rear door. Jaquelyn started to get up slowly, favoring her chest. She took one more look around the wild jumble of bags, silt, stones, and glass—their bower for almost three hours. "What should I do?" she asked the Monkey.

"Hi, Ma'am," he said respectfully. "You stay right where you are. I'll give you a hand." His manner was both cordial and take-charge. She allowed herself to feel a little safe. The Monkey placed his large hands around her waist.

Jaquelyn reached towards the open door with Jack's smiling face above it. "I guess we have to leave our little home now. I couldn't have gotten out of here without help."

"OK, Ma'am," the Monkey said. "Here we go!" He lifted her through the opening easily. Jaquelyn grabbed Jack's hand and slid her legs up through the opening with the Monkey's assistance. Then she paused to sit on the car for a moment, saw the crowd of people on the road waving as they saw she was at least mobile, and felt the rain on her face. She shivered and slid carefully to the ground with the help of the two men, still protecting her chest. "Ribs hurt?" the Monkey asked.

"Yes, I may have a fracture or two. What happens now?"

"We create a harness out of these belts and ropes and send you across." Jaquleyn looked at the wild water and had a moment of doubt about how the harness would affect her ribs. "Don't worry," the Monkey said. "The harness goes around your legs and hips." He quickly arranged the jumble of belts and created two openings for her legs. Jaquelyn stepped into the harness gingerly and was belted in around her waist. Then the Monkey connected the harness to the overhead rope. "OK, we're ready. You don't have to do anything. We'll pull you across. Just relax." Jaquelyn obeyed awkwardly. She was used to getting herself out of jams.

The shivers took hold of Jack again as he watched her limp body hanging from the harness. As the captain and the younger men started pulling on the draw rope, Jaquelyn moved in short jerky spurts, her feet dangling just a foot or two above the wild water. They grabbed her as she reached for a limb of a bush on the bank and passed her through several hands up the steep bank. The Monkey pulled the harness rope back to his end of the overhead line and started readjusting the harness.

"Don't forget the baggage, particularly her computer," Jack called out to him. "That's really important to her."

"Let's take a look," the Monkey said and opened the hatch. The large suitcase was within his reach and he grabbed hold of the black handle.

"My God, this is heavy. What do you have in here?"

"Papers and clothes, and they're all wet. Here let me help."

"I've got it." The Monkey used a lot of his strength to pull the large suitcase through the door and let it slide off the car onto the wet earth. Jack turned away from the Tercel and let go of any preoccupation with the other luggage. The trip across the swollen gorge only took a moment before strong arms helped him up the bank. On the mainland at last!

As it turned out, the hot shower and bath would have to wait many hours. Instead they were ushered quickly into a four-wheel drive ambulance that was waiting on the utility road. The paramedics strapped them into stretcher-gurneys with their heads in precautionary rigid neck braces. Then heart monitors were stuck to their chests. When asked if she had any pain, Jaquelyn acknowledged her aching ribs, so the two young paramedics initiated an IV drip. She had already identified herself as a physician, which made them a little nervous. Obviously, they didn't get many opportunities to apply their medical training, since they had a terrible time getting the needle into her veins. Jack decided not to mention his rib pains. The drive to the emergency room was uncomfortable, but at least they were dry and beginning to warm up. The ER staff was cordial and efficient, but the room was air- conditioned. Finally a nurse found some dry clothes in the lost and found and their shaking stopped. "He's going to need some stitches in his hand," Jaquelyn informed the nurse, who took a look and agreed. Urine, blood tests, and X-rays of Jaquelyn' ribs proved negative for fractures and internal bleeding, but her discomfort suggested some hairline fractures that didn't appear on the film.

They had to wait an hour for Seppe to come and pick them up. It was late and almost nine hours since the moment of trying to cross the bridge when they finally returned home. The bath and shower were divine, although Jack had to keep his cut right hand dry by wrapping it in two plastic bags and hanging his arm over the shower door. Jaquelyn reveled—gingerly—in her tub.

They were too achy to snuggle and fell asleep holding hands, still in a state of gratitude and mild disbelief about it all. The next morning several friends called to see how they were doing and to inform them they had made the front page of the Big Island Daily. When they finally got a copy of the paper, there was a large picture of their car on its side up against the tree. The caption read, "Elderly couple rescued by Firemen." "How dare they call us *elderly*," Jaquelyn reacted with a big grin. "They didn't even get close enough to see what we looked like!"

The wild ride in the gulch created a number of synchronicities. Jack's son Eric told his father a few days later that on the day of the great rain, three thousand miles away in Portland, he was doing his usual morning meditation when suddenly a most unusual thought appeared out of the blue: "I wonder whether I'll still feel connected with Dad after he dies."

Such is the mysterious power of initiation.

7 ❧ Discovering the Larger Message

A few days after their harrowing experience in the gulch and several unsuccessful attempts to find a new car, J&J finally had the time to reflect on what had happened during their wild ride. The early morning conversation took place in bed—a "horizontal council" they came to call it. The room was still dark with only a hint of light in the eastern sky, as Jack sleepily reached out for Jaquelyn.

"Ooh, careful!" her voice startled him. "I'm still really tender. My mind keeps on repeating familiar phrases like, *You never know when it will happen,* and *It may come as a thief in the night.* Jack held her tenderly as she continued. "Those familiar words have a whole new meaning now. The power of that elemental force that carried us like matchsticks whirling down the gulch reminded me of all that—and we called it in! Apparently that means we need to learn how to embrace nature with skill and love and humility, and certainly with respect. We're like children who don't know how to do all that yet. Another phrase comes to me from the Bible that has to do with the Messiah returning. It goes something like, *You need to fill your lanterns with oil and keep them lit. Stay awake because you never know when the Messiah will come.* Death is like that too."

Listening to her reflections, Jack remembered how she had spoken of the Christmasberry tree while they were still in the car. "Tell me again what you said about your connection with the earth, as you were watching the water swirling around the tree and eroding the little patch of ground holding us."

"I've always trusted your love for the earth," Jaquelyn replied, "and how you put your hands in the soil. You love to swim in the ocean, even when it's cold. You enjoy a connection with nature that I really don't have. So when I was sitting in the overturned car and we were afraid to breathe because it might dislodge the car, I really looked at that tree. It wasn't a big tree—the trunk was maybe six or seven inches in diameter—but it had many branches and we were caught in a few of them, like an embrace. I had a love for the earth and the tree in that moment that I had never felt before. That love may help my own healing, because I've been pretty ungrounded since the plunge. I need to add more appreciation for the power of nature to my spiritual awareness. Our capabilities are definitely being honed, not necessarily to do something special, but to be stronger vessels for healing."

"It's interesting how much of this is biblical for us," Jack observed. "While I've been writing these last few days, *Thy will be done* keeps coming up. Now you've added *the thief in the night* and *keep your lanterns lit*. As I was listening to you, I also heard, *He giveth and he taketh away*. The earth does that! We were swept away by the water and then saved by the tree and the piece of earth under it. If that patch had been just rock, there would have been nothing to stop us. That tree grew on the edge of the gulch, nourished by the water that flowed through it from time to time. So the very force that swept us away also saved us. That familiar paradox of nature teaches us not to polarize with labels of good and evil. That way of thinking continues and is increasingly terrifying. . . I also watched fearfully as the soil was eroding around the roots of the tree and we inched towards disaster. Then, after we knew we were going to be OK, I looked at you and you were absolutely exquisite. Your face was bathed in radiant light."

"From all those angels," Jaquelyn responded matter-of-factly.

"Including you—and, yes, we were blessed with angelic presence. The other moment I keep replaying is when I looked down the Cane Road after we cleared our gate and approached the bridge. As we watched the water coming in pulses like surf, an unfamiliar part of me took control. The sensible thing would have been to wait in the car for an hour until the water receded enough for us to cross. We might have just made the plane or you could have taken the later one that night. That was the rational path, but the part of me that took over wasn't rational. We were meant to encounter the full force of nature and, as you said, we were completely in its powerful hands."

"I think you're putting a spin on the story," Jaquelyn warned. "Maybe you felt more powerful than the water and thought you could handle it. You're implying that we wanted to have this experience so that we could sense—"

"Oh, no! I didn't *want* what happened. Neither of us did."

"You mean you're saying all this in retrospect?"

"Yes," Jack responded. "I woke up from my altered state as we tumbled and felt the pain of what I had done. I've been living with that decision ever since. To cause you pain, to almost cause our death is unthinkable. I drove into self-destruction and destruction of the person I love—'like life itself,' as we often say. Spinning is a danger, but I'm talking about the big plan, the universe's plan. That perspective is important. Otherwise, one disappears into self-judgment, which is another—and dark—aspect of the ego. Apparently, there was a deep place in me that wanted to break the chains of my usual restraint. But that might be putting a spin on it too. I woke up this morning feeling the weight of what Seppe called 'my stupidity.'"

"He used that word?"

"He asked me if I had ever done anything in my life more stupid than driving into the water. And I said, 'It was beyond stupidity. It was a moment of insanity.'"

"I would definitely call it more insane than stupid," Jaquelyn agreed.

"In a strange way it wasn't about poor judgment. Rather it felt like I surrendered judgment, surrendered reasonableness, surrendered—"

"Be careful!" Jaquelyn warned again. "I wouldn't describe it that way. It was more like a little boy saying he's going to take on a grizzly bear. There's a part of you that pushes the envelope on the physical level."

"Yes, I see that. I see what got me into it. I'm not trying to give that a spin. I'm trying to see the bigger picture. What this event has accomplished is to create an additional week together in this training course we call our relationship. One teaching seems clear. If you plan to explore natural healing, first get to know nature in its raw form—along with acknowledging stupidity, ego, the boy taking on the grizzly, however you want to describe it."

"We have to have the guts to call it crazy too," Jaquelyn suggested, "although I see what you're trying to say. We've been asking for empowerment and so the teaching is, *get ready to handle it!* I didn't want to go to D.C. with work piled up, so that's why I planned to go back to California almost two weeks before the big meeting. So much for plans! Now I'll have a lot of work to do when I return, including two local presentations that I have to bone up on."

Jack was still not clear. "How do we accept that the plunge was both an initiation and the result of stupidity or at least an error in judgment?"

"*Error in judgment.* I like that phrase better. We looked at the situation and made a judgment. You were decisive."

"It was a moment of madness and incredible hubris, as if I could part the waters. Totally insane! Maybe that's what it takes to kill the ego."

"The challenge is not to have the operation kill the patient," Jaquelyn added. "Above all, the accident has been incredibly humbling."

Seeing that the meaning of the wild ride was going to take more time to resolve, they shifted their attention over the next few days to buying a car. This time their efforts were rewarded in the form of a 1995 Toyota Avalon in remarkably good condition. They celebrated the new acquisition over lunch in Kona and decided to have a council that evening to celebrate.

Jaquelyn delighted in a long afternoon bath. She arose from the water looking like a river nymph, and put on a light blue transparent tunic. Then she arranged her hair in a loose bun on the top of her head and added a cloth flower. Jack took in her beauty with a surge of gratitude. "Not only did we purchase a vehicle today, but we had a wonderful late lunch all alone in Michelangelo's overlooking the ocean. We pretended we were a couple on vacation. We even had a beer in the afternoon!"

"What a wild man you are!" (*laughter*)

Jack wanted to give clarity another try. "Right now I'm seeing the whole adventure from a more playful point of view. Meditation students have their fierce Zen master. We have the force of nature on the path of relationship. The message I'm getting now is that we have to learn how to make the shift in consciousness that we experienced in the gulch in a way that is not so hard on the body. So rather than this being a singular experience—"

"It's a harbinger of what's coming," Jaquelyn interjected.

"Yes, to be healers we have to have strong footing. You actually got quite grounded during our council in the gulch, watching and appreciating the tree and the earth around it."

"I felt they both had life and spirit, and were totally connected to us."

"It's *Wankan Tonka*," Jack offered, "the spirit that dwells in all of nature. That's what the Native Americans call it. For those on our path, that spirit is particularly heightened by intimacy."

"When I invite that energy into my pelvis, it becomes my earth, my ground. I didn't use to think about the spirit in nature very much, to tell the truth. I just lived life from that place in my body, not really appreciating the earth or giving my groundedness any real attention. But when I was soaking in the tub this afternoon, I explored different levels of consciousness awakened by the gulch and before long I was way out there. For a moment I thought I might be losing my mind, but that shifted and then I realized I was being baptized! Hands were pushing me into the water. There wasn't any emotion to it, just hands submerging my body in the water."

"In whose name were you being baptized?" Jack asked with a touch of awe.

"I don't know. It wasn't clear. There was no sense of a mother god or a father god, just the baptism. And then there was another shift and I was imagining myself presenting in Washington, D.C. at the big conference. I heard myself say . . . um . . . I heard myself say . . . " (*sigh*)

"It'll come back," Jack reassured her. "Don't worry."

"We've had tastes of the elemental power of nature on our walks here along the Cane Road. Now our feelings about nature have a deeper resonance. When we are in harmony, our resonance with nature expands into erotizing everything without even thinking about it. Then I see the joyous life force, in everything."

"That's a great way to describe exactly what I've been experiencing."

"How wonderful!" Jaquelyn exclaimed.

At that moment Jack had a strong impulse to transmute their erotic energy into a healing state as they had been planning for so long. Their bodies were sore; making love still seemed days away because of the shock and trauma of the wild ride. Jaquelyn read him immediately. She had been sitting on their bed, leaning up against the white plaster wall under the silk Tibetan tonka, but without a word she shifted to make her left rib cage more accessible. In his mind's eye Jack gathered up the resonant feelings they had both just acknowledged and imagined them filling, first his heart, then his arms, and then moving down into his hands. He made a few passes carefully over her ribs, staying several inches away from her body.

At first, the sensations were familiar from all the years of scanning body energy fields at the Center for Healing Arts, but then something shifted. Not only did the boundary between Jack's hand and Jaquelyn's body disappear, but he felt in resonance with a unifying presence that surrounded them both. As Jaquelyn relaxed, she felt a slight stirring in her pelvis for the first time since their adventure. The body tenderness that had persisted since climbing out of the car began to ease. The pain diffused under the warmth of his hand. Jaquelyn felt comfortable for the first time in days.

Then in the space of a few minutes another shift occurred as she lost awareness of their separate selves and a single entity became the focus of her awareness. For a moment Jaquelyn wondered if the entity was their *healing Third*. Then even that thought disappeared, leaving only a witness awareness of their union. She felt that the shift was similar to what had happened as they plunged into the gulch, but this time the witness seemed to know exactly what needed to happen.

Jaquelyn broke the silence. "Turn your hand over. Then the healing will go in the other direction and heal your cut."

Jack followed her guidance in silence. "That was powerful," he said finally. "It felt like we were merging cell by cell—wait, it's happening again! We're having a glimpse of the healing field we've been tracking for so long." He lapsed into an ecstatic silence that resembled what happened when he entered her during lovemaking. The sensation, although subtle, was unmistakable. He let out a sigh of delight.

Simultaneously, Jaquelyn moved into her physician's awareness. "Take the energy directly into the cellular level of your brain."

Jack nodded and did his best to follow her guidance. Jaquelyn had waited for this moment a long time, not at all sure that it was possible. Now she knew that their Third could become a healing field. "Just imagine that our bodies are changing shape, elongating and expanding."

"That's exactly what I'm experiencing! It's transformative. I cannot believe what's going on here. My hands are immersed in this awakened field that is primal and creative."

"Primal ooze," Jaquelyn suggested. "We're not familiar with it yet. We haven't seen into the essence of it, but we're feeling its power right now."

They surrendered to the healing field, drawn by its magnetism in much the same way as they experienced making love, but now with new awareness. Punctuated only by an occasional sigh from Jack, they interwove their fields in a way they had longed to do for so many years. After what seemed an eternity, another shift into greater intimacy inspired words to flow again.

"Did you feel that change, just then?" Jaquelyn asked in a lover's voice. Jack nodded. "It's like we're being shown the possibility of actual merging."

"The awakening is palpable—and what a rough awakening it has been, like in the Sundance, when the participants pierce their chests with arrows and hooks. Our initiation had a strong touch of the shamanic."

"The wounded healer can lead to deep levels of consciousness," Jaquelyn added. "There must have been something thick in us to need such a big clobber."

"I certainly feel my density," Jack acknowledged.

"To get a jolt of this dimension is teaching us to transcend our bodies." Jaquelyn took his hand and held it gently, placing her palm over the bandaged finger to reciprocate the healing she had just received.

"I can feel how your love allows me to heal the parts of myself that doubt and hold back from fully embracing what we're being shown."

"The Eros energizes your body," Jaquelyn commented, "and the body energizes your mind. Soon you'll be just like me!" (*laughter*)

"Your hand feels so healing, as it transmits . . . sweetness." He was suddenly overcome with how dear she looked. "You're so cute, showing up tonight wearing that shimmering top. You're like the goddess coming out of the river with a flower in your still wet hair."

"And she's a little cold too. Let's have the heater." Jack lit the propane heater and they fell back into the healing state simply by joining hands again. Then slowly their hands began to move as if each were a complete body arousing the other for lovemaking. Soon the mutual caressing of their fingers moved them towards merging and the touching changed from gentle to firm, as if directed by a master conductor. Within a few minutes their fingers joined together tightly in a final surge of movement—and then were still.

"That was like an electric shock," the goddess said.

Her consort agreed. "Our hands danced into consummation. We could have gone on forever."

"As that was going on, I traveled to D.C, and was behind the podium again, giving my speech to the DAN! Community. . . *The kids are calling us. They're calling us to be wiser and more conscious. We're making great strides, but we can't sit on our laurels. We need to find new ways of healing that will reach all the children. Many have no access to treatment. We need to join forces with whomever can help us fulfill our mission.*"

"Hallelujah!" Jack shouted. "I hope you really share with all that passion."

"As I told you, hearing myself giving the speech started in the bathtub right after the baptism. I watched it all, like a movie."

"It's your ministry. Would you like to do some more healing? I feel we'll be guided."

Jaquelyn nodded. "You could work on the other parts of my body that are sore." With a few groans that favored her aching ribs, Jaquelyn turned slowly, searching for a comfortable position. The moving activated further pain. She didn't like feeling so tender, so it took a few moments for her to surrender. "Even though you're not touching me yet, I feel like you're reaching right into my flesh. I totally trust you."

"This level of trust and knowing comes from—"

"—being lovers," Jaquelyn interrupted. "If you love somebody enough, you know how and where to move your fingers. Your lover's flesh becomes your flesh. You know their body as well as your own."

"Let's see if we can completely dispel any awareness of separate bodies."

Jaquelyn yearned to feel his touch in that magical place in her mid-back above the heart that often yearned for contact. "If you move your hand up about three inches on my back, I can shift further into the merged state." They had come to see that place on the back as the human end of a virtual umbilical cord that connected each of them with their Third. Jack had noted long ago that the spot was located where Don Juan used to tap Carlos suddenly to shift him into "second attention."

"OK, that's where I'm heading," Jack said and felt an expanding surge of warmth flood his loins. He was following instructions now, although he wasn't sure from whom.

"There's such a yearning in that place in my back. It's like a gaping vagina, sucking and wanting something to enter that will fertilize and expand its power. The desire is sexual and universal, like all women's yearning for full acceptance and empowerment—along with a mate to help her become enlightened."

Jaquelyn's voice had dropped into a lower pitch, as she let the erotic life force in his touch arouse her despite the trauma they had experienced. This "goddess voice" took him to the place of wanting her, but he knew that was not where they were headed, not right now. That would come later, perhaps in a few days, perhaps not until after she left and they were together again. Now his fingers were ready to make love to her back. As they slowly crept higher towards the spot longing for touch, he imagined that he was caressing her breast, then her nipples, and finally her labia. The simple movements along her spine created a new kind of foreplay that had a different intention. Jack touched the magic spot on her back lightly, withdrew for a brief moment, repeated that movement and then, finally, arrived fully. He increased the pressure slightly as he circled the place of desire. He could feel the opening tangibly and gently massaged its "lips." Jaquelyn let out a groan, as if he had entered her fully erect, and then she took several deep breaths to slow down the approaching climax.

"Hold on," Jack said in a quiet voice. "Something new is allowing a deeper transmission. Are you ready?"

Jaquelyn's groans and breathing continued as she embraced the flood of feelings emanating from the spot in her back. The sensations were now expanding throughout her body. She knew that experience with her genitals as the source, but this was new. "Yes," she said finally. "I'm moving into complete trust now." Within a few moments healer and healee had disappeared, as do lovers at the height of passion.

The merging also stirred the man's playfulness. "Ah, yes, Jack and Jaquelyn are emerging from their ordinary meek selves into the *Elderly Couple!* We've had Superman and Spiderman and now we have the *Elderly Couple* emerging mostly unscathed from the wild river!" They both broke up with laughter.

"I'm very tired," Jaquelyn said finally. Jack nodded. They both got ready for bed and soon fell asleep, once again holding hands.

8 ❧ Making Love Across the Pacific

The implications of Jaquelyn's tub-baptism remained elusive in the days before she was to leave for California, until Jack talked with an old friend who called to see how they were doing since the "accident." Linda had been deeply involved with anthroposophy for many years and, when she heard Jack's description of Jaquelyn's tub adventure, she told him that Rudolf Steiner—the Austrian philosopher, educator and founder of anthroposophy—had commented on John's river baptism of Jesus in several of his writings. According to Steiner, in those days baptisms were not just symbolic events as they are now but actual near-death experiences. It started with John who, because of his own revelations, held Jesus under water just long enough for his "astral and physical bodies to begin to separate" (Linda's words). That allowed him to "see God," which was John's intention, according to Steiner. All the early baptisms were done that way in the years that followed the ministry of Jesus.

The explanation immediately clicked for Jack, not so much in regard to her experience in the tub, but rather as an explanation of what happened to Jaquelyn in the gulch when the water was rising and the fear of drowning had gripped her. Just in case they had failed to see the gorge experience as an initiation, Jaquelyn was given a second and far less threatening direct experience in the comfort of her tub—her favorite tub of all time, because it provided a large picture-window view of the riparian landscape and banana trees on the east side of their house.

After she returned to California, Jaquelyn hit the ground running, attending to her patients with autism, speaking at a few local autism meetings, and preparing for the big conference in D.C. Meanwhile, except for occasional trips to town to get mail and swim in the local pool, Jack remained at the Blue House, absorbed in his writing. Naturally, each time he drove across the bridge, their adventure filled his thoughts. On days of heavy rain his mood would shift and he'd relive those few wild moments, even feeling a touch of the fear he hadn't experienced then. They both came to accept that closure would take place in its own sweet time.

Although they checked in with each other every day, their first council at a distance took place almost a week after Jaquelyn had left and a day after she had driven to Santa Barbara to give a talk. She had tried to get someone to go with her, knowing she was still shaky and in pain, but no one was available. Driving home alone along the coast highway late in the evening, she found herself fighting large waves of fatigue. Afraid to stop by the side of the road in the dark by herself, she fought the tiredness in all her old familiar ways—pinching herself, singing out loud, turning up the radio—all to no avail. Deep exhaustion was slowly taking over her body. Then quite suddenly she had an image of her twin brother, Wendell, calling to her through the veil to join him on the "other side." His cries were intense and needy, qualities he had suppressed during his life.

Wendell's pleas did not appeal to Jaquelyn at all, but her curiosity and protective instincts joined with her exhaustion to draw her towards the veil. Like Jacob grappling with the dark angel, she fought Wendell off, feeling alone and abandoned as she drove in the darkness. The struggle continued for several minutes until she finally managed to image Jack vividly. As Wendell faded, the veil between the worlds closed again and she found herself approaching the familiar environs of Zuma Beach, north of L.A., with a great sense of relief. Jaquelyn made it home to the condo, shaky and completely spent, to find a phone message from Jack. He had called her at just the time she had been struggling with the pull from across the veil.

Jaquelyn was too tired to return his call that evening and instead sent him an email the next morning describing her experience. During the first few years after he had ended his life, Wendell had appeared in her dreams on a few occasions. But he had never reached out the way he did on the road the previous night, and she was still shaken by his anguished invitation to join him.

The wild ride had already catapulted them further into the work they called the *crossing yoga*—a set of relational practices that would help a mature couple make the final transition consciously—and together, if possible. These end-of-life practices and redirecting their erotic energy into the realm of healing were just two of the deep intentions that the gulch adventure had already begun to illuminate. It would take years for the full harvest, but already death was no longer primarily a topic of reflective contemplation. Overnight it had become a real and inseparable part of life.

They had arranged a specific time to council, but Jack was twenty minutes late finishing a gardening project and showering. In that short interval, lying on the bed in their condo with pillows piled on Jack's side to simulate his presence, Jaquelyn allowed herself to consciously return to their wild ride. Instead of replaying the moment of hesitation before they plunged or feeling the power of the roaring water, her imagination took her swiftly and unmistakably to a place "between the worlds." She felt an intense curiosity about death followed by a rush of the dread of drowning. Then suddenly the veil parted, wide open and inviting. The pull and the fear were almost equally strong but, with an act of will, she stepped back into life and the portal closed. It all happened in a flash, like the moment in the car when the water was rising. She got up from the bed and walked around the room to calm herself, wishing that Jack would call. Her heart was still beating rapidly when the phone rang.

Jaquelyn started right in to describe what had just happened while she was waiting for his call. As they talked, she felt the ground under her feet again. "Just hearing your voice brings me back. I see more clearly now that we were a unit in the gulch, an integrated entity. I think our bond actually kept us intact."

"Yes, something unusual happened," Jack agreed. "There's no other way of explaining how little we were hurt."

"My strong right tennis arm kept me hanging onto the ceiling handle."

"The Powers-That-Be said, 'You want to learn the crossing yoga? We'll show you what it's like. You may not realize what you're asking for."

By now Jaquelyn was more than ready to explore the bigger picture. "We don't have teachers to tell us about the crossing, so we were given an exceptional opportunity to experience a part of the passage directly."

"As the crossing yoga evolves, I think the normal ties that connect us with the world will become severed, strand by strand. What we need are practices that dissolve those links in as gentle a way as possible. We cut a whole bunch all at once in the gulch. Your adventure driving home yesterday and what just happened before I called are clearly related after-effects."

"Yes, we have to stay together now with our hearts open in order to handle what's coming through. I lost our connection for a moment yesterday because I was so tired and felt alone. A part of the other world is available to us now since the wild ride, but it can be dangerous for one of us to enter that consciousness feeling alone.

Jack agreed. "Whether we're physically separated or not, if we disconnect from each other, even in a subtle way, we may be asking for trouble. We also have to take good care of ourselves and, for example, not drive when we're tired. It's not a question of bravery. I didn't feel brave in the gulch. Did you?"

Jaquelyn laughed. "Not at all! I felt like a shivering orphan."

"I did ultimately find my protective role with you, but mostly I was overwhelmed by love. That image of you with the wet hair and shining eyes stays with me. Your whole face was radiant. I don't usually see energy fields clearly, just little wispy ghosts, but your aura was vivid. Sitting in the car in the middle of the water, we were both so alive!"

"Well, if that ride didn't wake us up, I don't know what would—

and I'm still hurting. My body is having a rough time. How's your hand?"

"I took off the bandage. The scar looks like a permanent wedding ring. In those moments, when all other reality faded into the bright light of love, we must have said, 'I do' again. You were exquisite. What are your physical talismans of the wedding, besides your aching ribs?"

"Well, I don't care as much about my appearance as I did before," Jaquelyn answered."I still like to look nice, but it doesn't matter in the same way. If I smile at myself in the mirror, I look cute and if I frown, I look older." I've been going around in old slippers without makeup, wearing old-fashioned clothes, not fussing with my hair for a change."

"That must be liberating."

"But I still wanted to be beautiful for you tonight before we talked, so I had a bath and put on soft clothes."

Jack smiled and wished he could leap across the Pacific. "Did you close your eyes and imagine you were in your favorite tub, looking out at the bananas trees?"

"Yes, and now I'm lying in the bed with the pillows piled up on your side, as if you were here. Because of what just happened before you called, I was wrapping my leg around the pillows and remembering how much I trusted we would get through it all when we were swept away."

"There's so much happening now. Your experience yesterday was another death encounter, a scary one. In the space of two weeks you've had three different near-death experiences . . . we have to come up with another word for them. They're actually trainings. We're in boot camp for the crossing yoga."

"With so much to learn," Jaquelyn added

"Indeed! The way Wendell called to you was spooky and not only physically risky because you were driving in an exhausted state but also psychically dangerous. Those kinds of experiences are like hidden reefs to a sailor. One has to be really careful."

"I couldn't get out of the grip of it for the longest time."

"The bottom line is that every moment is precious and anything can happen, just as it did while you were waiting for me to call. At least the third exposure was less dangerous."

"I did have fear," Jaquelyn acknowledged, "but I was finally able to witness the opening in the veil with only a little trembling and then I could move away."

"The progression of our training is remarkable. Hopefully, it will continue more gently. In the past you've been the one who usually brings in the teachings for us, sometimes with a bang, like these last two experiences. I usually get the teachings more over a period of time, incrementally. What's different about the gulch is that we both plunged in together—literally. In that moment our patterns disappeared."

"Does that mean that I won't be a few steps ahead of you any more when we take a walk together?" Jaquelyn asked, laughing.

"Somehow I knew you were going through something intense when you were driving back from Santa Barbara. It wasn't so much a thought as a shift in my mood. The day was overcast here. You know the scene—a large dark cloud covers the sky except for a blue band just above the ocean. I sensed something was up and then I got the email describing what happened that you signed YELP, instead of YELW. The typo gave me a laugh."

"Maybe unconsciously I wanted to see how the old boy would respond to 'Your Eternally Loving *Pussy*,' rather than '*Woman*.'" (*laughter*)

"I have to confess that, if we were together right now, I would have trouble keeping my hands off of you. If I could be as restrained when I'm with you as I am on the phone, our lovemaking would be even more extraordinary."

"Promises, promises," Jaquelyn said, laughing again.

"I'll have to lure you back to the Island and show you."

"I could never lure you here." Jaquelyn's tone was suddenly serious.

"You could lure me anywhere, Baby, even out of this beautiful place, and that's saying a lot. Our initiation didn't happen some place distant from where we live. It happened right here! The gulch is our eastern land boundary! I see the Christmasberry tree every day when I drive by. From where I'm sitting here in the bedroom, it's probably no more than two hundred yards away as the crow flies. So every time we make love here, we'll be near that moment of—"

"—death and awakening," Jaquelyn interjected. "You know what? Talking to you is helping me relax and feel less pain. I've been tense all week, like in continuous fear contraction."

"The drive back from Santa Barbara undoubtedly reinforced that," Jack noted. "When fear looms, maybe we have to be in a continuous state of love-connection in order to feel safe. That's one of my better propositions!"

"We've been building up to that for a long time," Jaquelyn agreed.

"The plunge into the gulch was like the beginning of a new marriage. When the divine man and the divine woman are wedded in a near-death ceremony, their vow is to be eternally aware of each other. I finally see what you've been talking about all these years."

Suddenly two birds celebrated Jack's realization by singing brightly in the Island dusk. It had been dark in California for some time, when Jaquelyn heard the dialog over the phone. They were both silent for a while, connected by the birds' song. Jack could feel his body arc over the Pacific and enter the bedroom of the condo. As he imagined holding her, he came surprisingly close to actually feeling her body. "Did you feel that?" he asked.

"Of course," Jaquelyn responded immediately. "You couldn't have felt it unless I did too."

"Our connection is so palpable that it's just as if you were here. There's no separation."

"I know. I feel the touch of your body through your voice. As we continue to be apart, we will develop new ways of creating tangible rapport."

"And then as always, the challenge is to embrace that state and simultaneously have the physical dimension enter in a natural way," Jack added.

Jaquelyn smiled. "I knew you'd find a way to bring it back to the physical."

"We need to be together more to do our relationship work and take care of each other. What we still have to do on the Mainland is not clear."

"How about a completely new place—neither Hawaii nor the Mainland?" Jaquelyn wondered. "When I tune in, my sense is that we will be serving as elders living out our time on the edge of a community—not necessarily one like Ojai. The location could be anywhere."

"That community could be here," Jack responded. "Something is building on the Island. The workday with all our neighbors was a big success. Many people showed up to work on our shared water system and we had a picnic lunch under the trees."

His comment left Jaquelyn feeling a little distant. "I have to confess, that even though I miss you, there's something very comforting about being here in the condo. City living has a cocoon quality that feels protective. I never see neighbors. There's something about our plunge that leaves me unsure I want to sell this place, even though I was ready to do that before. Hawaii has become our spirit place, and this is our workplace. But, if I didn't have all the conferences to get to easily, I'm not sure I would want to live here either. Maybe we're becoming children of the universe."

"I'm getting a lot of messages now to put roots down here," Jack responded, feeling uneasy about their different perspectives.

"If we just stay open and don't get attached to anything, we'll be directed to go to the right place where we'll do the most good . . . I wish you were here to take care of me right now. I'd ask you to get me some ice cream."

He felt an urge to get on a plane. "You've got my number completely, Baby."

"Goddess has *our* number."

"That's a good title for the book. You have to be a little crazy to travel our path."

They were both silent, contemplating the implications of his words. Then Jack consciously flashed on what they had come to call *Rumi's field*—the one the Sufi poet describes in the poem that begins: '*Out beyond all knowing of right doing and wrong doing, there is* a field . . . I will meet you there . . .' "I was just imagining our physical connection and ended up holding you in Rumi's field. Even at a distance, I can feel it in my body."

"Are you erect?" Jaquelyn asked. "Are you feeling aroused?"

"Aroused without being erect. If I can be in this state when we're together, you could express your full erotic power and I could dance with you without falling into our usual sexual patterns. We could go completely into the fire and maybe find the connection we had in the gulch through lovemaking."

"That might be even more risky," Jaquelyn said laughing.

There was another long pause in which a silent invitation was accepted on both sides of the ocean. They "kissed" almost three thousand miles apart.

"Did you feel our bodies just now?" Jaquelyn asked incredulously.

"I could actually feel your lips on mine. I felt your tongue and how it moves in my mouth."

Jaquelyn had a sudden impulse. "I want you to do an experiment. Go into my bathroom and open the cabinet to the left of the sink." The tone of her voice stirred his sleeping serpent. "Do you see the toothbrush?" Jack saw several regular toothbrushes, but she wanted the vibrating one. He found it among the bottles. She told him to take the brush back into the bedroom. "Now imagine that we're kissing each other," she said in her sultry voice. "Then turn the toothbrush on and bring it to your lips."

Jack followed her instructions, as he had done so often on their erotic journeys, delighted to be in the hands of the goddess again. When he touched the vibrating brush to his already aroused lips, the sensation was so strong he immediately pulled the brush away. He tried again—and again—each time holding the brush to his lips a little longer, yielding a little more, like when they made love. Then he pressed it harder against his lips, entering the stage of lovemaking when they devoured each other. The sensations spread from his lips to his now wide open body, and soon his loins slowly announced their presence.

"Let me share a little of what's happening here," Jack broke the silence, his voice now husky. "Your imagination is inspiring! Obviously, we were both feeling I was inside you just now and you were becoming fully aware of your goddess beauty."

"When your cock is inside me, it's like open sesame or *shazam*. Doors open up and a new awareness seems to spread out forever. I'm sorry that men can't feel that kind of spreading surrender."

"I'm learning to feel what you feel, so I can experience a little of what you're describing," Jack reassured her.

"If the man truly surrenders when he enters the woman—if he lets his cock be the carrier of all he has to offer—then his whole being enters the woman. That's the gift the man can bring. Stillness is part of that. Our sexual communion is movement and stillness together, mostly without a lot of words. The stillness brings me out of my familiar cultural roots and takes me into the core of nature."

"I like that," Jack responded, stirred by her insight. "Stillness shows us a way that Eros can transcend ethnicity patterns and deep personal patterns as well. The kind of lovemaking we're talking about would help you slow down a bit. I feel your body wants to slow down. You don't have to run everywhere."

"It's a habit," Jaquelyn explained.

"Yes, just like some of my mind patterns. We can change all that. I'm imagining that you're here on my lap in tantric position with me inside you. We're in Rumi's field, so there's no physical awkwardness or discomfort."

"Sounds great! Actually I'm losing weight, so by the time you see me I might be able to live out your dream and float on your cock."

"What a wonderful idea!" Jack exclaimed, his voice more husky.

"Practice for when I'm with you." Jaquelyn's voice was both challenging and seductive.

"I'm entering you in the deepest way."

"Feel your balls getting swollen—just a little and it will be ecstatic," Jaquelyn advised.

"What we're doing right now is really quite satisfying. Are you feeling OK?" Jack asked.

"Yes, because we're making the best of being separated! It's delicious."

In that moment Jaquelyn gathered her courage to ask him what she had been wondering about for several days. She began in a steady voice that was in marked contrast with the way she had just said *delicious*. "Did it ever occur to you to surprise me and come to D.C. for the DAN! party Saturday night?"

In a flash Jack felt like a tightrope walker in the middle of his act when suddenly a giant hand plucks the cable. "Uhh" was all that came out at first. Finally he added, "That thought actually did go through my mind once, maybe even twice, over the last month or so."

"Now that daughter-Leslie is coming and staying with me in the hotel, you're uninvited from that fleeting fantasy. But I can still get an enormous charge out of imagining it . . . I would be at the party, the belle of the ball, and you come up to me and I just pour out love for you. I'm filled with light all evening and carry that through the night and into Sunday morning to give a spectacular presentation."

Once again Jaquelyn had shared a fantasy of his love being more exuberant and, once again, Jack felt his limitations viscerally. He became aware of a pain in his chest and his mouth suddenly went dry. A gentle but palpable sadness passed through his body. He asked her for the exact dates of the party and the time of her presentation. The space between them become very still. "Why do you ask all this?" Jaquelyn said in a voice that conveyed her vulnerability. Would any man ever love her enough to live out such a fantasy?

The tenderness in her voice broke his heart. "Your scenario is so touching. I feel your sadness—or at least I feel sad. Yes, it's probably my sadness because I didn't give the idea more weight."

Jack's non-defensiveness allowed her to let go of her fantasy. Immediately she felt a familiar surge of love pass through her body and the erotic field they had created at a distance returned. "This is the way I want to feel when I'm making the presentation in D.C. in front of a thousand people," Jaquelyn thought. Then she imagined—no actually saw—him enter her again, not genitally but in the form of a wave of erotic energy interpenetrating with hers. She shared the image with him.

"That's what you can tune into when you're making your presentation," Jack suggested, his voice intimate again. "At any moment that you want a little more juice or need to take a breath, you can tune into that image. Even when you don't do it consciously, the image will be there. I'll meditate with you exactly at the time you're presenting. What a training these past few weeks have been! Our relationship is literally driving us into in a new level of love that allows us to face death more consciously."

"Yes," Jaquelyn agreed, "and this remote council is also part of our training for when one of us crosses. As I told you in my email, I actually saw a passageway through the veil when Wendell called to me like a hungry ghost. Do you think that means there's astral stuff to be cleaned up?"

"Definitely! The pull from a hungry ghost usually arises from unconsciousness."

"The attachment has to go both ways or Wendell wouldn't have manifested like he did," Jaquelyn agreed.

"Any part of you that needs to be needed would make you vulnerable to his yearning."

"It doesn't make sense that I would need him in that way. I get so much love from you and others. Maybe it's just an old habit, a hangover from taking care of him after he got polio. It's mostly that I feel sorry for him, like he's still wandering around the universe."

"There was a strong oedipal connection between the two of you that never really got resolved before he died. You were so much the woman for him—mother, advocate, sexual icon—and baton twirler. He told me unabashedly about his love for you once. I'll never forget that moment. Maybe his attachment is keeping him stuck in-between the bardos, and that's why he reached out so strongly. You were so large in his life. On the other hand, you don't have to abandon him either."

"I had the same protective pattern with Wendell that I still have with Richard. That's why I sometimes confuse their names. I have to let them both go even though it's painful, so that they can get on with their journeys, one in this life and one in the other."

"Yes, we each have some attachments to clean up," Jack agreed. "One can never control these kinds of primal forces, but if one is conscious of them, they don't possess us."

"And the primal force with Wendell and Richard is the protective mother?"

"Yes. As we have been discussing for years, men also have been wounded by the patriarchy in many ways particularly by not being conscious of their fear of women. Wendell constellated that wounded male for you—in the womb! You came out first, already one step ahead, just like you are with me when we're on a walk. The man is always trying to catch up with you. I know that so well."

"Then you're the one who can help Wendell," Jaquelyn responded. "If he could identify with some of the strengths you have, then it might be easier for both of us to let go of our attachment. You have to get in the act somehow."

"Are you suggesting we attune to him now?"

"He was so wounded as well as courageous," Jaquelyn added.

"OK, let's be silent and we'll see where we go."

They entered a meditation that slowly and carefully opened the gateway to the world of hungry ghosts and wandering spirits. Jaquelyn spoke after a few minutes. "It was healing for Wendell that I fell in love with you, because you had some of the same physical insecurities about your ability to be a lover that he suffered. So, if he can feel your empowerment and identify, maybe he can move on. When he appeared to me that time right after the suicide, his shoulders and head were bright but his lower body—the paralyzed part—was blurry and undefined. We need to hold an image of that filling out, so his pelvis becomes glorious too, like his brain and heart and sense of humor were. Then he can let go of his attachment to me, and I don't have to feel the need to take care of him anymore. We can become buddies and friends!"

Jack could hardly wait to share his part of the meditation. "I was with Wendell and felt a swelling of energy in my loins. I turned to him and said, 'Here, have some of this.' For a moment I felt his shame about how the paralysis had shaped his sense of manhood. Then the scene shifted and I was pushing him in his wheelchair. It was like watching a movie. After awhile I stopped and said, 'I want you to get up,' to which he responded, 'Don't do that number on me.' Then I said, 'No, this is for real. I want you to get up.' As he struggled to rise, still angry with me, I pulled the wheelchair away. All that happened quickly. Then I said, 'OK, I've taken the chair away. What are you going to do?' As the movie continued, it became clear my assignment was to help him learn to stand and walk, step by step. Apparently, he's still crippled where he is now."

"The polio took over his body identity completely. You were doing a healing through the veil."

"*We* were doing the healing," Jack responded firmly. "Even though we're an ocean apart, I felt we were doing the healing together."

"Yes, I was focusing on his lower body coming alive," Jaquelyn acknowledged.

"I don't think we would have developed these capabilities if we were together all the time. Being separated this past week gave our erotic connection a chance to shift into healing mode. You've wanted to do this kind of healing when we're together, which is a challenge because of my attachment to our physical connection. But I'm ready now."

"Particularly when I'm not there," Jaquelyn said, laughing.

"Well, I'm still in training. If you were here, I'd be all over you— no, actually, I wouldn't. I'm really learning to play in the aroused state. That's much more fun for you."

"Yes, because then I can be wildly seductive, rather than trying to deflecting your advances," Jaquelyn explained. "I'm getting sleepy. Is it time for us to say goodnight?"

"Sure, sweetheart. This has been really productive. Just stick with me Baby and the ride will get less bumpy."

"I'll stick with you forever. You're my man."

"YELP, forever. Your new signature says it all."

"I still don't know how the *P* got there," Jaquelyn responded playfully.

"Well, *P* is certainly the prime letter for genitals."

"*Prick, penis, pussy, pootang*—no, that's for fucking."

"So on this profound note, we'll say goodnight."

"Goodnight, sweetheart. I love you."

"I love you."

9 ✍ The Raging Bull Becomes a Lover

Although the councils at a distance kept the flow going, being separated after the wild ride in the gulch was a stretch for the initiates. On top of that, Jaquelyn's body was still aching, and she needed Jack's physical presence for healing and support. Washington, D.C. had gone well and they had stayed connected during the conference, but intimacy at a distance was obviously no match for celebrations in the flesh. Jack finally got the message and returned to California earlier than planned.

As they reconnected at the condo, it became clear that the initiation in the gulch had affected their sense of home in different ways. As you have heard, Jaquelyn had grown fonder of their place in the city as a result of the wild ride. As spring turned into summer the park across the street from their condo provided as much nature as she wanted. For Jack, the opening to love they had experienced in the gorge left him feeling that they needed the land, soft air, and the ubiquitous presence of the ocean to create the bridge between Eros and healing. As a consequence of their differing perspectives, they put the decision to move on hold.

Jaquelyn continued to struggle to find right-relationship with her DAN! colleagues and deal with the many autistic patients she was treating. An updated edition of her book was about to appear in response to its wide acceptance not only in the U.S. but abroad as well. *Children with Starving Brains* had already been translated into Indonesian and Turkish; a pirated Chinese version soon followed. Busyness kept them in California during the fall and into the holidays, which did indeed include spending several delightful days at the condo with Chelsey. Despite the passage of time, body aches and pains continued to remind Jaquelyn of their wild ride. Her bottom rib hurt on the left side just below her heart, and there seemed to be a small area of fibrosis there as a physical reminder of the wild ride. Although he tried several times, Jack was only able to provide temporary relief working with her energy field.

When J&J finally returned to the Island in mid January, it only took a few days for their rhythm to slow down and the focus of life to move towards greater intimacy. Dreams and messages from Third consciousness soon made it clear that it was time to pick up the threads of their erotic healing path once again. Jaquelyn found it a little easier to say "no" to prospective clients and conference leaders when the requests came from across the Pacific. Jaquelyn worked on the new edition of her book while Jack returned to the garden and the water—his two other "mistresses," as Jaquelyn liked to call them. Cozy evenings in their bedroom soon graced their journey again and, as often happens, the surge of intimacy stirred a few shadows that eventually demanded attention.

Close to bedtime, about a week after their return, Jaquelyn was surprised by a sudden desire to make love. Usually they planned their evenings of intimacy at least a day in advance but this time her need arose spontaneously and she was waiting in bed when Jack came into the room at ten-thirty, looking like sleeping beauty in her silky chemise. Jack got the message immediately and quickly disrobed. It had been a long day of writing and, although his heart was wide open from starting to work on a new poem as a surprise for Valentine's Day, he felt a little tired and strangely far from aroused in the usual way.

They snuggled for while as she explored his face and chest with expert hands. Jack took his time caressing her hips and approaching the swell of her breasts, only to leave that delicious landscape repeatedly to tease her. By the time his fingers finally arrived at her nipples she was aching to welcome the familiar surge of energy that sprung from breast to heart, and from there flowed on to her genitals and the rest of her body. Soon he was hard enough to enter. She didn't want to extend the play this time. The hour was late and she was hot.

When he began the familiar phallic dance at the goddess-gate, Jack realized something was different. The pleasure seemed more expanded, as if his whole body was about to enter her, not just his cock. As they undulated slowly, even Jaquelyn's groans created a new, otherworldly resonance for him. He knew that she wanted to climax this time from the growing abandon of her movements. Her will to come and playfully bring him with her would be hard to resist—and he knew that was exactly the challenge.

They played together like two musicians searching for the main theme, he going further and further into an unfamiliar, transcendent world, partly because he was trying not to come but mostly because something entrancing seemed to be leading him there. Jaquelyn had been close to climaxing for a while when he finally entered fully. Her mood that evening included the fantasy that he could make her come by threatening dominance if she didn't surrender. But Jack seemed to take a step back each time she approached the point of no return, rather than being the reckless lover she wanted at that moment.

Finally, after several retreats from culmination, Jaquelyn's irritation broke the silence. "Where are you, sweetheart? I'm not feeling you. I don't think I've ever felt like this before—a little distant, not really involved, even . . . (*she paused and realized she had to say the word*) . . . bored."

Jack heard her voice clearly but from a distance. "I'm here with you," he responded.

No, you're not, she thought and told him so. As they talked Jack lost his erection completely, stayed inside her a few minutes and then withdrew. He was still at peace, despite having left her hanging. Jaquelyn wondered if something was really off in a way they had never encountered before. They held one another for a while and finally fell asleep, each in their own separate world. She couldn't remember that ever happening before.

The next few days were filled with bits of debris from the experience. Jack tried, without success, to describe what had happened until finally they called a council, agreeing it would not be followed by lovemaking as usual. He lit the candle with an observation: "Clearly, Dr. McCandless has a bit of a charge around the fact that our lovemaking the other night faded before she was ready to stop. She has the presumption to think that she's running the show. For a while our connection was absolutely delicious—and, yes, different—which is one of the reasons I wasn't upset by your digs today. I think I know what happened."

"You do?" Jaquelyn was incredulous that he knew and hadn't said anything.

"Yes, at least for me. I tried to tell you, but—"

"—you were close to coming, so you pulled back," Jaquelyn offered.

"That might have been a factor, but primarily I found myself in a new, more transpersonal place, and I'm just learning how to navigate the new landscape."

"Humph," Jaquelyn said in disbelief.

Undeterred by her skepticism, Jack went on. "There's a gate into the erotic world that we might call the *vagina of the great goddess*. When we begin our foreplay, I can tell how far we are from the gate using the erotic sixth sense you've awakened in me over the years. It's like the knowing we have of each other's bodies and our erotic imagination give us an aerial view of where we are in the landscape of arousal. Sometimes I see that we're close to the portal already, while at other times we're still at a considerable distance with a lot of territory to cover. In the old days I would have described this distance psychologically as what we needed to process so that our bodies could celebrate."

"Do you have any idea of what separated us during our last lovemaking? I ask, even though we've decided lately that we don't need to process everything."

"Yes and anyway much of our processing gets done nonverbally as we approach the gate. Our bodies seem to guide us into what needs to be done to make love in that moment. So, while I was writing today, I asked the Third what was going on and was told, 'You're learning more about the practice of transcendent love—which, by the way, plays a significant role in healing at a distance.' The challenge is that we're both attached to the passion of our physical sexuality. Even though the gate was far away when we started making love last time, I felt trusting. I know you have deep knowing in your goddess body. I trust that."

"I used to think I did too, but I'm a little shaken up right now," Jaquelyn responded quietly.

"When I looked at the distance from the gate last time—I'm just remembering this now—I decided to approach the situation more consciously. I first went down the familiar road that makes me feel really turned on—you know, cocky and hard. That path is a mixture of the overwhelming passion to surrender and the desire to penetrate. But when I went down that familiar path last time, *nothing happened!* I managed to side-step self-judgment for which I was grateful . . . and then I saw the two of us as if from a distance. 'How dear we are,' I thought."

"Like children in the garden," Jaquelyn added.

"Without any of the pretensions we've had in the past, thinking that we know what we're doing. I'm feeling more humble now at the same time that we seem to be becoming more empowered. It's a curious paradox."

"I know what you mean. The empowerment for me is not so much out there in the world anymore. It's more internal."

"Yes." Jack agreed. "The other night was one of those rare moments in our relationship when I was the one exploring new sexual terrain. In the past it's always been you. That the old path to arousal wasn't working surprised me, so I looked more carefully and saw both our old pattern and the new transcendent path that was happening spontaneously. If the new path would serve us, I knew I could go there. Then I realized—I'm just seeing this clearly now—that *there are many paths to the gate,* many possibilities, not just the old one and the one we had stumbled onto. In a way multiple paths are what you've wanted all along. With that awareness, I became lighter, which is why I didn't slip into self-judgment after leaving you high and dry. Then a few moments later my center of gravity shifted."

"Away from your cock?"

"Yes, but even a bigger shift took place. I was suddenly *at* the gate, although I hadn't approached along any familiar path. I can tell when you're running the familiar kinds of images about wanting to be overpowered, even if you don't share them with me verbally. That's a part of what makes you such an incredible lover. You sprinkle the stew with a vast array of spices. So soon my cock felt like it was stirring and probing you. We were doing a delicious energy dance, but I could tell we weren't in resonance. I almost always follow you sexually, but this time I felt something else was guiding me."

"It would have been wonderful if you could have told me," Jaquelyn said sadly.

"I didn't really know then what was happening. I'm seeing most of this just now."

"I understand."

"If everything had been blissful as usual," Jack continued, "we wouldn't be having this conversation and discovering there's a new and vast array of paths to the gate. The challenge was that you had a strong expectation last time. You were hot."

Jaquelyn caught his touch of defensiveness mixed in with the spin. "The expectation wasn't in the mind; it was in my body. My body wanted to make love and discharge."

"Maybe we're not supposed to. Maybe we won't discharge this whole stay on the Island as part of the commitment to writing. That's the way it felt the other night. Of course, that could change."

Jaquelyn felt as if the air had been sucked out of the room. Would she feel suspended like this for weeks? Her dependency on him for release slapped her in the face, and she didn't like it one bit. But it was true that she had often challenged him to shift consciousness during lovemaking. She had also been on his case to take more initiative. Her words of upset faded and instead she ended up coughing.

Jack softened immediately. "Don't get me wrong. I think we need to make love, whenever we want to—and maybe even more than we normally do—but in new and different ways that don't involve discharging."

"That's great," Jaquelyn said gamely, coughing again. She took a sip of sparkling water.

"It could be that a kiss would encompass the whole lovemaking, a kiss with the quality of ecstatic communion."

"I hear that. I also hear that you feel released from my sexual mentoring. That's good."

"The detached erotic state that took hold of me is what you have been trying to teach me for a long time," Jack continued. Jaquelyn knew he was spinning, but she let him go on.

"What I did the other night was to release the way I usually become aroused enough to become present in a new way. Apparently my usual consciousness frame was shifted towards witnessing our lovemaking from Third Presence."

"Words, words. What you really mean is that there are times when you're not aroused, so you have to learn new ways to get there. Before I lost you entirely the other night, I felt myself reaching pinnacles of ecstasy but then I plummeted into dark scenarios when I couldn't figure out what was happening. I flirted with both extremes, making up fantasy conversations with you, like being thrilled by your commanding presence, even threatening to spank me if I didn't surrender. That stirred memories from my early childhood of getting attention from grown men without understanding why. So I touched a powerful light, and then when you got soft I was sent down into dark, shadowy crevices. What you're saying now is that we have to move out of those more familiar ways of arousal and be open to new paths."

"Our instructions are to be with whatever is happening in the moment," Jack responded.

"Yes and when I'm really hot like that, I occasionally imagine you saying, 'Spread your ass wider or I'm going to turn you over my knee and spank you until you're begging me to fuck you.' I want to be able to include *any* fantasy in our lovemaking but I just can't imagine you ever saying that, so I have to say it to myself."

"It never occurs to me to run that particular scenario, but I could."

"I've asked you to," Jaquelyn continued. "I've said you need to discipline me, to spank me like my uncle did that time when I was about ten. That image really turns me on when I'm in a certain mood. I said all that, and never another word about it from you. I'm only going to ask for something like that once or twice."

"What nonsense are you talking?" Jack reacted. "We're in this together. Keep asking! We both know the other is almost always doing their best."

"But if we hold certain images that don't click with the other, then we shouldn't pursue them anymore, right?"

"Wrong! You're still focusing on how far apart we were. The game is to pay attention and learn how to play each other's instruments and close the gap."

"I like the sound of that," Jaquelyn replied.

"I didn't plan it, but the center of my awareness of us during the last lovemaking moved almost entirely from the genitals to the heart, which is what you've been asking for, although obviously not that night."

"You've been treasuring my breasts a lot lately, and they're close to my heart," Jaquelyn responded, trying to feel closer.

"I could make love with you for an hour just touching your breasts. They are becoming more and more radiant."

"I never had much feeling in my breasts. They were so tender I didn't want them to be touched—nor my clitoris either. Prior to you, I didn't want anything sexually besides a cock. You changed all that years ago. Now we're starting to explore a whole new world when we make love. It's liberating to think that we can explore together rather than my trying to direct the situation and ending up disappointed or even mad."

"Then we'll have lots of colors on our palette and be in the moment," Jack affirmed.

"I wanted you to fill me completely last time. I needed the physical discharge."

"And I left you hanging, which a man who's learning to be a lover never wants to do. But we can get the teaching as long as we don't interpret the experience as a failure."

"If you could just have said something." Jaquelyn was not quite ready to let go.

"Of course. I will do my best to be verbal in the future, and you can always ask too."

"I did say, 'Where are you?' I asked you if you were in a trance. What else could I have done? You said, 'No, I'm here.' That's all you said."

Jack didn't want to go down the same path again. "You don't have to do anything. I'm learning. You're still my primary teacher—and teachers are always learning too."

"By having tough students to shape them up," Jaquelyn responded.

They battled on for a while and then decided to eat, hoping that might shift the mood. Jack prepared one of his special egg frittatas accompanied by a salad. He put some Chopin piano music on the stereo. That stopped the growing irritation but didn't draw them any closer. They enjoyed the meal, mostly in silence. After dinner, they made one last attempt to reconnect. Jack began.

"I must have had a dash of sternness in my voice or—"

"No, smugness," Jaquelyn corrected him. "I have problems with that."

"Well, it couldn't hurt for me to be more humble in what I say. I feel a certain amount of exuberance about finding meaning in what's happening, and maybe I need to tone down the rhetoric."

"You deserve to feel exuberant. At least our wounds serve to keep us from getting inflated."

"Yes, but I question whether we need them for that purpose anymore. Our relationship does a pretty good job of keeping us honest, although I'm probably easier on you than you are on me," Jack noted. "Maybe that should change."

"Promises, promises! You *could* be more courageous putting out how you feel."

Jack met her challenge. "You've asked me several times to help free us from any addictive sexuality. That's what I've been trying to do. I'm just following my instructions. There's no need for you to feel so distressed, and, obviously, I have to find a way to communicate that doesn't sound like I'm spinning. On the other hand, *I don't have to do anything.*"

"You have to eat chips." Jaquelyn's sudden shift in tone disarmed him.

He had just reached for the Tostitos again and stuffed several more into his still talking mouth. "You're right. I'm addicted to chips. That's where I've transferred *my* sexual addiction."

"From wheat to corn."

"But my real addiction is to you," Jack responded, "and you don't want me to change that at all."

"I think your addiction is more to relationship, and I happen to be the one you're intimate with. I'm the default setting."

He felt the familiar mixture of teasing, insecurity, and criticism—and he didn't bite. "I don't feel that way."

"Really?" Jaquelyn said in disbelief.

"Nope. I'm not addicted to relationship. In fact, I'm weary of relationship."

Jaquelyn never thought she would hear those words leave his mouth. "It's always exhausted *me!*" she said, laughing. "It's hard work."

"I know," Jack said, enjoying her surprise. "I want the world to hear this. *It's always tired her out, folks. And now it's finally tiring me out too. So we both need to shape up!* That's what you said to me in the early years: 'Shape up, Jack, it's hard to live with you.'"

The mood had shifted by the time they started cleaning up the dishes. "Cooking gets your creative juices flowing," Jaquelyn said, feeling a little better. "You used to cut roses. Now cooking is your meditation—lucky me! To help our lovemaking be more of a meditation, I'm going to practice moving the sexual energy up to the heart, the throat, and the Third Eye."

"Far out," Jack said, as the last mazurka came to an end. They went to bed that night feeling that they had stepped back from the edge of a cliff. As it turned out, however, the cliff remained close by.

The following evening Jaquelyn had to share what had been stirring in her all day. "I can't remember the last time I felt this way. In fact, I'm not sure I ever did. I'm actually not turned on to you. Your body still felt sweet to me last night, but the turn-on wasn't there. I never thought I'd feel that way. You have to give me time to adjust to what's happening in our intimacy. It's big for me, bigger than you can imagine."

They had counted on their sexual connection since the beginning, even when there had been anger or major upsets. So Jack was puzzled. Was Jaquelyn punishing him now for not being satisfied? He didn't think so. Her vulnerability was more due to something deep in her core identity that had been shaken. Perhaps he was also being tested. He knew her words would have terrified him in the past. For so long his manhood had depended on her finding him more or less irresistible. He felt the shadows trying to seduce him, saw his own fear as if from a distance—and took a deep breath. There was no point telling her what he thought was happening yet another time. He wasn't that sure himself. Smug, he thought, that's a laugh!

The next few days were sprinkled with sporadic conversations about their erotic limbo, but they never found common ground. Then on the eve of Valentine's Day Richard called to ask his mother to pay for fixing his RV. He had been living in it for a year now, moving the old vehicle from place to place in the San Fernando Valley, near their condo while he tried unsuccessfully to find work to support himself. He had helped Jaquelyn with her nutritional supplement business for a while but with the move to Hawaii she had taken over the reduced activity herself. Although he had creative and computer skills as a graphic artist, Richard seemed to have lost the ability to work for others or even get something going on his own. So J&J had been supporting him—and becoming increasingly concerned about the growing enabling pattern. Now radiator problems had rendered his RV non-drivable, and he was facing a familiar dilemma—no money to fix and move the RV to avoid police impounding it again for parking it in one place for too long. Jaquelyn came into the kitchen, her heart pounding, to tell Jack she was inclined to shell out the money once more so that Richard could repair his aging home on wheels. Had she not felt so strangely distant from Jack, she might have told her son that he had to earn the money this time. Jaquelyn identified that as the right response, but their erotic disconnect allowed her maternal instincts to take over. The idea that he might end up literally living on the street was unthinkable to her. To be shaken loose from the identity of sexual priestess and mother at the same time was too much.

When she told him the situation, Jack went into a long monologue about why she shouldn't bail him out again. Listening to his disapproval made her feel progressively more distant until finally his voice sounded like the fingernail scrapings of a sermonizing father on her maternal blackboard. She blew. "You have no heart for Richard! You never have—and I'm just a mother who can't let go of her son! Without the RV, he's homeless! You don't feel any compassion for his struggles and limitations!" Jaquelyn hurled the words at him as she leapt out of her chair and started to leave the room.

Her eruption poured oil on his sleeping fire. Jack had no idea that he was a sleeping fire, mind you. He thought they were slowly getting through the momentary challenge to their erotic life. In a flash he was a raging bull.

"No you don't!" Jack shouted and followed her into her small office. "You're not going to do your hit-and-run number this time. We're having a conversation that you initiated and because you don't like what I'm saying, you spew out a lot of lies and then disappear!" His voice scared her. The woman's primal fear of being hit flashed in front of her. Jaquelyn followed him back into the kitchen and dropped into the chair again, her body rigid.

Jack was already in an altered state, crashing around in the kitchen, flinging pots on the floor and slamming his open hand down on the counter as he reiterated how much he had given Richard for so many years. She watched in horror as his voice grew louder and a can of cashews hit the floor. Would she be next?

He was possessed—except for a small, quiet, presence witnessing it all in disbelief. Years of accumulated frustration around Richard welled up and broke through the restraint of his usual patience and understanding. "Don't sell the condo! Just go back and live there with Richard!" Jack shouted. "That's what you really want to do!" Another pot hit the floor as his clenched hand came down on the counter again. His voice was already hoarse and raspy.

When Jaquelyn saw he was not going to turn his rage on her physically, she grew strangely calm, as if she had found the eye of the storm. "Do you want me to leave now and go back to California?" she said in a steady voice without emotion.

Jack had no doubt that her question was real. He knew if he went a step further and said "yes," she would leave. He had one of those "drowning man moments" when everything they had shared, worked for, and dreamed about paraded in front of his wild eyes. He knew if they separated, his life would veer off into a cul-de-sac of despair. Not only would their mission be over but he would lose the heart of his life. There would be darkness and pain. He could not live without her. What was he thinking? Who was the creature crashing around in the kitchen? It was all insane. Time slowed down to a crawl. He saw the Third shaking its head in disbelief. No matter the rage he had no choice. After what seemed forever, the fire receded and the raging bull in him finally found a different voice.

"No, I don't want you to go back to California," he shouted.

"Then why did you say that?" Jaquelyn asked, both the wise woman and a child in that moment.

"To give you a taste of your own medicine," Jack heard himself say and wondered if that were really even a part of the truth. Sometimes she did make statements at times of deep feeling that he knew she didn't really mean, but he had learned to handle that over the years. Whatever had unleashed the outburst, the reality of their love started to rescue him from anger. Perhaps the Third had remained present enough to show him the way home. "I wrote you a poem for Valentine's Day," he blurted out, almost saying *fucking poem* but those words died with his fading rage. "I wanted to surprise you tomorrow but, believe it or not, I would read it to you now if it were finished. I don't have the last stanza yet."

Hearing he had written a poem reached across their separation. She had enraged a man again. She had done that with her father and others—and Richard too. Now it was Jack. It wasn't the first time with him, but he had never stormed about so wildly for so long. She wondered if his fury was the result of his still unconscious fear of women. Perhaps for the first time, she actually felt how a man can be entrapped by his love and simultaneous feelings of inadequacy. These realizations arose out of the wisdom of her woman's body, not through her head. She felt the power she'd had since growing breasts to attract *and* enrage men. She saw that the turn-on fantasy of having to surrender to the man in lovemaking was associated with these patriarchal patterns. She knew it was time to let that all go and risk finding out who she was without all that cultural baggage. It felt like a death, so she knew it had to happen. Jaquelyn almost blessed his rage.

Meanwhile, Jack was still stomping about in the kitchen. The lava continued to flow but the volcano had stopped erupting. "We can't go on like this," he said hoarsely. "I don't know where all this anger comes from, but we have to make changes. I'm through with the old Richard story. It's in your hands. I can't be caught between not wanting to abandon him to a life of dependency and enabling him any longer. I can't have him disrupt our relationship in this way. The triangle is destructive for all of us—and I see my part of the pattern. Yes, my compassion could be greater—and I trust the mother in you will find a way for us to work this out together. We have to! The old pattern has to end."

The anguish of still parenting a grown dependent son had again turned Jaquelyn away from doing what she knew was right. But she simply had to help Richard. He would have no place to sleep at night without the RV. Men don't understand how a mother feels, she thought, as she entered that archetypal place of refuge.

Jack wondered what had possessed him. Clearly, he had been stuffing his feelings about Richard, so he needed to be more current about that ongoing drama. But Richard was only the catalyst for something else that had been brewing all week—and perhaps a lot longer. In the past their powerful erotic bond had dissolved his anger again and again, but even a break in that rapport didn't fully explain the explosion. As he slowly put the kitchen back together, he got a glimpse of what might have happened. *The raging bull—a* wild part of him that lived in the cellar of his being—had broken loose. His unexpressed and unconscious masculine rage most likely had been an obstacle to their deepening love—until that moment in the kitchen. That frustrated, exasperated and fearful wild man had not yet said "I do" at the sacred alter of their Third—until now. Now the wild man had emerged and said, "No, don't leave. I do not understand how or why, but I know I love you. You are my mate." In a strange way the whole week had been orchestrated to make sure that no part of him was left out of their journey. The insight left a sense of awe in its wake. *Be careful how glibly you claim relationship as your spiritual path*, he thought.

The next morning the cold water at the local pool hardly put out Jack's fire. In the afternoon he finished the last stanza of the poem. Further reaping of the harvest arrived the following evening during J&J's celebration of Valentine's Day.

10 ❧ The Goddess Pays Jaquelyn a Visit

Considering what had happened the evening before, they felt strangely lighthearted when they sat down for their traditional Valentine's council.

"There are three possibilities," Jack began. "We can completely ignore what happened last night and not process it at all; we can do our best to witness what happened; or we can do what we usually do."

"Beat it to death."

"Yeah."

"There has to be a better option than that," Jaquelyn said hopefully.

"The middle option seems the best to me, although I'm game to just go on and follow our commitment to not process so much."

"I'm still too confused to go on," Jaquelyn acknowledged. "I want to pretend we were in a movie last night, playing the roles we were given. Tonight we're going to shift into the audience and watch the drama again to see what really happened."

"Beautiful!" Jack agreed.

"OK, but first I want to tell you something that happened to me in the bathtub a little while ago. I closed my eyes and imagined you in the water with me. We were just playing around, and I let you know that I didn't want you to tell me what to do, except maybe in our sexual life. Whether I'm right or wrong is beside the point. I just don't want *anyone* telling me what to do. Like it or lump it. You're more willing to wrangle all the time but to be honest I don't want to be bothered. I just want to follow that spirit in me that doesn't necessarily have anything to do with sanity or reason. Maybe that's self-indulgent. I don't know."

"That was beautiful." Jack couldn't help laughing. "Your honesty is disarming."

"I'm like a kid," Jaquelyn confessed. "I want to do just what I want to do."

"Absolutely. You witnessed your own monologue beautifully, including the indulgence. Go on."

"I was trying to analyze my sexual feelings in the warm water when I remembered a resident in Ob-Gyn during my intern days at Cedars of Lebanon Hospital. This guy did an experiment involving women wearing Tampons in a bathtub to see how much water went into their vaginas. They didn't want pregnant women to sit in bathwater in case their vaginas opened up enough to let dirty water enter the uterus. Are you following me?"

"Yes, although I have no idea where you're going," Jack admitted.

"I was inspecting the water flow into my genitals when spontaneously I did a continuous Kegel exercise—contracting the genitals, holding the tension, and then pulling the energy up my spine. I was also making those Sanskrit vowel sounds associated with each energy center. As I held the Kegels, I could feel a force moving up my body. I wanted to stop it at various places, including the heart, but the sound wanted to go right to the top of my head. The crown sound is supposed to be *AI*—as in *aye*, you remember—but somehow mine was *EEE*, the sound of the sexual center. I was struggling with the two sounds, trying to get them together, so I didn't have to be in just one or the other. Are you still with me?"

He nodded hopefully.

"I looked at the force moving up my spine—Kundalini, I guess," Jaquelyn continued. "When I have an orgasm with you, I don't hold back at all. I just spread more and more, letting the energy go out in ripples and waves into the universe. I noticed that holding the Kegel contractions in the tub led to just the opposite. The energy was going in and then up. It was amazing to me that this kind of energy could remain internal and move up, rather than out."

"What happened when the force entered the crown?"

"I don't know if I got that far. When I reached the top of my head, I almost lost consciousness. The only thing that maintained my presence was the debate between *EEE* and *AI*. The *EEE* representing my pelvis still wanted to maintain its identity as the focus moves into the domain of *AI*, which represents something like, *I am god/goddess*—you know, the transpersonal crown energy."

"Wow! You've created a ceremony in the tub that could reconcile flesh and spirit *in the body!* That's what we've been dealing with these past few days."

"It's incredible that our struggles would move to such a tangible level!" Jaquelyn exclaimed.

"Sound has always been extremely important for you."

"Yes, going back to my Oklahoma church days, when the congregation spoke in tongues during the wilder part of the service."

"Maybe we had to have the explosion in order for this realization to come about," Jack suggested. "Apparently, it's hard to get each other's attention at times."

"I think it's more about me pushing away from you enough to feel that we're not codependent, despite how present you are inside of me most of the time now. There must be a more creative way to discover that beside what happened yesterday."

"I would hope so."

"How would you describe the energy you were in yesterday?" Jaquelyn asked.

"Rage, existential rage." Jack said the words with a growl.

"Was that erotic? Is there such a thing as erotic rage?"

"It was a displacement of erotic energy. Obviously we're not dealing with our sexual energy very effectively right now."

"Where the hell *is* our sexual energy lately?" Jaquelyn exclaimed.

"Yours seems to have disappeared and then I started to feel the same way. Although I know it's impossible not to be sexually attracted to each other, it shakes up my world when I don't feel it."

"I agree that the attraction is always there, so when we don't feel it, that suggests the energy is being expressed in another way."

"Is that sublimation?" Jaquelyn wanted to know.

"Not in this case. Anger is not a useful path for sublimation."

"So, it's displacement."

"Exactly—into rage." Jack explained. "We're sculpting each other and when the clay is hard, a certain level of frustration finally arises."

"That brings recklessness?"

"Yes, although it was more explosive than reckless. I don't usually feel reckless. You're the more reckless one, but when I'm taken into the presence of the raging bull, I see now how unstable I can get. If we're not in balance, the energy can go wild. Passionate love can be dangerous."

"Can you make that last statement more personal?" Jaquelyn challenged him.

"I became violent in response to your inflammatory words. We're doing full-spectrum healing now and so, if the shadows are not included, they catch us by surprise. Since I trust that all our experiences are interconnected, the Kegel exercise you were doing might have something to do with what's been going on."

"Our ultimate goal seems to be creating an Eros tsunami in our relationship."

"A tsunami arises when two huge underwater earth plates begin to move against each other. Perhaps the two plates are the two of us or the two sounds!"

"Yes, and the tension between them must be relieved. To create a giant wave of Eros, we have to live through the movement of the plates. In other words we have to survive our personal unconscious earthquake."

They both fell silent for a moment contemplating the metaphor. From earthquakes it was easy to shift to volcanoes and the card with the painting of Mauna Loa erupting that Jack had presciently chosen for Valentine's Day. It was time to give her the poem.

He had always thought of Mauna Loa and her sister Mauna Kea as huge volcanic breasts, particularly in the winter when they wore their snow-nipples with goddess splendor.

"When a volcano erupts, it's like a breast pouring forth fire," Jack said out of the silence.

"That's wonderful; say it again."

"The volcano is an explosion of fire from the breast of the great mother. The milk of a volcano is the molten lava, and as you saw yesterday, I erupted. Still, a small part of me was watching the whole scene. So I wasn't completely lost in the violence. I would like you to read your valentine poem now and then we could work with the sounds."

Jaquelyn nodded, settled back on the Third's pillow, and read his poem slowly, stopping now and then to reread a line that particularly touched her. She kept shaking her head incredulously at the density of the imagery and how aptly it described their relationship at the moment. He knew it needed more work, but that didn't matter. The poem was just for them.

"You've never written anything like this before," Jaquelyn said admiringly. "Each line says so much. It's a precious gift."

"Thank you. The still emerging lover wrote it for his goddess. Listening to you read the poem somehow allowed me to witness my anger more freely—and that was a precious gift. The bar is set high now. We cannot tolerate any denial of our own darkness. I'm glad I was able to finish the poem, despite the explosion. Apparently the underwater earthquake is still in process."

A few days later Jaquelyn opted to stay home while Jack joined his daughter Baki and her family at the beach. On his return Jaquelyn wanted to talk. He could tell she felt more relaxed, even inspired, but he had no idea what had caused the shift.

Jaquelyn began to explain. "I looked at the whole situation today, starting with the need to break out of our sexual patterning on the physical level so that we could move the Eros further into spirit and healing. Then there's the part of me fighting like mad to keep it just the wonderful way it has been. It's like a civil war! Meanwhile you're mostly being dense about it all, thoroughly enjoying our physical intimacy, while I'm bitching and moaning and lecturing. Then all of a sudden a week ago, at a time when I really needed to ground myself by making love, you journeyed into another world. It was a shock to my psyche, when you faded in me and pulled away that night, I actually didn't know who I was for a while. The time we had made love before that seemed like a memory of a memory. It's mystifying to me that you were able to make a physical change so rapidly. Then the next morning, I had the unique experience of not wanting you to touch me. I can't remember ever feeling that way before. I've been hesitant to tell you that part of the story."

"I felt pushed away, so thank you for confirming that," Jack responded. "I did a lot of self-witnessing today too while I was swimming. There's an ongoing pattern in our sexuality of you wanting me to make you surrender when I'm fully tumescent. Before we met, I was far from that kind of a man sexually, but slowly I've tried to play that role since it works pretty well for us. Now we're supposed to break that pattern, among others, and so I took a different path to surrender last time. The story that arose in me went something like this: *Jack, this call to spirit is bigger than your sexual desire. You have no choice but to bow to its power. Let the energy pour into you.* I was into wanting to be overcome too. I just had a different surrender story going. In a way it's like what happened to you in the bathtub yesterday, trying to bring the *EEE* and the *AI* sounds together. The last time we made love I was the *AI* and you were the *EEE*. The two sounds coming together might dissolve our remaining boundaries between flesh and spirit."

"Sounds totally shape where I go in my head—and in my body," Jaquelyn picked up the thread. "I respond to all the sounds around me too, including the sounds of your anger the other night. But then my fear diminished even though you were still thrashing around."

"That's because there was a corner of my awareness watching it all," Jack offered.

"The part that kept you from actually breaking something or hurting me?"

"Yes, it's clear that I stayed away from you and chose things to throw around that wouldn't break. Yet I was still out of control. Maybe I'm spinning but perhaps I had to enter the darkness to risk emancipating oneself from the tyranny of control. Obviously, that can be dangerous."

"Well, dangerous or not, we've been tumbling in another kind of gulch these last few days," Jaquelyn said with a sigh. She was tempted at that moment to share what had happened to her while he was at the beach, but she wasn't quite ready and decided to wait until after their regular meditation the next morning. Just the decision to hold the experience a while longer was a significant and empowering change for her. Maybe it was the fear of his reaction and the freshness of the experience, or maybe it was the need to first find a new voice that was more uniquely hers. In any event the meditation the following morning brought Jaquelyn new insights about the power of sound to enter the spirit world and left her higher than a kite, as well as ready to tell her story.

She asked him to remain in the small room where they meditated. The space was actually an alcove that was separated from the living room by decorated Japanese sliding doors. The outer wall had built-in shelves that housed their collection of talking pieces and other ceremonial remembrances. Two white wicker chairs, a low wooden coffee table, a bookshelf, and a standing lamp completed the simple furnishings.

"Sounding all started before I met you," Jaquelyn began, "when I joined the Self Realization Fellowship and was given the mantra HRIM. The woman there pronounced the I like in the word trim, and that's the way I said it for years when I meditated. She also told me that it was my own secret mantra that shouldn't be shared with anyone. Then years later, after you and I met, I was reading about sacred sounds and there was HRIM right there on the page, identified as the mantra of the divine feminine. It wasn't secret at all! So I went to see Judith Tyberg, the author of *Language of the Gods*—you remember. I pointed to the mantra in my book and she belted it out the correct way—HREEM! The long EEE activated my sexual center and then expanded through my whole body. That was my real initiation, and I've been using that mantra ever since. She explained how the HREEM had to go through the heart, whose sound is HUU, in order to reach out to the other—who, for me of course, was you in the physical world. From the heart the sound goes into the throat, AHH, and then on into the brow or Third Eye, OM, in order finally to be transformed into the crown sound, AI. That's the key to bringing all the sounds together. The crown sound has a subtle kind of Y in the middle of it, like in the word aye."

"When my heart is open," Jaquelyn continued, "I'm in touch with the sun and the beauty of the ocean, and the blessings of being alive. The heart is also the place where we merge during the still moments in lovemaking. Those moments allow my orgasmic sounds to move into the AI, which is about searching for union on a higher level. Just now in our meditation I made the choice to go beyond the physical world of relationship, using the crown energy to boost me. There was a moment of feeling the loss of that delicious connection with you, but I'm on a mission now and so I honored my intention to go further. As I did, I felt the AI electrifying my head in an extremely subtle way. Then the sound went out and out . . . encompassing everything. The AI is that place in the crown where we make the transition from the body to formlessness. To bring it back into the physical plane, I would have to add the M, so the sound would be AI-M. Without the M, the AI takes me out beyond form and sensation. I don't bring anything back, just the sense of having touched the mystery that sends vibrations down through the body. But I don't want to return all the way into my body. I want to hover a little above my body in a spirit world that I can actually sense and know consciously even in my body. So the sound I want is somewhere between AI and AI—M, with just a hint of the M."

She continued by describing how she had played with these sounds like a musician discovering a new instrument for sending the body into ecstasy. "When I moved back into the sexual center, I felt the yearning for union with the other that's awakened by our lovemaking. Now we have a choice. We can embrace the moment of merging, as we have done in the past, or we can go further by allowing the rising Kundalini to be initiated—which leads to celebrating the universal force. It's our union at the sexual center that is the source of both options. Having the choice is what is really new."

She felt ready now to share what had happened the day before while he was at the beach.

"Yesterday I was in a terrible place. The morning after our abortive lovemaking a week ago was unique in my life with you. I can't remember another time when you have reached out to me and I thought I don't want you to touch me! I actually recoiled. I had an expectation the night before that something extraordinary was about to happen just before you withdrew, and that plunged me into a state of confusion. My whole body was set up for lovemaking, so it was a shock to the system. My first reaction was anger, wondering if there was some part of you that wanted to frustrate me because I was asking you to let go of your sexual patterns. But then, trusting what is guiding us now, I realized that it was your unconscious genius to allow what happened to actually happen. I don't give you credit for it, and I don't blame you for it. So I couldn't really be mad at you. I knew it wasn't anything you did deliberately to hurt or defy me. For a while that morning, I was lost in a flood of feelings about how hard it is for men and women not to hurt each other."

Jack listened, knowing Jaquelyn was headed for something that would be challenging. The only time Jaquelyn built her story slowly was when she was planning to share something that would reshape their relationship.

"Then you left," Jaquelyn went on, "and I was so glad you did. I felt enormous relief to get out of your field. I needed some time to get back my bearings and find out who I was. I have been so influenced by our connection that I was lost, lost in an astral forest. You left and I let out a huge sigh of relief. The fog lifted and the air cleared—and the sun came out, literally. Our relationship is so intense, so thick, that it penetrates every aspect of my actions and my being. I can lose who I am.

"The sun was shining on the floor in our bedroom, creating a lovely, inviting spot," Jaquelyn continued. "So I sunbathed in the nude and warmed myself. The air was beautiful and the birds were singing. I was a jewel in an incredible setting. I lay there in the sun and went into a deep meditation. I felt my womanness and how hard it was to resist the pull and yearning for penetration. Then I found my fingers exploring myself. I let them enter. I felt the energy build. I couldn't penetrate far enough for a full climax, but I could feel the energy building. The orgasm was soft and flowed all over me. For the first time in my orgasmic life I did not have an image or a feeling of a penis penetrating me. Then I realized what was happening. I was feeling the goddess. I was experiencing the goddess in myself and I was feeling the collective goddess, an incredible maternal being encompassing all the power of women to be ferocious, say, like Kali, and to change the world. I also felt the goddess's sweetness and how she was all of nature—the sun and birds and everything, all together. She was my divine counterpart. I couldn't condense the core feminine manifestation of life as the great mother, or the great warrior, or the great anything, because she can shape-shift and create whoever she wants to be. These creations manifest most powerfully in the feminine body, and I felt the deliciousness and the interiority and the secret mystery of all that in my own body through our lovemaking. I've always had an intimation of some powerful awakening force, but I had no idea what it was, even though I touched it when I was very young. Then it had to do with Jesus and my father—with love for something much bigger, but always masculine, always masculine, until that moment in the bedroom.

"So I lay there feeling the warmth of the sun penetrating me like a lover. The sounds of nature also entered my body and I felt how delicious it was to be this incredible receptive vessel. I realized that the goddess was enjoying her goddessness through my woman's body. My body and my genitals are jewels that are filled with light and sounds that are all a mystery. I began running my fingers over my clitoris. For years I had no awareness of my clitoris and wouldn't allow anyone to touch it. But through our lovemaking and your gentleness and your incredible mastery of sexual energy, it has been awakened. That's a powerful gift for a woman that has to be handled well. You know all that. I could feel the womanness in my clitoris as the more tangible and external counterpoint to the interiority of my secret mystery place of divine creation. In a way my clitoris felt like my masculine counterpart, able to emit energy and penetrate like the male organ. I could feel all that, but there was still a distinct feminine aspect to the clitoral emanations that were subtler, sweeter, and deeply connected to that inner place of union. Perhaps that's the great difference between males and females—the interiority of that secret place where the sexual chakra is awakened by union with the other. The fertile power of creating a new being lives there. I could feel that the goddess was pleasuring me and that I was pleasuring the goddess. There were waves of sweetness in my orgasm I had never felt before, waves of ecstasy all through my being that didn't stop with my physical boundary but expanded outward. I felt I was sharing this incredible touch of the divine, this union, with the whole feminine world. I felt the powerful yearning of men to penetrate women so that they can touch what I was experiencing and be transformed."

Jack was mesmerized as Jaquelyn went on with her story. "And in that state I realized, despite the hard work I had done to heal the addictive aspect of my sexuality and the imagery of being forced to surrender, that you knew somehow I still had this divine story locked up in my being. In the goddess's presence I had none of those fantasies—no fantasies at all, in fact. It's a blessing that those old images and fantasies are gone. My old buddies that could always get me off are gone. I don't need them anymore. They've taught me and helped me in many ways. I'm feeling incredible love and appreciation that you had the wisdom and the genius to do what you did. I felt compassion for any pain you may have felt, but you were sure enough of yourself to handle it. Even though you might not understand what I'm telling you, you have more confidence than ever before. You're holding your own. It is your strength as a lover, along with our meditations, that have created a womb for me to birth new levels of my feminine.

"I have enlarged myself in our union," Jaquelyn continued, "by taking in the divine feminine in a way that is powerful for me and I believe can be for all women. I want to share this and help women find a way to invite this experience. I hope they don't have to reach 73 and have a man like you to do it. I want to find some way to help women realize they really are goddesses. The horrors of what happens in some cultures, like the clitorectomy practices in Africa, literally relegate women to biological mothering. A clitorectomy is one of the most inhuman acts I can imagine.

"After I had my love affair in the sun with the goddess, I looked into the mirror and saw myself with short hair—and so I cut it, just like that. It could even be shorter in the back. See how lovely it is?" He looked carefully and agreed. "I wanted to surprise you. When my hair is shorter, it makes my head look poofy and cute and young. Longer hair drags me down. With the empowerment by the goddess, I just went snip, snip, snip. And then I went snip, snip, snip some more. I tapered it and trimmed it, and felt very beautiful."

Her hair was such a place of vulnerability that for the goddess to empower her in that way was a major step. Jaquelyn wasn't quite finished sharing her revelations.

"I also saw my whole relationship to Sri Aurobindo in a new light. I realized that he and the Mother had started something that needed to be expanded. The Mother ran the ashram and was creative in the outer world. He carried the interiority. They reversed the traditional roles. Aurobindo moved from the role of teacher and activist in the world to having a love affair with his feminine. Our path is similar in some ways."

Having shifted from her personal story, Jack found his voice. "Maybe it's because Aurobindo has had such a deep influence on you that we have gone through a similar cycle. You've gone out into the world as a physician and I am becoming more interior as a writer. You entered DAN!, a club of mostly male researchers and doctors devoted to healing children and brought your goddess gifts to all of them. Finally your wisdom allowed you to step back from the worldly pattern when you realized how exhausting the work had become.

"Sitting here, listening to you is wondrous," Jack continued. "I'm so grateful. We are being guided and have to trust what happens is part of the teachings. That's particularly hard for a man when he leaves his woman high and dry sexually! The lovemaking was so different that night. Our bodies felt strange, without the awareness we usually have. We plunged, like in the gulch, only this time I was the one to say, 'It's OK, sweetheart. We're in this together.' So, the next morning, when you were feeling don't touch me, I could easily have gone into a reaction. But again trusting the guidance, I just lay there a while and then I said, '"Let me just hold you.' That brought your repulsion back to neutral and your charge disappeared.

Yesterday when I left for the beach, I knew it was right not to pull you into a day with the family. I don't feel fear listening to your story of the goddess's penetration. It's the natural harvest of all that has happened recently. The divine feminine mystery has been born in you. To celebrate all that I have to transform any part of me that would limit you or hold you back in any way."

"Does that trouble you?"

"On the contrary. I was just thinking, how lucky can a man be to dance with the mystery—and not only when we make love."

11 🐦 Ode to the Goddess

By the summer of 2005 Jaquelyn was also prepared to leave the rush of Southern California and begin to moderate their busy lives by making the permanent move to the Blue House. But before she could appreciate the possibilities of living a more 24/7 life with Jack, Jaquelyn had to deal with the sadness of leaving her family behind, particularly Chelsey and Richard. That took a while . . .

J&J moved just after Thanksgiving, 2005, and because of the timing, they were not with children and grandchildren either on that day or Christmas Eve, as had been the ongoing tradition in Jaquelyn's family. In fact, it was the first time in thirty years they failed to gather for at least one of those holidays. That made the move across the Pacific especially bleak for Jaquelyn.

On their anniversary the day after the Winter Solstice, J&J had made love passionately, but even that didn't seem to shift Jaquelyn's mood, nor did the lovely walk along the Cane Road that preceded their council on New Year's Eve. It was clear that dealing with the fallout from the move would be the theme of "ringing in the new year."

Jaquelyn suggested they start off the council with a long meditation, during which she struggled with judging herself for feeling so closed down. After they finished, Jack asked her to speak, but she declined, so he picked up the Peruvian rattle they were using that evening as a talking piece and began.

"Our Third seems far away. I had some trouble making the connection, but I finally got through. We definitely have lost something these past few weeks, despite our wondrous anniversary lovemaking. During the meditation, I got a few hints about how to move forward, one of which had to do with letting go of our old stories—yours about the woman having to follow the man literally across the ocean, and me, the subtle way my father controlled my mother's movements by taking care of her so devotedly, particularly towards the end of her life. But the main thought that came through had to do with what you said last night when we had dinner at Café Il Mondo."

"You mean about not wanting to be here without you?" Jaquelyn asked.

"Yes. It was the intensity of your comments and the particular phrase, 'I'd be packing my bags in a moment, if you were to disappear.' I didn't believe you in the restaurant, and I was encouraged just now in the meditation to stay with my disbelief that you're here only because of your love for me."

"But it's true. That's how I feel."

"We're here, both of us, to take the work we do individually and together to 'another level,' to use your favorite phrase. We've created a space for this to happen on a spirited piece of land and in a community that's supportive—let me finish (*Jaquelyn had started to reach for the rattle*). What's partly in the way of embracing that vision is this old story of the woman being caught in the patriarchal trap and having to follow the man, like your mother followed your father from Oklahoma to California." He put the piece down seeing how eager she was to speak.

"My mother *hated* leaving Oklahoma," Jaquelyn began. "She had friends and family there and didn't want to travel across country in a weird-looking vehicle my father had welded together in his car repair shop. The appearance of our van really embarrassed her. We were all so unsophisticated. I thought our 'wagon' was neat. What did I know? People called us *Okies* and made fun of us, as my father drove the family west, picking fruit and fishing. He was having a ball; my mother was miserable. I can't help but feel a little that way moving here."

"I get it. And I have to confess that I've reminded myself of my father on a few occasions these past few weeks, as my taking such good care of you veered towards a pattern of control."

"I've got to find some way to get out of this funk. I'm clear about my depression from leaving the family, but now the problem seems to be that my heart isn't open. I haven't felt yours very open either. To explore the new levels of healing with Chelsey that we've been talking about, we have to be in resonance with each other."

"Yes, and we have to give ourselves a little time and space to do that. It's only been four weeks since the move."

The challenge had been identified but, as the conversation continued, they both realized the mood was not going to shift. So, instead of continuing the council, they decided to listen to one of Jaquelyn's guided-imagery healing tapes while they held each other in bed. As he often did, Jack fell asleep before the imaginal journey was half over. Jaquelyn lay awake for a while, still longing for her darkness to lighten, until sleep brought its welcomed relief. Midnight and the turn of the year passed without their notice.

J&J awoke the next morning feeling humbled and grateful for the dawn of a new year. "We're like newborns," they both agreed. Holding each other in the embrace meditation, they found humor in the dramatic pace that had taken over their life since their initiation in the gulch. They saw how each time a crisis loomed, they ultimately found guidance through the wisdom of their relationship. "There has to be a more conscious way to journey forward now," each of them thought at various times during New Year's Day, in between receiving phone calls from friends and family. By the end of the afternoon, they were both ready for another council in the hope their Third would offer new insights.

The need for guidance during the council on the first day of January helped them to embrace reality in a new way. They used the occasion to take stock of their relationship from a broad witness perspective. In particular, Jaquelyn realized that she had an actual visceral reaction to Jack's imperfections because of how her vulnerability had increased along with her love. The council also emphasized her need for greater access to a witness state that would allow her to accept him, at least in that moment, imperfections and all. "I won't stop trying to perfect your ordinary self," she told him, "but our Third is calling me to do that with more compassion. Of course, I want you to do the same for me! Making the big move raised the bar and we contracted. I'm seeing it all more clearly now."

Their council continued in a lighter vein and ended in a state of silent gratitude. Jack's final words were clear and heartful. "On the path of becoming the lover of the goddess the man must also face the bleakness of Kali. Even though temporarily he may have become the 'enemy,' his Beloved still needs to see herself—darkness and all—reflected in the mirror of his love. That makes me think of that great Leonard Cohen song, 'Dance me to the End of Love.' I remember one verse by heart:

'Dance me to your beauty
With a burning violin
Dance me through the panic
Till I'm gathered safely in
Lift me like an olive branch
Be my homeward dove
And dance me . . . to the end of love.'"

To mark a new cycle in our big story and as a preview of coming attractions I'd like to offer one of Jack's poems—a favorite of mine. It was written in an honest but playful mood as a thirtieth anniversary present for Jaquelyn a month after the move. He had no idea how prescient it would be.

Q and A about the Goddess on Our Thirtieth Anniversary

How angry can the goddess be when loving a mere mortal threatens her power?

Imagine Pele just before her hot juices burst from the caldera
To create a new shore as her boiling blood enters the sea.
Imagine Diana in full command of her celestial stallion
As she rides to the hunt from which no creature escapes.
Imagine Kali, hungry for yet more violent men
To follow those still warm on her lips

I don't need to imagine . . .

I know fire eyes that penetrate to oceanic depths
When this mortal fails to show up with every cell.
I know the pounding heart that fears being hunted
When I elude the search for radical honesty.
I know the feeling of being devoured by ecstatic love
With every touch, kiss, and encounter with your mystery.

How unpredictable can she be when her feelings are fully awakened?

Imagine a wind that shifts in every moment, swirling eddies
Mixed with blasts from whims of goddess breath.
Imagine sea changes defying the most seasoned sailor
Struggling to maintain course and command of ship.
Imagine the sudden seismic trembles of an aroused Gaia
Impatient with the dishonoring of misdirected men.
Imagine the white inferno at the core of a sun
That makes life possible on only one of the planets.

I don't need to imagine . . .

I know sudden shifts of mood that destroy all expectations
Demanding present moment, only moment for survival.
I know the sudden swell of a gale overtaking my boat

Even when the bosom of harbor and home are in sight.
I have been shaken like a rattle of unsuspecting stones
When my affirmation slumbers or is slow in coming.
And I have been burned to a crisp by the wind whipped flames
Of a stormy heart in the tempest of her transformation.

And how sweet can my goddess be when her love calls for communion?

Imagine a voice that sings with prolific passion
As the gates of heaven open wide in surrender.
Imagine a breast so nourishing for the soul
That all other fare leaves only a wanton appetite.
Imagine desire boundless in the swell of hips
That would test the talents of a Michelangelo.
And imagine a sun rising on a new wondrous world
Where making love has become an ultimate practice.

If this be our path, then what is the koan that captures the secret of the journey?

Devotion, discipline, and ancient mantras?
The chakral hum of seamless mind, heart, and body?
Acts of bravery slaying a multitude of dragons?
Searching for sacred secrets at the boundaries of awareness?
Yes, all of these and more.
But my goddess says simply:
"All you have to do is make me happy."

Part III

❧

Creating a New
Mythology of Relationship

12 ✒ Third Consciousness as Healer

Before we begin the next story, I need to fill you in on the status of J&J's health. When Jack had Lasik surgery in 1990, the ophthalmologist made a diagnosis of glaucoma, particularly in his right eye. That initiated a series of medical treatments, including drops and several outpatient surgeries. Jack supported these conventional treatments with a daily set of eye exercises and a healing meditation that helped to stabilize his condition. In addition, he and Jaquelyn shared a dream of finding a way they could use their strong erotic connection to bring about further healing and even a reversal of his glaucoma. They were well aware that the latter possibility flew directly in the face of conventional medical wisdom.

When they moved to the Island, Jack's Los Angeles ophthalmologist referred him to a protégé whose office was in Kona, so the journey to the tourist center of the Island became a quarterly pilgrimage. Many months without a checkup had passed by the time of the first appointment in late December of 2005. The diagnosis was not encouraging. The optic nerve in his right eye showed further deterioration and there was some peripheral nerve loss in the left eye. Even though he had recently passed his driver's test successfully, the trip home that day was filled with foreboding about the future.

Meanwhile, Jaquelyn had experienced a few episodes of atrial fibrillation and so was in the process of readjusting her treatment for mild hypertension. These medical realities expanded the already hot topic of healing, previously focused largely on Chelsey, into their own bodies. J&J were thrust into the dual roles of healee and healer, which naturally further deepened their intention to use their strong Eros-bond for healing. They saw the mission in much the same way the traditional shamanic healers used their connection with the spirit world to manifest healings. For J&J this transcendent healing state became increasingly identified with Third Presence.

After the sobering visit to the ophthalmologist, Jaquelyn took on the task of healing Jack's eyes with a passion. By early January she had already recorded a few guided healing meditations for him to use on a daily basis. In addition, she suggested they visit an herbalist they knew in Hilo to explore other healing possibilities.

So on a bright and blustery day in early January they made the pilgrimage to the "Big City" to have a session with Stan, the herbalist. An additional purpose of the trip was to buy a Sears garden tractor for mowing the extensive hillside and meadows around their home, one that Jack could actually sit on! Stan examined Jack's eyes and came up with a number of homeopathic remedies that he felt would at least stop further loss of the visual field.

"Don't let these medicines get warm in your car," Stan suggested at the end of the session.

"I'll put them in the trunk under a towel," Jack responded as they emerged from the traditional house in the old part of Hilo. He opened the trunk of the Avalon that he had parked in Stan's narrow driveway. The passenger side of the vehicle was up against a row of hibiscus bushes. Jaquelyn was standing to his right, her back brushing up against the hibiscus hedge. He dropped the bag of remedies into the trunk and reached for a large beach towel to wrap around the small package.

"I think the medicines would be cooler under the front seat," Jaquelyn advised.

Jack didn't agree and felt a touch of annoyance. Nevertheless, he handed her the small bag, which Jaquelyn took in her right hand as she began to move between the car and the bushes to carry out her plan. In the next moment two events took place simultaneously.

Jack slammed the trunk lid down vigorously and Jaquelyn pushed away from the car with her left hand to get past the bushes not noticing that she had rested her hand on the open rim of the trunk. Her scream was restrained but chilling. "Quick, open the trunk," was all she said in a voice so low that Stan, only twenty feet away, already greeting his next client, didn't notice.

Jack looked in horror at Jaquelyn's left hand, whose fingers were no longer visible. He quickly reopened the trunk, as an image of severed fingers flooded his vision. "Oh, my God," was all he could say.

Jaquelyn clutched her left hand with the right as the blood began to flow from a cut on the ring finger. She shifted into medical emergency mode instantly. The fact that it was her own hand that was injured didn't seem to matter.

"I need to squeeze the fingers tightly to stop the bleeding and get some ice right away."

"I'll go back inside and get something to—"

"No, don't go back," Jaquelyn said in a harsh whisper. "Get in the car and drive." They slipped into the car immediately and found a small package of Kleenex to wrap the wound.

"What can I do?" Jack groaned. "I'm so sorry."

Jaquelyn felt only a limited amount of pain and was thinking clearly. "My ring finger is probably broken," she told him in a matter-of-fact voice. "It wasn't your fault. I shouldn't have rested my hand there. But you did park so close to the bushes that it was hard for me to get by." He nodded, feeling totally responsible. "I can't see what the damage is until I clean off the blood. I have to get some ice on it as soon as possible."

"Let's go to the emergency room and have them take a—"

"No," Jaquelyn interrupted. "That's the last place I want to go when I'm bleeding. All you do is wait." She knew ERs from her medical training and was sure she could give herself better care. "Let's go to Café Pesto and I'll clean up my hand in the bathroom. Then we'll get some ice in the Health Food Store."

Jack backed out of the driveway carefully, so distraught that he wanted to reverse time and eliminate what had happened. He actually had a flash of a climactic scene from an old *Superman* movie when the Man of Steel does exactly that in order to undo some unthinkable disaster. They drove the half mile to the restaurant in a few interminable minutes, while her hand bled profusely, wrapped in the wad of tissue. By the time he left her off and parked the car, his heart was pounding rapidly.

Jaquelyn entered the ladies room quickly, brushed past the woman drying her hands with a rushed "I've just got a little cut and need to clean it," and turned on the water. She felt the sting immediately followed by a flash of sharp pain that shot up her arm. She hit the soap dispenser with her right hand, feeling grateful that it was the left that had been injured. *I'd be out of tennis for a long time if it were my right*, she thought. Then she realized that two-hand typing at the computer might be impossible for a while. She had a moment of anxiety, and then another wave of pain brought her attention back to the competent job her right hand was doing to clean the wound. The left hand was still relatively numb, and she could see that the cut was quite deep, but she was no longer sure that any fingers were broken. Even if they were, there was nothing else to do but bind all her fingers together to create a natural splint.

Jaquelyn was still in the bathroom when Jack came into the old building that housed Café Pesto. He began pacing in the small hallway outside the restrooms, smelling the familiar odor of disinfectant. A woman soon came out, smiled at him, and said nothing. Clearly, Jaquelyn had been discrete. Finally Jaquelyn appeared, the bloody hand wrapped in paper towels. "I need some tape to hold these two fingers together and some ice," she said calmly. "Let's go to the Health Food Store," she said still in a quiet, steady voice.

They walked down the block to the store and, while she looked for ice, he found Band-Aids, a roll of gauze, and some tape. "They don't have ice," Jaquelyn said rejoining him, "but I remembered the trick of using frozen peas instead." In a few seconds she had her wounded fingers surrounded by a pea-poultice. The cold gave her immediate relief and comfort, knowing that the swelling would now be under control. He couldn't believe that only fifteen minutes after the agonizing moment in Stan's driveway, the feeling of crisis was already abating. They returned to the car where Jaquelyn applied the

Band-Aids and wrapped her fingers in gauze. Jack's fingers trembled a little as he cut strips of tape to secure the bandage. He asked if he should apply the tape.

"No, I'm doing fine," Jaquelyn said quietly. "It's clever of you to have a knife in the glove compartment." In a few minutes she was done.

"How is it feeling?"

"Not too bad. Even if my finger is broken, all they can do in the ER is what I've done. Thank God for the rubber seal on the trunk. I would have lost fingers for sure without that."

"Are you sure we shouldn't check in at a hospital?" Jack asked.

"Very sure," Jaquelyn responded in a confident voice. "Now let's go and buy your garden tractor."

The sudden shift in focus stunned him. Once again he had caused her injury and pain. Why wasn't he more careful? Can we really go on with the afternoon as if this were only a minor problem? Yes, the clear answer came back immediately. "You are remarkable," Jack said with as much admiration as she had felt from him in quite a while. "And I still can't believe what happened."

"We'll figure out the why's later on," Jaquelyn said with a smile as they drove off. She continued operating in her calm medical mode while he ordered the mower and they drove home. As they pulled into the garage, Jack suggested they have a council preceded by a healing meditation—if she were up for it. Jaquelyn readily agreed.

After the meditation, Jack lit the candle and began to share what he had experienced.

"I saw the cut healing and the swelling going down. It didn't seem as if any bones were broken. I hope that wasn't wishful thinking. I saw that I could help ease your pain."

"Great! I think my hand will be OK."

"Then I shifted to taking a look at why it happened," Jack went on. "That produced some fairly shadowy reflections that are not easy to share . . . I let myself go back to the moment when I closed the trunk lid and saw that I had a touch of irritation because you didn't like how I was dealing with the medicines."

"A touch of patriarchal anger?" Jaquelyn offered.

"That fits."

"You were saying the other day how unspoken thoughts or feelings can have power in the world of actions. We're not used to living in such rarified atmosphere. We have to be more conscious."

"In the moments after your scream, I felt enormous remorse that I had hurt you."

"Did you think I was holding you responsible?"

"No," Jack responded, "it was like a very minor version of what happened in the gulch. We were together—and you were wonderful. You took care of yourself. I hardly did anything."

"Your care was essential," Jaquelyn assured him. "There wasn't really much you could do about my fingers. Even with my shadowy mind, I couldn't make anything out of the experience during the meditation. Of course, if you had parked in a better place . . ."

"As I pulled into Stan's driveway, I actually wondered whether I should park along the curb," Jack confessed. "Sometimes we're given little hints that we have to learn to follow."

"Particularly lately. I tend to go with those flashes; you tend to give them more thought. You're getting better, though."

"Whatever the meaning of the accident, I felt the depths of our love today in little ways, like this morning when I complimented you about your hair."

"You don't know how happy it would make me to have an easy hairdo that you liked," Jaquelyn said with a big smile.

Jack laughed. "I think I have an inkling of how you feel, having studied at the *School for Hair Awareness* for so many years. Our recent hair conversations should have alerted me to your vulnerability right now and the need for me to stay conscious. A similar momentary loss of awareness occurred when we made love last time and my finger got under your clitoral hood."

Jaquelyn remembered with a shudder. "Yes, that was another time when you went a little unconscious."

"The sexual energy was so strong that we both got carried away. It was painful for you, like an electric shock. How do we stay as conscious as we need to be? Can our love and Third be empowered enough to see accidents before they happen?"

"We know we're both becoming part of a shared entity—literally, not metaphorically or in some abstract spiritual way," Jaquelyn responded. "That's the incredible truth about relationship that we're learning and it is our sexuality that holds the Third together. So, as long as our erotic life is strong, the answer is yes."

"That inspires me to share something else that's close to the edge." Jack's voice sounded vulnerable. "In those firsts few moments in Hilo today when I felt the anguish and I really didn't know how seriously hurt you were, I thought about tennis and your computer—and in those few moments I said to Spirit, 'Better something happen to me than—'"

"Oh, honey!" Jaquelyn felt a flash of empathetic pain.

"Then the thought dissolved and I was left with a deep sense of loving you."

"Yes, I understand that kind of feeling, particularly as a mother."

"Maybe what inspired my thought is that I'm learning to love you like a woman can love. If the way I already love you expands like that, then—"

"—we will find the healing state we're searching for together," Jaquelyn finished the sentence.

"Yes, finally, it's clear. We need to embrace being lovers as our full identity."

"Nature designed it so that people can fall in love soon after they are ready to be procreative," she went on. "Until recent times humans didn't live much longer than that child-bearing period. But now we live into our eighties and even nineties with enough accumulated wisdom and experience to support a new kind of love and creativity."

"So rather than creating children," Jack chimed in, "we can create a field—Rumi's field! That's what the *Flesh and Spirit* practices can do. Every couple on the path can contribute to the actual bonding of flesh and spirit at the heart level—literally."

"The heart is the common ground where they merge," Jaquelyn agreed.

"Our home here on the Island could be a place where that actually happens. When we came here to live, we said all we would do is make love, meditate, and write."

"Can I have that in writing?" Jaquelyn responded with a smile. "But don't give up your caretaking. I love how you take care of our nest."

"I want this place to be as beautiful as possible so that you feel completely at home."

"Befitting the jewel that is the goddess—which means that you can handle any hairdo, right?" Jaquelyn started to laugh in that contagious way that he couldn't resist and that often felt like an invitation to make love. "I think you're going to have to accept that your spiritual path is totally inseparable from my hair. At least for this goddess, hair is part of the journey. It's been fun to have this new, wild hairdo after six years of having it totally straight."

"It's wonderful," Jack agreed, "like your hair in that little picture on my desk that someone took when you were on television years ago—wild and pouty and sexy. Every time I look at it, it turns me on."

"Ho! Open up your heart and make room. There's more of that juice comin' through!"

"I'd like to do a healing on your fingers," Jack offered. "Why don't you get comfortable on the bed."

Jaquelyn agreed—for the sake of his remorse as well as her fingers. They entered an altered state almost immediately as Jack made several passes over her wounds. Then a thought intruded Jack knew he had to share. "You've told me a few times recently that you're afraid to love me as much as you do because I might take you for granted. I wonder if there needs to be an act of faith that goes beyond all my possible imperfections."

The day's adventure had left Jaquelyn open and vulnerable. "What's to lose? My resistance is all a bunch of ego stuff anyway."

Her immediate lack of defensiveness was irresistible. After a few moments of intense silence he leaned over and let his mouth touch hers gently. They held the kiss for a long time without moving.

Finally, Jaquelyn pulled away a little. "Did I activate you by saying 'What's to lose?'" Her voice was soft and inviting.

"Yeah, that's the spirit of what we're doing right now—throwing our conscious fears and barriers into the fire. There are probably many patterns that don't serve us any longer."

"When you love someone the way I love you, it gives me a healthy willingness to take risks." Her voice had that purr that came straight from the goddess. This time the kiss went deeper into an exploration of tongues and mouths that was soft and gentle. When they finally disengaged, they looked at each other in wonder.

"I would miss you terribly if you were to die," Jaquelyn said out of the silence, her face radiant with an almost childlike vulnerability. "The idea of life without you is . . . unthinkable. Before that happens, I want to love you in a way that won't be so painful if you're not embodied. As the veils get thinner we'll learn how to still be connected, even if one of us makes the crossing first . . . Even that will be alright," she added with just a touch of a smile. "I trust we will find a way."

Her words were like a harbor for a weary sailor. "It's late and I'm ready to hold you," Jack said, knowing they would not make love because of the hour and all that had happened that day. Just holding each other would be a healing gift from the goddess. They were not disappointed.

13 &s Chelsey Embodies the Third

As J&J focused more of their erotic energy on healing, Jaquelyn's fingers improved rapidly. Naturally, working with Jack's glaucoma was a more challenging long term task, but they both felt that the healing quality of their intimacy had become at least a stabilizing influence on Jack's eyes. As winter turned into spring, the trade winds, the ocean, and the fertile volcanic soil drew them closer to nature, to each other—and so also to Third consciousness. Once they adjusted to the move, I found it easier to reach them on the Big Island than in California and so I celebrated the wisdom of their westward migration. Many couples underestimate the importance of where they live in shaping the character of their relationship. I assure you that J&J in Los Angeles was a significantly different couple than J&J in Honoka'a. "Of course," you say, but I mean different in essential erotic ways, not just different in the pace and patterns of life and the effects of interacting with a different community. I'm referring to the way the erotic quality of a relationship connects directly to nature. Let me explain.

The heart of the shamanic healing tradition lies in the inseparable connection between the shaman and nature. The jungle healers listen profoundly to their indigenous plants in order to understand their medicinal and mind-altering capabilities. Contemporary culture is finally beginning to appreciate that these healers are—literally—in loving, intimate, and physical relationship with the plant medicines they use. The desert healers of Mexico are similarly in direct mental, spiritual, and physical relationship with the sacred plants they utilize to expand their consciousness and guide their culture. I am like these shaman in many ways. In brief, my effectiveness in guiding J&J depends significantly on their connection with nature.

In particular, I welcomed the eventual inclusion of psychoactive plants in J&J's ceremonial life together. The first half of their lives had involved only the occasional use of alcohol, but the 1970s brought some experimentation with a variety of substances, including cannabis and ecstasy. Jaquelyn had tried LSD in the 1960s, years before they met, when "acid" arose as a new and hot topic for progressive physicians, but Jack was not drawn in that direction. For him, meeting people such as Terrence McKenna and reading all the Castaneda books opened the doors to indigenous plants, with psilocybin the guide he felt took him most directly into home ground. Jaquelyn found mushrooms disturbing and unappealing, particularly after an experience in the high Rockies when they both followed Terrence's guidance to up the dose to 5 mgs and make the journey in separate rooms—and in the dark. That was her final mushroom trip! Jack experimented with psilocybin a few more times after that, but lack of availability and being unable to share the experience with Jaquelyn soon brought his limited explorations to an end. They investigated ecstasy for a year or so, but the physiological effects of amphetamine were not to their liking.

Eventually, they both discovered that cannabis served as an effective ally of their relationship and, slowly over a period of many years, they made occasional use a part of their ceremonial times when they were alone and at home together. The plant helped them to let go of the fullness of their active lives more easily and served their relationship in several ways. For Jaquelyn it usually brought a slower body rhythm and liberating relaxation. For Jack it tended to support his exuberance as a lover, both with words and his body. Most importantly their ceremonial relationship with cannabis became a useful context for explorations of Third consciousness. Over the years I made sure that they viewed the plant as indigenous healing medicine in the traditional shamanic sense—which was not hard for me to do, particularly after Jack's diagnosis of glaucoma and his discovery that cannabis helped to reduce his ocular pressure.

Nature entered J&J's life on the Big Island in a number of other compelling ways. Jack had been a devoted residential gardener all his adult life, with roses as his primary focus. It is no accident that Jaquelyn's discovery of his potential for meditation occurred early in their relationship, when she was watching him do the annual pruning of the more than fifty rose bushes at their adobe home in Calabasas, California. She saw what she described as "pale purple lights" around his head and knew he was meditating in a way that she had begun to experience in her new Transcendental Meditation practice. When he joined her at dusk that day and she told him what she had seen, he accepted her affirmation of his meditative state, even though he had no previous training or experience. Until that moment, it had never occurred to him that he was in deep contemplation when he was with the roses.

J&J's move to the Island's year-round embrace of fertility further inspired Jack and, eventually, the vegetable garden he and Seppe created became the source of much of their food. Growing one's own vegetables helps a person become a true lover of the soil. Specifically Jaquelyn soon realized that Jack's deepening earth connection was actually being transmitted to her through his touch during lovemaking. Unlike Lady Chatterley, Jaquelyn had both the gardener and her chosen life partner combined in one man.

Jack's devotion to his weekly swim in the ocean also added to the deepening intimacy. To give you a brief example, here's an experience he shared with Jaquelyn after a swim one day:

"I was appreciating the ocean in all its pristine beauty when I realized I was telling you the story of my experience swimming out beyond the surf, *as I was living it*. In particular, I was sending you descriptions of what was happening in my body. The realization was subtle but startling. You're the main character in my life story, of course, but you're also its major context because, even when I'm not with you physically, I still relate my life to you. The situation is analogous to how devout religious practitioners live their life in inner dialogue with their deities. Whether it's God or one's intimate partner, this level of connection is what I have come to call 'living story.'"

"It's clear that we're characters in each other's stories, "Jaquelyn responded, "but actually *living* that consciously, as you say, takes it further."

"In addition, sharing my experiences with you as I live them, and vice versa, actually radically changes the experiences themselves. Eventually, our stories begin to merge tangibly into one joint story. In other words our life actually becomes a living story, even if only our Third can understand its full meaning."

As you might imagine, all this delighted me, but where the notion of living story really became creative had to do with Chelsey. To give their healing efforts coherence and direction, they had both come to frame their goal for Chelsey in terms of her ability to have an ongoing intimate relationship—assuming, of course, that was her destiny. If J&J could imagine Chelsey's gradual healing taking place through a fictional but realistic relationship with a young man—they called him Damian—then that story could constellate a healing field in which Chelsey at least would be inspired to relate more actively with her family and particularly her friends at school. For a child with autism this vision is invariably an ultimate goal. The actual story of Chelsey's relational life might not end up sharing many details with the fictional one—no matter. The healing field created by the story would support Chelsey's true relationship journey, whatever that was meant to be.

The seeds for all this were planted in 2006 when J&J arranged to have Chelsey, then twelve, stay with them at the Blue House for a whole month during the summer. Just before Chelsey's visit, Jack flew to Israel alone to perform a wedding for a couple that he had worked with for many years. The bride to be was a *sabre*, a native Israeli, who was instrumental in initiating and nourishing the council work in Israel and who hosted J&J during their many visits to the Middle East. The work in Israel is another adventure whose threads we'll pick up later. The wedding turned out to be on the second day of what became known as the "Lebanese War." Jack flew home just hours before the airport was closed to commercial traffic.

Jaquelyn met him in Los Angeles a day before the annual family summer party at which they were to pick up Chelsey and take her to the Blue House. A few weeks before that a colleague of Jaquelyn had offered to lend them a portable hyperbaric oxygen tank (HBOT) free of charge for the month. Jaquelyn couldn't resist seeing if Chelsey could be helped, as were some other children with autism, by spending several hours a day in a pressurized environment of enhanced oxygen that was analogous to being about fifteen feet underwater in full scuba gear. So the tank was shipped from the mainland and was waiting for them at the Blue House when they arrived with Chelsey in late June. It took Jack most of a morning to assemble the seven-and-a-half-foot long thick canvas vessel supported by a metal frame. The oxygen generator and compressor made a humming and chugging sound, respectively, that soon became a familiar part of each day. J&J each took turns doing the "dives" with Chelsey, while the other monitored the tank. Portable DVD and CD players kept Chelsey's restlessness from getting out of hand inside the chamber.

The usefulness of the tank's environment for healing never became clear. It was the physical closeness they each shared with Chelsey in the tank that proved to be the source of whatever healing took place. Swimming in the Honoka'a pool, trips to the beach, a weekly horseback riding class for special-needs children, endless hours on the swing that hung from a eucalyptus tree near the house, field trips to Taco Bell and the hot pool south of Hilo, baths twice daily and lots of music and books filled the other hours of Chelsey's visit to the Blue House.

Unlike when other friends or family visited, J&J were not shy about making love while Chelsey slept in the nearby guest room. In fact, knowing she was sleeping peacefully not far away made it easier to dedicate the "merit of their practice" to her healing. After the three of them had settled into a good rhythm with the HBOT dives and other activities, they could no longer resist the yearning in their bodies. They were hungry for intimacy and hadn't yet celebrated Jack's safe return from the Middle East. The consummation fulfilled their expectation, as Jack described in his journal the next morning while Chelsey and Jaquelyn were still asleep.

Last night we made love in a way that was distinctly transcendent and reminded us of the picture of Siva and Shakti in deep communion that hangs on the wall by my side of the bed. All this happened after we had a council in which we acknowledged that we really aren't clear about the path of healing for our young—

At that point Chelsey entered the bedroom in her pajamas with sleep still in her eyes. "Hi Chelsey," Jack greeted her. As usual, she didn't respond, so he went on writing until she let out a remarkably realistic coyote howl to re-announce her arrival on the scene. Jaquelyn opened her eyes, saw that Jack was already awake, and closed them again.

"Grampa?" Chelsey began.

"Yes?"

"Can I have some Kocoa Krispies, please?"

"Yes, in just a few minutes," Jack responded. "Let me finish this." Chelsey wandered into the living room and put on some music.

What else do I recall about last night? I remember having the image of the two rainbows I saw from the top of the land several months ago, the lower one being undefined and nestled underneath the full and vivid one above. The double rainbow is such a perfect metaphor for what we're doing with Chelsey now . . . As usual it's been a wonder to surrender again to her feral nature. Last night, we acknowledged that, whatever else is being accomplished, we're giving her family a break for a month. That we know for sure. Everything else about Chelsey's healing is speculation, although there does seem to be some noticeable improvement in her ability to communicate.

At that point Chelsey reentered the bedroom determined to satisfy her need for Kocoa Krispies. Jack gave up trying to capture any more of the evening and made her breakfast.

The days with Chelsey were full-on, so it wasn't until a week later that they managed to schedule a council while she explored the world of Tele-Tubbies on Jack's computer. He began:

"I think our friend is preoccupied for a while so we can really talk. One topic might be turning up the heat in regard to her awareness of others. If Chelsey's meant to have a Damian in her life, we need to help her move in that direction in whatever way we can."

"Yes, we're about a quarter through the month with her," Jaquelyn responded, "and it feels like this has been an adjustment period for us all. She's not quite a teenager, but her recent physical maturity is startling. She still has a total lack of inhibition and self-consciousness about her own body. That has its good points. It also generates concerns when I think about the future. The adjustment has been hard for me. For one thing, I always anticipate that she's going to be less impaired than she is."

"That's because the Chelsey who lives inside you is not the actual Chelsey. Maybe it's her perfected or unimpaired feral self, both of which are delightful images that we both hold. Also, you're so identified with her that your reaction may have to do with feeling your own limitations."

"Yes," Jaquelyn agreed, "I want to write about the emerging divine feminine and I don't know if I have the capacity to do it. The classical feminine image that the patriarchal world tries to perpetuate is the nurturing mother who is focused primarily on raising children. We have to be shocked—women as well as men—into embracing a much larger vision of the divine feminine. The need for the goddess to enter our world screams at me. Women have been brainwashed, as you said coming home in the car with Chelsey from the hot pool the other day. Even though some more enlightened men like you are in touch with the feminine and the need for true equality between men and women, we are still all subject to the incredible imprint that gives men superiority and higher spiritual ranking than women. This awareness has made me so reactive—mostly angry—that I can end up wasting energy, as you have pointed out. Yet, there's a part of me that knows the wrathful goddess has to make up for the deadness in men, particularly those in power now. Some liberal pundit said it well the other day: 'The gnomes reign now in this country.' World events seem to be leading towards the need for a dramatic opening to a new goddess of love . . . Yes, I'm like Chelsey in a way. Until a few years ago, my innocence about what really goes on in the world resembled hers and my worldly consciousness is still emerging. I'm like a gorilla glimpsing its future as a human and wondering where all that sophisticated evolution is going to come from. Of course, gorillas don't wantonly kill each other or destroy their environment, but you know what I mean."

Her last image was so striking and unexpected that Jack was speechless—and so she went on.

"When I read what's going on in other countries—the hierarchy of male power, the ownership of women, and the horrible misuse of authority—I have more of a sense than ever before that the collective feminine has to break out into new awareness. The old tradition that men need to benevolently take care of women—the benevolent owner tradition—is a major obstacle to the empowering of women. We may even have to take a deep look at the traditional nurturing role of women. That role has diminished for me and now I want to kick ass! If women are in the nurturing, forgiving, loving, serving kind of consciousness that progesterone and estrogen produce, it's so hard for them to make the big changes needed in the world. I think the nurturing part of women needs to be balanced by the empowered feminine consciousness that is emerging. The nurturing may even have to be subdued for this to happen. Women have to show power!"

Jaquelyn was on a roll, charged by the now familiar combination of anger at what was happening to women in many parts of the world and the exhorting of the emerging missionary goddess. He tried to listen more deeply when she hit her stride like this, so he could take in her full passion. Having his attention, Jaquelyn went on.

"If this new power has to enter in a way that makes men more afraid of women, at least the fear will be overt rather than hidden the way it has been for eons. You're as enlightened as anybody, although you still have inklings of that fear at times. You've said to me that I'm imprinted by the patriarchy even more than you are. You tell me that my fierceness is, in part, the struggle with my own inner patriarchal demons. But women may have to go through that in order to reach another level of empowerment. You have to hit a mule with a two-by-four to get it going. I believe the feminine has to hit the male—and female—world in some way with an energetic two-by-four! I do think there has to be a shock, whether it's the cosmic tilt of the earth moving on its axis that's being predicted or the date of reckoning envisioned in 2012. Something big has to happen!"

Finally, Jack had to speak. "OK. The danger in what you're suggesting is that the two-by-four is still the old power pattern, although the hand that does the bashing would be the feminine rather than the masculine."

"Yes, and—"

"Let me finish," Jack shot back quickly. "What you're saying is part of what needs to happen, but it's not the whole transformation. For me, the biggest step is to move into another level of conscious relationship between men and women. This is the issue we debate all the time now. I'm suggesting that this angry, activating energy become part of something even larger that has to do with deeper intimacy. One doesn't have to exclude even the vengeful feminine in this larger context—obviously humans could use a major rewiring, as the insanity of what's happening in Israel and Lebanon now makes clear. Most leaders today don't know how to change the way they function basically, and part of the solution is the emergence of powerful feminine leadership, as you say. I couldn't agree more. However it happens, men have to get it, and they're more likely to get it on the path of intimate relationship than getting beat up by an angry goddess. Our relationship has been tempering for both of us. I'm learning to recognize the patriarchal remnants in me, so I don't try to contain your power unconsciously. We may be getting different messages. Mine is that men need to see the goddess fully in their women—and to know that it's to their distinct joyous advantage to do so."

However diplomatic his language, Jaquelyn felt contained and that made her restless. But Jack held on to the talking piece.

"Your pitch right now may be to own that part of you that is the Amazon queen. However impaired, we've seen over the years that Chelsey has the same regal essence. Despite her impairment, she's imperious too."

To Jaquelyn's relief, Jack put down the Brazilian rain-stick and got up to pee. Talking about Chelsey reminded Jaquelyn that they had not heard a peep out of her for quite a while. "Better have a look at Chelsey while you're up," she called after him. He found Chelsey in her room, playing with her tape recorder, happy as a clam. He told her to join them in the council. She picked up the recorder.

"No tape recorders in council," Jack called over his shoulder as he headed back to the bedroom. Chelsey entered a moment later making a string of weird noises, tape recorder still in hand.

"Come over and sit in this chair, honey," Jaquelyn spoke hopefully. Chelsey did one of her long vocalized throat-scraping in-breaths—and recorded it. She kept on playing back the sounds and recording new ones despite their requests. The scene seemed destined for chaos. "We need to pick up the stick again so she's knows we're really in council," Jaquelyn suggested over the din.

"I don't think that will make any difference," Jack said still engaged in their dialogue.

Jaquelyn began to lose focus. "Take the tape recorder from her, will you—now?"

Jack wrestled her gently on the bed and took the recorder. "You can get a book, if you like," he added.

"DVD player!" was Chelsey's response as she tried to get up from the bed to get the portable device they had been using in the tank.

"No DVDs," retorted Jaquelyn "and no weird sounds, only talking."

Jack was ready to get back to their council, but he had to shout to be heard over Chelsey's now unrecorded noises. She had no interest in joining a council of the sort going on. As she grew louder, he raised his voice. "We each have different messages, and I trust they fit together." Chelsey suddenly plopped down in his lap, all the while making louder and louder throat noises. "Since my message is about relationship," Jack went on, "I have to find ways to connect with your passion. Otherwise, I become part of the enemy."

Chelsey leapt up and started rolling on the bed. Jaquelyn had to literally shout to be heard. "You are talking about a kind of consciousness that might possibly exist some day in a country like ours, where women are pretty equal and have a lot of privileges. I'm thinking more of—"

"GameBoy!" Chelsey yelled from the bed, trying to find a way to tune out their interactions so lacking in the loving flow she had come to associate with council. They ignored her one-word command as usual. Jaquelyn didn't miss a beat:

"—a world in which men shit on women, beat and kick them around until they have no self-esteem." Chelsey repeated her demand, to no avail. "Until you have respect, you can't really love someone. I'm only saying that the first step has to be that men recognize women have innate power. Until they have respect for women's power, they cannot possibly reach the level of love you're talking about."

Chelsey maintained her monologue of throat sounds, alternating her regular voice with repeated throat noises, as if she were mimicking the heated discussion she was witnessing.

"My job is to help men do just that," Jack said above the din.

"Yes, I agree." Jaquelyn responded. "You may be able to reach the group of more enlightened men, but it's going to be hard to reach fundamentalist Christians, Muslims, and Jews because only something shocking will get them to look at a woman and say, 'This is a being I should respect, love, and cherish in an entirely new way.' You can lure a few men on the fringes, but unless something revolutionary happens, you are not going to change most men. I think you're very idealistic and, yes, I agree that my anger is in the style of the old patriarchal pattern, but I feel that's a necessary step to achieve a new level of consciousness. That's my opinion." Chelsey was beginning to take long, loud, in-breaths as she continued the parallel dialogue with herself.

Jack picked up the piece. "You have to watch that your perspective doesn't become a self-fulfilling prophecy that deflects us from the yet deeper intimacy that we're facing. We both hold the vision that our service in the world is sharing our relationship, but we may have different roles in fulfilling that vision. I don't think it's naïve at all to call in the power of loving relationship. In fact, that's what has to evolve. Is it going to happen in our lifetime? I don't think in those terms. The change is so immense that all we can do is take little steps. I'm left with trusting that, whatever it is that you have to do, we will continue to deepen our path. If the emerging goddess avoids relationship, that clearly will not serve."

She could hardly believe her ears. What was he thinking? Chelsey started jumping up and down on the bed. "I could not possibly do what I need to do without our relationship supporting me," Jaquelyn retorted, the heat rising in her voice. "I couldn't even say what I'm saying without our relationship. Your words are totally confusing to me."

"You say that, but from my point of view you don't function as if that were true!" Jack retorted, his voice rising as well. "Something is missing between us in this council. We're not communicating!" Chelsey was now jumping up and down on the bed, reaching heights comparable to her trampoline leaps at home. "There's something missing in the way you describe your mission that separates you from the masculine. You feel in a polarized state to me."

"I said that women have to wake up too," Jaquelyn countered.

"I'm not talking about that," Jack once again shot back. "I'm talking . . . about . . . I don't know what I'm talking about! Unless you and I can integrate our perspectives so a third view emerges, our relationship won't really serve the mission. I'm singing my song and you're singing yours. We're trying to find a third song. So you're right; it can't happen without our relationship being clear, and that's precisely why we're struggling."

By this time the bed was groaning under Chelsey's gymnastic feats, effectively drowning out both of them. Chelsey seemed quite aware in her unique, non-cognitive physical way that Jack was missing an even larger picture than the one he was trying to paint for Jaquelyn. With each leap on the bed, she spoke her piece silently but with increasing clarity:

I'm getting really upset. My body is getting tighter and tighter. That's why I'm jumping. Can't you see that you've lost the safe place between the two of you that I love so much and makes me want to be with you? Why can't the two of you see that?

A skilled witness would have added:

You're reacting, Jack, because you're afraid she's going to get busy and pay less attention to you. You say it's about the relationship, but it's also about your desire to be the primary focus in her life. Exactly the same is true for you Jaquelyn. You want to be the center of Jack's attention as much as possible. It's an old and familiar story. Still, you do have a point, Jack. Jaquelyn is on a roll and doesn't see the broader implications of her fierceness. She is still the Amazon queen in some respects, despite all your wooing. You'll never be comfortable with that. The argument isn't going anywhere. You've each made your point. Cool it!

Chelsey was now reaching heights of more than three feet in her jumps.

"Chelsey!" Jaquelyn shouted. "Stop jumping, you're destroying the bed. Stop! Come, sit with us." Chelsey slowed down a bit but continued jumping. She still had a lot of tension to release. "Chelsey, I told you to stop, right now!" Jaquelyn repeated.

Jack got up quickly, put his arms around their mentor, and wrestled her down on the bed. Embracing her broke through his unconsciousness, and, with a rush of understanding he transformed all his pent-up energy into tickling. They ended up rolling on the bed laughing, grandfather and granddaughter, their foolishness healing what had been happening in the council. "Well, sweetheart," Jack called out to Jaquelyn from the bed "whatever midcourse correction we needed, Chelsey's done her part. Our friend knows exactly what she's doing. Council's over. It's my turn to be in the tank."

Chelsey got off the bed and went looking for the portable DVD player and *Alice in Wonderland*. She could hardly wait to get into the tank with him and play their new game, "pickin on grampa's head." Jack was more than ready.

14 ❧ Goddess Arising

The last story gives you a playful glimpse of how integral Chelsey had become to J&J's relationship. That summer was perhaps the peak of her impact since, as she grew older, her mother felt that she needed more time with her peers. Chelsey made only two more summer visits to the Blue House after 2006, once the next year and then again in 2010 for just ten days.

You may be wondering about the reference to the game of "pickin' on Grampa's head" at the end of the story. I could give you a direct explanation, but Jack wrote a poem about his playful healing times with Chelsey that includes a description of the HBOT experience, game and all. Here are the relevant verses:

In the tank one day she discovered my thinning hair
No longer hid the barnacles that come with age
And many years of sun in the garden and swims in the sea
These encrustations seduced her irrepressible fingers
That never rest until she finally falls asleep, exhausted

After I parried her pickings for several days
She upped the ante on this wacky way we have
Of connecting through her stubborn synaptic system
"Walking to picking grandpa's head, yes," she says gaily
"Noooooooo," I whisper into her ear in self-defense

We played out this ritual in our capsule, in the car
And at the beach, each time changing the tone, pitch, and length
Of the "No," until her delight knew no bounds
And I was as foolish as a grown man can be
When love for a child goes beyond his comprehension.

&

Now I want to tell you about a magical flower. In February Jack had seen a lovely orchid at the local farmer's market that he knew would find a welcome home in Jaquelyn's office. The five-limbed purple beauty lived a radiant life for well over a month, and when the bloom finally dropped, they found a sunny corner of the dining area for the green stalks to carry on in memory of their beautiful ancestor. The plant soon became a part of the clutter of magazines and books piled next to it on the wooden window seat near the table.

About a week after Jack returned from taking Chelsey home, Jaquelyn was looking for a missing book in the stacks on that window seat. Even though they were both delighted to be alone in their bower once again, she had been missing Chelsey a lot that day, particularly her unique feral innocence. When Jaquelyn came upon the half-hidden flower pot with its clump of green, reed-like shoots, she couldn't believe her eyes. There hidden among the rushes was a small new bloom, just as lovely as its ancestor. Since those kinds of orchids rarely re-flower unless they are in the ground, she took its birth as a sign of Chelsey's future healing. If the orchid could regenerate, so could Chelsey emerge from her impairment. The orchid became part of the setting of their councils for many weeks after its discovery, including the council described in the next story. This tale gives further insight into the important matter of how self-involvement—in this case, Jack's—gets pruned along the path of evolutionary relationship.

The summer clouds that had piled up along the ocean horizon to the east were turning pink in the reflected light of sunset as Jaquelyn began by commenting on Chelsey's innate playfulness:

"As we've said many times, you and I are pretty serious characters. Certainly I am. For you to have the kind of fun with Chelsey that you do is so good for her—and for you. I often heard you guys laughing in the tank and realized that you and I don't share that kind of foolishness very much, except sometimes in our lovemaking."

"Yes," Jack agreed, "the goddess takes many forms that reveal her omnipotence, but she can also be quite playful, even foolish. We may experience her somewhat differently because she has so many facets, and we have varying agendas and missions."

"I didn't have an agenda that time alone in the sunlight," Jaquelyn affirmed. "The goddess totally surprised me."

"By the way she penetrated you?"

"Every cell was penetrated, not just my vagina."

"I just realized something about your rite of passage with the goddess. We tend to objectify and anthropomorphize the divine— see it 'out there' somewhere. So you say *she* penetrated *you*. In fact, you were actually *in a goddess state of consciousness*."

"We definitely merged, "Jaquelyn mused, trying on his perspective. "It was so overwhelming that I didn't really know what was happening until afterwards. I was lying nude in the morning sun that was streaming in the window. The sun was part of me. The sounds of the leaves moving in the wind were part of me. I connected with the fish in the ocean. I was part of it all. It was an extraordinary feeling, like a continuous orgasm without any spasm. Yet with all that happening, I felt completely still."

"You became the goddess and described it in terms of being penetrated because that's your familiar path to ecstasy. By the way, that also implies that our lovemaking is a state of goddessness for you, which is so validating for me."

"What happened that day did have a resemblance to our sexual merging, but it was important that you were gone. I don't believe that 'she' would have appeared if you had been home."

"Yes," Jack agreed. "It's so fortunate that our gender struggles don't seem to negatively affect our lovemaking."

"In our lovemaking, the gender differences are absolutely delicious. Considering how we can battle, we are fortunate that our differences usually create sparks of Eros."

Jack had been staring at the new orchid bloom while they talked, which reminded him of an image he'd had when they first discovered the flower. "Just look at the orchid again for a moment. She's maturing now, but when she first reappeared, I saw a maiden on the path of empowerment. I saw a nubile beauty, a sprite, coming through the reeds that grew along a riverbank."

"I can image that now even when she is more mature," Jaquelyn was delighted to enter the fantasy.

"When we make love, I never know who is going to appear at the river. Often it's the younger woman, since your body usually feels youthful to me. Sometimes, when you're into your mature power and manifesting the wisdom of the goddess, you remind me of Isis or Sophia. Whoever appears, my challenge is to make love with her so we can enter the state of goddessness that we've been talking about."

"Sounds good to me. You've been doing that for years."

"*Learning* to do that," Jack countered. "Our lovemaking has been an incredible training program."

"Talking about the maiden orchid makes me think about the powerful—and still mysterious—role Chelsey has played in our life. What is at the heart of it?" They both paused and took a deep breath in honor of the scope of the question. Jack spoke first.

"Chelsey was sent in for many reasons, mainly because we were lacking something."

"I needed to open my heart more to the mystery of the feminine," Jaquelyn suggested.

"We were each stuck doing our individual assignments, and despite the *Flesh and Spirit* intensives, we were not working together enough. We lost track of our relationship in some ways and forgot that it was the context of our entire mission. Chelsey helped us to remember that. Now we're the gatekeepers of each other's forgetfulness. When we started our journey years ago, you challenged me to keep an image of you in my heart even when I was involved with other people and projects. Now I see that really means staying in reverence to the goddess, but it took a while for that practice to become a part of my path. You know about the goddess. She lives in you. I discover her as an explorer entering the unknown landscape of my lover. My practice is to not lose track of that."

"And, going back to Chelsey, that includes playfulness," Jaquelyn reminded him.

"She allows me to be a fool, and I'm much more balanced when I have that option."

"Do you feel safe with her in a way that you don't with me, not only because she's a child, but because of her unique kind of innocence?"

"In a way, yes," Jack confessed, "and also because expressing myself with more playful abandon is part of her healing. I get to be more full-spectrum in helping Chelsey be more relational. By the way, I mentioned the possibility of there being a 'Damian' in her life at least half a dozen times during this last trip, and she seemed to pick up on the game of having a future partner. If we hold the image of Chelsey becoming more aware of others so her relationships can deepen, that will allow her more options in the future."

"Yes!" Jaquelyn agreed enthusiastically. "The Damian story is just our way to help Chelsey have the choice to manifest who she's supposed to be relationally."

They drifted into silence for a while on the wings of Chelsey's possible healing, both looking at the orchid once again, until another image arose for Jack. "The five limbs of the flower's presence are so in balance. The way the lower limb is expanding now suggests a maturing of her genitals, her womanliness. That mystery is too powerful for a man to understand fully. If he dares to know her secret parts, it means he is willing to die . . . I'm willing!"

"Promises, promises." Jaquelyn's familiar mantra brought the usual laughter.

"Touching that fire is dangerous because it's so hard to stay conscious when we're in a merged state. Perhaps mindfulness can be an ally that balances the ecstatic state of the goddess that we're seeing reflected in the orchid. Mindfulness could help us stay conscious no matter how powerful the lovemaking becomes."

"Shadows participate in creating the balance too," Jaquelyn added. "I remember you saying recently that ecstasy is both dark and light in its moods and colors. The darkness helps to recognize the light, and we need light to see into the darkness."

By this time, the conversation and the orchid's presence had left them both feeling amorous, but when they held each other a while later, it was gratitude for the Third's patience and wisdom that flooded their embrace. So to honor gratitude, they restrained the familiar magnetism, dedicated their embrace to "balance," and finally fell asleep in the unseen arms of gratefulness.

As they were gathering for meditation the next morning, Jaquelyn felt the goddess hovering about, waiting for silence to make her appearance once again. They emerged from meditation forty minutes later.

"It was a powerful meditation for me," Jaquelyn began, "maybe because we restrained ourselves last night, but mostly because I've been gathering pieces of a major realization, ever since your explosion in the kitchen months ago. I began by using *HREEM* to help me get through all the layers of my busy mind, and soon I felt a familiar, wonderful stirring in my sexual chakra that suffused my whole being. Then I moved into an insightful state. . . . Lately, I've been feeling the need for more self-assurance, so I want to report to you what I experienced just now without worrying about whether I'm being inflated or presumptuous." Jack nodded in full support and she went on.

"I realize that when I projected Jesus onto you very early in our relationship—you were giving a talk and I saw a golden light around you—I was fulfilling my father's admonition to 'love Jesus Christ with all your heart and soul.' Since he also thought the Jews were the chosen people, I was killing two birds with one stone by seeing you as my personal Jesus. More tangibly, I was also seeing your potential in a way I had not experienced with any other man. Ever since that moment—and empowered by the depth of our sexual connection—I've been on a campaign to perfect you.

"When Israel first beckoned us, I saw what that would mean for you and supported your going alone the first time. I had an intuition that it would be a place where you could tap into a new level of recognition through your gift of teaching council, your wisdom as a therapist, and all the other gifts you bring. I knew you would come back feeling more realized because of people's reactions and projections, which is exactly what happened—but I had some concerns. I don't have much innate narcissism, but when I see any imperfection of that kind in you, it's almost more painful than seeing it in myself. In a way, I've always put you ahead of me because, as a woman, I'm culturally imprinted to believe I can't be the kind of divine being and have the wisdom that you seem to have. But that imprint has been slowly disappearing. In the last couple of years I've been getting a lot of worldly ego support through a level of recognition that I never received before. When I had the epiphany with the goddess in the sunlight, I started having a feeling—without an image of how it might actually happen—that something powerful would eventually constellate for me around us going to the Holy Land. I had a strong, womanly realization that felt analogous to how Jesus talked of 'Father in Heaven.' For me the realization of divinity is 'Mother in Heaven.' I call that 'all-consciousness' the *Great Mother*. I saw, even way back during our first few journeys to Israel together, that we could enter the Holy Land in a way that would help people see the couple as avatar. As far out as it sounds, we've even talked playfully about being disciples of Mary Magdalene and Jesus who were returning to the Holy Land to continue the work."

Jack was listening intently and had no need to speak, so Jaquelyn continued.

"Our relationship and my love for you and Chelsey have taken me beyond myself, closer to that place where the promise of realization becomes tangible. I know that my path is through my erotic connection with you. It has nothing to do with how you look or the size of your cock or your personality. It's totally a gift of the divine that is beyond my comprehension. You have been brought into my life to help me discover my own divine consciousness and—this is what's not easy to share—I feel I have a chance of being closer to that divine consciousness than you do to yours. You are so accomplished and developed that you can stay right on the edge of realization, but the very capacity that you have is like an obstacle to your total surrender. Your mind can wrap around anything and produce so many insights that you never quite get to full surrender. I'm not handicapped by that kind of mind."

He waited to feel a reaction to her words, but this time there was nothing; no response welled up. He continued to listen with no inclination to speak. In fact, what he did feel—and that surprised him—was a sense of agreement with what Jaquelyn had said! She went on.

"Of the two of us, I am the one who will move into the state of surrender needed for realization first, because I have already touched it at times, mostly when we make love. Yet often—paradoxically—I can't quite get there on my own. Once I get near to it, the shift happens for you too because we're so connected. So when anything is off in you—*anything*—I see it as an obstacle to my own realization and have a big reaction. You have a kind of self-absorption that sometimes can't get out of itself enough to take the leap. Your mind and intelligence are gifted in helping other people to break through, but for you to leave your mind enough to touch the needed surrender yourself is another story. I have an overactive imagination, but my mind doesn't grab hold of things and wrap itself around them in the way yours does.

"If I'm on the verge of realization, I know I have to be with you and immersed in our erotic consciousness to get there," Jaquelyn continued. "That's the field that can overcome all my obstacles and my fears and cultural imprints. But that erotic field is so powerful that it catches me the way your mind catches you. The vehicle that can take me to that place of magic also becomes the obstacle, because it's hard for me to get into that erotic field and not be consumed by it at the same time. The period of abstinence that we had after the blowup in the kitchen months ago took me closer as did the goddess-in-the-sunlight experience. The time with Chelsey and the orchid and maybe even our conversation about balance last evening may have played a part. Who knows? For whatever reason I finally got clear today in our meditation. I saw clearly and simply that I need you. We have agreed to come into this lifetime to take the leap together. Aurobindo said it would take 300 years, but with erotic energy as the fuel, the process is accelerating and, I believe, will eclipse any barriers that might keep people from ultimately recognizing their divinity. We know we have a divine spark in us, but to really feel it throughout our whole being the way that Jesus did—and I suppose the way that Buddha did too—is another matter. The way to the true Christ is through love and surrendering to something greater than yourself—*within yourself!* The church lost that teaching in its desire for money and power."

Jack recognized that she was streaming now beyond her mind in just the way she had been describing. He remained silent, mesmerized.

"I saw that my vision about going to the Holy Land was based on Mary Magdalene being given the recognition she deserved, beginning with the fact that she was the one through whom Jesus re-entered this world after the crucifixion. As we begin to create the new evolutionary mythology, I've come to believe that the miracle of Jesus' resurrection was primarily a result of their relationship. But Jesus had to pursue their vision of divine love based on the culture of the time, which meant that Mary would not be given appropriate acknowledgment. When you read the gospel according to Mary, it is clear that the core vision of divine love is all there, even in the fragment. Clearly she shared the wisdom that he taught, but their world wasn't ready for them to be recognized as a pair. It's taken this long to come to the threshold of that recognition.

"I see that our love and our connection can take me to a place of realization. If we are exquisitely together, that realization will be a mutual experience. I see that happening. You doubt your capability as a healer. That struggle is about your mind getting in the way. You don't want to be presumptuous, so you end up thinking you can't do it. There's fear of having that level of empowerment. Can you be clear or pure enough to become realized in a way that won't harm anyone? I feel we are close to that level of empowerment. I know we will do it together, if we do it at all. When you said this morning in bed, 'If we can't do what we're being asked to do, who can?' you were right on. We've been given the incredible gift of our connection. It's definitely divine. There's no other explanation for it, since we're just ordinary, physical human beings. We don't have any unique capability, other than the gift we've been given of knowing that spirituality, love, and sexuality can ultimately evolve into an inseparable affirmation of life. That's where the feminine must come in powerfully. The goddess of everything tangible in the world has to join with the old images of God to allow that to evolve. We are disciples and emissaries of that union, which now has to be manifest beyond anything we've ever known."

Jack continued listening, fully engaged by Jaquelyn's streaming thoughts. "We're right on the verge of that union—and it's very scary. I pray we have the juice to do it. The key is for the old patriarchal Jesus story to evolve into a new awareness of the potential divinity of human beings *in life*. The fact that we use erotic relationship as the path to this awareness doesn't mean that everyone has to do it that way. Other people will have different paths, but once a community of couples breaks through, once even a few couples get there, then . . . just look at how Jesus' realization changed the world. Consider the power of that! For such a realization to occur only once in the last two thousand years and affect millions of people is incredible. I know how all this may sound, but I don't feel inflated or conceited. We've been given a gift, and we have a responsibility to embrace it, to hone it and be the carriers of it. We are among the ones to do it. We've come to believe that Mary and Jesus had the same kind of union that joins body and spirit that we're pursuing, but that part of the story has been totally denied and buried for all these years. They called her a prostitute. Yet the story remains in the New Testament that it was Mary who first saw Jesus and allowed him to re-enter the physical plane. That was the miracle. In a way their consciousness together has permeated the whole world for centuries. I'm winding down. Do you understand?"

Jack had listened in a way that he had never listened before. He felt no resistance and no need to speak. "I do," was all he said—and then he smiled, recognizing in that moment he had spoken the vow for a new marriage. They were silent for a while until a few more words floated up to the surface of his consciousness, carried by an unexpected wave of tears. "I have just two brief comments: one, I'm ready to take that step with you, however it comes; and second, it doesn't matter to me how unique we may be. What's important is for us to do what we're being asked to do. My guess is that similar and analogous movements are happening all over the planet. Conscious evolution is becoming a necessity."

"I agree, and still I'm concerned that a lot of people won't have a clear understanding of the evolution that needs to happen," Jaquelyn responded.

"Each couple that's on the path of relationship has a piece. It's not just one way or one kind of relationship that is bringing this new awareness into manifestation, just as you say. There are probably unusual ways in which the evolution of Eros is happening that you and I might not even recognize."

"Yes," Jaquelyn said, comforted by his words. "In the big picture it doesn't matter how each of us is doing it. I've always seen that the book will be one way to share the message."

"And Mary's Gospel is a piece of the story," Jack added. "It's all beginning to fit together. I've been tempered in our fire and I feel I can take the leap now. Surrender is an act of enormous self-confidence. Otherwise it's more of an abdication."

"What's exciting about the writing is that, if we're this close to the awareness and see it even before it fully manifests, you can tell the story compellingly enough to transmit the message we've been assigned."

"The writing process itself—for us and hopefully for others who tell their story—will become part of the manifestation process."

"And it's also in that spirit that we've imagined the possibility of a Damian in Chelsey's life," Jaquelyn added, closing the circle. "We want her to have that choice. Even if she doesn't fully free herself from impairment, if we see her in a relationship clearly enough in our minds to create the story, then that possibility will be there for her to choose, if that's her heart's desire."

They looked at each other with a mixture of love and awe that would soon become a frequent companion to their new marriage.

15 &s Ten Clues to Walking the Path of Relationship

As you might suspect, J&J's focus on transforming scripture didn't stop with exploring the true nature of Mary's and Jesus' relationship. Once whetted, their appetite for changing the immutable Western biblical perspective grew stronger as they began to glimpse the possibilities of the new relational paradigm being revealed to them.

In simplistic terms, the mythology of a culture can be seen as its "collective living story," which means that the creation of a mythology for the new relationship paradigm will depend on many people sharing their personal stories about intimacy over a long enough period of time to permit the new collective story to emerge and be recognized. This may take generations, depending on how long the old stories persist. The more these long-held stories are openly debated and transformed, the more the new mythology can take hold of the imaginations and belief systems of the culture. The challenge is to balance change with cultural stability. This need for stability suggests that the early phases of the new relational mythology will necessarily involve transforming the old stories into bridges to the future. Such transformations always involve a lot of thinking out of the box and risk-taking. Obviously, stories held devoutly for thousands of years are not changed easily—and for good reason.

Jaquelyn's early Christian imprinting was instrumental in J&J's focus on transforming the Jesus–Mary Magdalene story. In Jack's case long-held curiosity became the doorway through which transformation flowed. He had always been intrigued with the story of Moses and the Ten Commandments, particularly the part about Moses having to receive God's word twice, since that detail heightens the drama of the Passover story that his mother made sure was a part of their family life every spring. As far as Jack could tell, everyone seated around the Pesach table assumed that the same collection of "thou-shalt-nots" had been delivered the second time as the first. But was that really what happened, Jack wondered. How do we know that the first set of tablets contained the same Ten Commandments that have formed the backbone of religious law for millions? Suppose the first set of inscriptions were different—say, geared for a more conscious populous and therefore inappropriate for the Hebrews Moses found dancing around the golden calf. Suppose the first set of tablets contained a far more sophisticated message that might be useful *now*, Jack imagined playfully.

For years he did nothing about such conjectures, until it became increasingly evident to J&J that human evolution required a new set of fundamental teachings, including the familiar Ten Commandments. The resulting exploration took place in the spring of 2007, ironically during their (nontraditional) celebration of Passover. I was particularly taken with the way they used the Passover story itself to make the transition into a markedly different vision of the "Promised Land."

Jack wanted to celebrate Passover in part because it was their first April at home in the Blue House (they had been in Israel the year before) but primarily to see how they would transform the traditional ceremony to serve the path of relationship. He gathered together a bottle of red wine, some spelt crackers that seemed a good substitute for matzo, a larger candle than they normally used for council, and donned the red Israeli yarmulke that had perched on the bookshelf in the living room since their move. He planned to say the prayers for the wine and crackers in Hebrew, these being the only Hebrew prayers he knew, and was tickled at the thought that Jaquelyn would offer a dedication while lighting the candles, since that was traditionally the role of the women of the household. They gathered in the bedroom for a Pesach council. The food would come later.

Since Jaquelyn was not familiar with the Seder, Jack shared the tradition of seeing the ceremony as a metaphorical journey out of bondage (in Egypt), through a challenging period in the wilderness (the Sinai), during which the struggle with fear, doubt, and materialism (idolatry) leads ultimately to Judaism's major sacred teachings (the Ten Commandments) and—finally—realization in the Promised Land (arrival in Canaan). In response to the question, "What is your Egypt?" Jaquelyn immediately identified hers as the intense fascination with the gory physical details of the widespread pathological treatment of women and children, particularly in the Middle East and Africa. She felt Jack's Egypt had to do with his tendency to lead a patterned life. Jack's take was that his bondage had to do with vestigial self-involvement and the resulting inability to fully surrender to the goddess along the path of relationship.

Let's pick up J&J as Jack is talking about the time in the wilderness when the people are starting to build idols to worship because they are losing faith in Moses and his brother Aaron. They fear they'll never get to the Promised Land, and so they succumb to the prophets of Baal:

"Moses sees that they have left bondage only to take on another form of slavery, so he asks God, 'How do we shape up this group?' God says, 'Leave the people for a while and come listen to me,' so Moses goes up the mountain to get the—"

"—word."

"Right, leaving Aaron in charge of the tribe for a long period," Jack continued. "Moses gets in touch with God directly and inscribes the visionary teachings he receives on a set of tablets. This is where the story gets interesting. As far as I know, no one is sure what Moses wrote down on the first set of tablets because he destroys them when he returns and sees that his people's idolatry has become ecstatic and obsessive. So the quest for guidance is temporarily postponed, and Moses goes back up the mountain. He realizes that the people didn't know what real freedom meant, having been enslaved for so long. So again he asks God to give him a vision that the people can follow in order to survive the wilderness and get to the Promised Land. Once again God provides the teachings, and Moses dutifully inscribes what we now know as the Ten Commandments on the tablets he brings down the mountain. The First Commandment is clearly responsive to the problem of idolatry. "There is only One God and I am that God! Don't worship any others!' This teaching has been seen as the monotheistic awakening in Judaism— essentially the realization that we are all part of *The One*. But in the context of the Old Testament, it carries the 'do not' flavor that permeates all the commandments.

"Now you and I are searching for a new story," Jack went on, "hopefully with more affirmative teachings. The Ten Commandments don't seem to be working very well. We're still fighting over whose god is the true *one* God, with murder and rape as or even more prevalent than ever. In many ways people are still stuck in the wilderness of confusion and unconsciousness. We don't really understand the First Commandment and so, in the spirit of evolution, we ask—playfully—what did Moses bring down the first time? More to the point, what would a contemporary circle of evolutionary visionaries come up with now? I'm suggesting that we create *Ten Clues*—let's not call them *commandments*—to the new relationship story you and I are tracking now and see what kind of a promised land they lead to. The commandments are about carrying out or not carrying out certain actions. We need affirmative clues that go deeper into the nature of spiritual reality and help us create a foundation for *all* our actions. I know it sounds presumptuous to—"

"—Stop!" Jaquelyn interrupted him. "It's not presumptuous." Her voice was both pleading and demanding. "The world is ready for them now—in fact, desperately in need of new teachings. If we can receive them, they could be useful. I believe that!"

Jack embraced her challenge, was silent for a few moments—and then stepped through the doorway to the *cosmic library*, the name he gave to the storehouse of collective wisdom. "OK, the first clue is similar to the old one but expressed affirmatively." He paused and the words came to him after a few moments:

"I. The divine is manifest as wholeness, as the oneness of all. All gods and goddesses, all divine images, are manifestations of this oneness."

He had crossed the threshold now and the insights flowed. "The second teaching is one I've said to my clients a million times:

II. There is only relationship. The divine is manifest in the interdependence of everything. There is no consciousness without relationship.

"Of course," Jack went on, "relationship is not restricted to couples or parents and children or other familiar kinds of relationships. We include human connections with other creatures, with place and, of course, with whatever people hold as divine. Each kind of relationship has its own particular nature and place in the oneness."

"Our path of relationship covers many of the bases," Jaquelyn affirmed, delighted with what was happening.

"Let's drink the first cup of wine to that. I'll say the blessing in Hebrew. You light the candle. I know the prayer for the wine. A woman usually says the prayers when lighting the candles."

"I can fake it," Jaquelyn said with a smile.

They poured a little red wine and Jack said the prayer. Then Jaquelyn lit the candle: "As a wise man I know so well has been saying for a long time, 'relationship is all there is.' Here we are in the wilderness of exploring intimate relationship. Once the lovers expand out of themselves enough to really know each other, they enter the *queendom of goddessness*. In deeply experiencing the connection between self and other, the lovers capture a glimpse of oneness and enter a new era. The book *The Secret* and the new Esther Hicks book are best sellers, number two and number eight. Millions of people are reading about the simple idea that strongly holding positive images will help us all build a better world. We're part of it all. So the people suffering in the wilderness and waiting for guidance are respectful and ready this time. It is thousands of years later and finally we are ready to hear the new teachings. We are ready to bring a new vision into the desert—and then let it expand everywhere."

"That was quite a blessing!" Jack said joyfully. "The Promised Land has to be all of the earth, just as you say." He had covered his eyes with both hands, imitating the tradition of women praying on Shabbat. "I think you're supposed to cover your eyes because the divine light is so bright. But you know that literally. Even our council candle hurts your eyes now." He took another sip of the wine, and this time held it in his mouth for a long time. "Rolling the wine around in my mouth, I taste the earth as well as the grapes and it is—"

"—smoky, sensual, and earthy," Jaquelyn finished his sentence.

"Yes! Now let's tune in to see what the third teaching is."

"I think it's about manifestation," Jaquelyn suggested.

"We started with the mystery of oneness. Next, there is only relationship. What follows? I think manifestation comes later," Jack responded.

"The birth of the child?"

"There's something before that, something that we've learned already." Jack could feel it, but the words were not quite there.

"The way we're learning to know each other as we merge is so expansive," Jaquelyn offered, doing her best to attune to Jack. "We become so much larger as our awareness of other grows."

"Keep on talking," Jack urged, closing his eyes. "I'm riding your energy to get the teaching. The essence is clear; just let me get the words." He paused . . . and the words came:

"III. Erotic love is the spirit of the divine."

Jack elaborated. "The divine manifests relationally. This teaching finally defines spirit, which has been elusive for us and many others—in terms of erotic love. The definition is still elusive, but we know more about erotic love than we know about spirit, so it's a step in the right direction. We approach the mystery of the divine through the heights—and depths—of erotic love. What flows through the divine body—the divine spirit—is erotic love. It's a full moon tonight; a Pesach full moon is quite powerful, according to tradition."

"I'm so glad we're doing this Seder," Jaquelyn exclaimed. "Now can we manifest the baby, the divine child?"

"Spoken like a true mother-goddess! OK. Let's see what's waiting to enter." He did his best to move out of thought. "The fourth clue has to do with the manifestation of the divine, like what happens when two people make love who have traveled the path long enough."

"Yes," Jaquelyn agreed, "the divine can manifest in physical ways or in actions or in energy going out into the world. Just like the yogi meditating in a cave helps the world, I have to believe that the world is a better place after we celebrate our union ecstatically."

"So how can we put all that together?" Jack wondered "The clue has to do with the consummation of two novitiates when they celebrate erotic love." Jack fell silent, trying to let go of all the ideas and words for a moment to glimpse the underlying clue. It materialized slowly:

"IV. The divine is manifest when two lovers fully consummate their relationship—when they merge totally."

Jaquelyn nodded. "We feel the divine around us when we make love. We're embraced in a divine field and become god and goddess. We are that!"

"Exactly! We're in transition from the 'I Am That' paradigm to the '*We* Are That' paradigm. Of course, for this clue to be relevant for a wide variety of relationships, we have to understand the word *merging* to mean coming fully together in any profound way, not necessarily sexually . . . OK, now what's the fifth clue? This has to take us further into the manifest world."

Jaquelyn was in the flow and responded immediately. "We have to find a way to reach those who are ready to hear about the possibilities of relationship in the same way people were ready to learn about the law of attraction in *The Secret*. We need to help people understand the transcendent joy that relationship as a path can provide lovers—*and* the planet. The world would be a different place if more people knew that path."

"Again, when you begin to flow, I just ride your wave," Jack said delightedly . . . "The fifth clue has to do with the divine being more readily manifest when there is alignment, when you know who you are and know your particular capabilities. Although early in my life I wanted to be a master cello player, I soon discovered that I didn't have the talent. We come to know who we are after getting excited, working hard, getting bumped around—and persevering."

"You're a master pussy player!" Jaquelyn countered. (*laughter*)

"Thank you!" was all Jack could say. His talent had finally been identified—and by a representative of the goddess! "I'll add that to my doctorate. I'm an MPP, as well as a PhD. OK, your humor ushered in the fifth clue; it's about resonance:

"V. The Divine is more readily manifest when one is in alignment and resonant with one's true nature, one's true voice."

"We need to go deeper to get the next clue," Jaquelyn suggested. "It's about surrender. We need to fulfill our service to others in the same spirit as when we surrender to making love. That's what produces the necessary alignment, resonance, and acceptance that allow the divine to manifest. Our challenge is to carry that level of alignment and resonance out into the world more tangibly than we do now. The *Flesh and Spirit* practices do that but we need to go further."

"As we will when we start sharing and writing about the crossing yoga. All of these practices interrelate and overlap to some extent—which gives us the sixth clue," Jack said with delight:

"VI. The complete surrender to erotic love brings a resonance and alignment that are the model for manifestation of the divine in all situations.

"In other words," Jack elaborated, "one becomes a lover in the world using divine sexuality as the doorway but without getting stuck crossing the threshold. It's basically what you've been trying to get me—us—to do for years. The sixth clue speaks to sexual intimacy as the inspiration and then going beyond it to manifest the divine in all our relationships and worldly service."

"To make this clue more applicable to more couples, the word *erotic* might be replaced with *spirited*." Jaquelyn suggested.

"Right on! That's almost implicit in the way we've been using *erotic*. Also note that, like the others, the sixth clue is worded in an affirmative way, but it implicitly alerts us to attachment as a primary obstacle to surrender."

"I'm not sure I get the obstacle part."

"Being attached to our sexuality has been our challenge in one way or the other for years," Jack responded. "Almost every time we make love a moment arises, usually early on, when you have to ask me to stay conscious. Sometimes it's when the kisses get too wet or I lose sensitivity in touching your nipples. Usually one reminder is enough and I'm OK for the rest of the journey. My unconsciousness in those moments reveals my attachment, however subtle. Years ago, I used to call you back to earth when you blissed out during love-making, so we've helped each other stay present at different times. Now we're both trying to stay awake as we explore a new kind of stillness during lovemaking. Staying conscious in that ecstatic state and the sixth clue are all related. The sixth clue says that once we master conscious lovemaking, we can do anything from that level of awareness—writing—anything!"

Jaquelyn was fully involved in the game now, which allowed her to leap. "You garden from that level sometimes. I know you do . . . I think the ninth clue has to do with the Bardo of dying and the markers along our path that we establish when we make love. The tenth has to do with the crossing yoga. So now all we have to discover are seven and eight."

"How clever of you to jump to the end! Then we can bridge to the clues we've already been given. OK, let's get nine."

Jaquelyn saw the clue clearly. "It's about the journey through the Bardo of dying. The teaching has to do with establishing mark-ers, reference points, to keep us on track and conscious, so we don't disconnect from the light at the end of the tunnel."

Jack took in her words and searched for the underlying teaching. "Towards the end of our lives we are being asked to leave markers that transcend death. Our books and even projects like the ones in Mali and Israel can be markers. It's the level of consciousness they manifest that makes them so, not so much the projects themselves. And each time we make love the opportunity arises to leave a particular kind of consciousness marker. So let's see how we might phrase this clue." Once again, the words came to Jack out of the silence:

"IX. Transcendent actions (actions that manifest the divine) can leave markers—heartprints—that are recognizable to practitioners and serve as lighthouses in the Bardo of dying."

"I love *heartprints*," Jaquelyn exclaimed. "I don't think I've heard you use that phrase before . . . OK, now let's see if we can get the tenth."

"The tenth is easy," Jack replied immediately. "It's about life being eternal. How you experience death depends, to a large degree, on a new awareness of time. So:

"X. Consciousness and what we call life are eternal—out of the reach of ordinary time."

The word *eternal* inspired him further. "The notion of eternity gives us a hint about the seventh clue. It might be about time—perhaps that amazing koan Tarthang Tulku gave us so long ago:

"VII. Time is Prana.

"In other words, time is inseparable from the breath of life, from spirit."

Jaquelyn nodded. "Then the eighth clue has something to do with the world at large, some way of bringing all the other teachings further into the manifest world. Part of our service is to be part of gatherings devoted to creating an Eros presence on earth that so many traditions have envisioned but eludes most people still. In that sense, *our Third is like a personal messiah*, Jack. Maybe we are preparing to be one of the avatar couples that William Erwin Thompson spoke of years ago."

When she called him *Jack*, he knew that Jaquelyn meant business. He listened carefully.

"The rise of the couple as potential avatar is part of evolution now—with that level of Third consciousness at which couples create a literal force in the world."

Jack suddenly saw the teaching:

"VIII. Anything that can be imagined can be manifested, but only if there is sufficient collective consciousness and resonance for its realization.

"This clue includes the power of affirmation, the law of attraction—all that stuff," he added.

"Yes, this one comes after the time clue," Jaquelyn agreed, "because knowing that time and consciousness are inseparable is really a prerequisite for the Law of Attraction. OK, but where does the importance of community come in?"

"It's implicit in the eighth clue," Jack explained, "because like-hearted groups are necessary for gathering enough consciousness for manifestation. As people wake up and begin to relate in new ways, they will form communities that create a critical mass of consciousness. This is already a familiar teaching and is beginning to happen. For us it means gathering with the couples that do the *Flesh and Spirit* practices on a regular basis."

"OK, the clues feel complete," Jaquelyn reflected, "but somehow they seem masculine to me, although less so than the stern tone of the Ten Commandments. Maybe it's because Moses only knew how to listen to the masculine divine, not the goddess. The feminine needs to be brought in and the clues expanded in some way."

"OK, let's do this in the spirit of Passover," Jack suggested. He poured the third cup of wine. "OK, I'll say the prayer again."

"The same prayer?" Jaquelyn asked.

"Yes, you say it four times at the Seder."

"Why don't we say a new prayer that includes what we've just learned?"

"Great, you say it," Jack responded, appreciating her innate resistance to tradition.

Jaquelyn nodded. "The first few clues are about the nature of the divine—how we are all one and so already merged—and suggest that the joy of realizing all that can be reaped in the passion of our relationships—in what is challenging, fun, sexy, and *alive!*"

"So the first two clues are intrinsically both male and female," Jack observed. "There's nothing patriarchal about those two."

"Right," Jaquelyn agreed. "The third clue says that true erotic love, conscious erotic love, is the spirit of the divine—"

"—which is totally gender-balanced."

She nodded in agreement. "And which is essential in all intimate relationships. Then the couple becomes a more powerful force in giving back to the world. The clue about consummation has to do with lovemaking transmitting the joys and blessings of heaven on earth. Each couple's influence goes out into the world, whether it's from their writings or their role in the community or just being at home working. I feel enormously blessed and elated that I've been given this assignment with you. It's more inspiring than anything I could have ever imagined."

Jack laughed. "You did imagine it, because the only way anything can be manifest is by—"

"—yes," Jaquelyn joined him. "I did imagine our lovemaking, and that has been my home ground and inspiration, because it's in our union that I touch divine consciousness. I am ready to do anything with you. We have an enormous capacity to image, and so what we image has to be right on. We can have differences in how we image as long as we both choose what's good for our relationship and the whole community. And that brings us to the next clue, which is the magic of manifesting in community when people image the divine together—"

"—and bring sufficient resonant consciousness to actually make it happen," Jack added.

"Yes, and that's exactly what we're doing in Africa," Jaquelyn affirmed. "As wild as the vision is, the HIV/AIDS Project in Mali is going to happen. We're actually going to find out if the low doses of Naltrexone that I've used with hundreds of autistic kids is useful in preventing HIV-positive adults from developing full blown AIDS.

It's our mission! Eventually, the medication will be available to heal the orphans and the babies that are dying now—and that will inspire people to get these kids into better family situations and schools. Beyond all that, conducting monthly councils for the adult patients we're testing worked out amazingly well. New approaches will keep coming down the pike for curing AIDS and helping contain HIV, but the council part of the program is evolutionary, since it changes the relationships between men and women.

"That reminds me of the photo," Jaquelyn continued. "It was a brilliant idea for me to put that picture I took of you looking at the Niger River on my computer. I feel your beautiful muscles inside the shirt I gave you. You are so dear just looking out over the water. You're happy just being near water, even though the Niger, as it goes through Bamako, was too polluted for you to get in! I see you gazing at that river probably ninety-five times a day, and every time I feel a surge of love . . . It's such a blessing to be able to do all this with you."

Jaquelyn went on for a while longer in the same inspired vein, celebrating the implications of the clues, while Jack listened with great pleasure. By the time she finished, there was a huge grin on his face. "So I conclude from all this that the ten clues are gender inclusive. What's different is that the woman tells the story differently. I gave the bare metaphysics of it, while you used the clues to create a visionary goddess story. I loved how you did it . . . I think we can claim that the clues are gender balanced."

"And it's delicious to express the meaning differently," Jaquelyn added happily.

"Now with the ten clues in hand, maybe we can shape up and eventually get to the promised land."

"The traditional commandments may have been necessary all these years," Jaquelyn responded, "but we're ready to see a whole new promised land now as evolution becomes a co-creation of men *and* women. We've transformed the old story, but more changes are needed. The new story wouldn't have a solitary man receiving the teachings. The visionary would be a couple or there would be a whole circle of couples and singles."

"Indeed!" Jack affirmed. "In the new mythology relationship will have to play a central evolutionary role."

The word *evolution* thrust Jaquelyn abruptly into the present. "Relationships could play a strong role in the 2008 race too. The Obamas are a strong team. But Bill Clinton needs to do something really loving for Hillary by showing that they have some juice between them. We know they have deep love and respect for each other, but—"

—they don't seem to have much juice," Jack agreed.

"If they could erotize their relationship, she would win the primary and the election in a breeze. As a woman, I have to get that message to her."

"In exchange for her getting Bill's foundation to give the Mali Project a grant?" Jack asked playfully.

The fact that a colleague of Jaquelyn's knew one of Clinton's inner circle and had offered to hand him a grant proposal to complete the Mali Project suddenly became part of their Pesach celebration.

Jaquelyn lit up like the Northern Lights. "I'm going to do it! I'm going to write a letter to Bill and say, 'Look, the world is waiting for you to show some hair and do your best to wake up the erotic part of your relationship with Hillary. Use your charm and power in the sexual arena to stir the pot. She'd win the primary in a breeze. I'm going to do it! I'm going to do it tomorrow!" She leapt up from the rocker and was literally dancing around the room, clapping her hands. "It's so exciting. Don't let me forget this. Woo-hoo! Hot damn! We might as well have fun fulfilling our assignment."

Jack hadn't seen her so jubilant in a while.

"The Seder was really good!" Jaquelyn added settling back into the rocker.

"Yes, and now we get to sip the wine once more and eat before we say the ending prayers—which might not be traditional at all," Jack said suggestively. They dined simply and then, as you might expect, celebrated lovemaking as their promised land.

16 ❧ Revelations in the Bathtub

The ten clues provided a foundation for the new mythology that was emerging for J&J. The clues also created a bridge to Jaquelyn's increasing fascination with the ancient goddess era and its brutal demise in the hands of the early patriarchal cultures. The more she read about that early period in human history, the more she knew the goddess had to return to redirect the suicidal impulses of the patriarchy and inspire a new era of erotic love. This vision was a tangible evolutionary experience for Jaquelyn. As you already know, she felt the goddess's presence in a personal and physical way, literally in her own body.

In the spring of 2007 the emergence of the goddess took another leap forward as a result of a psychic reading with a man she had worked with before in Sedona. He seemed unusually attuned to Jaquelyn's uniquely empowered erotic nature, and so his readings always inspired her in a productive way. In fact, on more than one occasion his counsel left her wishing that Jack had more of his natural gift for recognizing and appreciating those mysterious qualities she had begun to gather together under the heading of the "nature of the divine feminine."

Jaquelyn sought the reading because of the challenges she was facing disengaging from her prominent position with the DAN! organization and her sadness that Chelsey would not be visiting the Blue House that summer for the first time in several years. The spaciousness to embrace new inner and outer initiatives was obviously growing and she needed to check out what was emerging with a sympathetic and objective source.

Jaquelyn's reading with the psychic inspired a long monologue about the emerging goddess, which she recorded while luxuriating in her bath overlooking the banana trees. Contemplative tubs had become one of her favorite ways to connect with the divine feminine, along with making love and council, of course.

Later that evening, she and Jack meditated together, during which the goddess appeared vividly to her. Jaquelyn shared various parts of her experience, finally summarizing it all with just a few words: "The goddess is yearning for relationship and has decided to be intimate with a man. She's come back to earth again so she could magnetize the man and manifest in human form."

Jack was delighted. "That explains why there are these two people totally in love doing a wild dance along the path of relationship. As I let you—and her—in more deeply during the meditation, I realized the book I'm writing is really a joint book. I'm just the scribe. We need to talk about that but first let's hear what you had to say in the bathtub after your session with Ron." They put on the tape and listened for a while:

"Once again I feel I am moving into the core of the feminine universe. Emanations seem to be going out from me. The oceans don't stop them; the sky doesn't stop them; the mountains don't stop them. They radiate out to infinity. I know these emanations touch the world in many different ways, one of which is encountering the feminine collective in Israel and Africa. Having met many women in these two places and reading the news about what's happening to women all over the world is deepening my identification with female empowerment now. What started with my reaching out to a few of my close women friends has turned into a yearning to have tangible and virtual gatherings of women to share visions of empowerment. Some of my women friends, as well as Jack, have told me that they can't embrace some of the violent, Kali-like images I want to evoke to scare the men into waking up. I realize that the violent ways I want to punish the men reveal that I am still an emerging goddess with a lot to learn. But I feel that the door has been opened and I'm on my way.

"The reading with Ron helped me to see that my real love is to tell women about the emerging goddess and the fear men have of her that is reflected in their behavior all over the world today. The common denominator of all the atrocities done to women is the fear of the feminine. I think the original impulse for union in the universe was totally mutual between the masculine and feminine spirits, but the feminine is actually what manifests spirit. The feminine creates matter, and so everything we see, feel, and know in the universe is born of the feminine. She invites and magnetizes. She's been given enormous sexual magnetism so that she can invite male godness to manifest. She's the adventuring spirit that came to earth to get the lay of the land and saw that her spirit needs to materialize. She wants her god-man to come into her and fill her and help her see herself as goddess."

Jack couldn't resist reaching out to stop the tape when he heard the phrase lay of the land. "That's another great title for the book, Jaquelyn: The Lay of the Land, because 'lay' has at least three different meanings. The songs the troubadours sang were called lays—and your songs are ecstatic. The idiomatic meaning of the phrase has to do with knowing your way around the land, which in this case means around the goddess's body. And, of course, you're the lay of all lays! Your words are inspiring. Men have to understand that they need guidance from the feminine to become lovers. Of course, a certain amount of resistance is fun, as long as it's erotic."

"Resisting can lead to creating erotic games and so much learning," Jaquelyn agreed. "As we know now, all there is . . . is relationship."

"Yes, the universe is one huge relational web that knows itself only through relationship—through its innate interconnectedness."

"Is that why autism has become one of the major diseases of the century?" Jaquelyn asked.

"The autistic children reveal both the toxicities of our civilization and our limitations in relating. We all exhibit autistic symptoms to one degree or another. So Chelsey is on a mission."

"Ron agrees. He actually said, 'She's served her mission by getting you to learn what you've learned and to write the autism book.' Then he told me that my work and the book are my ways to become well known in the world, so I will be a thread in many people's lives. Eventually, it doesn't matter what the thread consists of. Once it's there, it can be used for other purposes. If I start vibrating at a certain frequency, that frequency will create a transmission for everyone who has ever heard of me or read anything of mine or heard me speak! Isn't that exciting?" Her almost childlike joy was so dear to him that he could hardly refrain from folding her in his arms. "When I'm happy, I can imagine myself radiating out in every direction, into every person, just like Ron predicted."

"Listening to your tape, I felt what an honor it is for a man to be able to share the path with a woman like you. Being given this assignment means I have the potential to embrace the emerging goddess in a fully alive woman. You keep upping the ante in the game of surrender. Listening to you I caught a glimpse of why I've been struggling recently. The bar is getting higher all the time."

"Good! I hope it makes you a little more easygoing," Jaquelyn said in a teasing voice.

He felt the comment like a gentle blow. There was a definite silence. "I already think of myself as easygoing."

"You're slow going, but that's not what I mean by easygoing. You move rather slowly and have consciously disciplined yourself to do that. I was thinking more of being sharper, more alert."

"Like you!" Jack matched her teasing voice.

"Yeah." They laughed. Such humor is the mark of a man who is learning how to love the embodying goddess.

"It is difficult at times," Jack went on. "We have such different patterns. When we're in our erotic state, it works—and at other times we struggle with our stuff. Maybe you've been wondering, 'is this guy ever going to get it?' There's a particular doorway that I can't seem to find right now. It's hard to describe, but I feel how you yearn for me to find it. Maybe there will always be more doorways."

"I know what you're talking about, although I can't name it either. But I do know we're looking for it together and it has to do with our sexual connection. I want to be in that level of ecstasy and awareness and love, with all the choices we have then, even when we're not making love and even if the goddess coming through me is Kali, the bitch, the powerful one, wanting to kill violent men or cut off all their cocks. The other extreme—yes, I am black and white sometimes—is the sweet, adoring wife who never questions the power and superiority of the male."

"It's a stereotype, but that kind of woman is not doing her evolutionary job," Jack responded.

"Yes, but many powerful men marry women like that. Bill Clinton is an exception and look what's happened to him and our country. Men have to learn to handle powerful women—even Kali—if the full goddess is going to manifest."

"Exactly!" Jack agreed. "Part of our challenge is helping men understand that they are to be actually re-created in their relationships with women. They can't embrace the goddess without a full transformation of their essential manhood. Some men know this, even consciously."

"In particular, men have to discover what their phallus is really for," Jaquelyn continued the thread. "A woman wants her lover to be connected to his phallus consciously enough to know that it belongs in her spiritually and even physically, as well as to him."

"Yes! When he enters his lover, it's like the salmon going back upstream, the ferry boat docking. As a kid I used to watch the ferries docking at the tip of Manhattan. How the boats fit exactly into the docks fascinated me. I see now I was really watching the phallus re-entering the land—the woman. When we make love, I 'land in you.' In this moment it feels like my phallus is already in you, even though we're sitting three feet apart. When my physical cock actually enters you—when I dock my cock—then the vision is realized. What more could a man want?" (laughter)

"I've never been able to figure out why men don't see that," Jaquelyn added in her innocent voice.

"I need to sell them on it. Basically I'm a salesman, like my father."

"Yes, you're a consciousness salesman."

"My body feels different having heard your words tonight," Jack explained. "I feel lighter. (He put a hand over his lower torso.) This part of me used to be sleeping until you activated it."

"I knew cocks when I met you, but I didn't really know a man until I loved you," Jaquelyn's voice was soft and vulnerable.

"It was perfect for me to find a woman who is centered in the place of my insecurity. It was an incredible fit. The man's self-confidence has to be really strong to walk this path. There are many men who end up being manipulated by their women."

"Yes," Jaquelyn agreed, "women know sexual seduction, but that's all part of the game . . . (silence) . . . Isn't it?

Jack laughed. "Indeed! You have the most incredible mixture of innocence and sexual wisdom. Maybe they go together. It's so clear that Eros has to be the core of the new mythology. We've become so encumbered with the patriarchal legacy. Mary and Jesus must be lamenting—'Oy vey! After all that we went through!'"

"Profound mutual recognition and responsiveness are essential," Jaquelyn added. "When I call, you often show up right away. But sometimes when I want you to be really present, you say, 'give me time.'"

"Yes, I keep on discovering hidden pockets of non-presence," Jack acknowledged. "Many men have parts of themselves that are independent of each other, like regional warlords. Each part owns its own territory and makes agreements with the other warlords. Woman is more of a whole interrelated piece."

"Piece of ass! (laughter) Let's listen to the rest of the tape." Jaquelyn punched the start button.

"The woman wants her man to come into her and fill her and help her see herself as goddess, as an expanded magnetic feminine being. It's a wonderful dance. There's no problem about who's on top, who's the more powerful. Their merging is beyond all that.

Competition is irrelevant. Our focus is on men and women because that's what we know the best. All intimate relationships are equally potential and should be totally honored. I also want to include the individual healing that is part of our path—the relationships with the inner man and inner woman—so it's best to use masculine and feminine rather than man and woman to describe what we are learning.

"The masculine can actually fill and fertilize—and complete the feminine. They complete each other. This aspect of the feminine does not come from Diana, the lone warrior. Rather, it comes from a place of in-loveness with the union with her god-man, her partner. The nourishment she gets from him and their relationship fleshes out the inspired image of the feminine divine I've been picturing and talking about for years. There's a parallel arising of the masculine too, but the man's challenge is greater than the woman's in some ways because there are already established patriarchal patterns and doxologies that get in the way of his awakening and surrender as a lover.

"The evolving feminine is building a brand-new temple on the virtual or imaginal plane by integrating the collective energies of all women. As we awaken and come to know this temple, evolution will accelerate. What I'm yearning to feel intensely is the enormous beauty and power and deliciousness of the collective feminine. It's like a beautiful, succulent flower with a most wonderful aroma that makes you want to surrender. Women are made to attract gods. Rather than looking down on that attraction as something dangerous or evil, this magnetism should be celebrated, honored, and worshipped. That's what I'm about—and the time to build the temple is now. I need to magnetize other women of like mind to gather together.

"When I stay on the edge making love with Jack, I actually feel I am capable of transmitting energy in the powerful way I envision. We can focus that transmission on Chelsey, for example, to help mobilize her stem cells and connect the dendrites in her brain. We should do that in a disciplined way on a regular basis. Then there are our friends who are ill and need support. On the other hand, there are companies making medications who have lost their way and fallen into making money as their ultimate priority. They need to see how their policies affect the millions of children and the poor who are dying of AIDS and who cannot afford their medicines. Most important, I need to connect with the unknowable, unseeable, unfathomable, and eternal divine feminine. I have to start writing my book and plant the seed.

"I dreamed last night that I was with Chelsey. We were walking at dusk on a road with our arms around each other. She was just about as tall as I am now and we weighed about the same. She's solid muscle and I'm made of seventy-five year-old flesh, but we fit together. I felt she was totally recovered and conscious and feeling my love, and I was feeling hers. In the dream the love was full and beautiful. The dream helps me let go of having to be with Chelsey and get on with the other work that calls now. I know she's going to be all right, no matter what. She is a goddess and has taught me a lot about goddesshood. I'm enormously grateful to her and to Liz for letting me explore so many kinds of treatments and even encouraging me. I have to finish up with autism. I've made connections with lots of autistic mothers, and when I move into the next phase I can use my strong connections with them to transmit the vibration of the new collective feminine. That's a delicious thought.

"Then there's the challenge of changing men's behavior. To do that, I have to actually enter their bodies. It's from knowing Jack's body so well and feeling that deep union with a male that I will be able to move into the collective masculine and penetrate its whole being. A current mission for me is to create a single unified male entity that incorporates every one of the thousand males that performed the atrocity of stoning that young woman in Iran. Then, when I enter that masculine being, the thousand men will see the girl they murdered rise up in resplendent goddesshood, totally translucent and emanating a brilliant light. Dumbstruck with her radiance, they will realize they have killed a woman who embodied the divine feminine, as do all women. Basically they will be fried—baptized—into being men who totally honor and are in love with the feminine. It will be like they have gone crazy and, the more one of the men gets it, the more he will spread the word. They will become emissaries of the new feminine and do their best to change the world before all the honeybees die . . . I'm a dear friend of the honeybees.

"I have to write in the first person and talk about how my sexuality emanates and transmits the divine feminine. That will magnetize the women into entering this collective and changing the world. Join the circle! Don't be afraid of your sexuality! Rejoice in it. It can be your pathway to knowing your divine self and creating an erotic world in which people love and help each other and find ways to regenerate themselves. Once the sexual energy is turned on and fully infuses our physical being, it can expand into the spiritual dimension to erotize everything. An erotic world has been promised. The feminine has to manifest that world now and men are to be fully a part of co-creating it. Then men and women together will recognize that the divine feminine is the only force that can overcome the patriarchal power that has demonized us for so long."

When the tape was over, J&J sat in silence for quite a while. Finally Jack found his voice. "I'm impressed. Your words turned me on. I want to hold you."

"I thought you'd never ask."

"Before we do, I want to share something with you. I've been aware of this for a while, but it's just now getting clear enough to describe. As we complete our councils and begin to head into making love, the intensity between us gets stronger almost every time. Then, as the build-up peaks and I begin to touch you, I get a message about the unawakened terrain that is to be illuminated by our passion—the Eros field—that we're creating. The terrain feels like part of our own personal landscape, but I feel the awakening also contributes to the evolutionary awakening. Other couples on the path contribute in their unique way."

"Our lovemaking is a devotion to the goddess," Jaquelyn added, "which reminds me of how the Hebrew god, Yahweh, came to be. Did you know that in early Gnostic Judaism, Yahweh had a lover, the goddess called *Astarte* or *Ishtar?*"

"I remember vaguely. Tell me the story."

"When Astarte was reigning," Jaquelyn explained, "the image of the male god Yahweh first arose as her lover. She was a descendant of Isis and the other early goddesses. Yahweh and she were the first god and goddess pair in those days."

Something stirred in Jack's imagination. "Yahweh becoming a god as Astarte's partner suggests that the entire patriarchal period has been about *men growing up to be lovers*. We needed the patriarchal era to balance the long period of goddess worship. Now that the patriarchy is drawing to a turbulent close, we need to reinvent our sense of deity, not as individual anthropomorphic entities but *as relationship itself*. I think that's what the process of erotizing the unawakened landscape through lovemaking is all about. Each time the terrain we're being asked to illuminate is different, depending on where we are along the path and the full potential of the Eros field we've created at that moment. When we can't keep our hands off each other, the terrain is smaller and not as starving for Eros as other portions of the landscape may be. When the energy is high but we are not champing at the bit, or if there are shadows that haven't been faced, then the terrain I see is larger—even vast—and has the feeling of never having experienced Eros before. Every time we illuminate new terrain, we get more familiar with the expanding landscape and so become more empowered—and now I really can't keep my hands off you!"

They lay down side by side on the bed while he took her hand gently in his. For several minutes they remained motionless, intrigued with how long they could resist the magnetism between them. This game of playfully refraining from the temptation of love had become more subtle of late and generated a huge wave of energy when they finally surrendered. This time they rode the wave so far into new territory that the surroundings seemed almost impersonal. Finally, Jaquelyn had to speak.

"I just felt like I was a black hole. I've always seen the black hole as being intensely magnetic, not for physical objects but for energy itself."

"Yes," Jack agreed, "the black hole is about energy disappearing from one dimension of reality to another."

"Yet it is still a pulling, a mysterious pulling. On the physical

level the connection between us is extremely magr
because of some mysterious forces that exist on a mo...
Beyond the physical, maybe our magnetism is about the energy of
surrender. So what is the pulling of the black hole and what does it
have to do with relationship?"

"As I understand the physics," Jack began slowly, "the energy that
moves into the black hole disappears from the ordinary universe in a
sort of energy death. The rebirth happens as the energy reappears in
a new dimension, which we can think of as another universe, now
that the multi-verse theory is gaining acceptance. The black hole
is needed to account for the flow of energy between the universes.
Looking at the physics relationally, we can say that during intimacy
it's male energy that enters the black hole, which is itself female.
The female receives the male and "he" disappears—dies—as he
enters her, to be reborn in another universe. I'm reminded of what
happens to the male tarantula when he enters the hole the female
digs to lay her eggs."

"That image works for the crossing yoga too," Jaquelyn added.
"That journey starts with entering the black hole at the end of life
and then goes through the transformation of consciousness that
leads to the universe we call death."

Jack couldn't resist touching her breast near the nipple as lightly
as an angel's kiss. "Your flesh is getting more and more to be an
organ of ecstasy."

She groaned with pleasure. "This is magic. There's nothing like
it . . . oh, honey."

They disappeared for a while into the lover's black hole as his
fingers slowly approached her now erect nipples and, ever so lightly,
touched the taut flesh and her ring of Venus.

"Shall we have the chocolates now?" Jack asked.

"OK . . . see what an easy lay I am?" (laughter)

They unwrapped the small coin-shaped candies slowly. "Eating
the chocolate reminds us that we're still in our bodies, black hole
and all," Jack said hopefully.

"Chocolate increases the endorphins. Acupressure, sexuality,
dark chocolate, and vigorous exercise all increase endorphins." He

loved when the doctor and lover came together. "I'm imagining the chocolate is your tongue," Jaquelyn added seductively, as she let her tongue awaken the fullness of his lips, daring him to resist the temptation to join in. He stayed completely present—and still—allowing her to continue her exploration without restraint until that was no longer possible. Even then he held back the growing temptation to devour her completely and let her tongue lead the way. Finally, their dance took them out of time, as the merging of mouths had its way. After what seemed a very long time, they both fell into stillness again, simultaneously.

"That kiss was like an entire lovemaking in itself," Jack finally broke the silence. "By being as still as I could while you danced around the fire, I finally understood what you've been talking about all this time about rushing into merging."

"Ummm," the goddess replied.

"Do you think Mary and Jesus were practitioners of this stillness and used it to penetrate the veil through lovemaking. Could they have seen death itself as an extraordinary part of making love? Could this be part of what they meant by eternal life?"

"If they are our erotic ancestors, the answers must all be yes," Jaquelyn responded without hesitation.

"So lovemaking is the heart of the crossing yoga."

She shivered with delight. "That's a date, honey. What are you doing New Year's Eve?" She sang the words as a line from an old song, stored along with innumerable others in her musical archives. He laughed with just a touch of fear.

The invitation returned them to their bodies—which were waiting not so patiently to connect. In a few moments the fire began to roar. "It's like the lightning the other night that filled the sky," Jack said with a touch of awe. "We're becoming intercellular," he managed to whisper, "We're occupying the same space!"

Jaquelyn groaned inaudibly, wanting him badly now. "Becoming love's body is such a joy. The goddess is here!"

They surrendered to her presence and, as he approached the gates, she shuddered again and let out a soft moan that spoke of the almost painful nature of such pleasure. "Every cell is aware of the merging now," Jack whispered, as he slowly entered her with a slight pulsating movement. Again moans were her response. Then they paused and were still, he only just past the portal. That allowed her to find her center again and begin a slow rhythmic movement that challenged his stillness. He met the challenge.

"This is even beyond stillness," Jaquelyn spoke out of the silence.

"I'm learning how to relax through layers and layers of arousal," Jack responded. "When the stillness is this deep, you can do anything you want, and I can embrace it."

"Are you sure?" Jaquelyn asked in that same irresistible tone that suggested both angels and devils, as she undulated more intensely on his magus-wand. It was her goddess dream come true. Jack found a place of such open surrender that she could dance forever. A few moments later, when he began to touch her nipples again, she became still for a moment, groaned again and felt a uterine contraction that was fully orgasmic.

"When the baby nurses, the breast sends a message that contracts the uterus," Jaquelyn said reverently. "This is divine."

Then he moved further inside her—and stopped again, still a ways from what was possible. He determined how deeply he should enter by the soft goddess sounds that came through her from a place of primal erotic wisdom. "I can feel how the goddess is guiding all my movements through the sounds you're making. Your breasts are incredibly aroused, more than I have ever experienced before. The little buds of pleasure are all celebrating."

"They're devotees worshiping the goddess of nourishment," Jaquelyn whispered.

The rain began to fall more heavily as her breathing became heavier. Soon the goddess songs came forth in full voice, rising and falling in perfect rhythm with the sounds of the rain on the blue roof. The lovers of the goddess listened reverently to all the music.

17 ✒ A Moment of Suspended Horror

As it is with lovers, time is remarkably fluid in telling their story. The summer and fall of 2007, as well as the winter of 2007-2008 were busy times for J&J, including return trips to Israel and Africa, and a number of *Flesh and Spirit* trainings. There are many tales that could be told but what calls me to share next is the re-emergence of the power of nature that fueled the wild ride in the Honokaia Gulch. In the spring of 2008 the mission of that manifestation of the goddess to shape their relationship arose spontaneously once again. The adventure involved their daughter Elissa, her then-husband Tim, and Elissa and Tim's son, Nicholas.

The scene is one of the Big Island's most beautiful places—Kealakekua Bay, on the leeward side of the Island, about forty minutes south of Kona. The marine preserve there had been the place where Jack first swam with dolphins and was a favorite destination for J&J during their early years visiting the Island. The north end of the bay is considered among the best locations on the Island for snorkeling, and the resident pod of dolphins still swims into the preserve almost every early morning to this day.

The early morning sky promised a glorious day. Tim had worked out an ingenious rig for the car that held the fiberglass kayak firmly on the roof. A second kayak, an inflatable Sea Eagle, was in the trunk, all set to go. They pulled out of the driveway at six-thirty, hoping to get to Kealakekua before the dolphins departed the bay, as they did most mornings by nine. Jaquelyn had contemplated backing out of the long day, but she hated to be a spoilsport and, besides, snorkeling at the far end of the bay was one of the few water adventures she still enjoyed. Neither she nor Jack was counting on seeing the dolphins, much less swimming with them. But when they wound their way down the steep road to the ocean from the main highway, they noticed a covey of kayaks all gathered in one place in the middle of the bay, near the bottom of the cliffs where a large landslide had occurred during a recent earthquake.

"I think we lucked out," Jack said hopefully, as they started to unpack the car. The old concrete pier at Kealakekua was made for larger boats, not kayaks, but none of the locals wanted to make it more accommodating for fear that even more tourists would invade their popular paradise. The pier was constructed of heavily graveled concrete with two ten-foot notches carved out of the south-facing side. Depending on the tides, the notches were either two or as much as four feet above the water level—just right for motor boats but a real leap for those in kayaks that ride low in the water with their gunwales only a few inches above the sea.

It took them only twenty minutes to inflate the Sea Eagle, load their gear, and get ready to launch. The surf was relatively calm. Jack dropped into the stern of the fiberglass kayak, and Elissa took the bow with Jaquelyn in the middle seat. Their launch was far from graceful, but they just laughed at the awkwardness, eager to get out into the bay to see why all the other boats had clustered. Tim and Nick had no trouble dropping the lighter inflatable into the water and jumping in.

Just approaching fifty and in excellent shape, Tim was completely at home in the physical world. His strong, dark features and matching full head of hair created a striking presence. A gaffer by profession, he had a rare knack for making and fixing things, and a deep love of nature. At fourteen, Nick physically resembled his father and shared his love for the mechanical world. He was equally fortunate to have also inherited Elissa's unusual intelligence and perceptive sensibilities.

They paddled around the end of the pier and headed north to join the other kayaks that had formed a large circle in the middle of the bay. The Kealakekua Preserve provides a dramatic setting for the many snorkelers who visit regularly in kayaks or tour boats. Multicolored cliffs, covered with a variety of small trees, ferns, and exotic foliage, tower almost a thousand feet above the water along most of the shoreline. The cliffs gently melt into the ocean to the north, where the Captain Cook Monument is situated on a small grassy knoll adjacent to the sea. The monument is not imposing, although it marks the spot where the ubiquitous explorer is said to have met an untimely end at the hands of the locals due to some unspecified "misunderstanding." Perhaps they grew tired of European explorers "discovering" paradises that had long been known and revered by indigenous peoples. There is a small pier in front of the monument that, together with the nearby rocky shoreline, serves as base camp for the many swimmers who make their daily pilgrimage to Kealakekua.

The water in the bay is sometimes that beautiful blue-green that blesses Hawaii, although in recent years the volcanic activity of Mauna Loa, to the southeast, fills the sky with enough of Pele's breath to often veil the sun and leave the ocean a flatter blue-gray. That afternoon the sky was slightly overcast with "vog" from the new Kilauea fissure, but the air temperature was still comfortable because of the veiled sunlight filtering through.

They saw the dolphins swimming among the kayaks from a distance. "Go for it," Jack shouted. "Jaquelyn and I will stay with the boats."

The next hour was blissful. The resident pod of spinner dolphins was feeling playful and showed off for the small assembled flotilla. The adolescent spinners in particular burst out of the water repeatedly, their silver-grey coats glistening in the hazy sunlight. J&J happily watched their family's joyous close encounters with the magical ocean creatures. After almost an hour the dolphins began to work their way towards deeper water, making larger and larger circles around the boats. For the finale, a few of the younger dolphin spun skyward exuberantly as they disappeared into the sea-haze. Tim and Jack then headed north towards the monument.

Being with the dolphins and now paddling with Elissa in the bow, her lean graceful figure and long blond hair tied back in a ponytail, felt like a divine gift. Father and daughter enjoyed an easy closeness, a well-earned harvest of many years of facing their shadows whenever they arose. In a month she would turn fifty. Just the fact that the youngest of his children was approaching the half-century mark brought Jack a smile of disbelief. He paddled in rhythm with her strong strokes, stretched his legs around Jaquelyn in the middle seat and gave her a squeeze of gratefulness. She turned with a knowing smile. Words were unnecessary.

As Jack scanned the shoreline around the monument, he realized with a rush of adrenaline that landing the kayak was going to be tricky. The surf was already heavier than at the pier. Watching the sets of larger waves crashing against the rocks led him towards a small cove, protected by a string of large boulders. Tim followed him with the inflatable, trusting that Jack had been there before and knew the best place to land. It had been many years since their last visit, however, and Jack realized that he no longer had the same confidence handling the kayak that he used to have. The realization was momentary, and he was not aware of having immediately suppressed it.

One of the reasons the far end of Kealakekua Bay is prized for snorkeling is the shape of the reef near the monument. A great variety of coral grows just a few feet from shore along a seabed that slopes downward gradually for about thirty feet. At that point, it drops suddenly, disappearing into a hidden world of dark blue shadows more than sixty feet below. The water is so clear that, on a sunny day, one can see to the bottom of the reef.

They snorkeled for a while, each mostly in their own world. By the time Jack was ready to come out to rest, Jaquelyn had been ashore for half an hour. She watched him walking in among the mixture of coral and rock near the small pier, stumbling and trying to keep his balance in the increasingly heavy surf. A man sitting near her also noted Jack's struggles and offered to help, but Jack shook his head and said, "No thank you."

In the next moment, a large wave tossed him against an underwater rock. She could see him grimace. That he was unwilling to accept assistance when he obviously needed it bothered her. That was not one of his better characteristics. She watched him carefully to confirm that he was OK and teased him about refusing help, as they sat on the pier together watching the others reveling in their explorations of undersea life. By early afternoon, the vog had thickened and they were ready to make the return journey across the bay.

The surf was significantly heavier than in the morning with large sets of waves rolling in every few minutes. Other snorkelers were already having difficulty negotiating their landings and departures from the monument. Jack tried to regain his old feeling of being in command of the situation, but the calm center he once knew as an experienced canoeist eluded him. Their departure was not pretty, including one moment when the fiberglass kayak turned over in the heavy surf, spilling out all their gear. They finally got it together and paddled briskly across the bay, talking about their good fortune in having a marvelous day of snorkeling, plus time with the dolphins. Their gratitude moved them into an altered state that the ocean and its creatures so often induce. In less than half an hour they were all within a hundred yards of the pier.

The surf had increased further during the return trip. They could see the waves crashing against the rocky end of the pier and along the shore on both sides. It occurred to Jack that this was not going to be an easy landing. "Maybe we should wait for Tim and Nick to land and get their help," he wondered to himself but didn't act on the thought. Later he found out that the same idea had occurred to Elissa as well, but neither of them had said anything to the other. Instead, Jack brought the kayak close to the larger of the two notches in the pier and set about timing the landing to take place in between swells. As he steered the kayak closer in, the scene before him felt slightly unreal, as if he were in a dream. Once again, he let the awareness pass. The kayak heaved with the waves, rising and falling at least three feet with each swell, while he did a draw stroke intensely with one end of his double paddle. Slowly the distance between the pier and boat narrowed until Elissa felt it was safe enough to make the leap. She rode a swell and stepped into the notch a foot or so above her, throwing her paddle onto the main level of the pier and quickly turning around to help Jaquelyn.

At that moment, Jaquelyn stood up unsteadily in the center of the kayak and acted in a way that added to Jack's already dream-like sensation. In the days that followed he would associate that state with the one he had entered during that fateful day four years earlier when he approached the bridge over the gulch in the pouring rain. Ultimately he came to understand the state as being "between the worlds" in the shamanic sense, neither fully on the physical plane, nor in the spirit world but somehow caught in-between. That was not a good state to be in when docking a kayak at an unwelcoming pier in heavy surf!

Jaquelyn stood in the heaving kayak, now about a foot or two from the pier, clutching her damp towel. Having a strong impulse to be unencumbered, she tossed it to Elissa. The towel never completed the journey and instead fell into the water between the pier and the kayak to sink quickly under the heaving surface.

"Why did you do that?" Jack heard himself say with a touch of irritation—and immediately wished he hadn't spoken. Jaquelyn heard his tone and felt reprimanded, but there was no time to deal with the towel, as a large swell moved the kayak away from the pier. He paddled furiously against the surf and once again brought the boat up alongside the pier. When he looked up he saw Jaquelyn still standing, unsteadily in the kayak, uncertain about what to do. The shelf in the pier seemed so high. She hesitated and then grabbed hold of Elissa's outstretched arm with her left hand. Her back was to Jack, who was still in the stern of the kayak trying to hold it steady. Another swell raised the kayak and dropped it further from the pier, just as Jaquelyn made the leap. What happened next they would replay over again in the days that followed, searching for other choices they might have made that would have led to a different outcome.

Jaquelyn began to fall into the water between the pier and the boat as Jack, paddling vigorously, watched in horror. The scene unfolded in that terrifying slow motion that often accompanies a nightmare. He lunged forward in the kayak, prepared to block her fall at all costs and avoid the fate of the towel. Jaquelyn realized that she lacked enough strength in her left arm to pull herself all the way up using Elissa's hand, but she held on for dear life as more hands on the pier suddenly came forward to help.

They came a moment too late. Jaquelyn hit the pier first with her right calf and then her head. As she spun around, her left arm twisted grotesquely in Elissa's outstretched hand. A primitive howl of pain tore out of Jaquelyn's mouth—an animal voice belonging to the bones that were being twisted and broken. One foot was in the water, her only lifeline her left arm now at a strange angle to her body, still desperately holding on to Elissa's hand. The other helping hands grabbed for any part of her body they could reach.

Jaquelyn's eyes were closed and her face, white as a ghost, as they gathered her battered body on the concrete ledge. Jack never remembered how he got out of the kayak or how it got pulled up on the pier. The next thing he knew he was bending over Jaquelyn, as she lay on her back, her right hand grasping her head near her left eye. "My head," she groaned, more worried about that than the searing pain in her left arm. There was blood oozing from a cut near her left eye, but Jack could see that it was superficial. Suddenly, a young woman materialized out of the crowd and knelt down next to him. She told Jack not to move Jaquelyn at all as she assessed the grotesque bulge in Jaquelyn's left arm just below the shoulder.

"I'm a doctor," the young woman said to Jaquelyn, who nodded appreciatively. Jack still seemed caught in nightmarish slow motion. *Could this really be happening* flashed repeatedly through his mind, not yet grounded in any coherent reality.

The pain helped Jaquelyn make eye contact with the young woman. "You're a doctor," she repeated in a thin voice. "Is my head OK? I saw stars when I hit the pier."

The young woman looked carefully at the wound, dabbing it with a Kleenex. "I don't think it's serious," she said. "It's your arm that's hurt. I'm a pediatrician, just graduated from Stanford. I'm no expert, but I think your arm is broken or at least dislocated. It's completely out of shape." Jaquelyn fully concentrated on her arm for the first time. Jack grasped at what the young woman had said. "Yes, dislocated. The arm looks dislocated, not broken."

Once again, a familiar, calm doctor presence arose in Jaquelyn that knew immediately how badly her arm had been injured. The young woman asked her to describe the pain on a scale of one to ten. Jaquelyn thought carefully before answering: "It's a seven or eight." Jack could hardly bear to see her lying there, shock-white in her blue wetsuit, looking vulnerable and wounded. The young doctor asked someone to call 911, while she stayed with Jaquelyn, comforting her and talking about what happened to keep her from retreating into shock. "How did I get up on the pier?" Jaquelyn asked.

"We all helped you up," the young doctor said and continued on about her recent training to maintain Jaquelyn's attention. Jaquelyn reciprocated, identifying herself as an autism specialist who had written a "widely read book." The two doctors chatted about autism as they waited for the ambulance to arrive. Jack couldn't fathom the calm conversation taking place.

"Thank you for taking such good care of me," Jaquelyn said, after a pause in the exchange. The pain had increased. She thought about all the times she had been on the other end of an accident, comforting someone and taking the proper action. Jack, still in a daze, touched Jaquelyn's right leg.

"Ouch!" Jaquelyn yelled suddenly, for the first time discovering the large hematoma on her right calf where it had hit the pier hard.

"It's a bad bruise," the doctor said, "but not serious, I believe. It's your arm I'm worried about. I'm pretty sure it's broken."

"Or dislocated!" Jack added, still in denial and feeling the first wave of guilt that he had not taken better care of his woman. All he could do was continue kneeling by her side and looking into her eyes, so filled with vulnerability he could hardly bear it.

By the time the ambulance and two paramedics appeared a few minutes later, Tim, Elissa, and Nick had loaded the fiberglass kayak back on the car, deflated and packed the Sea Eagle, and gathered all their gear. Elissa found out where they would be taking Jaquelyn and asked Jack for the keys to the car. "We'll follow you to the emergency room. Don't worry about anything. We've got all our stuff. You go with Jaquelyn in the ambulance."

"Yes, I want to do that," Jack responded and finally got up from his kneeling position as the paramedics deftly slipped a small stretcher under Jaquelyn. They rode together in the ambulance, sirens wailing, to the hospital south of Kona.

As soon as they entered the ER, a large, cheery nurse took over. The first step was to get Jaquelyn from the stretcher to a bed, cut her out of her wet suit, and help her get warm. That took many blankets because of the fierce ER air conditioning. Pain medication followed. A doctor finally appeared, a tall man obviously from the South. "Your arm looks broken to me," he drawled. "Let's take an x-ray and see." They wheeled Jaquelyn out of the ER into radiology and took a series of pictures. Each slight motion needed to get the right angles for the x-rays sent a shot of hot fire down her arm. She was glad to get back to the ER. Jack sat by the bed, called Elissa on his cell phone to let her know what was happening, and held Jaquelyn's right hand.

"Is it like childbirth?" the nurse asked Jaquelyn, making conversation while they were waiting for the x-rays to be developed.

"Worse," Jaquelyn responded. "The pain is stronger and there's nothing good to come out of it at the end." They laughed. The x-rays came back a few moments later. They were not pretty.

"Looks like at least a triple humeral facture," the doctor said without emotion. "I'm not an orthopedist, but it's a nasty break." Jack felt another wave of grief. "How would you rate the pain," the doctor went on. This time Jaquelyn gave it a nine. "You can take another Vicodin," he responded and the nurse produced the small white pill immediately.

"There's no orthopedist on call right now," the doctor drawled on, "but I'll see if I can get a hold of one on the phone. Even though the break is a bad one, we usually don't operate in situations like this. We just let the arm heal on its own."

"I want to do whatever will allow me to play tennis again the quickest," Jaquelyn responded with a sinking feeling that getting back on the court might take a long time.

They experimented with a few different kinds of slings until they found one that seemed to work. As soon as they strapped her in fully, she felt a little better. With her arm kept close to her body, the pain was bearable.

Jack asked the doctor a lot of questions about how such a bad break could heal on its own. "By just the force of gravity holding the bones still—we don't set breaks like this one," was the answer, but that didn't make much sense to either of them. The x-rays showed at least a one-inch displacement of bone in the upper humerus. It was hard to look at the x-rays without grimacing. The idea that these twisted and flayed bones could somehow come back together seemed unlikely. "I'll try our orthopedist on the phone again and get a consult," the doctor said and left the ER. He came back empty-handed a little later, just as Elissa, Tim, and Nick arrived in the waiting room. They decided to go home and arrange to see their own orthopedist the next day. The nurses gave them a rousing send-off.

The trip home was filled with little groans from Jaquelyn when her arm got jostled and much revisiting of the landing scene with many "what ifs." It was a restless night for J&J. A visit to the local orthopedist the next day confirmed the treatment. He suggested only a weekly checkup and x-ray to confirm that progress was being made.

In the weeks that followed Jack plunged into his new occupation as nurse/caretaker with full devotion. In particular, Jaquelyn's daily bath became a loving ritual for them both. Jack filled the tub, tested the water, and helped Jaquelyn in. First she squatted in the rising warm water and then slowly slipped off her haunches, holding firmly onto him with her right arm. She could soap parts of her body with her right hand but she needed him to wash her right side and back. The tenderness Jack felt taking care of her moved him close to tears.

One of the times he helped her out of the tub and settled her on the towel-draped three-legged chair in her bathroom, he was reminded of an Aldous Huxley novel he had read in college. "Such is the Kingdom of Heaven," he said out loud, as he was drying her feet.

"What's that about?" Jaquelyn asked.

"Oh, I'm remembering the last line of Huxley's *Point Counter Point*," Jack answered with a dreamy smile. This elderly couple is finally able to love each other without major obstacles, and in the book's last scene they're taking a bath together. 'Such is the Kingdom of Heaven' is the last line of the book. Those words have always stayed with me."

"Do you see us as elderly?" Jaquelyn asked, smiling.

"I feel ageless, if you really want to know," Jack replied. "Drying you like this takes me back to when the kids were little, and I bathed them almost every night. It makes me feel really tender when you're vulnerable. For you to need help on this level is so rare and goes against your passion for self-sufficiency." He carefully blotted the moisture between her toes, trying not to press on her hematoma as he moved up her body. Drying her thighs and genitals provided a delightful range of mixed feelings. "This is such a joy for me. I thought our relationship was already as multi-dimensional as it gets, but bathing you takes us to a whole new level."

"I've never needed anyone to wipe my ass before."

"I would do that with pleasure as well."

"Fortunately, I can do that with my right hand."

"It's so strange how the universe works," Jack mused. "You already struggle with how much you love me, fearing that you depend on me too much for what sustains you. Now the injury makes all that look tame."

"It's like the goddess wanted me to be humiliated."

"I think the word *humbled* is more appropriate," Jack suggested.

"You always put a more positive spin on disastrous events."

"It's hard for me to think of the gulch as just an accident, but I agree it's even harder to see your broken arm as more than that. Still, we had so many warnings that something wasn't quite right before the landing."

"The wild goddess teaches us once again," Jaquelyn allowed, "and I'm OK with learning from whatever happens."

"I want to be sure we don't make the same kinds of mistakes again. I seem to have a tendency to do that. I feel guilty that the physical part of the process often ends up playing out in your body."

"I am hurting, and it's going to be a long time before I can play tennis again," Jaquelyn groaned. "This 'learning experience' is happening in my body, but there's no reason for you to feel guilty. You did the best you could. I'm not as strong as I used to be, and I lost my balance—and I didn't follow my instinct not to go in the first place."

"But clearly I wasn't conscious enough," Jack added quickly. "Our ecstatic time with the dolphins and snorkeling left me in a less grounded state. But we'll get through it. You may be playing tennis sooner than you think."

Jaquelyn's patience was challenged in the weeks that followed. The "jello" state of the new bone growth that filled in the gaps took a long time to reach the firmer plastic state and then still longer to harden up into real bone. Then there were setbacks caused by overuse and an occasional inadvertent bumping. It took several months until Jaquelyn began to forget that she had an injury and until late August before tennis became a possibility. Jaquelyn's arm would never be the same. The new bone was larger and created a sense of unbalance that took time to integrate. For a while, trying to put food in her mouth with her left hand comically ended up hitting the cheek near the corner of her lips. She had to learn where her mouth was all over again, like a baby.

Two months after the nightmare, Jack returned to Kealakakua with two of Jaquelyn's daughters and a grandson, who were visiting. Needless to say, Jaquelyn stayed home. The family repeated the scenario of that fateful day exactly, arriving early at the bay with the two kayaks and all their gear. The surf was up this time as well and the launch was challenging, but they managed without mishap. The dolphins had already left, so they paddled on to the monument to snorkel. When the waves showed no sign of subsiding, they decided to return a little earlier than planned. On the way back across the bay, Jack noticed the tell-tale arcs of a small pod of dolphins just ahead. It was early afternoon, so the sighting was unusual and led to floating gratefully in the presence of the dozen or so mostly resting spinners for ten minutes. One young adolescent did manage a joyous leap before they all sounded and disappeared.

Jack noticed his heart was beating noticeably as they approached the pier. The sense of *déjà-vu* had been happening all day for him, but this was the moment he dreaded. This time he was in the stern of the inflatable kayak with Jaquelyn's oldest daughter, Leslie, in the bow. Her younger sister, Adrienne, and Adrienne's son, McCabe, were in the fiberglass kayak alongside them, with the sixteen-year-old doing a good job in the stern. Fortunately, the surf had subsided somewhat by the time they were ready to land. When someone on the pier asked whether they wanted any help, Jack accepted without hesitation. The landing went smoothly.

A few minutes later, as they were packing up all the gear and loading the car, Jack noticed a middle-age couple approaching the pier in a rented kayak. They seemed undecided about how to land. The woman's eyes revealed a hint of fear that Jack recognized. "Would you like some help," he shouted loudly to be heard above the surf. The man eagerly took him up on his offer and Jack guided them in carefully, finally grabbing the kayak and holding on while first the woman and then the man got out, timing it all with the swells.

"Thank you sir," the man said several times, repeating it again a few minutes later as they were about to drive away. That's the least I can do by way of redemption, Jack said to himself.

18 ❧ Returning to the Holy Land

The end of 2008 and the beginning of the following year were also times of extensive traveling for J&J. They visited Israel in early November (voting in advance by absentee ballot) to facilitate relationship workshops, council trainings, and women's and men's circles. The time in the Holy Land also involved helping the group of council practitioners there to build a cohesive organization that was sustainable in both programmatic and financial ways. Then they flew west, for a three-week stay in Mali to support the HIV-AIDS study that was finally ready to enroll patients. The route from Tel Aviv to Bamako included a change of planes in Ethiopia's capital, Addis Ababa, where maintenance delays created an unexpected one-night layover. It was en route to Ethiopia that they got the news of Obama's strong victory in the presidential election, which, to their delight was being loudly celebrated in Addis Ababa, as well as in many other cities in Africa. As they walked around the shops and government buildings in the city, they were greeted by many wide grins and shouts from young people: "We love America. We love Obama! Obama is our man!" The shining smiles gave them a surge of hope that life could change for many people, even those in Africa.

The time in Mali was productive, although the local officials revealed a knack for creating administrative hurdles hitherto unknown to human bureaucracy. The highlight of their trip was facilitating an advanced council training with a group of mostly Muslim men and women who were completely baffled by the empowered nature of their facilitators' relationship and, in particular, by Jaquelyn's outspoken, no-holds-barred way of communicating. By the time they boarded the flight to Dakar in route home via Atlanta and San Francisco, it had been almost seven weeks since they had slept in their own bed. Christmas was only a week away. As you might imagine, they felt like kissing the ground on arriving at the Kona Airport.

J&J celebrated Christmas alone. After the long trip, they welcomed the quiet time, although not being with family still felt a little strange. Their council on Christmas Eve took on the flavor of a marriage renewal ceremony to which Jaquelyn invited Mary Magdalene and Jesus. That inspired idea led to a playful evening that honored their spirit teachers.

As the year ended J&J felt as if they were navigating a worldly river whose current was growing stronger all the time. It would be only six more weeks before they were to return to Israel, this time to conduct the "shared society" initiative you've already heard about. The basic idea was to use the practices developed through the *Flesh and Spirit* work with intimate couples as a basis for establishing direct, compassionate interactions among Arab, Jewish, and Christian leaders. They hoped that the intimate atmosphere of Third consciousness would overcome traditional cultural barriers and even subdue the historical hostility between the light- and dark-skinned brothers and sisters that can be traced back to biblical times. It was an ambitious approach, and they both knew that the possible outcomes included at least a mild disaster. Needless to say, I fully supported their vision, and I'm glad to report that their growing trust in the wisdom of their Third kept their spirits high during the days before the departure for California, where they were stopping for a week to see family, before flying on to the Middle East.

During the last night at home, Jaquelyn invited Jack into her ceremonial bath for a council. She was stretched out languorously in the water when he came in with a candle. He sat on the small three-legged teak stool that lived next to the tub and once again took in the perfect balance of her voluptuous breasts, the swell of her hips and the long slender beauty of her legs and thighs. He noticed all this beauty with both the familiarity of the lover and the witness perspective of a man who was about to share his beloved with people in distant worlds. Jaquelyn had on a yellow terry cloth hair band to hold up her curls so they wouldn't be straightened by the steamy hot water. Outside the banana trees moved gently in the late afternoon breeze. Three bunches hung from the cluster of stalks, all still green and small. As always, the fruit and purple flower at the end of the thick ribbed stem hanging below fascinated Jaquelyn. She studied them every time she had a bath, marveling at the wild unself-conscious sexuality of nature.

Jaquelyn waited for Jack to speak first. On the eve of their departure he was in a retrospective mood. "I'm pondering a basic question we've been chasing all these years. Why did you find me sexy and choose me as your next man thirty-five years ago? I was quite overwhelmed then—working twelve-hour days running a school, fighting with my board, not feeling very juicy, but still getting involved with several inappropriate women. It wasn't a good time for me—perhaps the darkest period in my life. Maybe my woundedness was a setup for you. The wounded male has always been an archetypal draw for you."

"Yes—and was I in for a surprise!" Jaquelyn responded. "I could see that you were wounded sexually but I felt the potential. So I told you that your sexual teacher had arrived."

"Yes, and you are still my teacher, although now we've become really matched."

"It is a compliment for me to hear that," Jaquelyn said with a smile.

"So here comes this unsuspecting guy who's offered a deal by a goddess-in-the rough. She says to him, 'Look, the only thing that's going to save you from a miserable two-dimensional life of a mathematics professor slowly drying up from lack of Eros is a woman who is so grounded in her sexuality that your mental powers and shadows will not deter her.'"

Thoroughly enjoying his story, Jaquelyn let out what could only be called a carnal laugh. "I read every man I met then as a possible lover and needed to see potential in order to be motivated. I was 'a devout crotch watcher.'"

"Lucky me! Little did I know that thirty years later I would still be in awe hearing the goddess songs. I'm beginning to listen to them more consciously now, although that's a challenge, since I'm usually way out there by the time you sing. Listening attentively often leads to my further initiation into the nature of the goddess. If I really take in the songs, I might be inspired to join you. I think you would appreciate a collaborator."

"Yes, and one with more humor," Jaquelyn added.

"Yes, my humor index could use a little raising . . . OK, so tomorrow we fly away singing our songs together—and adding a touch of humor. We need to be in the state we're in right now when we're in Israel, which includes me wanting to devour you!" He allowed himself to look at her reclining body without restraint. Jaquelyn was still fully stretched out in the water, her "burning bush" (as she named it irreverently after their last visit to the Holy Land) just below its surface. As she stirred, the water gently caressed her breasts, like the clouds that gather around the peak of Mauna Kea after a rain, he thought.

"Just devour me every moment we're there and don't think of anything else," Jaquelyn agreed. "Then our work will flow naturally."

"Our friends in Israel are counting on our relationship to empower the shared society intensive, although they don't understand exactly how that will play out—nor do we. We're trusting, though because the path we're on has blessed us so in so many ways."

"We're saying that our way is *a* path now; we're no longer saying it's *the* path," Jaquelyn noted.

"That's good because the challenges continue, like not abandoning myself to the ecstatic feelings of merging when I'm inside you."

"I want you to become the poet-lover when you're inside me. You can't just indulge the ecstatic feelings. You have to keep on returning the energy to the lovemaking."

"Yes," Jack agreed, "and the more I do, the further out you can go."

"I trust that."

"Then we get to hear the divine songs."

"And one of these days, you'll want to tape one," Jaquelyn added with a smile.

He felt the slight dig. "It's true, we haven't recorded any deliberately."

"Listening to them could entertain us in our old age." (*laughter*)

"Now that we're talking about it!" Jack offered, "I realize I'm being transformed by the songs."

"Maybe they will become duets, with you writing the lyrics."

"In a way our council dialogues before we make love are the lyrics. "Then later you add the music. When you're in that energy, you are irresistible."

By this time, Jaquelyn had gotten out of the tub, dried herself, and slipped into the familiar soft green housecoat. Meanwhile Jack prepared the usual plate of snacks to assuage her hunger during council. While they were eating, a gecko appeared on the outside of one of the small bedroom windows behind the dresser, creeping up on a moth.

"One of our pets is here," Jaquelyn announced

"We're part of their food system, since our light attracts the moths. The geckos are family for you."

"I love watching animals of any kind. The sweet potato you brought from the garden that looks like an otherworldly creature is fascinating to me. Watching her grow with shoots reaching for the light intrigues me. She's a being with arms stretching upward just like me. I want to grow plants that have strong healing powers. Taking care of them would change my consciousness."

"That's already happening by growing veggies in our garden," Jack commented. "These two rice crackers take the place of the communion wafers in the traditional ceremony. The crackers honor that old tradition and transform it."

"The other day I had the image of my broken arm as my personal cross to bear, since the new bone configuration has that shape. It's as if Jesus were living inside that part of my body now, as I heal. I feel my remaining Christian roots have gathered around my injured arm. I think all the rest of me has been cleared of early imprinting. As we heal my arm, we're replacing the cross of Jesus with a new version of the story that no longer requires anyone to be crucified for the sins of humankind."

"And simultaneously, I'm accepting Jesus in our version of his life with Mary Magdalene," Jack added. "That's deeply healing for me—for us—and a good preparation for Israel. I wasn't aware until this moment that I was still holding some shadows about Jesus, although as a Jew that's not uncommon. The level at which we have to be transparent and non-judgmental now means that I can't hold those ancient feelings. We have to be able to live in the consciousness of our lovemaking to pull off what we're going to be doing in the Holy Land."

"Every time we're in council, we say that we're being asked to live in the state of making love as we go about our work in the world," Jaquelyn said slowly, choosing her words carefully. "It's not hard for me to be in that state of intimacy with you, even when other people are around. That's the challenge anyway."

"Your bringing the cross into your body is a brilliant way to transform your Christian story. You were attracted to me because of my sexual wound and my potential, which you framed by identifying me as your Jesus. Mary needs to have her Jesus. You said that you wanted me to be—

"—a sexy Jesus," Jaquelyn completed the sentence for him. (*laughter*)

"Yes, and now, more than thirty years later, we're celebrating the whole story through our mission in Israel. Part of that means conjuring up the authentic Jesus, who had to be a wild, swarthy, revolutionary rabbi, not the usual blue-eyed, pink-cheeked, Christian imago. Eating this cracker means that I'm finally willing to acknowledge that the real Jesus—the historical Jewish Jesus—is part of my ancestry. Along *our* path, ingesting the 'body of Christ' means that I'm accepting lovemaking as the central practice in my life as part of the transformation of our patriarchal world with all its glories and horrors."

"Sounds good to me," Jaquelyn spoke her familiar affirmation with the usual smile. "I trust that our relationship will contribute a drop of healing to the thousands of years of patriarchal dominance. Now we're supposed to eat the wafers without any more words."

They took several minutes to eat the small crackers, with each bite taking in a little more of the story of Mary and Jesus that had followed them for so many years.

Finally Jack spoke again. "It must have been so hard for Mary to watch her lover die slowly on the cross. That may have something to do with the ongoing controversy about his penultimate words: 'My God, My God, why hast thou forsaken me?' Some scholars conclude that Jesus was comforting himself by reciting the beginning of the twenty-second psalm. Now, thinking of Mary, his words may have expressed the final pain of separating from her. They trusted that their relationship was strong enough to bridge between the worlds, but the risks were enormous at the moment of death."

"But they did stay connected through the three days until Mary brought his spirit body back," Jaquelyn affirmed. "They succeeded in doing what they set out to do, and I see the depth of our intimacy making that possible for us too. I could never explore the veil and come back without you, but *with you* I can go back and forth, exploring and learning about the terrain. We trust our intimacy that deeply."

"Every time we make love, you go to new places in your body and invite me to join you. You show me the new landscape and then I try to describe it to you."

"It's simple. I love to be with you and wrap myself around you like a snake. Then I can sing my songs."

"Even though we co-create the music, I'm still a little shy about the songs," Jack confessed. "Actually I'm in awe of them."

"Yet you know every sound I'm going to make from the way you penetrate me. You're like the conductor, complete with baton. I'm just the orchestra."

"You contain all the instruments," Jack acknowledged with a smile.

"You have the baton."

"It was my passion to be a symphony conductor when I was very young. I've told you before how I used to play classical records and conduct the music in our living room in the dark. I wanted to be a musician until it became clear I didn't have the talent. And now I'm making music with my cock."

"Of all things!" Jaquelyn exclaimed.

"The last instrument in the world I would have imagined mastering! There are so many unexpected blessings along our path!"

"Aurobindo says we take our current psychic life with us through the veil. So, if we continue to make music as we do now, then we are more likely to have a more conscious life going through the veil. If we don't, we probably will become unconscious at death, like when we're asleep and in-between dreams."

"OK, on that high note, it's time to eat the second Brazil nut," Jack suggested handing her one.

"Yum! They're very sexy, aren't they?"

"Chewy," Jack replied. "I've been devouring you all this time. You love for me to explore you with my tongue and mouth, so you can be awakened in a way that only the cock can eventually satisfy. You love to create two rivers—awareness and desire—when we make love."

"I make a science out of that," Jaquelyn acknowledged.

Jack paused, noting that swirls of smoke were coming out of his mouth as he talked. They had noted this phenomenon several times in the past, once even in the local movie theater, but most often during their councils. It seemed to signify a state of heightened consciousness.

"What *is* that smoke?" Jaquelyn asked.

"I don't know. Perhaps it has something to do with moisture condensing, since it looks like one's breath when it's cold outside. But it definitely marks a shift in consciousness, like the ringing in the ears that people speak of when they are in a heightened state. Maybe it's a cloud of erotrons!"

"*Erotrons?*"

"I've been playing around with the physics of relationship again," Jack confessed, "like we used to do in the old days. I've been calling it *quantum erotics* because it's analogous to quantum physics."

"The mathematician cannot be denied!"

"Basically, I think of *erotrons* as elements of love that can be in either particle or wave form. It just occurred to me that the smoke we see around our heads could be erotrons in particle form."

"Whatever you call it, the smoke moves around your face, like an aura," Jaquelyn observed . . . "OK, are you ready for the last Brazil nut?"

"This last one is a big test of consciousness," Jack said playfully. "Eating this is going to make us so erotic that I will have to stay especially centered. The temptation is to devour the nut the same way I want to devour you."

"My nut looks like the head of a cock—sort of."

"Your words sent a tumescent pulse through me. I hope the Israelis have Brazil nuts. We're going to need all the support we can get. Most of the people gathering for the shared society intensive won't know more than one or two of the other leaders."

"I can already feel some strong connections happening in the women's circle," Jaquelyn added. "I'm so turned onto women now that I want to write a book for them."

"Do it! We could even begin the intensive by sharing how our personal story led to that moment. We could say, 'This drama has been unfolding for a long time.'"

"I love it! I can't think of a more perfect way to start."

"They'll be expecting a pitch for cultural peace," Jack added enthusiastically, "so we could immediately go to the personal level, maybe even tell them about our—"

"—discipleship with Mary and Jesus."

"Even that!"

"It's pure opera," Jaquelyn exclaimed with delight.

They were silent for a while, looking into each other's eyes until Jack spoke again. "In this moment I cannot feel any fear in loving you more all the time—and that trust extends to Israel. I no longer feel any apprehension about our gig."

"As long as you love me totally, there is nothing to fear," Jaquelyn agreed.

"I have memories about the fear of loving that are all fading as our love deepens. A new simplicity is arising."

"The truth is enormously simple. It's present in the passion we're discovering in our lovemaking and will help us make the crossing. Sometimes we touch that simple truth when we're talking too."

"I just got a glimpse of the flow of energy in the next thirty-six hours as we fly away," Jack interjected. "I want to hold you. Your beauty is overwhelming right now."

"That's because I have finally fallen deeply in love," Jaquelyn said in her innocent—and wise—voice.

"Humans are evolving now to the state where Eros can wrap his wings around Psyche. Love will finally embrace the human mind. My love for you is becoming the environment of my mind. The male and the female are simultaneously re-creating each other now. Many people are doing that now—*together*. Co-creating a new relationship reality with spirit actually works." Jack said the last words in a passionate whisper, which sent a pulse of energy up Jaquelyn's spine. She rarely heard him speak so affirmatively. That opened her heart, and love's body followed immediately. It was as if a warm, pulsing, golden light was slowly turning on inside her. "You're beaming," Jack said simply.

Jaquelyn let her robe fall open and they were silent for a while in the stillness of Eros. "It's indescribable," she said finally.

"I just made love to you in the imaginal realm. Now let's see if we can make love while we continue talking."

"Every time feels new and goes beyond where we've been before. Let's lie down on the bed and just hold each other to see how long we can allow the energy to build without moving. We're in her hands now."

They arranged themselves in the embrace meditation as usual and actually managed to remain still for quite a while. In the silence Mary Magdalene and Jesus appeared to Jaquelyn clearly. She had to tell him about it.

"I felt Mary and Jesus inhabiting us in order to feel the kind of sexual energy humans can feel now. They are ready to share the secrets of union from the other side with us, so we can learn to make love once we're there."

"It's a training program!" Jack exclaimed. "We're being trained in the art of spirit lovemaking by receiving their guidance until eventually we're ready to make the crossing."

"At the same time Mary and Jesus expand in the sexual arena by inhabiting our bodies. That's how they catch up with the times, rather than still living in the Holy Land of 2,000 years ago. Perhaps they didn't have the chance to experience the full mystery of fusing their bodies in lovemaking that we're exploring."

Jack was reaching the boundaries of his restraint. "My back aches for your touch—you know the spot—yes, that's it. Every touch feels like making love now. Everything is both heart and genital now. I remember your goddess songs the last time we made love. I listened closely—and heard surprise in your voice, like you were seeing the beauty of who you truly are. You sang, 'If I am being loved this way, I must be of the goddess.' A woman has to move out of our patriarchal culture completely to see her full beauty and divinity. I am inviting you to leave the patriarchy with me."

"The last time we made love, there was a split second when I thought I had the choice to move beyond life," Jaquelyn acknowledged, "but I didn't go because I wasn't sure you were completely with me."

"I wonder if that was the moment when your singing sounded like a glorious celebration of the goddess. The next one after that had a touch of the blues, as if you were acknowledging how hard the path has been for so many women. There was even a touch of, 'I'm not sure we will ever make it' in your voice. The goddess songs are so varied."

"I'm not aware of those darker themes when I'm singing," Jaquelyn replied.

"They are encoded in your DNA. Of course, the main message I hear is from a woman joyously celebrating union in her body. A man can get close to that by being inside the woman when she's in that state. Then he approaches ecstasy."

"When her songs are coming through me, I'm not thinking, but afterwards it has occurred to me that maybe the goddess was really too feisty at one point a long time ago."

"Too feisty?"

"At the time of the turning from the goddess's time to the patriarchy, all her lands were being taken by nomadic herders. She was sexy and threatening to the men and to their new emerging cultural structures. When the men had been with their herds for a long time, alone and without women, they began to sack the villages and kidnap the women. Eventually they decided that all women had to be subjugated—and that plunged them into the darkness of the early patriarchy. Now, finally, that era is ending as enough of us are supporting the birthing and recognition and strengthening of the feminine divine in women and in our relationship with the earth. With the rebirth of the goddess, we need to have courage to live our path fully, whatever it takes, just as Mary and Jesus did. They had the courage to accept that one of them had to cross before the other. Clearly that was to be Jesus."

"That was their story," Jack added. "Although that could happen for us too, I don't think it has to."

"Oh no! We're on a path that's teaching us how we can cross together."

"We're coming out of an era in which fear predominated and in which love was characterized primarily as a struggle between the sexes or a more or less ascetic connection between humans and a projected god-figure. The consequences of continuing in this vein are too great." Jack was suddenly aware of a heightened flow of energy in her. "I feel the pull of what is happening in your body. When you take the goddess energy into your flesh and all the layers of your feelings, her presence becomes extremely real. More people have to bring the goddess in deeply like this in order to get it—"

"—*together*," once again Jaquelyn finished his sentence.

When they made love later that evening, the goddess joined them in some of the ways they had imagined—and a few they hadn't.

19 ❧ Lovemaking in the Veil between the Worlds

The journey to the Holy Land was full-on challenging, intense—and successful beyond their expectations. The shared society work, which came to be called the *Inbar Initiative* after the kibbutz where it took place, turned out surprisingly well. J&J returned home in early March tired and satisfied, ready to do an intimate debriefing on their own holy ground.

This next story moves us towards the completion of their work in distant lands. They were to return to Israel again in 2010 for a final tour of duty, but the peak experience remained the shared society initiative at Inbar. The Africa HIV-AIDS program would not be completed until the middle of 2011.

Although they didn't talk openly in Israel about their own take on the Mary–Jesus story, as they had planned, their connection to the biblical couple had a strong influence on what happened at Inbar—and afterwards—as the next story reveals.

A week after their return Jaquelyn had an insight that she was eager to share. She called for an open-ended council for that evening and suggested they commit to just that part of their practice without the usual shift into lovemaking. Jack readily agreed.

"I was reflecting on our trip," Jaquelyn began, "and how Jesus and Mary have been teachers for us, starting way back. My dad always dreamed about going to the Holy Land, but it wasn't a dream of mine when I was growing up. So our strong focus on Israel in recent years carries a touch of irony. That we are expanding on what Mary and Jesus started so long ago seems grandiose—and yet it makes sense. We feel they are our ancestors in the lineage of courageous men and women who embrace both sexuality and spirituality in their intimate lives. I *know* they saw how these two streams are inseparable, but in their world Mary could not be recognized for her significant role in their work together. Has anything really changed? What I'm really trying to tell you is that I felt like Mary at Inbar and afterwards. Everyone wished I had been more active and told us so in the debriefing circles."

"Yes," Jack agreed. "I was the dominant one at Inbar, the patriarchal facilitator, if you will, and you were in the background, as Mary had been. The analogy is valid. As with Mary, you knew that I couldn't have facilitated were it not for 'us' and your ongoing initiation of me. But it takes time to change the story. The number of people who can handle our story of intimacy is growing even if slowly. The *Flesh and Spirit* work is spreading in various ways now. Years ago we had trouble working together leading workshops. We had different styles of facilitation and were competitive at times. We worked through those issues, and I trust we'll work this out as well, since we are committed to dancing together 24/7 even if it's—"

"—painful?" Jaquelyn interjected.

"No, it's wonderfully challenging."

"You had a look on your face that suggested pain."

"Well, it is a lot of work sometimes that is—"

"—delightful." Jaquelyn finished his sentence once more. "I don't see it as work at all. I can't think of anything else I'd rather be doing, so how can I call it *work?*"

"*Work* is not a bad word for me," Jack responded. "We live an interdependent life and serve each other with a kind of love that always seems to be in motion. When I'm in that state, during our intimate times, for example, you're astounding and dear—and all I want is to be your lover. That identity fills me; no part is left out.

Then we have other patterns that apparently still contain patriarchal remnants, whether they're part of your inner masculine or patriarchal dregs I bring. The initiative in Israel was a setup for those shadows. I had done most of the logistics and preparations for Inbar, so I needed to keep my hand on the wheel."

"That made it hard for me to jump in, particularly since I was a little nervous to begin with," Jaquelyn commented. "Despite presenting at all those autism conferences, I always get stage fright. So I just let you do most of the facilitation. I had my moments, particularly when the men and women met separately, but you were on a roll most of the time."

"Yes," I understand Jack said with a sigh, "and many people wanted to hear more from you, but they still spoke of what we did as a *we*. I tapped into our joint energy throughout the three days. I couldn't have facilitated were you not sitting next to me—and you did contribute significantly at times. We were holding a lot. The participants could have rebelled at any moment."

"I know people felt the *we*. I'm talking about the balance," Jaquelyn reiterated.

"As the work continues, I agree there must be more balance. I trust the transpersonal dimensions of our love will break whatever patriarchal patterns remain for us."

"We were so close in the weeks leading up to Inbar," Jaquelyn persisted. "Then it became much more of your show. After we came home, it felt like you went into your own world to integrate what had happened. So these past few days I've been wondering whether our identification with Jesus and Mary has influenced our balance. We've described what most likely happened to them two thousand years ago from our point of view and how we are carrying their legacy, but now we have to actually *embody it!* We're deeply involved in Israel and you're a Jew, although not a religious one. I was born a Christian and saw you as Jesus. And it gets even more complicated because the Jews believe the messiah is yet to come, so traditionally Jewish mothers are hopeful they will give birth to the true transcendent one. I wonder what is it like for a man to have a mother who thinks her first-born son might be the messiah—and loves him like your mother loved you."

"I don't think my mother believed in all that, although the image might have been buried in her unconscious," Jack replied. "That whole story is mostly a playful metaphor about Jewish mothers, but perhaps it's still spiced with a dash of reality."

"Then to marry a woman who sees you as Jesus means you're getting it from both ends. Are you feeling fried in the middle of all that?"

"I have felt fried at moments," Jack acknowledged, "but I'm not complaining. I take the Jesus projection as part of the way you're transforming your Christian legacy. Your notion of Jesus came mostly from your father's traditional daily prayers, as well as church. As you know, I see Jesus as a swarthy Semite and revolutionary *rebbe*. We've been able to hold these different images productively and even integrate them so we can be more in alignment. More recently we've come to see that Mary and Jesus must have embraced their relationship as a path of awakening, perhaps by adapting the old goddess practices or the esoteric aspects of the Kabbalah. Before the recent renewal of interest in Jewish mysticism, I didn't realize that those old teachings were so focused on relationship and love."

"I took my father's admonition to 'love Jesus with all your heart and all your might' quite literally. That was a major part of my imprinting."

"You wanted your lover to be Jesus. You wanted it all. I'm OK with that. The projection has helped me to grow."

"Yes," Jaquelyn affirmed, "and now we're preparing to do our version of the practices that allowed them to connect through the veil. They are our ancestors in that sense at least. Mary not being Jewish is another similarity."

"The interweaving of Christianity and Judaism has been a theme in our relationship since the beginning. That's one reason our Third has a quality of reconciliation that has been helpful in the shared society work. Inbar was the beginning; now it is up to our colleagues in Israel to pick up the threads and carry the initiative forward."

"Hopefully, we planted seeds at Inbar that with time and nourishment can play a part in helping to avoid the ongoing cultural polarizations and also help to heal the great rifts *within* each of the main cultural streams. If greater equality between men and women can become a growing reality in that part of the world, then the vision of creating a shared society in Israel will be given new life. All these issues have to be healed simultaneously in an integrated way to make real progress. It's an immense challenge."

"Yes," Jack agreed, "at Inbar our Third was like a stem cell that has the potential of healing the old cultural mind-sets. We began to build an intercultural Third in the group by stretching our own Third beyond its personal nature."

"What we're doing seems so ambitious that it's hard to share the vision with others."

"I understand," Jack acknowledged, "but Inbar took place. It was real. Third consciousness itself is evolving."

"Inbar was an initiation for us. That's why I cried the second night at the kibbutz. That afternoon our circle told us that something tangible was happening, and that really touched me."

"It's as if our Third went international and said, 'OK, if these guys are going to be useful in the last cycle of their lives, they have to learn how to transcend their personal experience of Third consciousness, enter into the cultural arena, and transmit that consciousness to others. So let's create an opportunity for them to raise the bar *in* their relationship and, at the same time, take them *beyond* their relationship.' Our Third came up with the perfect solution—the Inbar Initiative! That fulfills that old vision of ours that the deepening of relationship begins with individual couples moving into Third consciousness, and then spreads to groups of couples and singles, and eventually to the larger community."

"Despite the success, we have to be careful we don't overestimate what took place at Inbar," Jaquelyn cautioned. "Also, I wish we had found the guts to talk about Mary and Jesus. I see her increasingly as a powerful manifestation of the priestess-goddess. Although patriarchal eyes saw Jesus as the visionary and Mary as more instinctual and intuitive, we suspect that they actually played different roles at different times, like any couple on the path."

"Yes, in some ways you're the classic visionary and I'm more like Mary, the metaphysician. That's only one of the reasons I've always held your Jesus projection loosely. What I do hold strongly is being your lover whose mission is to reveal and reflect your divinity."

"I always feel my goddessness when we make love," Jaquelyn said with a smile.

"That fulfills the main intention of your so-called *projection*, so we shouldn't use that term any more. Simplistically, it's been about depowering your Christian imprint, as well as part of my training."

"You seem quite clear lately. Have some of these thoughts and ideas been moving through your mind the past few weeks or are you being more or less spontaneous now?"

Jack paused to take in her question. "I have scouts on the edge of my perceiving mind that gather information, but they don't knock on my consciousness door right away. Then a council arises or we lead a program like Inbar that generates a call for insight. That leads to the knock on the door and I'm given the information I need to assess the situation *at that moment.*"

"Is that how our version of the Mary and Jesus story was revealed to us?" Jaquelyn asked.

"Yes, over time, with the visionary input from you being most of what my scouts picked up. M&J were in a perpetual battle with the Jewish patriarchy. All that finally took its toll, and Jesus chose to sacrifice his own life—which of course included the ending of his embodied relationship with Mary. Jesus was indeed betrayed by most of the apostles, not only in the specific ways the Bible teaches but, more significantly, because the apostles' love could not overcome their patriarchal limitations. It's a different world now, and you're being asked to chronicle what it's like for a woman to become a relational goddess in this transition between a dying patriarchy and the birth of the relational era. The goddess era was dominated by a life-affirming feminine principle. The patriarchy basically became an individualistic era shaped by the creative, immature, and violent aspects of the masculine. Now we are entering the relational era, in which the masculine is hopefully mature enough to enter into intimate partnership with the emerging divine feminine. Personally, my job is to keep reflecting how much I recognize, accept, and love all aspects of your emerging feminine, not just the sexual. There's always more to say, but I think you know by now what it's like to make love with you. It's in all the other areas that I have to remind you of your goddessness now."

"Yes, I need to be a writing goddess," Jaquelyn concurred.

"Indeed! Writing your story is an affirmation of the emerging goddess-hood in you and other women. These stories are part of an evolutionary wave beginning to crest so they won't sound pretentious."

"Our relationship will keep us both honest and humble," Jaquelyn assured him.

"People will be moved to hear what sexuality is like from a woman who has a deep and life-long connection with the erotic goddess. You have a lot of wisdom about sexuality that comes from a different source."

"Different from yours?" Jaquelyn asked.

"Of course, and different from most women's. What I know about the deep sexual world has mostly come through your wisdom and direct connection with the divine feminine. To be able to be in love with a woman with your knowing is a blessing, which is also how Jesus must have felt about Mary."

"She was trained sexually in the goddess temple practices. We need new forms of those practices now—badly."

"Mary was so empowered that imagining any patriarchal stuff in their relationship is a stretch," Jack added, "and yet there must have been times when she felt frustrated, as you did at Inbar. Let's take stock. We received a certain kind of validation in Israel. What are we to do with that? Regarding the shared society work, the council group in Israel needs to take the initiative; that much we know. I see our focus being more on our ultimate intention to learn how to make love as we prepare to leave our bodies."

"When enough couples learn how to make love at the end of life," Jaquelyn added, "each in their own way, then the collective resonant field will manifest and begin to permeate the culture. What a transformation that will bring! We're getting closer all the time!

Another question is, how will the expanded Third we birthed at Inbar affect our intimacy?"

Jack's face lit up. "The sex we had a week ago was absolutely . . . I don't have the words."

"We had just gotten home after a long journey, so we just let loose without directing the energy anywhere. Unbounded passion led us all evening."

"Yes, and when we tried to play out the same script again last night, our bodies said, 'No, now you need to start learning how to use the energy in new ways'—in ways that bridge the physical plane and the spirit world."

"Yes!" Jaquelyn agreed, "and when you are not fully in your body, some archaic insecurity gets triggered in me—*the man could leave at any time.*"

"I stayed inside you last night even though I didn't stay hard. I didn't pull out suddenly."

"I'm talking about pulling out energy, not so much your cock. *Pulling out* isn't the right phrase anyway. It's more that you drifted into mental narcissism. Our lovemaking gets better and better, so if you're not fully present, like you were the night after we got home, I begin to wonder. That night I told you I've never been happier in my life."

"After such a glorious moment, the Third often picks up another piece of shadow for us to work on," Jack reminded her.

"Last night it seemed as if we stopped right in the middle of my orgasm."

"Your orgasms are extending—and becoming legend. Yes, we did stop. I suspect you entered a new ecstatic place and somehow I lost track of you. To build trust we have to deal with that, which is exactly what we're doing. Then, as our faith builds, you can continue to embody the divine feminine, step by step."

That triggered a question for Jaquelyn. "Does the hundredth monkey phenomenon work for the emerging goddess? Will the hundredth woman who really gets that she's a disciple of the goddess—and that all women collectively are the goddess—manifest the field for all women?"

"On our path she'll be doing that in relationship, so the hundredth woman *and the hundredth man* will cross the threshold together. It's the hundredth *relationship* that will actually create the critical mass. Don't forget our bumper sticker: **Aquarian men and women are going to get it—*together*.** We're a good example. You explore new terrain, and I find a way to describe the landscape you've uncovered. We have to be working together consciously in almost perfect balance to do what we're being asked to do . . . I just had a playful idea about our writing."

"I've been stuck, so tell me."

"Suppose I finish my book and you read it," Jack imagined playfully.

"And I say, 'Oh, my goddess!'"

"You love the book because it's a long love poem to you about our life together. However, there might be a lot of stuff that you don't see the same way. You'll want to respond."

Jaquelyn's face lit up. "So then I write, 'This is really what happened, girls. This is the real scoop.'"

"Yes! Basically, as writers, we're both inviting people to live an erotic life in all its flavors, not just chocolate and vanilla. That's what we did at Inbar. No pair of leaders that went into the center knew each other very well, and most didn't know the other person at all. One was always from the Arab culture and the other a Jew or Christian. Yet they connected. There was Eros even between Rebecca and Hussain. That picking names out of a hat created the pairing of a conservative Jewish doctor and an Arab community leader from the West Bank was cosmic irony. I felt elated when they hugged after the final council, remembering what Rebecca had said when they started their council: "You're the enemy! I wouldn't have come had I known a person like you was going to be here.'"

"And then there were the Arab and Jewish business leaders who ended up together in the center," Jaquelyn remembered. "Both had lost a son in the fighting. By the time their council was over, they were in tears and talking about their shared longing for peace. I'm so grateful for what happened."

"We're both growing, and when either one of us leaps forward, it may take some time for us to consummate the movement sexually. That's probably what happened last night. When we finally do our homework, the lovemaking is inevitably sublime. What that means is that apart from a few zigs and zags here and there, our lovemaking is steadily on a curve of increasing ecstatic union—which means the adventure will continue through the crossing."

Jaquelyn laughed at his leap of faith. "Good thinking. Is that the erotic mathematician speaking?"

"I'm just extrapolating."

"That's a vision that needs to be shared with a lot of people."

"It's one of my unassailable assumptions," Jack agreed. "My primary axiom is, 'Wherever the lovemaking takes us is where I want to go.' It doesn't mean we won't have bumps now and then, but they're getting rarer." His focus was shifting. "I would either like to eat you or some food."

She laughed again. "I have to have a bath before you can eat me, and it's already eight."

"Are you saying you want to eat first?"

"Well, I like to get it out of the way."

It was Jack's turn to laugh. "I wonder if we'll ever transcend the food–sex question. In any event, our challenge now is to make love along the bridge between life and death—and track each other all the way. My love for you always inspires me to find you."

"Your cock's love or your love?"

"Hopefully, they're the same," Jack assured her. "Tonight we're going to make love in the veil between the worlds. We've been approaching that slowly. Last night I lost track of you, so tonight, I accept the challenge to find you wherever you are, and then find a way to ground our bodies."

"I think I'm flirting with entering a state that usually implies being on the other side," Jaquelyn said in a quiet voice.

"Is that where you went last night?" Jack asked with a touch of fear. "We know that people who anticipate the crossing for years shift consciousness accordingly, so we'll learn more as we attempt to make love in the veil. Our bodies still have to be present but perhaps in a very different way."

"When we get very still during lovemaking, we touch that place in between the worlds more easily than if we're active."

"You've been saying that for a long time, and you may have noticed I am stiller now, although probably not as much as you would like."

"The challenge is that I want you to stay hard even when we're not moving," Jaquelyn explained.

"That's the state where my mind is most in resonance with my body. But, if we're still, you usually lose your tumescence. I want more stillness *with* tumescence. That's why I've been telling you to put your head in your cock. Then we can enter the veil. When you stay hard, we can bring back the information that we discover there."

"Is it putting my head into my cock or my cock into my head—or does it matter?"

"I think your cock's in your head quite a bit. You think about sex a lot. So it's the other way around that is needed. When you're really aroused, your cock seems to have a mind of its own. That's the kind of mindfulness I want you to practice. Maybe if you could find a way to channel Jesus more directly . . . When you're sleeping—before you start making bubbling noises—you look like a god to me. Sometimes I get mad at you when I feel that way because it makes me so vulnerable. If you would channel Jesus and get some guidance from him, I might feel safer, like I did when Mary came to me in the tub that time to tell me she was ten years older than him and his intimacy teacher. That made sense to me and reduced my fears. When we're in lovemaking consciousness, you could access him wherever he is. Jillions of people connect with him all the time."

"Yes and some women even see him as a lover. I've never really felt his full presence—like smelled how his skin smells. I haven't gone that far. Is that what you're asking me to do?"

"I'm asking you to access him, however you do it," Jaquelyn repeated. "At the end, he did cavort between the worlds and so he has something to teach us."

"Why not? For years we've been fleshing out their story as part of our path. Maybe intimate direct access to both of them is the culmination of all that. I'm game!"

"I've always believed that Mary and Jesus used their powerful attraction to each other to go back and forth across the veil."

"Yes," Jack affirmed. "Eros *is* connection, and so the challenge is to stay consciously connected as the energy builds in our love-making. This should prepare us for remaining awake as we make the crossing. We've had a glimpse of that state when we're making love and perhaps also in council without even touching each other."

"We've been talking about being in that consciousness no matter what we're doing and whether we're together or not. That's where we need to be to transmit Eros."

"Lately, we've been feeling that our lovemaking could be the time when we actually make the crossing. Dramatic as it sounds, both of us have had that experience recently."

They were silent for a few minutes while Jack tried to make the connection with Jesus. To support him Jaquelyn held an image of Mary. After a few minutes Jack smiled. "What I have to do in order to make the connection with Yeshua personally is to confront—"

"—what your mother would say."

"Exactly! I have to face two thousand years of Jews having to deal with the figure of Jesus. That's another reason I've held the story lightly and like to use his Hebrew name, Yeshua. Then I don't have to face that long historical shadow head on. But now that's exactly what I have to do if we are to really empower our work."

"You have to experience all the feelings," Jaquelyn agreed.

"Yeshua did go way beyond the Judaism of his day."

"And we're doing the same."

They dropped into silence again and this time the clouds parted and Jack caught a glimpse of what they were meant to do—just a glimpse. "Not surprisingly, getting closer to Jesus has to do with healing," he said with a touch of awe. "Whatever else he was, he was a healer."

"Then, if you connect with him, you can support changes in the body of someone we want to help, like Chelsey," Jaquelyn responded quietly.

Despite their agreement earlier in the day, they both knew the next step in connecting with Mary and Jesus would be to make love.

"What do you want to do?" he asked.

"I want to go to bed," she answered. Was it Mary or Jaquelyn speaking?

"I like when you invite me," he answered, knowing she would lead him to where she had gone the night before—to continue their exploration of making love in the veil between the worlds.

20 ❧ Goddess Songs

The interweaving of the Mary–Jesus story with J&J's work in Israel and their exploration of the crossing yoga gives you an idea of the more spiritual portion of the body-spirit continuum that lies at the heart of J&J's vision. At this point, for balance, I would like to give you a taste of the more physical part of the continuum that also continued to deepen in parallel with their adventures abroad. Ultimately, it is deceptive to distinguish spiritual and sexual aspects of J&J's journey, since intimacy was sexual and spiritual for them simultaneously, as you have heard. Indeed, the inseparability of sexuality and spirituality lies at the core of their evolutionary message. Still, some stories emphasize one portion of the Eros spectrum and some others.

This next story takes place right after a weeklong gathering of experienced F&S facilitators at the Blue House. The training had gone well. All eight participating couples had studied with J&J for years, and a few of the more experienced duos were already leading their own workshops. With the five-day facilitator training under their belts, the whole group was empowered to take the relationship work out to a wider audience in the U.S., Europe, and Israel.

As a consequence of having worked well together, J&J's usual debriefing process went smoothly and, when they met for council the day after everyone left, Jack was longing to hold his goddess. With a house full of people, more than a week had gone by since they had made love. Then as the council started, Jaquelyn surprised Jack by asking him to summarize his early sexual development in the same playful spirit as she had shared her own youthful experiences during the training—much to the delight of all those present.

"As I'm sure you can feel," Jack responded, "I can hardly keep my hands off you, but I'm fine playing with the assignment and see where it takes us. So here goes. . . . When I was an adolescent, there was always a sense of something looming in the distance—intercourse—that was never going to happen, mostly out of my own insecurity as well as the strong taboo that was present in the 1940s. I remember at least one occasion when I ejaculated in my pants. It was not an artful time. There was a lot of petting, mostly kissing and groping of breasts."

"Did anyone ever complain that your kisses were too wet?"

"You're the only one who has given me that feedback, which I need now because our kisses go so deep. I was surely less wet then!"

"You're a wonderful kisser," Jaquelyn reassured him. "Sometimes you just lose consciousness. I do too."

"Our mantra now is, 'the more conscious we remain, the deeper the Eros.'"

"Yes, the challenge is to simultaneously witness the passion rather than letting it sweep us away. That's what we continue to learn every time we make love."

Jack nodded in agreement and went on to chronicle the sexual life of his first marriage and the years that followed when he became the headmaster of an independent school. He did his best to add a few juicy details he hadn't shared before.

"As you know," Jack continued, "because of the deep bond with my mother, the incest taboo shaped my inner feminine image in a way that drew me toward young, vulnerable women—a dangerous challenge for a headmaster of a co-ed high school! It was an intense and dark time for me in many ways. Eleanor and I had separated and the two older kids were gone, so only Elissa—sixteen at the time— was left at home with me in our Calabasas adobe. I was by myself a lot since she spent much of her time with friends. Not surprisingly, I had little sense of the direction of my life apart from what was going on at school. A typical workday lasted at least twelve hours.

Then, at the height of my obsession with Rosa, we met and I spent nine months in the group. That started my rebirth. Your sexual energy was different from that of any woman I had ever known. You entered my tinder-dry erotic landscape and lit a fire. Although I'd had glimpses, I didn't know the extent of that terrain, and so my strong erotic thoughts and feelings soon scared the shit out of me. Your patience was such a blessing!"

"There was no other game in town," Jaquelyn said with a smile.

"It took seven or eight years for that roller coaster to settle down but finally we were graced with a deeper love I had never experienced before."

Jack's words turned her on, which Jaquelyn honored silently by inviting a kiss with her eyes. It was a gentle one, a brush of the lips that just hinted at what was possible. She was delighted. He sat down again and continued. "All the religious stuff about the wickedness and sins of the body is just the opposite of what can finally emerge now as love and sexuality and consciousness all evolve together—although I do understand why the path of intimacy has taken all these years to emerge in the mainstream. It takes a lot of commitment and tons of hard, devoted work."

"Let's take some of this energy we're generating in this moment and see what you can do with this leg of mine," Jaquelyn proposed. "It's been really aching since I strained it playing tennis a few weeks ago." He nodded and reached towards the rocker, placed both hands on her calf, and imagined a flow of energy going through the sensitive area. She felt the warmth of healing right away and told him so.

"Something seems to be guiding me," Jack offered.

"I am totally surrendered."

They were silent for several minutes, until the flow of energy suddenly expanded. The rush made them dizzy. "That was a challenge," Jack managed to say.

"I almost lost it."

"Me too. I felt our erotic energy shift into the healing mode immediately and then, at a certain point, the field suddenly blossomed. Our desire for each other keeps on building and, in turn, increases the effectiveness of the healing. Why more people don't use their erotic energy for healing is a mystery to me. Of course, it takes a lot of preparation and attentiveness to get here."

"Your hands are transmitting intensely. That's got to help my leg. Thank you."

"I want you to stretch out your legs and put your feet on my chest," Jack requested. "Then I can hold your calves and continue the healing and bring both legs into balance. Let's see where that takes us."

They shifted positions so that he was directly beneath her thighs with his legs under the rocker. When Jaquelyn placed her feet on his chest, she felt an immediate surge of energy move up her legs and into her loins. "It feels like I'm about to give birth," she said.

"The circuit that connects your feet with my heart is also flowing into my cock—"

"Mmmm," Jaquelyn purred.

"—which is creating a kind of tumescence I've never felt before."

"*I'm* feeling it too."

"Naturally!" Jack exclaimed. "That's the nature of this kind of resonance. We're in an erotic state where what each of us desires is exactly what the other is compelled to do—healing and all. This is what merging erotic fields can create."

They fell silent again in the same position. She could feel how her feet were drawn downward towards his loins and, as she slowly bent her knees and he leaned forward, his mouth came closer to her genitals. For a while they were wordless until Jaquelyn spoke. "Are you OK?"

"I'm fine. We've created a powerful circuit."

"You're being asked to go beyond me all the way to the goddess," Jaquelyn said invitingly. "Do it consciously!"

Her words opened a door and he felt another rush that threatened to sweep him away. "I'm being blissfully annihilated. The magnetism between us directly invites surrender."

"Yes, and the surrender leads to further attraction, which creates an erotic–surrender spiral that takes us into a new level of awareness."

The spiral moved Jack's hands slowly from Jaquelyn's calves to her lower thighs. The shift created the feeling he had already entered her. "The flow between us is filling our entire sensory reality. This level of desire will eventually color all of reality for us."

"The world could sure use a hell of a lot more of what we're doing. We need to bottle it and give it away for free!"

Jack could feel the irresistible call of her yoni and let his hands move up her thighs still further. "Oh goddess," he said.

"This is near Chelsey's bedtime. Why don't we send her a blast of healing energy?"

Healing at a distance was not exactly what Jack had in mind at the moment, but he was game. "Wonderful idea," he said in a tone that opened her heart still further. He imagined Chelsey curled up in her bed in Phoenix. The phonograph was playing Kenny Loggins' lullabies, and she was absorbed in her Game Boy. He imagined them both meditating in her room, quietly activating the dormant dendrites in her brain. Connecting with Chelsey cooled him down a bit and kept his hands from moving any further—for a while. Soon he felt the pull again.

By this time Jaquelyn knew she had to have him inside her. She reached out towards his body, touched his chest and moved downward until her hands found his partially erect lingam. It responded immediately to her caresses. "Humans are evolving, Baby," Jaquelyn groaned.

"We're both creating a whole new set of loins. It's actually been happening for a while."

As they talked, Jaquelyn let go of his cock and he moved away a bit to take a good look at her. She was wearing a loose silk tee-shirt that hid just enough to create a longing to see more. Her eyes were shining and her mouth was slightly parted in an irresistible way. Jack moved his lower body completely under the rocker and spread her legs slightly with his hands, now high up on her thighs just below her mound of Venus. She slid down in the rocker to meet him, until her genitals were only inches from his already open mouth. They had never been in this position before, and she let her imagination run wild. In a moment Jack had reached that place of shared desire where giving her pleasure was all he wanted to do.

Slowly his fingers gently massaged the outer lips of her vulva, alerting them to what was about to happen. He surrounded her clitoris with gentle caresses without actually making direct contact. He wanted to save that for his tongue. Jaquelyn knew exactly what he was doing.

"You are so hot," Jack whispered the obvious. His comment aroused her still further. Was there no limit to the feeling of abandonment and arousal, no outer boundaries to their merging? They were ready to live the question. "This is a whole level of surrender I've never known before," were his last words as he moved forward and buried his mouth in her mystery.

Slowly, Jack's tongue explored her outer labia. She tasted sweet and of the goddess, with a hint of soap and oils mixed with the subtle muskiness of her silky emanations. Jaquelyn moved her body further towards him so he wouldn't have to strain, but he had already shifted further under the rocker. Soon his tongue, now fully awakened and acting on its own, responded to her yearning to be explored—and then devoured. His tongue found her clitoris, filled with the blood of arousal, now larger than he had ever known it before, and moved gently in arcs of joy.

Jaquelyn made soft noises that created a distinctive goddess song, different than the ones she sang when he was inside her. This song spoke of the earlier times of goddess worship when humans were still in awe of the divine feminine and lived their lives accordingly. Timelessness called his tongue to go deeper, and her whole lower body began to undulate slowly. Jack's lips were now pressed softly against her vulva, moving in a slower rhythm than his tongue, which, on its own, had fully entered the birth canal seeking the source. Lips and tongue created a counterpoint of pleasure as they moved in different but completely harmonious rhythms. As he pressed in further and felt her body yearning to be penetrated, he wondered whether his mouth and voice would forever be transformed by their explorations. 'Have I reached the G-spot?' Jack wondered and went still deeper. Tongue, mouth, and thought—all together—approached the inner gates of heaven in a dance of adulation.

Worldly time passed, unbeknownst to goddess and her lover, until finally they knew it was time for him to enter her in the phallic way. She sent the message silently. He received it and began a slow withdrawal, like a lover leaving his bower and lingering at the doorway, still in the wake of ecstasy.

"I was getting a little worried about your neck being uncomfortable," Jaquelyn said in a quiet voice.

Jack laughed. "Are you joking? I was lost in joy. My whole body was inside you."

"And now I'm ready to make that a reality," Jaquelyn replied, still in the quiet voice that went right to his loins. It was time to pass the baton from tongue to phallus. Jack was kneeling in front of Jaquelyn now, so she easily reached out and began massaging his loins playfully, staying away from his cock. He groaned with pleasure, anticipating how she would soon initiate the cobra's dance of arousal . . . In a moment they were in the full tableau of an ancient time: he kneeling before her throne, she with both hands on his now fully aroused man-ness, performing the secret mudras that only the goddess knows. Jaquelyn was smiling now, knowing they would soon disappear under the spell that was flowing through their bodies. Feeling her smile, he opened his eyes and they both laughed.

"This is a level of surrender I've never felt before," Jack whispered.

"Can you levitate, Baby?" Jaquelyn asked, wanting to feel his arms around her and him inside her so badly she could hardly stand it.

"Oh, goddess, I'm ready," Jack responded and got up off his knees so they could navigate the short journey to the bed. Watching her move, he thought he saw sparks of energy flowing from her hips and buttocks. "My goddess is a-fire," he whispered. As they pulled down the bed covers, it started raining softly, so they climbed in under the covers and listened to that goddess voice together. By the time they rolled over into the familiar embrace meditation, their bodies had already begun to merge. The boundaries of their bodies disappeared so quickly that they were swept away—and again started laughing. The playful mood continued as he started caressing her breasts. When Jaquelyn reached for his cock, she had the distinct impression she was touching her own body.

"I have just what you want," Jack whispered.

"Yes, yes," Jaquelyn responded playfully. "Please, my ass is on fire. I want you. That's all I want."

"But first I want to taste your lips and devour you a while," Jack responded teasingly. The long kiss took them to places that they had reached before only with intercourse. "It's a miracle," was all they could say after they finally caught their breaths.

"Thank you, goddess," Jaquelyn's voice was full of gratitude." Do you think we'll be given angel status in heaven?"

"I don't know about angels, but I feel so grateful for what we have been given right here in this bed. Each time we make love, we die a little more. At this rate heaven can't be too far away."

Whatever separate identity remained was consumed in the fire of another kiss. Then the angels danced for a long time, while the goddess sang.

When Jaquelyn shared her songs of love, Jack was so much a part of their creation that little of his consciousness remained to reflect on the nature of the music. But later he sometimes likened their lovemaking to two experienced instrumentalists improvising, each player inspiring the other—or, more accurately, both becoming inspired by their musical Third. Sometimes it felt like desire itself wrote out the notes and guided their fingers. Once while Jack was inside her and simultaneously bringing her to clitoral climax, Jaquelyn felt like his celestial lyre. Several times already he had imagined his phallus, flute-like in her gifted fingers, wanting to release its music deep inside her.

Reflecting afterwards on her songs offered Jack new insights about the goddess. Her arias would usually begin with soft, husky "Oh's" from her chest and throat. These sounds seemed like wild birds caged too long, now needing their freedom. Jack noticed that Jaquelyn sometimes cleared her throat or coughed shortly after he first entered her in order to open the passageways for subsequent singing—like a diva doing exercises before a performance.

Then, as he penetrated her further and the energy poured through his heart and magic flute, the "Oh's" sounded more strongly, like stage whispers invited into full-voice by an appreciative audience. The first few were still gentle and soft. They spoke of the goddess arising from her sleep after centuries of waiting for her lover, then stretching her limbs to prepare for lovemaking while calling to the night creatures to gather and listen. These calls to nature were often so poignant and primal that Jack would ask her how she was doing, and Jaquelyn would come a bit closer to earth again and translate the sounds into words of appreciation and love, such as, "Goddess is with me," or "My heart is full of gratitude."

But soon, as the orgasmic state approaches, Jaquelyn's songs become more dramatic and varied, gaining in volume and bursting with color. Starting with golds and pinks, the goddess adds purples, deep blues, and reds from her palette. There is a moment when the song becomes a cry of the women long denied their rightful voice who will not be silenced any longer. Hints of pain, a touch of anger and even lament enter the changing pitches of the music. On occasion, the songs become a celebration of the goddess returned, the end of exile from the Garden—paradise regained—at least in the body of one woman.

Sometimes the song line rises and falls, gathering more power with each cry and breath until pulsating cries tumble out of her like wild, crazy laughter. Jack always marveled at how those repeated rhythmic calls of love seem to touch that part of nature beyond human civilization, particularly as he moved in further and approached the portals of birth. At times he heard the goddess's anguish over how humans had turned away from her vision for the earth and its lovers. Then, suddenly, the song would shift into paeans of gratitude that her lover had finally appeared and recognized her divinity.

Because the goddess arias have many verses and their orgasmic chorus is slightly different every time, this music of lovers connects us with all our ancestors, human and otherwise. Sometimes, stirred by her lover's courage to enter the holiest of holies, aroused and vulnerable, a new wave catches the initiate unawares and the pitch and pace suddenly shift into wails of desire and the incantations of a priestess speaking an otherworldly language of love. The sounds tumble out—no, burst out—into a world that has rarely heard such music and so is dying from deafness to ecstasy. He was sure that Jaquelyn, the woman, didn't know consciously what she was singing. Yet Jack knew beyond a shadow of doubt that their goddess-mentor had been training them for years to make such music. She had taught him how to move in and out of her grottos of love like the air in Bach's organ responding with joyous surprise to his genius. She was the singer, for he rarely joined her arias save when their bodies yearned to share a climax to their lovemaking.

Jaquelyn's singing spoke of her body's unique orgasmic experience with Jack. In her previous relationships and in their early years, Jaquelyn had a defined uterine climax that lasted as long as a minute or so and then subsided in a way that was not unfamiliar to the roughly one third of women who enjoy such "inner climaxes." He had been awed—and taught—by the power of these moments, which eventually helped him stretch out his own ejaculatory experience. Then, in the late 1970s and 1980s, they rode the wave of interest in Tantra, called it "sexual communion" (after Da Free John), and discussed non-orgasmic sexuality enthusiastically in their work with other couples, always stressing that it was both the man and the woman who were equally involved in exploring the practices they were pursuing—unlike in many of the ancient traditions in which only the male practices lovemaking as a non-physically climactic meditation.

In more recent times, Jaquelyn came to experience a new orgasmic self that was far more expanded, complex, unpredictable—and astonishing. Her climaxes expanded both in terms of personal pleasure and duration. Once, when their lovemaking seemed in harmonious two-part counterpoint with the rain, she spoke of glimpsing the goddess's "eternal come." After lovemaking, she often spoke of having felt a radically new kind of orgasm, which they realized arose out of Third consciousness more than her individual neurology and emotional reactions. Gradually Jaquelyn's orgasms took her further into a transpersonal state, where her body seemed no longer to be governed primarily by the familiar laws of human biology. Climaxes took place on multiple levels, sometimes with accompanying images, but increasingly imageless and primarily energetic, as if each peak was associated with a different erotic reality. Despite the complexity, she always knew her expanding orgasmic nature had to do with the goddess celebrating their deepening love.

In a state of awe after lovemaking, Jaquelyn often wondered how such blessings had come about. The fact that a man like Jack loved her the way he did validated her connection to the goddess that had blessed her at least since adolescence. For Jack, becoming the lover of the goddess had been initiated by Jaquelyn's challenge at a time when his sexual capacity was still largely shrouded by insecurity and inexperience. Her increasingly passionate desire for him to enter her with his full being when they made love and the passion of her songs told him repeatedly that he was making progress along the path. Each time they made love was healing for him and verification for them both. They sometimes laughingly admitted to being totally addicted to their lovemaking and called it "ecstatic co-dependence."

On a few occasions Jaquelyn said she didn't have a way to describe what it was like to make love with Jack, which amused him no end because of the artistry of her singing. That he was the only one to hear her arias made the music even more precious. His occasional "brava's" were enthusiastic: "That was magnificent. You were incredible!" Even though the songs of the divine feminine could not be readily shared with others, they both came to believe that the goddess songs, as personal as they were, belonged to everyone.

When Jack entered her, Jaquelyn returned to the old myth that speaks of the time when woman and man were fused together and then cleaved by the gods and goddesses because of hubris. Merging in lovemaking was the path to primal wholeness and a measure of the divine spark in their union. When Jack entered her, this mystery was solved in her flesh and increasingly in her spirit. When Jaquelyn told him she had trouble bringing back the fullness of their experience, he would answer, "Stay where you are and sing and I will find you." He knew the sounds she made gave his lover's body all the guidance it needed to track her anywhere. None of that process went through his mind, of course. It was his body that knew the way. So each time they made love, they evolved out of the old myth, coming closer, step by step, to the full promise of male and female union once again—this time, they trusted, with sufficient humility to avoid pride and arrogance.

Jaquelyn often spoke of cellular union when they talked afterwards. It had been she who sensed the presence of their Third palpably that morning many years before when they were in an embrace meditation. Now her whole body entered that state of awareness, each cell joyously celebrating its surrender of sovereignty to the magnetism of wholeness. As the fusion deepened, she experienced being in both cellular and Third consciousness simultaneously—and came to realize that fusion had been one of the goddess's deepest and oldest yearnings.

Through their lovemaking and, in particular, the songs, Jack began to understand that the essence of the divine feminine had to do with a kind of body wisdom that included all of evolution before humans while also holding the promise of what was yet to come. This wisdom is not immediately available to men, although they can come to embrace it—primarily through their bodies, not their minds—when they love courageously enough for their psyches to become devotees of love. That is at least one way the male mind can become an initiate of the goddess and transcend the patriarchy that has so imprisoned it all these years.

21 ❧ Approaching Pure Desire

Because our reflections on Jaquelyn's "goddess songs" cover a lot of possibly unfamiliar ground, I'm inclined to share another story that provides a more concrete taste of the nature of J&J's intimacy. The time is a warm day in August about a month following the last story. After the Flesh &Spirit training, Jaquelyn drifted back into work overload and Jack found himself slipping into judgment about her long days at the computer. She was aware he had pulled in his usually expansive erotic field, except when they fell asleep holding each other at night. When she felt distance between them, Jaquelyn's first instinct was to invite lovemaking, which was usually more than sufficient to "get the old boy going," to use her playful words. As you will see, this time a rather long journey back in time was needed before J&J were ready to re-enter the mysteries of the goddess together.

They agreed after breakfast to have a date that evening, which set erotic expectations going in both of them. As the hours passed, Jaquelyn felt the goddess enter her over-busy life again, slowing her down and reminding her that all she really wanted to do was to "meditate, make love and write." Jaquelyn planned to bathe in the afternoon, so they could start their council in the light and, hopefully make love before dusk.

Jack also set about preparing his lover's body for their sacrament—and his mind as well. As our last few stories have described, he had come to see each love-making as a joyful excursion into a particular relational landscape that needed erotizing. When they had been dancing with shadows, the terrain might seem quite barren at first, but the council invariably provided enough insight to allow their lovemaking to work its magic.

As he showered, Jack imaged their upcoming council and was surprised to see a wild landscape with clusters of upturned earth and boulders strewn about. The territory to be "brought into the fold" was large enough to leave him wondering if it would take all evening for him to rise to the occasion, figuratively and literally. That the evening would be full of surprises was immediately confirmed when Jack appeared in the bedroom, prepared to sit in his back-jack on the floor at the foot of the bed as usual. But Jaquelyn was not in her usual rocking chair, although she had prepared the central alter with a few talking pieces and set out the Third's pillow. Instead she was sitting in the only other chair in the room, an old Hawaiian plantation rocker, since it afforded better light for reading from the two manila folders on her lap.

Jaquelyn didn't look up when Jack entered the room. "Uh, oh," he thought, pulled out the padded back-jack from under the bed and settled into it while Jaquelyn continued to read, fully absorbed. After ten minutes passed, she spoke for the first time, without looking up. "I want to read you some early writings that I discovered in two old files this afternoon while I was looking for something." He nodded, lit the candle in honor of listening and sat back. She began to read without identifying the source.

I am feeling my body's love for Jack and the sensual memory of the state of fusion we were in Friday night that created a delicious presence in my flesh. This presence is always there but when I am conscious of it, I feel in a dance of ecstatic motion different than anything else I know in the physical world. Feelings are my pathway into this world where flesh tingles and feels lighter. Here there is aliveness in the relationship among all my cells—a mutual awareness and recognition that feels electrical and wondrous. A subtle chill comes over my back and moves down my spine ending in my buttocks and pussy, that mysterious hub of my energetic being. All roads lead to pussy because I've dared to speak the "eeeeeeeeee sound" a few moments ago. Jack turns me on when he says strongly (for him), "I want to make love with you tonight." So I bathe and anoint myself with lotions and creams and oils and slick-um, and present myself to my king as he lies in bed working his cross-word puzzle. We are shy and a little awkward at first. It's been a long time since we've made love, maybe about a month in physical time but eons in soul time. Are we still the same people? Maybe our sense of togetherness will have changed . . .

Jack gave her words full attention, primarily in response to their exuberance, but also because they were so different than the images he had just received in the shower. The next part of her reflections had to do with sexual desire:

The soft touch of his fingers sends a powerful vibration into my body. I feel and see a deep orange glow in my lower back that spreads around my vagina, arousing me. A tiny familiar fear also accompanies the intense pleasure. Will I be satisfied? Once it is aroused, the yearning deep in my vagina aches proportionately to the distance from physical union with a hard and vibrant penis. I feel like there is a huge magnet pulling cock into my sexual center. The force feels like unattached desire. Is it possible to feel pure sexual desire without any object or goal? Can fully awakened sexual desire be manifest spiritually? Can there be pure sexual awareness without desire? Is that what intimate love becomes? Desire for penetration suffuses my whole being. I feel myself arching up to welcome him and draw him into me. I love the pressure of penis entering me, opening my secret pussy petals and slowly, lovingly nailing my body to the cross of life . . .

The wild brilliance of her writing and particularly the final image of his phallus leading to her crucifixion was so outrageous that Jack knew the words reflected her intention to further dispel the Christian message imprinted during her childhood. Jack thought of the clusters of earth and boulders again—and surrendered fully to listening.

As cock moves slowly, deeply, and repeatedly in me—never the same way twice—I find myself instinctively moving to join him in mutual exploration. I embrace him, enclose him, suck on him with my whole being. I vibrate in resonance with him. My vagina is becoming a tunnel of juicy fire. I am breathless, motionless, timeless, a vessel of pure pleasure so intense it's beyond the personal. I cannot help telling Jack how much I love him—oh, so much. I am completely open and trusting. Jack moves gently, slowly in and out of me, creating an incredible flow into us from the timeless creative patterns that shape men and women. Soon my brain is gone. I'm just all pussy; that's all I am, all I want to be. I am in heaven and want to stay as long as possible. The joy is without attachment or yearning. We can stay here indefinitely since we are totally fused. I feel such overwhelming love for you my dearest warm, alive, familiar, safe, adorable, masterful, gentleman-lover-father-son. We create the Holy Ghost with our union! We peak for long moments, then release a tiny bit, and then peak again in varying rhythms and pastels . . .

First the image of the crucifixion and now the Holy Ghost! Associating that part of the Trinity with their Third had apparently been in Jaquelyn's imagination for quite a while, although he wasn't sure when she had written those ecstatic words. She went on to finish the piece.

I hear and feel a low moan in response to my heart opening. I sense a stream of fire come from cock deeply into me in that exquisite moment of soul-fusion just prior to physical climax. Jack catches me in a second peak of divine ecstasy and we ride it to spasm together. Serpent power in the root chakra is ignited and starts moving up my spine, into the emotional and heart centers. All tension is released slowly and with great satisfaction. I can't remember anything quite like it. In this moment I feel whole and truly unattached.

Jaquelyn stopped and looked at him for the first time. "Do you remember that? I wrote it almost ten years ago."

"The moments you were describing stir many memories," Jack replied. "Yet parts of it could have been written recently. It's beautiful."

"I was quite surprised how poetic it is. I don't think of myself as that kind of writer."

"But you are pure poetry as a lover and that's whose voice we just heard. 'She' can write your book."

"The question I posed about unattached desire is interesting," Jaquelyn observed. "I started asking years ago. I still think it's possible."

"We're getting closer all the time. When we make love I hear myself urging you—and me—to embrace desire absolutely, to obliterate everything else but desire. Maybe, if there is only desire, there's no room for attachment. Maybe we can squeeze out attachment by turning directly into desire and embracing it. That means we're moving against the long history of teaching that desire as an obstacle to enlightenment, if not outright sinful. Ours is an outrageous path from the traditional religious point of view. It's obvious from the writing that the goddess and you have been working together for a long time."

"For eons, actually," Jaquelyn affirmed. "You and I are like fish in the water of desire. Desire is our total environment when we make love."

"Exactly! Since most of us get attached when we desire something or somebody, the erotic path to detachment may seem impossible. But when we actually do the work, the state of consciousness we enter turns out to be real and transpersonal."

"You have to be pretty pure or the desire will burn you up, as does the desire for power, for example."

"For eons men have feared becoming consumed by desire," Jack added, "even when it was for the woman they loved. So men separated love and desire, making one of God and the other of Satan. The traditional church has labored to build a wall between God and eroticism, but now that wall is crumbling."

Jaquelyn nodded, but she was ready to move on and without pause started reading a letter to Jack, written in early 2004, a few months before the gulch adventure. It was during a time they were apart a lot and shortly after Jack had had a series of erotic dreams about other women. After hearing the dreams Jaquelyn had spent a sleepless night and in her over-worked exhaustion had written him a letter the next morning—a letter she never shared with him. The last part of the letter went like this:

> . . . So I feel my life of trying to be normal is over. I just don't care anymore. If you need me to die to let you go and have a happy, normal life with another woman, like in your dreams, I'll be happy to allow that to happen. I have my ways. I'm not going to send this to you now because I don't have the time to start processing it, as I know you will want to do . . . It's done. —Jaquelyn

The shift in mood left Jack speechless as he tried to embrace her bleak, middle-of-the night resignation. He wondered whether the letter had come up now to honor unexplored shadows or to remind them how tenuous their foundation had been—and perhaps still was. The unsent letter was less than five years old!

He finally found his voice. "What's surprising about your letter is how recent it is. Something dark must have been going on with you to allow my dreams to take you down so far. I would have been shocked to receive that letter."

"I think it was just after we were at a DAN! conference together and had fallen out of sync. Do you remember?"

"Vaguely, yes."

"I think that's when I felt I had to pull away from work or lose you," Jaquelyn recalled. "I was tired anyway, but you were very threatened by my involvement."

Jack was beginning to feel some heat, both to have been set up for such wild swings of emotion and the old story that he had been threatened by her consuming involvement in the autism community. He tried once again to correct her perspective. "I was missing you. You were often traveling and gone. But I came to understand that you had to immerse yourself as totally as you did. You had so much to give the autism community and it was an opportunity of a lifetime for you. Despite the challenges, we also saw how much Chelsey and your work actually expanded our relationship. So the fact that you came to the edge in 2004 is a surprise to me—and humbling. I guess we, or at least I, needed to be reminded of that now."

"2004 feels recent to you?" Jaquelyn sounded startled.

"Yes! There must have been something missing in our connection for you to have gone to such a dark place. I don't remember us saying or doing anything to warrant that strong a feeling but there it is in black and white."

"You were sitting in the front row at the DAN! conference when I introduced you to the audience as my beloved partner. You acted surprised as if you didn't know what I was talking about. I don't remember exactly what happened, but the net result was that we didn't shine our light on the world in that moment. I was sad, even though no one else noticed. I felt that you couldn't really be fully with me during that very important period in my life. I was exhausted and frayed—and I was missing you too. I had come to use you for a lot of support and love and sex, so when that was not happening very much because of my busyness, I felt lost in the universe."

"Why is all this coming up now?" Jack wanted to know. "The range of feelings in these readings is amazing."

"Yes, and I have one more piece I'd like to read. This letter is from June 6th, 1974."

Jack took a deep breath. It was the letter he wrote to her just after the end of the group in which they met. Jaquelyn read it slowly.

Jackie,

Virtually all my feelings on leaving the group last Tuesday relate to you and so this letter is my response, since the group doesn't meet again.

The pain I experienced from your remarks at the end was the pain of something dying. That feeling was slowly replaced by great anger. It grew as I drove home and got so strong that I had fantasies of slapping you and struggling with you physically. (I can't recall ever feeling that way before about a woman.)

I felt your summary about me at the end had disdain and frustration and anger in it. I didn't feel any positive feeling, as I did when you spoke to the others. I felt a lot of what you said to me was on a new and more personal level. It wasn't so much what you said but saying it that way at the last meeting left me with a blocked feeling. I had no place to go with it, since we were not allowed to respond.

My first fantasy was that you did it to make very clear that our connection was entirely in the group because I felt so angry I wanted no connection with you in the future. But in the days that followed I continued to feel upset and unsettled and unfinished. I had a second fantasy that you were making one last frustrated attempt to make some meaningful contact with me.

You know, what really pierced me was not so much the "con artist" comment but the sarcasm behind the "sorry to burst your bubble" and the disdain for what you saw as my preciousness and inauthentic tenderness.

As I have been searching for the truth in your statements my anger has altered. I hear your message. I have heard it before but not so clearly. In fact I heard parts of it again on Wednesday from a former student who came back to visit.

What I felt die on Tuesday was the ability to come from that "game place" in me that is a major form of defensiveness. I have been trying to accomplish that for a long time, so I am really grateful to you. But I am still angry—and feel unfinished. I would like to talk to you. When school is over and your schedule permits perhaps we can have lunch. I would like that, although I am a little frightened when I think of it.

—Jack

"Oh my," was all Jack could say when Jaquelyn finished.

"You were very honest."

"I described the whole process."

"Even thanking me for what I said," Jaquelyn said with a smile.

"Our story is amazing to me. We are definitely a low-probability event! We came so close to not even starting our relationship in the first place—and then there were all those close calls in the early years."

"I was looking for old medical records today, because of a court case, and came across these files. I found a lot of stuff that's grist for my writing mill."

"The juxtaposition of what you chose to read and what's going on right now is startling," Jack said with a sigh. "Some of our current issues are similar, although they're much more subtle now, of course. You're getting busy again, for example, and that's making it hard for you to write. When either of us gets too busy, the relationship suffers. In the past you often felt the strain when I got over-involved with Ojai. Then the pattern shifted and you became busy too, often busier than I was."

"The sudden increase in my work on top of everything else has made life seem extremely intense lately," Jaquelyn acknowledged. "There isn't enough time."

"When we miss each other, it's like fingernails on a blackboard."

"Maybe we're just getting old."

Jack laughed. "That too! Your mind is a wild ride! I'm holding on for dear life. but I'm not complaining. I'm glad you never sent the letter."

"Maybe the gulch initiation was a response to the limitations in our love that were becoming so apparent when I wrote that letter," Jaquelyn speculated. "Nature decided to give us a glimpse of what love could really be. I don't know many people who talk about our kind of sexual love. Our flesh is so *young*. We're ageless when we're making love."

"Yes," Jack agreed, "and yet there's definite wisdom that arises from our bodies. You always tell me that my cock knows more than I do. I've begun to take you literally."

"So your cock has become your teacher."

"As dangerous as that is for a man, it is ultimately right-action on the erotic path of relationship. Serving you and our relationship are my mission. I trust I am transforming any part of my consciousness that could be called "non-Jaquelyn." As we've said before, part of women's anger towards men is that they don't love as fully as women can. Men can love god fully—and have. They love their children fully—sometimes—and their work—often—and they love their wives a lot—sometimes. But for almost all men, there's still the need for a quantum leap into the unbounded eroticism that many women know about and desire. I wouldn't say that your heart has always been open in terms of what you think and say, but in some very primal way you have always been a lover."

"I didn't know about unbounded love before I met you," Jaquelyn replied. "You taught me that."

"I learned about unbounded love in our relationship, just like you did. Entering that fire of the goddess is not a reasonable move for a man."

"It's only unreasonable from the point of view of the patriarchy."

"Yes," Jack agreed, "and we need to rescue reason from the history of the past four thousand years by surrendering it to a new relationship with the body. If we don't evolve a new kind of body wisdom, reason will continue to separate us from our flesh. The shadow story that has shaped the patriarchy all these years is the battle between the mind and the flesh. This war has to end and in the reconciliation we can fully explore the vast bridge that actually connects flesh with spirit. You embody that bridge, literally."

"Isn't Eros the bridge?"

"Both the bridge and the entire territory that it makes accessible. For us, the process of erotizing the landscape as we approach lovemaking is becoming tangible. Shadow material arises organically in our lives and our job is to erotize it, to incorporate it into our intimacy, particularly our lovemaking. We're giving Eros a tangible presence in our psyches."

"Yes," Jaquelyn affirmed, "and that presence is Third consciousness. The magnetism between us invites the substance of place into it." She was slowly making the landscape idea real for herself.

Jaquelyn's words stirred Jack into arousal. She had moved to the bed after the readings and was leaning up against the wall. He was sitting on the edge of the bed near her feet. The candle was on a plate between them on the bedspread. She could feel his shift immediately.

"Shall we pull the covers down?" was all Jaquelyn said.

"Sure. We've been talking for a quite a while."

"For years. I feel the connection between us all the time now, tangibly."

They removed the bedspread and pulled back the covers. While she changed into her loose-fitting top, he lit the four or five candles spread around the room. Then he took off his clothes and turned off the lights. Jaquelyn was confident now that they would connect and in so doing integrate the unsent letter of despair, a faint echo of which had emerged for her in recent weeks due to her busyness and Jack's withdrawal. She hadn't planned the council the way it went; the writings just fell into her lap. The goddess has a way of creating doorways.

By the time Jack slid one arm around her as she lay on her back, they both knew they were home free. The kiss started out gently. He noticed a new spicy taste on her lips, wondered what it might be for a second and then let go, inspired by her hunger. Jaquelyn felt she had been waiting years for him to want her as much as she wanted him. She appreciated his way with words, yet it was only when their bodies spoke to each other that she felt completely at home and sure of what was happening. Her sureness flooded him with the full light of desire. The kiss went from gentle to passionate gradually, artfully. Jack knew he was in the hands of his mistress and surrendered.

The evening's orchestration brought her to new heights of passion. Hearing her read the unsent letter had challenged Jack's love, which allowed Jaquelyn's desire to be expressed without restraint. Feeling that the goddess wanted him passionately expanded his sexual confidence to new heights. He took more risks than usual in the way he touched her. Just cupping her breast made her groan with pleasure. His usual pace would have allowed the delicate caressing of her breasts to take a while, but as Jaquelyn began to suck on his tongue in playful promise of coming attractions, he found his fingers already beginning to stroke the sacred circles around her nipples. She groaned again and began to move her pelvis as if he were already inside her.

Their pace accelerated like young lovers discovering each other for the first time, but graced with the body wisdom of elderhood. A vision of an eastern tantric temple priestess initiating her priestly lover danced through Jack's head . . . and disappeared. She had wanted him inside her long before the kiss started and now just imagining his aroused phallus set off a series of shudders like erotic waves breaking repeatedly on a welcoming shore. Her mind was in full service to love's body and Jaquelyn could feel the powerful magnetism drawing him into her. The inevitability of this man's full passion surrendering to serving the emerging goddess drove desire forward like a roaring fire through a dry forest.

The field of love they evoked was more than a match for the expanse of shadows they had been assigned. Soon, Jack was fully erect and Jaquelyn couldn't wait any longer. She ended the kiss but not before exploring his lips invitingly with her tongue one more time. Then, spreading her legs slightly, she reached down to find him. He had already shifted his body into their familiar scissors position and was ready to enter. She moved him up and down, slowly at first, caressing her vulva until it was glistening with anticipation. Then she ceremoniously moved him to the gateway and invited him in.

"I want you now," Jaquelyn said in a feline whisper. As Jack began to enter, she actually heard the sound of his blood rushing though his phallus like a mountain stream in springtime. For a moment she thought she would faint with pleasure, so she opened her eyes and discovered that he was looking at her in the candlelight. They were home. Thought abandoned them gracefully, as he entered her in stages until it seemed as if his entire body had returned to its place of birth. Then her body spoke in a language she had heard only rarely before, not in words but in shudders of subtle movements that had a life of their own. The goddess in Jaquelyn wanted to conceive again—not a child this time, but the lover she had imagined so long ago. "I want all of you in me," she said in a mysterious voice he had not heard before.

"All of me?" Jack asked, ready to fulfill her desire.

"Yes, every cell," Jaquelyn whispered.

Some hidden portal in his body opened spontaneously. He was caught up in a torrent of desire that had no beginning and could only end in his own rebirth. The cells in his brain, like those in his phallus, knew exactly what to do. He moved slowly, instinctively, trusting the orchestration, changing the rhythm like a gifted composer—now larger thrusts, then stillness, then slow movements that resounded in her uterus and lit a flame hotter than she had ever known. "I'm on fire," Jaquelyn acknowledged simply.

"I know," Jack responded in a whisper. They were the last words spoken, as the music took over completely, carrying them toward a Niagara they had not experienced before. Jaquelyn climaxed several times, singing those songs of the goddess that combined pleasure and pain in a way they had come to treasure. Jaquelyn felt his orgasm begin before Jack knew it was approaching—like the four-leggeds who anticipate an earthquake and scurry to safety before humans have a glimmer of awareness. But there was no escaping this earth-shaking eruption. Jaquelyn had a moment of fear, like the animals, but the physical outpouring of love was just what she desired—as much as anything she had ever wanted. It was not only Jaquelyn who embraced this outpouring. The merging of their bodies had also invited an embodiment of the primal goddess—the one who had visited Jaquelyn alone that day in the sunlight.

By the time Jack knew he was coming, he was in the midst of the rebirth. His whole body trembled in unison with hers. There was no separation, no separate thoughts, no separate body sensations, just one body giving birth to the lover of the goddess that would honor the dying era of dominator cultures and the beginning of the age of Eros.

Their shudders would have embraced pain as well as joy, but J&J's merger took them beyond both into a strangely peaceful field of love. Was it finally Isis connecting Osiris' phallus to her lover's body? Was it what the Kabbalists practiced in the stillness of the temple's Holiest of Holies? Was it the moment when Miriam saw Yeshua three days after his "death" on the cross? Yes, all of these stories and others had helped to create the field they had found finally after so long.

Then Jaquelyn came again, singing a quieter song this time that helped Jack realize what was happening. "I'm still coming," he whispered in amazement. "I've been coming all this time. I've never experienced that before."

"Yes, I know," Jaquelyn spoke with the insight of her body.

"And you came again just now while I was still in the throes of it."

"Yes, and I'm still—" Jaquelyn began to sing again, this time honoring that he was being birthed in that very moment. They celebrated together as a river of creation roared through them for what seemed a long time, slowly decreasing in intensity until they were finally able to rest.

After a while, Jack spoke. "I didn't know a man's body could do that."

"Only when two bodies become one in the presence of the goddess can that happen," Jaquelyn said without hesitation, once again in touch with the wisdom of the ages.

22 ❧ The End of Individuality

As J&J's stories suggest, the nature of intimacy is transforming the human psyche in a way that strongly embodies what people usually think of as "feminine" values. As the patriarchal vision of individuality reveals more of its violent nature, a new and more intrinsic relational consciousness is slowly arising to counteract the destructive forces. This is happening not only in the world of intimate relationship, of course, but also as a result of how economic, ecological, political and health realities, as well as Internet access, are creating a new sense of international community. The blessings—and agonies—of the evolutionary struggle will continue to be reflected in the stories I have yet to tell. This next tale, for example, gives us a further tangible glimpse of the emerging goddessness in Jaquelyn. The time is a few months after they facilitated the shared society initiative in Israel. The scene is again Jaquelyn's bathtub at dusk as she readies herself for an intimate evening.

Rather than languorously enjoying herself while viewing the banana trees outside the window and anticipating what was to come, Jaquelyn was "instructed" to ask Jack to sit by the tub and participate in what was becoming a part of her ongoing communion with the goddess.

"I wanted you here so I could share what `she' just told me," Jaquelyn began. "This time the goddess gave me specific advice: *You don't really breathe deeply enough*, she said. Hearing that, I realized there are actually times when I hardly breathe at all."

"That might explain the recent volatility of your blood pressure and mood swings. If you're not breathing deeply, then—"

"—my heart might get alarmed."

"Yeah," Jack agreed, "so taking deeper breaths would be healing and stabilizing."

"It's amazing to get such a direct and tangible teaching."

"Did she say more?"

"I asked to get in touch with people on the other side," Jaquelyn went on, "whoever wanted to come through. The first person that showed up was my dad. At that moment he seemed a lot like you, except that you're more sophisticated and educated. But I saw similarities for the first time. That allowed me to forgive him in a deeper way for his fundamentalism and the way he treated Wendell. Then, suddenly, Mary Magdalene appeared—once again. I asked her how it was to live in that world of two thousand years ago and wondered if she had a vision for me that could heighten the presence of the divine feminine. She didn't respond directly but a few moments later the goddess entered me in the form of a feminine wreath around my crown, like a garland of female angels. The circle was made up of all the aspects of woman, with every shape and every kind of attire represented. For a few moments I was in a wild state of ecstasy. Then I remembered I had written a protest letter to the main newspaper in Nairobi, a city of millions, where 95% of the women are genitally cut. My letter led to a vision while I was in the tub of all the women there joining hands and merging into a huge council of womanhood."

"What an inspiring image," Jack exclaimed. "May it be so!"

"Then my body became infused erotically in a way that was beyond my comprehension. I saw that a woman is more likely to welcome the goddess more enthusiastically when she is infused in that physical-erotic way than when she just thinks or writes about the divine feminine. When that energy is in your body, you *are* it, like when we make love. I want to simply be who I am and trust that, as she comes into me, I will be inspired to support the needed evolutionary changes. I want to have the courage to be part of the group that liberates women in a new way. Women have to actually embody the goddess energy now."

"What it boils down to," Jack echoed, "is helping people make the shift from external deity consciousness into awareness of the divine *in relationships*—all kinds of relationships. Then, for example, what Jews hold and what Arabs hold can be embraced in a larger 'Semitic awareness' that both incorporates and goes beyond their present identities and cultural stories . . . Tell me more about the wreath of angels."

"What flowed through me lying in this magic water felt like hot electricity," Jaquelyn explained. "The angels were all the aspects of woman. The wreath around my crown was like a live video describing the nature of the divine feminine—all of her. I could actually feel it tangibly."

"It's your goddess crown."

"If a sufficient number of diverse women would coalesce into a unified critical mass," Jaquelyn continued, "we could tip the evolutionary balance in the right direction. Initiatives like Inbar can also play a role. What happened there was unlikely—and wonderful—and typical of that crazy, visionary part of us. The field we generated together created a wild and wooly event, even though I didn't play as active a facilitating role as I will next time."

"Yes, we put all of our Third energy into the pot and asked the leaders to help us cook it slowly," Jack added. "We saw that what is needed in Israel and elsewhere is a broad cultural form of the Third consciousness we've been tracking for years. That's a major part of the assignment now."

"Well put."

"Our lovemaking is the standard for all of this," Jack affirmed. "For future Inbars we need to use the power and interconnectedness of the larger circle to bring us into a state of consciousness analogous to what we enter when we make love."

"Ho!" Jaquelyn exclaimed delightedly. "You're getting it."

"I do get it now, because we're co-creating it *together*—even at this very moment. Like the people from indigenous cultures that couldn't see the explorers' boats in the harbor, many women won't be able to see their full goddessness until their partners recognize them and invite the divine feminine into their relationships. For heterosexual couples, the new definition of woman-ness is interdependent with the new definition of man-ness. The awakening is simultaneous."

"I have something else to tell you," Jaquelyn went on in a softer voice."When goddessness comes into me lately, I have an awareness of the presence of *Jehovah*—that was the name for the New Testament god I heard most often growing up. In a way that `being' is more mystical, wild and irascible—and more appealing sexually—than the Jesus of my youth. Of course we've been retelling the Jesus story and seeing him in a more realistic light through his relationship with Mary Magdalene. Still, the 'father' is somehow more appealing to the goddess in me. You have some of that Jehovah in you. After we make love and all our femaleness and maleness have merged, I sometimes flash on the father god of my youth. I remember him harshly judging me for touching my genitals when I was a kid and sometimes the caricature of him that looks like Santa Claus comes up for me. The father god came to me a little while ago when you were in the bedroom just before I sent you a silent message to join me here. I wanted you so much that you actually materialized. You must have felt it."

"Yes," Jack acknowledged, "it was like a feminine energy reached out and started stroking me in a playful and seductive way. The game is that the goddess becomes highly magnetic and at the same time challenges her lover not to be easily seduced but to transform the arousal into expanded awareness. Then she can see herself more fully and manifest her power without her lover being consumed like the proverbial moth in the flame."

"Yes, that's how she materializes sometimes."

"And at the same time the man is materializing as her lover. I was in the shower a while ago, preparing my body for our sacrament. Shower time is always arousing for me, and usually includes a touch of tumescence and a lot of anticipation. When I got out and decided to just wear my robe tonight, I had a sudden, and quite rare, impulse to look in the mirror. As I wiped off the steam with my towel, I asked to see a reflection that would reveal any gap between my self-image and those reflected back to me by others, particularly by you. Then I asked my reflection, 'how authentic are you?' As I looked, I realized the question was being directed towards a younger part of me that has not been fully cooked until now. I saw this younger part acknowledging that it was ready to be integrated into the older, wiser part."

"I confronted you with an example of your less mature part when you answered the phone the other day," Jaquelyn reminded him. "I heard you say hello to someone and then slip into your oozing voice. The jump was too quick and too much. I felt it was not totally sincere."

"Yes, I remember. That's a good example. When I looked into the mirror I saw that there's still a place in me that is concerned with the impressions of others, a part that is not fully secure—like I still have a memory of immaturity. So later in the bedroom, when I felt the goddess in the tub telling me to, 'come and be my lover,' I closed my eyes and spoke to the image in the mirror once again: 'You can stop being my youthful memory and become the authentic being the goddess wants.'"

"I love it—and the reason she wants it is because she doesn't get to celebrate her empowerment alone in this new era of Eros. That's the heart of our challenge. Ultimately, there's no such thing as 'alone' in the era that's coming. We're all becoming aware that we are parts of a single vast and tangible organism—and now the goddess wants to make love with a physical man who is truly ready to meet her. As we simplify and become more authentic, she and her lover will consummate their evolutionary mission."

"It will take everything we are to do that," Jack added.

"That's always been true, Sweetheart."

"I see now why your father came in tonight—besides for your forgiveness. I need to be more of a man in his way. He had a certain kind of authenticity—you have it too—that I'm still developing. Basically, it's simply being who you truly are. Feeling your invitation from the tub, I took another step in that direction . . . Now it's time to consummate the shift."

"You seem like a poet and a musician right now, "Jaquelyn commented, "with your instrument all tuned, ready to inspire the goddess to sing."

With that Jack arose from the small stool by the tub and went to get something to eat. A few minutes later he returned with an apple carefully cut into thin slices, two Brazil nuts, some almonds and two rice crackers with brie—just as the goddess emerged from the bathroom in her blue robe, untied and open. Jack put the plate down and impulsively opened his own robe in response. In a few moments, they were sitting in their usual council positions—he in his meditation seat by the foot of the bed and she in the rocker. Jack described what was on the plate.

"The apple, of course, represents the fruit in the Garden that comes from—"

"—the tree of knowledge of good and evil," Jaquelyn chimed in. "Eating the apple in our present consciousness will take us from the old ways of the goddess—that means the innocence of the Garden—through the expulsion and into the possibility of a balanced relationship between man and woman in every part of the world." She paused for a moment, distracted by seeing his cock, already slightly tumescent. "I just realized something."

"What?"

"Your cock has a slight curve." Jaquelyn made a descriptive gesture with her hand. "I have a preference for that spot on the left side of my vagina that your curve just matches. It's half-way up the vaginal canal. When you're inside me, it's always a bull's-eye."

"The goddess has reshaped me to fit you perfectly!" Jack exclaimed.

After they each ate a rice cracker, a slice of apple and a Brazil nut, Jaquelyn smiled: "Since our lovemaking explores new territory each time, can you play a new role in tonight's celebration? I want you to know how it feels to be Jehovah exploring the body of the goddess. Can you?" He nodded as she spread her legs slightly to make room for him. "OK," Jaquelyn whispered in a voice that matched her movement.

"I will explore the land of the goddess—literally," Jack said in a whisper. He took a few deep breaths to slow down time and balanced his arousal by shifting into the witness state. Jaquelyn never took her eyes off him as he moved into his new role. Each looked at the other and saw who they had become.

"Jehovah" arose from his back-jack and approached the rocker on his knees. "I've come to worship the goddess," he said.

"The goddess wants a lover."

"I am that lover," Jehovah answered. "What the goddess wants is who I am."

"Are you prepared to show me with your body as well as with words that you are the lover I have wanted eternally?" the goddess asked invitingly.

"Yes, first with that part of my body from which words flow out," Jehovah responded. He leaned forward slowly until they both felt their lips touching, although their mouths were a still a few inches apart. "Your mouth is like a goddess shrine, one of her many shrines," Jehovah-Jack said. They both knew exactly what the goddess had in mind. At that moment to give the goddess pleasure became not only his desire but the only event in life that had meaning. Jack imagined he had become very small and was about to start the journey to his place of birth—once again. The goddess's soft sighs spurred him onward. Besides being his lover, she was also the *great mother* now—his and the mother of all the creatures in the universe.

Her pubic hair was soft and smelled slightly of fresh apples. Jehovah-Jack was in the Garden, approaching the tree of knowledge with his tongue while his nostrils admired the white and pink blossoms that were everywhere. He wandered in the lushness timelessly being guided by the breaths and moans of joy playing in the branches above him.

Jaquelyn felt her whole body come alive. In ordinary life she walked upon the ground but as goddess she *was earth itself*. As Jack's mouth articulated the wonder of his love, his gift for poetry entered her to celebrate her mystery—no, *the* mystery. Finally, she couldn't stand the suspense a moment longer. She took his head gently in her hands and moved it until his tongue hovered directly over Aphrodite's rose bud. He felt a wave of surrender begin to overtake him reminiscent of an ocean encounter with a strong current beyond the surf.

Jack's serpent tongue entered the channel of life deeply, while his lips were still encountering her portals of mystery. Everything was in motion now as he honored the goddess as she was venerated in the times of worship before men discovered their fear of the feminine. He was ready to die like the salmon, as long as it was in the pools upstream where he was born. A moment later, when he realized he hadn't been breathing, a strange sadness overtook him. He was not really going to die in that moment! He would have to take a breath again and deepen his love even more. Such is the power of Eros. Then Jaquelyn took his head in her hands again and gently lifted him until their eyes met. It reminded him of how a queen would ask a kneeling courtier to rise and join her on her throne or couch. They kissed, and he tasted the sweetness of the world in which he was no longer small or the salmon but her lover. Jack accepted the elevation and arose from his knees. Jaquelyn allowed him to help her out of the chair and into bed. He was hard already and she was ready.

As Jack-Jehovah entered her gently, he was rewarded by lyrical words and moans. "That curve in your cock fits me perfectly," goddess-Jaquelyn whispered. "Our bodies were born to make love with each other." The words helped her hold on to consciousness, so Jack moved in further, creating a new goddess song in which the in-breaths described new delights of pleasure and the out-breaths voiced sighs of gratitude. He slowed the tempo even more and moved totally into sensation, except for a moment when her songs spawned an image of waves on a warm beach, one swell followed by another slightly larger.

"The surf is up," Jack-Jehovah said in a whisper.

"Is that an invitation?" Jaquelyn-goddess asked.

"Oh, goddess, is that an invitation!" he responded, the whisper now stronger, as he penetrated further. The songs shifted again, adding varied colors to the music that celebrated the fullness of her surrender. Then the man stopped moving entirely and they took off on a flying carpet that soared over the landscape of love for what seemed like hours. There was no time now. They were out of the earth's gravitational field, hearts beating in rhythm, both well beyond any illusion of individuality. The woman spread her legs even wider, inviting him to fill her completely. He did, as the waves, now in slow motion, moved them to the edge of awareness.

23 ✺ Reliving an Old Myth

You have heard how J&J transformed the biblical Moses and Mary Magdalene-Jesus stories to create a path out of traditional Judaism and Christianity into the Aquarian Era. We have also mentioned a few older stories that played a role in J&J's creation of a new mythology of relationship, including the Isis/Osiris and Ishtar (Astarte) myths. Adapting or transforming these seminal stories from humanity's shared roots continued to be a thread in J&J's councils over the years, as they came to understand that cultural stories must evolve too.

Another tale that touched J&J in a variety of ways is the eastern myth of Kali and Siva. These two Hindu deities appear in numerous stories, sometimes as lovers and sometimes not. The particular myth that arose along J&J's path is the one in which Siva is sent to rescue Kali from intoxication as she was fulfilling the mission to terminate the lives of violent men. This myth was definitely ahead of its time in showing a level of sophistication about relationship that was not to be realized in the cultural mainstream until thousands of years later—in other words, until now. We pick up our lovers just as Jack is lighting the council candle. It is spring, 2009, shortly after the previous story.

"This council is dedicated to truth, whatever truth is—no, I dedicate our council to consciousness. Truth is elusive."

"Right, truth is relative, just like morality is relative."

"Cultural and religious traditions have often short-circuited the path of consciousness by claiming to know the absolute truth. Making such claims inevitably leads to—"

"What's that?" Jaquelyn asked playfully, looking at the bulge in Jack's silver-grey sweat pants he was wearing, along with his pink sweater.

"That's my cock"

"No, that's *my* cock," Jaquelyn corrected him.

"Oh, excuse me, you're absolutely right. I forgot—which brings me to Kali and Siva. I did a little research and re-read the story yesterday. There are now three traditional stories that play a role in our relationship: Isis and Osiris, Yeshua and Miriam and Kali and Siva. What is amazing is how the Kali-Siva story speaks to what you and I are facing *right now*."

"Are you're talking about the story where Kali gets inflated with the blood of the violent men she's devouring," Jaquelyn asked.

"As the story relates to us, *intoxicated* is the right word rather than inflated," Jack responded. "Kali has an addiction. Although you sometimes make really bold statements you're not inflated. That's not your problem. The challenge is more that you get intoxicated with the devouring Kali aspect of the goddess energy. This myth can help us."

"Explain how you feel I'm intoxicated," Jaquelyn asked.

"The devouring Kali in you wants to do away with patriarchal beasts, so women can be liberated and seen as divine. It all began with your father when he asked you to choose between sexuality and Christian righteousness. You had no alternative but to choose being the erotic goddess that you were becoming, even then."

"I remember when I went to get my dad when he was in his seventies and couldn't pee because of his prostate. I told him authoritatively that he was coming on the plane with me to Cedars of Lebanon Hospital in Los Angeles. He had never flown before. All the Jewish doctors took excellent care of him and, since he believed the Jews were the `chosen people,' he felt like a king. I was the `Doc' from that point on. When a falling tree killed him in his boat on the river while he was fishing a few years later, his wallet contained a five dollar bill, a picture of my mother and him just before they got married, and my business card! My father finally elevated me to goddess because of his adventure at Cedars."

"It was so good that happened before he died," Jack affirmed . . . "So back to Kali and Siva. The story reveals the dangers involved in attacking the symptoms of a disease rather than the underlying causes—in this case Kali destroying violent men."

"I do have some of that anger about the patriarchy," Jaquelyn acknowledged, "but I'm very creative when I get going like that and accomplish a lot."

"Yes, that's true, and so did Kali until she got out of control."

"What's the timing of the Kali/Siva story historically?"

"It comes long after the Isis-Osiris saga, during the transition from the goddess era into the patriarchy," Jack responded. "The Egyptians embraced the goddess in some remarkable ways with the Isis-Osiris story being a good example. But their vision wasn't differentiated on the relational level; Isis was both the sister of Osiris and his lover. Although that story teaches us how the goddess eventually creates her lover, literally body part by body part, it wasn't until the birth of the new sky-god, Yahweh at the end of the goddess era that the differentiated evolution of the masculine really begins. The Jews called god Yahweh; the Christians eventually latinized the name by using Jehovah. With Yahweh we start the long journey of the son—the new male—becoming the lover, which is what the patriarchal era is all about."

"And the journey was brutal from the beginning," Jaquelyn picked up the thread. "Because women as representatives of the great mother goddess had ruled for so long, men had grown fearful and jealous of their power, particularly in the sexual arena. So they created their new deity as more powerful than the mother goddess and mortal men as more powerful than mortal women. Their new religion established men's control over women so men could fight the lure of sexuality. Theology was used to justify the stealing of lands and the murder of countless peoples. It became important for Hebrew men to bequeath their newly stolen lands to their blood sons, so women were relegated to status of baby-makers with no freedoms or human rights. Monogamy was instituted for women only while for centuries men were free to have as many wives, concubines and slaves as they wanted."

Jack nodded. "I understand. Monotheism really meant a monogamous god/*man* relationship, not god/human. In the goddess era sexuality was seen in procreative terms, probably with mostly elementary emotional overtones rather than the increasing complexities that arose during the patriarchal era—the era of differentiation.

"Everything became far less peaceful with the rise of Hebrew theology."

"Since the son had to grow up to become the partner-lover, most of the patriarchal era is about male adolescence. The patriarchy got caught in its own shadows early on because personal love hadn't evolved sufficiently to balance men's fear of the feminine and the relentless growth of male individualism. Now to pull us out of these patriarchal woes we're affirming that the son *has* matured sufficiently to become a true lover of the goddess in his woman. This maturation represents a huge leap in consciousness that has taken place in parallel with the bloody horrors of the patriarchy. It's because we're coming to the end of this cycle that the Kali-Siva story becomes relevant for us even though the myth arose during an earlier stage of the patriarchy—I think about fifteen hundred BC . . . Anyway, back to the story. Kali is out there with a sword—as are you—and she's gone berserk."

"Railing against the evils of the patriarchy," Jaquelyn chimed in, "cutting off the heads of despotic male leaders and the cocks of men who rape girls and—"

"It's the waves of anger that are addictive," Jack interrupted. "Killing off the patriarchy has taken the place of your mission to vanquish autism. It has been a challenge to deal with your ferocity and make sure our version of the Kali-Siva story ends well."

"I never thought of Kali as having a partner. It's hard to imagine even a powerful god like Siva being able to handle her."

"That's the point of this story. Here she is, wildly cutting off heads, feet, hands—and other body parts—and getting more blood-thirsty by the minute."

"If my fury reminds you of Kali at times, your challenge is to love me anyway," Jaquelyn reminded him.

"Exactly! Kali has lost focus and her partner Siva is to be the one who rescues her from intoxication. That's what all the other deities decide."

"He knows he has to make love with her to bring her out of the intoxicated state," Jaquelyn responds without hesitation.

"That's our version of the story for sure," Jack agreed, "and the traditional story gives us a context for doing exactly that. So Siva first covers himself with ashes to hide his divine light. He doesn't seek the help of any other god or try to stop Kali by force."

"He deals with her directly through the power of his love!"

"Yes, that's the crux of the story," Jack affirmed. "The myth gives us a clear direction and validation for what we're doing. Conversely, it shows us that our story is not only a personal story but is somehow connected to the evolution of relationship."

"I've been impressed with how you've been tracking the evolutionary aspects of our path these past several months."

"It is amazing how all the stories fit together . . . So Siva hides his radiance so Kali won't recognize him from a distance and lies down in the field of the slain. The moment of their encounter has to be spontaneous and intimate."

"That took incredible courage," Jaquelyn commented.

"And trust in their love. What blows my mind is that just a few weeks ago we had a council in which you challenged me to stand in for all men and face the goddess's anger. That's exactly what Siva did. He put his life on the line without any protection, trusting Kali would recognize him at the last moment and come out of entrancement."

"Are you saying that there's a danger the intoxicated Kali would come through me with her sword and demolish you, if I don't see you and love you the way I do?"

"It's a risk," Jack responded, "with death being a metaphor for separation. You might disconnect in a wild moment of rage at the patriarchy or even despair about life, as when you wrote that letter five years ago."

"But you love me enough that you're willing to take that risk." Jaquelyn was embracing the meat of the story now.

"Yes, and Siva covering himself with ash means I am willing to encounter Kali in the killing fields as the mortal man I am. Whatever divinity I have has to do with my love for you."

"Sometimes it feels like I'm living the lives of all suppressed women and those that die terrible deaths," Jaquelyn confessed. "You can lose your mind in that."

"I'm gambling that our love is stronger than your rage and can match the darkest shadows of the goddess—which is probably her intoxicated rage."

"Isn't that part of everybody's shadow?"

"Yes," Jack agreed, "but I would describe the primary male shadow in a different way. Fear is at its core."

"Rather than Kali's craziness."

"That's one word for it. As I said, I prefer, intoxicated."

Jaquelyn nodded. "Being intoxicated can come from living something so intensely that it's like a drug. That's actually pretty common."

"Yes, particularly if you're living out a deep cultural or evolutionary story. These myths are like grooves in our consciousness. The Kali-Siva story was told and retold. It was one way for people to understand women and their power. The Isis-Osiris story has a very different teaching in which the divine feminine is the primary healing force. Isis ultimately integrates the dark and light masculine and puts Osiris back together. That's why that ancient story relates to us."

"She puts him back together because she wants a lover." To Jaquelyn it was obvious.

"Yes, and that's the main point of the evolutionary story we're exploring currently. At the end of the goddess era, the divine feminine was getting restless and wanted a lover that could truly match her—just as you do."

"I feel you are doing that."

"It's the ultimate gift I have to give you," Jack responded.

"I gave you the gift of sexual love, so you owe me one. You give your gifts more consciously and graciously than I did. I couldn't help myself. I saw you as divine."

"You always say that you didn't do it consciously," Jack reminded her, "but your consciousness also includes your impulsive reactions— particularly those of your body. Impulse fuels your visionary capability too. That's the positive part of your impulsive side. Without that we wouldn't be where we are now . . . So Siva is lying there and doesn't know what Kali will do. When you're in that archetypal rage, I feel you might see me as one of the goddess's enemies."

"A patriarch."

"I've said jokingly a few times that I should wear a football protector cup when we have our councils. That would add a great ceremonial touch!" (laughter)

"Do you really feel the devouring Kali in me?" Jaquelyn couldn't quite identify with the raging goddess.

"Definitely! You've been wild at times."

"Have we ever made love when you haven't felt that I'm totally with you?"

"Never!" Jack agreed. "Our lovemaking is so wondrous that I would do anything to make love with you, which is exactly what Siva does."

"Does he have an erection?"

"No, Siva wouldn't have had an erection at that particular moment! (laughter) Wait, you're right! He is all erection, as in the Siva shrines, those piles of stones. They represent the full vulnerable presence of the erotic male."

"The total erotic potential of the male—magnetic and aroused," Jaquelyn emphasized.

"So Kali enters the killing fields with her sword drawn and, yes, I—Siva—do have an erection because I'm totally in love with you and know it's my erect self that you are more likely to recognize. The scene is a dramatic moment in the evolution of eroticism."

"I still turn you on even though you feel I'm intoxicated with rage," Jaquelyn wanted confirmation.

"Yes," Jack assured her. "I'm willing to risk having my manhood amputated if you don't recognize me. I'm counting on your love to awaken you from your trance, so you can see me as your partner."

"I did recognize you in the beginning of our relationship," Jaquelyn reminded him, "even though I didn't understand why. I believed in that recognition and hung in there despite your unconsciousness."

"What an incredible gift that was! Now I'm finally returning the gift. You gave that gift in order to evolve from the undifferentiated ancient goddess into the goddess-lover-woman. We're playing out that whole story. I certainly had, and probably still have, enough patriarchal stuff in me for you to go on a rampage. It's stubbornly buried in my DNA—and in how our language and art and advertising objectify women . . . So Kali comes to where Siva is lying all ash-covered, stands over him and looks down into his eyes. There's an intense moment of life or death trespasso—and then, sword drawn, she sees his radiant being under the ash. She sees her lover beyond her intoxication, beyond her mission. She sees the eternal light of their love. The goddess who knows death also knows love. You have a deep relationship with both."

"I am curious about death," Jaquelyn acknowledged.

"Yes, it's more about curiosity for you. So Kali and Siva connect. Their Third is strong enough."

"A woman needs that kind of recognition and love from her partner too, so she can forgive him for being a man." (laughter)

"That's how the traditional story ends in the references I found," Jack added with a suggestive smile, "but we can play out that moment further tonight when we make love. This story provides yet another connection between death and making love."

"We've been exploring that connection for a long time."

"Just like Siva I've been saying, if I die when we make love, so be it.'"

"What a way to go," Jaquelyn exclaimed. "Siva's act of courage and trust implies full acceptance of the goddess and initiates a new level of relationship. Kali had to go to the edge of sanity to bring it into awareness. Unless she expresses wild rage, the goddess is not complete. Death has to be faced for love to expand to a new level."

"We're approaching eighty. We'll be blessed to live ten more years. That's not a lot of time."

"I'd like to be around at least five more years after 2012 just to see what happens."

"Yes," Jack agreed, "however wondrous our relationship is going to be when we're out-of-body, our lovemaking is too ecstatic now to give up."

"Since it's been getting better and better, why wouldn't the ecstasy continue?" Jaquelyn asked innocently.

"Yes, and continuing the Siva-Kali story after the moment of recognition can be part of that. After their epiphany, they get to make love."

"Right now?" she said coyly.

He laughed. "Pretty soon—and let's do it on an empty stomach tonight. Then we can have a lovely feast later. Our lovemaking will be the consummation of a new marriage in which I embrace the dark goddess as you integrate her. The Kali energy will still be there in you, but if the man is sufficiently free of the patriarchy, maybe the murderous Kali won't have to be summoned again."

"You're inspiring lately," Jaquelyn said gratefully, "helping me to be more expansive and perhaps inflating me too. What you're doing feels so loving."

"I assure you that I'll watch the inflation. We do that for each other. Transcending the intoxication of your anger at the patriarchy will help your writing too."

"I hope so. I'm still having trouble getting started."

"You'll find your voice as our own story gets clearer," Jack assured her. "I need to enter a stronger writing field now as well. It's important that we create that field together. I need your help. Just like you need me to be your lover, I need you to be my writing partner."

"Sounds good. I don't want to feel neglected or left out when you disappear into the writing . . . After all the stories, do we end up just being Jack and Jaquelyn?"

"Yes, maybe also with a touch of Osiris and Isis, and Yeshua and Miriam."

"What happens to all the gods and goddesses as we move out of the patriarchy and into the Aquarian era?" Jaquelyn wondered.

"I imagine we will embrace their particular qualities more fully as part of life and not see them as the externalized divine protectors and judgers of humanity any longer."

"And the primary spiritual practices will be relational, like council and sexuality," Jaquelyn added enthusiastically.

"Exactly, and now I need to tell you what happened last night. After writing about Siva and Kali yesterday, I woke up around one or two am with a rush of fear imagining Siva lying in the killing fields so vulnerably. Was I being a fool to take that risk? I thought about your shadowy mind and your curiosity about death. I remembered how upset you were with me last week when I was driving on the Cane Road and a chicken darted out into our path. You were right; I was going too fast—the impact broke our plastic grill—but what stirred me the most was how you saw the incident as a preview of our own death. I lay there last night exploring all my feelings . . . and then I had a moment of real clarity. I saw how my reactions to your upset about the chicken were all vestiges of my old patriarchal consciousness. I saw we had to actually play out the moment of the Kali-Siva story when she looks down at his ash-covered body. There was no choice."

"Were we spooning when all this was going through your head?" Jaquelyn asked.

"We were lying on our backs, just touching. That position is quite erotic for some reason. First I got clear that we are not going to get killed in the car from my careless driving. I don't want top play games. Last night I was ready to embrace death with deeper respect and humility."

"Sweetheart, that means you need to slow down," Jaquelyn exclaimed. "The kind of intensity that comes out in your driving is what needs to change. It comes out in other ways too."

He felt the temptation to be defensive—and let it go. "Yes, I need to be more attentive."

"You have to let go any macho reactions to getting old or not seeing as well as you did before."

"Yes, those remnants of the patriarchal male are still in me and need purging," Jack acknowledged. "So in the middle of the night I turned toward you, covered myself with ash and lay down in your killing fields. I felt the goddess in you as you slept. After I made the full commitment to complete the Kali-Siva story, I fell asleep."

"Did you dream after that?"

"Not that I remember. When we woke up this morning, I wasn't in a hurry to tell you what had happened. I knew we had the day together and the story would unfold. Now it's time to play that out. Let's enter the story just before the recognition. You don't have to be Kali-like. We've called in the story. Let's see how it turns out."

"If we're headed for lovemaking I trust whatever happens," Jaquelyn added with a smile.

"Then I'll be able to have a Siva-like erection, so we can move into the lovemaking after the moment of recognition. You can apply Siva's testosterone to his lingam as part of the ceremony. We'll just go with whatever happens spontaneously, and talk about it later."

Jack seemed so playful to her at that moment, this boy-man—on the one hand supportive and there for her, even wise and courageous—while at the same time creating a mythological scenario like a young actor playing out a fantasy with his girlfriend in an empty theater. "You're so cute," Jaquelyn summarized her feelings with a laugh. They arranged themselves on the bed, side by side, and held hands. She knew that once they opened the sexual door, there would be no more conversation—yet she still had one more question. He sensed that and waited for her to speak as the buzz between them began to build.

"How is all this going to change our daily life?" Jaquelyn finally asked out of the silence. "Are we simply going to be more conscious about what is already happening or are there going to be some noticeable pattern changes?"

"I do see changes, like spending more time writing," Jack responded. "We'll be more selective about what work we take on and there will be more wild activities, like dancing on that boat out of Kona. Then there will be times when we really hunker down and spend three full days in a row just writing and making love."

"Sounds great to me!" Jaquelyn spoke her mantra with laughter. "I would like to achieve whatever I set out to do with a little less effort. I'd like not to worry so much about how I look or whether I'm getting enough recognition. That's all so time-consuming."

"Ho!"

"And I'm not going to wear high heels anymore! I don't care if people notice my beautiful legs."

"They're beautiful whatever shoes you're wearing," Jack assured her. "Actually being barefoot looks the best."

Jaquelyn was ready. "OK, let's get into the story," but as soon as she had spoken those words, she felt a cold chill pass through her body. "I felt an unknown thick energy inside me just now. It was dark and scary."

"Let's face it together. Here take my hand and we'll see what it is. You identify it."

They were silent until she spoke: "Perhaps traces of the patriarchy."

"Maybe it's my patriarchal residue or the patriarch inside you, that shadow that lives inside every goddess-to-be, however deeply hidden. Becoming aware of the inner patriarch is part of the woman's initiation into the divine feminine. She can't be free until all those judgments of women that she has absorbed during her life are brought into the light. Maybe you have to invite me to face your inner patriarch, just like I took on the goddess-in-you as my inner feminine. Then he won't take over at moments of unconsciousness. That would be a major step along our path."

Jack squeezed her hand slightly and took a deep breath. Jaquelyn felt safe enough to face her fear directly . . . In a few moments, to her great relief, she felt its impact begin to wane. She stayed with the dark presence for a few minutes, urged it out of its hidden inner chamber and turned it loose.

Jaquelyn's mood shifted. "Although the presence seems gone," she reported, "it left a shiny cloud in its wake, a pure clear darkness, not grey or dull. The cloud had a translucent blackness brimming with delicious possibilities."

"Perhaps it's a gift from the shadows to heal the intoxication," Jack suggested."Use the energy coming through my hand for support. Then you can tap into the cloud and do whatever you want with it." They fell silent again while Jaquelyn used his hand as a life-line once more. They stayed connected for what seemed a long time before Jack asked, "Where are you?"

"I went to the other side," Jaquelyn answered. "It was lovely. Were you there too?" Her voice was light and childlike—and extremely vulnerable.

"You are so dear to me right now!" Jack said close to tears. "I followed you everywhere to make sure you could find your way back. To go is one thing; to return is another. Tracking you eased my own vulnerability too."

"I was almost beyond being able to come back when I remembered that I was holding your hand. That saved me. It was an incredible moment."

"Our erotic connection was strong enough to take the risk, which is exactly what Siva did. I'm ready to be your Siva. I'm ready to be present and aroused, despite all of the anger that women have accumulated for thousands of years. Let's pick up the story where Siva and Kali look deeply into each other's eyes in the middle of the killing fields."

After a few minutes Kali-Jaquelyn spoke. "I'm drawn to your light body, even though it was hidden by ashes. You can't hide your presence from me. As we looked into each other's souls, I felt this incredible energy between our genitals. It's still happening. The energy is cycling between our genitals, our hearts and our crowns—and everything in between. It's so alive and real. Our Third is a flesh and spirit being! We are occupying the same space, headed for total body fusion. We are so blessed to be discovering all this." She squeezed his hand gently and asked, "Can we try to synchronize our hearts?"

Jack nodded and they re-entered the reverie. After a few moments, he spoke. "To slow down your heart all you have to do is image that we're holding hands, lying here quietly on the bed. You can use my heart beat as a template and then you won't have any problems with—"

"—tachycardia. All I have to do is infuse my heartbeat with our sexual energy."

"Exactly."

"I'm taking you in, Baby," Jaquelyn said in a whisper.

"I'm in our resonance, as if we're making love. I'm not so much penetrating you but energy is emanating from my heart."

"You're feeling the magnetic draw of my heart, the divine magnetism of the feminine."

"It's a different kind of magnetism that doesn't call for movement," Jack explained. "This ceremony is challenging us to be in stillness without grounding the erotic energy physically."

"This is the stillness that can balance your intensity that I was referring to before. Your intensity creates a driving force for motion that takes our Eros to familiar physical places. But if you stay in stillness, we can discover new dimensions of ecstasy." They both re-entered the merging spontaneously, still lying side by side on their backs holding hands. Jaquelyn began to feel a rising wave of energy starting at the base of her spine that took her breath away. "Oh, yes," she said almost inaudibly.

"I'm staying completely motionless," Jack reported quietly, "although I can feel the incredible pull to touch your body, your breasts, and taste the mystery of your kisses. Let yourself feel the erotic flow that's pouring out of me now. It's such a challenge to be still, covered in ashes, waiting, fully aroused, vulnerable—and yet trusting . . . A moment later he broke the silence again, "What are you doing right now?"

The question caught her on the edge of awareness, ready to ride the growing wave out." The Kundalini is roaring through my pelvis," she answered. "Usually it doesn't roar; it just starts uncurling. This is different . . ." Her breathing began to increase as if she were nearing climax, but their bodies remained still. "There's light floating behind my eyes . . . Touching your hand allows me to stay in my body. Your hand is the only link with the physical world."

Jaquelyn's words told him it was time to harvest their stillness physically. He began by touching her belly lightly with gentle strokes that slowly awakened her breasts. He answered their call . . . A little later the first kiss tempted timelessness, taking them into the fusion of lips and tongues and a world of sensation. When they caught their breaths again, Jack managed to speak: "The goddess's dream of a lover that recognizes her full divinity is finally coming true." Then Jack and Jaquelyn's ordinary selves disappeared again into the mists of Eros.

They remained still for what seemed a very long time, perhaps until the goddess had forgotten all the centuries of waiting, as she prepared for the joys of consummation. When the disciples stirred, ready to serve the story's conclusion, an unfamiliar fire arose in them. The woman noticed it first.

"My ass feels like it's literally on fire," she said.

"Yes, an ancient white fire. I feel it consuming our bodies, making them whole," the man responded.

"Ancient mysteries."

"I am willing to die now and disappear into you."

"I am ready to take you into me. Touch me slowly, lightly. Every nerve is awakened."

"I know."

They spoke only a few words after that, mostly in awe at what they were being shown. The consummation unfolded slowly, sometimes with hardly any movement, sometimes inspired by the wild passions of a loving Kali. When finally the goddess began her songs, this time mostly celebrating delight and gratitude, she was joined by Siva in full voice in a new way. The killing fields became a lover's bower, as their duet celebrated the wonders of evolution, the music as unfathomable as looking into an empty night sky and seeing galaxies.

24 ✧ How the Patriarchy Began

The Queen and
the Shepherd

By December of 2009 J&J had fulfilled their intention to turn over leadership responsibilities to the Israeli council group. Meanwhile the LDN-AIDS program in Mali was moving forward rapidly, as the local team finally hit their stride. Because these two major efforts now required less attention, J&J's ongoing exploration of the emerging mythology of relationship gratefully took up the slack.

In particular, they focused on the transition from the end of the goddess period into the dawn of the patriarchy, using a few of the traditional evolutionary stories, such as the Inanna myth and the more familiar Theseus legend. These stories describe those ancient goddess times when the queen chose a new consort each year, having sacrificed the previous one in a ceremony that honored the cycles of nature. The old myths were intriguing, despite not being substantiated by historians, but they lacked the intimate details J&J needed to build an evolutionary story. So J&J decided to make up their own version of the transition. The next tale describes how that came about . . .

It was raining and cool as they settled down for a council, accompanied by the propane heater's cozy hum. Jaquelyn lit the candle and began by describing her passionate conviction that the Abrahamic religions—Judaism, Christianity and Islam—all had become a major obstacle to evolution. Listening to her fiery words left Jack in an appreciative mood. "You still have a touch of the teen-age rebel in you, that 'don't-tell-me-what-to-do' energy that adds so much spiciness to our stew."

"I just finished writing about being thirteen and how my father was afraid I was going to marry one of those drunken Indians from the local reservation."

"You did marry one," Jack reminded her teasingly, "but he's not drunk, except with love for you."

"Promises, promises . . . When I started to develop, boys were suddenly drawn to me like flies. It drove my father crazy. When I put on lipstick one day, he called me a whore and washed my face with soap. I've been fighting the patriarchy ever since. He had a twinkle in his eye for women but he would never do anything about it because he adored my mother. His twinkle for her was the brightest of all. The Bible helped his restraint too. He saw it as god's word."

"As so many still do, but I agree that we can't evolve as long as what people have called god or the word of god is seen as *out there*, external. We still need a presence in our lives that guides us towards right-behavior and helps us to face fear but, as we've been saying, it's time for that presence to arise more directly from the intimacy of our primary relationships. The sense of divinity needs to move more directly *into* life and for us that means into relationship. That's a breath-taking shift that will sound terrifying and dangerous to biblical ears."

"I understand," Jaquelyn responded, "but the danger can be overcome. Although I have seen your godness for a long time, I can also see your personality quirks that piss me off. I'm not blinded by the fact that you are divine to me. I can still see who you are as a human being. That's been a tremendous gift."

"And an amazing blessing!" Jack added. "Your gift encouraged me to grow in areas where I was limited, mostly in the sexual arena at first. You were unmercifully tough on me in the group and then, after we were intimate the first time, you made it clear that if we were to be lovers, something had to change."

"I said, simply, 'I need you inside me longer.'"

"What a brilliant and compassionate way that was to let me know the rules of the game—and miraculously my more than twenty years of premature ejaculation cleared up in two nights. I had a lot to learn and was ready to learn it, even though I had no idea what the 'it' was."

"But I knew," Jaquelyn responded with a knowing smile.

"Indeed you did, and fortunately that was one of the few times in my life when I surrendered completely in the moment. Those times have been life-altering, which is one reason I don't surrender so easily. They're turning points on the path and have to be chosen carefully."

"I don't think you choose them. I think they choose you!"

"Both are actually true," Jack countered. "Let's say I have the illusion that I am part of the decision. That makes it easier for me to understand what happened and describe it later."

"You can pretend you understood after the fact, as you often do!" (laughter)

"Your gift of seeing the divinity in me—along with all my stuff—modeled that process so I can learn how to do the same for you. I shudder to think how long that has taken. In the beginning it was hell at times."

"Tell me about it!" Jaquelyn had little difficulty remembering. "But when in desperation I tried to explore my connection to another man who worshipped me, it didn't work. I think I already had my shield up. Just like the ovum does, I had closed the gate after I fell in love with you, even though consciously I was ready to leave."

"What a blessing that was! Most men have to work so hard to develop a shield like that. My inner feminine was an elusive and seductive goddess in those days, so I was far from loving in that way."

"I wonder if that's one of the reasons I'm so fascinated with all this goddess material now," Jaquelyn mused. "I've wondered about the divine feminine since I was a teen-ager but I hadn't any form or name or understanding of it, and no knowledge of the history of the goddess times. Now, as I learn, I'm actually having ancient memories in my body. It's an uncanny feeling. Did you know that in the old goddess tradition, when the queen took a consort for a year, his main job was to be the lover of the goddess? They actually called him that! I just read about it today. So I imagine what might have happened finally was that the queen began to fall in love with the new consort. He was a shepherd in the version of the story I was reading. There may have been a magical moment when the queen experienced a new kind of love beyond the usual goddess era sexual practices."

"A truly evolutionary moment! Obviously the 'shepherds' of five thousand years ago were not ready to face their fears of being intimate with their 'queens' and so the patriarchy was launched with fear at its roots. After many generations maybe the chosen kings grew in power and started to rule with the queens, until finally the men became the empowered ones and the women became their queens. From this perspective the development of the patriarchy slowly taking place in Europe and the Mideast could be described by the evolution of the relationship between a mythical goddess-queen and her shepherd-lover. It's only now, five millennia later, that men—and women—have evolved their love sufficiently to subdue the underlying patriarchal fear."

"Now the job of the queen's lover is to truly see her and love her enough so she doesn't want him 'to die.' Maybe when men love more deeply, they come up against the yearning to be 'the queen's lover,' in one form or another—usually unconsciously. That still can create profound insecurity. 'Will I be enough?' 'Will she leave me for another?'"

"Yes, this story is compelling," Jack picked up the talking piece excitedly, "because it's still going on now in the human psyche. As the woman on the path gets more goddess-like, her lover is continuously challenged to face his fear of being adequate and loving enough. Then, as their intimacy deepens and the woman surrenders to her love for the man, she further embodies the goddess and the evolutionary story spirals onward. This cycle is part of what energizes the extraordinary sexuality we have been experiencing lately. The more the woman embodies the goddess, the more profound her surrender and the more awakened the lovemaking."

Jaquelyn nodded. "And the more like a goddess I feel, the more I have primal memories. I'm the ancient goddess who is waking up from the trauma she received at the hands of the early Hebrews and the Christian church."

To confirm their inspiration, the goddess graced them with a burst of rain, as she so often did during their intimate evenings. It would have been hard to see the momentary deluge in any other way than a blessing. The sound was loud enough for them to pause and wait for the pounding of the water on the roof to subside. When it did, they went on co-creating the story of the queen and the shepherd. Months later, Jack wrote a poem about their ongoing weavings. Let me share portions of it as a way of describing what took place that December evening and the months that followed.

With the courage of woman's knowing she is part of nature
Millennia ago you birthed a vision of having a lover
And patiently, as history unraveled, held the dream and
Kept it alive in the hearts of those who see beauty in the
Limbs of a tree or a meadow of cows with their white bird-mates
Gathered at their feet until the flock flies to their next assign-
ment.

All these years you have lived your dream, weaving it into
The promise of evolution while waiting for the patriarch to
emerge
From adolescence . . . Now he appears—finally—to recognize
Your wisdom and beauty after centuries of wandering in the
wilderness
Simply because you asked him in a moment of love to see you
as a woman
—Whence he felt his loins leave his custody forever.

You have not been able to trust your lover until his manhood
   awakened
With a lucid love for his woman that ignited roaring wildfires
In his unconsciousness, searing every cell
Of awareness so to cleanse the blood on his hands
From all those falsehoods about women he never really knew
Hiding his fears in the labyrinths of scripture

To fulfill the promise of evolution you and your lover must turn us
From the fury that has burned through a nature now so decimated
That many fear the trees will die and the white birds will never
   land again
But rather soar into the sun with the message that the "experi-
   ment" is over
Done—finished—and a new vision of life is to appear after the
   last foul
Out-breath is taken by the world you birthed and cherished

You sense all this in the awakening bodies of courageous women
Co-arising in the streets of Cairo and Teheran—and in the
   darkest
Hearts of Africa where tribal battles have over-run the garden . . .
At times you suffer history in your body but more often now
You celebrate the awakening of love's body with your shepherd
And so calm the wild winds of your unbridled mind.

This moment has no precedent in the long experiment
We have no god or other ancient icons to pray to
Now the wisdom of your vision and the beauty of your flesh
Are the essentials for awakening and so I trust
We will make love in an evolutionary way
And so come to know that magic as our Great Turning.

When the rain stopped, Jack spoke. "As we're transforming the
story, I can feel stirrings in my body. The linkage between mind
and tumescence is amazing. The initiation for the man as lover of

the goddess means that tumescence becomes a mentor of his mind. Evolution needs that impulse."

"Sounds good to me!" Jaquelyn spoke her mantra with the usual smile.

Jack met the moment. "I'll give you the pleasure of full and direct visibility of my evolutionary status," he said quickly slipping off his black sweatpants and spreading his legs slightly. The tumescence was already promising.

A rush of color swept over Jaquelyn's face. "Beautiful!"

"Now we can see directly how our words affect the shepherd. You can shape the tumescence. You can play me—"

"—like an instrument." Jaquelyn loved finishing his sentences.

"Exactly. I'm being told we should be silent for a while—and then no holds barred. You tell me when you're ready to come out of the silence."

"That means a total surrender of control," Jaquelyn's voice was strong and inviting. "It's all or nothing for me."

"I am ready for the embodiment of passion that will celebrate the ancient goddess's evolution into being the lover-goddess. Her dream of a fully empowered lover is our creation myth for ending the patriarchy. Now, thousands of years later, you and I—and many others—can celebrate the realization of her dream." He looked down at his genitals. "As I'm talking, I can feel myself—"

"—rising to the occasion," Jaquelyn said with a seductive grin. Another burst of rain echoed their arousal. "Just the background music we need," she added.

Jack paused for a moment, noticing that a distinctly reddish light was emanating from Jaquelyn's face, the same light he often saw along the surface of the Cane Road when they walked at dusk. The glow starkly revealed her beauty in a new way. "Our connection is so tangible," he said after a few moments of silence. "How are you handling all this?"

"I'm stirred by the story like a lover," Jaquelyn responded. "It is caressing me."

"The light around your eyes is . . ." He had to stop. Her face was literally radiant. "It's like I'm seeing you for the first time. Perhaps it's the new story."

"I still look familiar, don't I?" As much as Jaquelyn had longed for his recognition, it was a little unsettling to hear him talk that way.

"Of course," Jack reassured her, "although your face keeps on changing in the light coming from your Third Eye—and now there's spirit smoke coming out of my mouth, whatever it is."

"Erotons, of course, since our Third Eyes are in resonance. Would you like to—"

"I would." Jack started to get up as he spoke.

"Is the shepherd—the evolved shepherd—ready?"

"Yes, I am ready to live the new story. Is the queen ready to become the lover-goddess?"

Jaquelyn answered with her body, as they began to celebrate the end of the patriarchy in their own intimate way. The goddess joined them with great rhythmic bursts of rain.

Part IV

❧

The Evolutionary Path of Relationship

25 &s Council as Foreplay

By the end of 2009, the myths and stories about relationship had interwoven sufficiently to produce a rich harvest for J&J. Jaquelyn's notion of the goddess being all women—actually all of nature's female creatures—had by then become a tangible reality for her. Jack saw this reflected in the imaginative ways she continued to discover new aspects of herself in their relationship, especially in council and, of course, during lovemaking. Meanwhile what Jack liked to call "combing out the patriarchy from his being" was in full swing—linked inseparably with the ongoing emergence of the erotic goddess in Jaquelyn. They both sensed they were being prepared for a level of fusion in lovemaking beyond their wildest dreams and, as a consequence, their councils increasingly became an integral part of their foreplay. The theme of fusion will unfold in several of the stories that follow, including the one I want to tell you now . . .

The early winter day started out sunny but by noon huge banks of moist grey clouds blew in on the trade winds. By evening the rain was coming down hard which, as usual, they saw as a blessing. In the afternoon Jack had planted beets and jicama in the garden. Working in the soil was one of his favorite ways to prepare for their intimate evenings together. They hadn't made love in a week but it seemed much longer, and so the conversation had already turned in the erotic direction as we tune in. Jack is speaking:

". . . I had waves of gratitude looking at our wedding picture today. When I compare my body now to how it was in 1975, I see that this seventy-eight year-old version is certainly far more awake sexually despite the trials and tribulations of aging."

"It's because of the deep Eros," Jaquelyn affirmed and was quiet for a moment. "What is amazing is that I don't have to actually have you inside me to feel our merging. Just imagining our connection makes lovemaking virtually tangible. I feel you entering me and I also penetrate you, until we reach that place of communion where we lose all boundaries."

"When we merge, I can sense all the different kinds of womanness you're bringing in lately. Just now I imagined making love with that beautiful lady whose picture was in the anniversary card you gave me yesterday. That shot of you on the autism conference circuit was delightful, although she's a bit of a mystery to me."

"I want you to know how much she is admired all over the world—and what a great lover she is too . . . Just looking at you now turns me on." Jaquelyn's voice invited spontaneous tresspaso for a few moments.

Jack broke the silence. "I just saw that the more tumescent I am in my whole being—particularly my heart—the more clearly you can see yourself reflected in my love. I also saw that our cells carry images from the past—thousands of them. The more we make love, the more—"

"—we heal the past and transform our bodies with love," Jaquelyn completed his thought.

"Then I saw a continuum of different colors, like a rainbow, that describes what's going on inside you. At one end is the domain of the Amazon queen, with all the vivid colors of the goddess era, and at the other end are the more subtle shades of the lover-goddess who is evolving now. You move back and forth every day, sometimes closer to one end of the continuum and sometimes the other. Part of my tracking you requires that I know where on that continuum you are at any given moment—not an easy task at times."

"I'm sure it isn't," Jaquelyn agreed. "The image fits pretty well. I do go back and forth, particularly when it comes to doing the women's empowerment work that seems to threaten you so much.

Why is my wanting to work with groups of women so frightening?"

"I may be in denial but I wish you could find a better way to describe my response. I don't feel the fear you keep bringing up. My primary question has been how much of the sorely needed empowerment of women is meant to occur within the intimate relationship setting."

"It seems to me women have to get strong first and then they can begin to relate to their lovers in new ways."

Jack nodded. "I understand that my saying women's empowerment is tied in with intimate relationship feels like a form of patriarchal control, and so the Amazon queen reacts. I've no problem with the strong desire you have to work with women. I don't think I ever had. The real challenge for me has to do with figuring out who you are in any given moment. There are times when I get an Amazon queen response, especially when I say something that feels restrictive to you—and then within an hour I can be dancing freely with the relational goddess again. I'm still learning how to handle the shifts."

"I can't stand to be restrained or limited in any way lately. Today I fired two patients who dared to question my advice. I'm cleaning house. Aren't you proud of me?"

"Yes—and let me assure you that even as she is being transformed, the queen in you will continue to be of service, assuming you use her power consciously. How useful my old king will continue to be is another question. The Amazon queen is changing and the lover-goddess doesn't want a king. She yearns for a lover."

"Yes" Jaquelyn exclaimed, "a lover who helps her to focus on writing her book. That's my primary purpose now."

"Indeed, and I want to further assure both the Amazon queen and the lover-goddess that I'm letting go any notion that intimate relationship is a *necessary* condition for women's empowerment. There are many paths, and I'm trusting that the timing and balance of women's awakening relative to their involvement in intimate relationships will work itself out in a unique way for each woman."

"The Amazon queen is still wary of men, and rightly so."

"Yes, which is why it's become obvious to me that for many

women, a major leap into individual empowerment may have to occur before their plunge into deep intimacy—as you've been saying. In a way your huge success in the autistic world was that kind of leap for you, and it shaped our intimacy profoundly. I've come to trust that our relationship will keep on expanding to embrace whatever you want to do with women—and for as long as you need to do it."

"I like the sound of that!" Jaquelyn affirmed. "And then all men need to do is to surrender to being initiated by their empowered women," Jaquelyn added in that voice that combined innocence and wisdom.

"Spoken like a true temple priestess," Jack said with a chuckle. "Aren't you lucky to have one for your very own?"

"I count my blessings every day, but the initiation has another—"

"What's the 'but?'" Jaquelyn interrupted in the same voice.

"The other half of the initiation process needs to be honored. The man is not just a lump of uninitiated clay. On our path at least, the initiation of the man as lover is inseparable from his recognition of the goddess in his woman. The two processes happen simultaneously. In the goddess era, the priestesses initiated men with whom they had little or no intimacy. Obviously in the relational era the initiation will be intimate and complex."

"But women still need to gather together to support each other's empowerment."

"Of course, especially the many women who are not in intimate relationships with men. Some of these women are becoming empowered in relationships with women, and many others through various professional, creative and spiritual paths. All those options are playing a role. We're not saying that empowerment has to take place primarily in deep sexual relationships."

"Although that is exactly what is so sorely needed now in the world," Jaquelyn shot back, shifting her perspective.

"Yes and other paths of feminine and masculine empowerment are needed too."

"Do you think women and men can be empowered on the relational path without the particular kinds of sexual experiences that have blessed our relationship?"

"Yes," Jack responded, "I think the empowerment lies in the love more than in the specific kinds of sexual interaction, but we don't really know—and it actually doesn't matter. We're here to bring a much needed particular flavor to the evolutionary feast. Not many people are doing what we're doing, as we keep discovering. We can do only what we've been guided to do. That doesn't mean that everyone or even many people have to end up traveling our path."

"I get it—and the essence of that path is the profound merging that's happening now, not only in our lovemaking but also in our councils and embrace meditations."

"Actually I like the word 'fusion' better than merging. Fusion has a quality of high energy that merging doesn't necessarily convey. Even when we're just talking like we are now, we know we can shift into a fusion state. Then our bodies feel like we're making love. We've always said that we want our whole lives to be lived at the level of our lovemaking. As that happens, what we share with others will become more apparent and effective."

The words invited them into a spontaneous meditation that lasted several minutes. Finally Jaquelyn spoke. "I feel the fusion in my genitals and in my breasts and in my heart. The energy opens inside my body, starting in the pelvis as usual. I've noticed lately that the rectum is activated too. Then the energy spreads. It starts someplace between the rectum and the sexual center and forms a shape like a cobra's hood. You know the shape I mean?"

"I think so. Go on."

"The cobra's hood collects the fusion energy and then expands beyond that container as the energy goes up the spine. The cobra becomes the Kundalini serpent with its tail growing longer as it approaches the crown, like a flaccid penis growing harder and longer as it rises—but still undulating like a serpent. Lately, your cock inside me feels just like that cobra. In my goddess wisdom I know an awakened phallus pulses during lovemaking rather than just thrusts back and forth—and I'm not talking about the final pulses during ejaculation. If we could experience the pulsing when you're actually inside me, I know it would be so powerful."

"Your image inspires a wild thought. As our fusion goes deeper,

I wonder if the aroused phallus inside the vaginal canal could act as a bridge of love that spans the transition between life and death. For that to happen the man's whole body, heart and mind need to be tumescent, which means he has to bring his full presence into his phallus. Then all of him ends up at the gateway to the womb and the full cycle of life continues."

"What a gift to see lovemaking as the bridge between the worlds, compared to the old story of the boatman rowing us across the river Styx—one by one! When I think about where we began thirty-five years ago, it is literally awesome to have arrived at this image."

"You were the teacher and I the student in those early years," Jack recalled.

"As time went on, I basically birthed you and shaped your manness to fit me exactly," Jaquelyn added with a smile.

"That's our version of the queen and shepherd story. We're living it out, including my tending to your flock too—mostly Liz and Richard and Chelsey . . . Now let me tell you what happened for me while we were meditating. I started out feeling the magnetism between us as usual. It's getting stronger all the time. Then, when I began to move into the fusion state, my whole body became phallic and my heart took on a luminous tumescent quality. When I looked at it carefully, I saw that it was actually our fused hearts that I was sensing. We create that when we make love, of course, but to be able to sense the same field in meditation is such a gift."

"A blessing!" Jaquelyn agreed. "What happened next?"

"After a few minutes, I moved into a transpersonal state that seemed heartful—and then Richard appeared."

"Our son Richard? That's a surprise."

"Yes, it surprised me too," Jack acknowledged. "He didn't speak but just looked at me expectantly. I stayed open and knew immediately that I had to welcome him into our life with a love that would be equivalent to inviting him to live with us here in Hawaii. My heart started pounding. On the one hand, we're both clear that we don't want to live with Richard—or anyone else for that matter—nor do we think that would help him in the long run. (Jaquelyn nodded vigorously) But I can still invite him into our home heartfully in a symbolic way. I struggled to approach that level of love, but when I finally got there I felt lighter and free. It didn't change anything about our decision to wean him from financial support. My encounter was on a different level."

Jaquelyn was all smiles. "Maybe what you just did will help release him to get on with his life—and that gives me another idea. I want you to imagine that you and I actually conceived Richard. Pretend he's our biological son now. The way you need to love him will follow from that."

"What a brilliant short-cut to what I just went through! Richard accepted me as his spiritual father when he visited us last summer, although I don't know if he would still own that. Your image takes it a step further."

"And liberates us all from the old triangle with his father."

"OK! When we make love tonight," Jack continued, "we'll actually conceive a new Richard who, we trust will find a clear path to independence. To help transcend the old patterns we could add a touch of humor too. We've been taking our parenting so seriously that there hasn't been enough levity to clear out the heavy shadows. Richard has a sense of humor that would help move us along. Our challenges are to let go what remains of your mother guilt that you didn't do right by him and my stepfather's limitations in loving. Then we can breathe clean air. The ability to do that deep kind of clearing is going to be useful, maybe crucial, in making the crossing consciously."

"Exactly! We're preparing."

"My meditation didn't end with the encounter with Richard. After that happened, the focus shifted again to rendezvousing with the goddess. As I approached her, I felt her magnetism and power, and then I felt a touch of fear that I might be engulfed when you and I fuse. But I persevered and when I actually imagined the fusion, I saw that it would be both ecstatic and annihilating. I realized there is no experience of ecstasy that isn't annihilating as well. After that teaching, an image came as a culmination of the meditation . . ."

He paused to catch his breath and she felt also for dramatic effect. This time she forgave him because his story amused and excited her. "Well, what's your image?"

"The scene arose out of the early days," Jack began. "Do you remember that video I used to show the kids at Heartlight—the 'Mystery of Life' I think it was called? It showed the man's ejaculation and the process of conception from inside the woman's body using fiber optics. It was astounding how the kids responded, especially the older boys. They totally identified with the sperm, fighting their way up the vaginal canal, striving and battling. They would cheer and root for one of the sperm to win the race. Only one gets the prize, of course, unless it's a multiple birth. While all this competition is going on, the huge ovum sits there like a space-ship, hovering in its fluid, round and mysterious, ready to accept just one of the frantic creatures struggling upstream. Once the lucky sperm penetrates, the video shows how she envelops him and closes the gates. The rest of his buddies die off and become waste material. I saw how the contrast between the sperm that enters and all the rest could explain at least some of men's innate competitiveness. The biology tells so much of the story."

"So?"

"So the man who aspires to be the lover of the goddess needs to do a ceremony in which he becomes the sperm that makes it all the way and enters the goddess-ovum just as the actual sperm did that created him. He also needs to be compassionate about all the other sperm. He needs to do this ceremonially, first in meditation and then in love-making."

"Sounds like Flesh and Spirit Graduate School!" Jaquelyn exclaimed.

"Indeed, and as he consciously enters the ovum that is the goddess seed itself, the man is annihilated. He becomes part of a new being that is jointly created with the goddess. If he can live through that experience, he will further fulfill the evolutionary promise of becoming her lover. The moment is ecstatic for the man and at the same time he has to let go of who he thought he was—fully let go. The sperm disappears inside the ovum never to be seen again. Conception requires the end of the sperm."

"The ovum changes too, don't forget! She is waiting for her man to arrive, inactivated but toti-potential with life. She is not fulfilled until she is entered. Then, when he enters, she embraces him fully and is instantly activated."

"And her embrace disappears him forever," Jack repeated.

"Why do you keep emphasizing that?"

"So you can begin to understand men's fear of women in a different way."

"Are you trying to make excuses for the patriarchy?" Jaquelyn challenged him.

"Not at all. Biology tells the story without sentimentality—just straight up, as they say here on the Island. The sperm has done its job and becomes part of something larger."

"Yes and so does the woman."

"Her change is from inactivity to activity." Jack needed to make his point. "His change is from furious activity to ecstatic annihilation."

"I'm not so sure. Anyway, the exercise is perfect. I see how that would shift a man's perspective about women in the right direction. So do we celebrate this birthing in a meditation?"

"Yes—and then also when we make love."

"Ah, another one of Doctor Zimmerman's famous foreplay scenarios," Jaquelyn responded with a smile.

"Of course. Isn't that what I'm supposed to do to keep you entertained?"

"Yes, and you do it so cleverly that it fools me every time. I think we're exploring metaphysics and all the while you're getting ready to take me to bed."

Jack loved the game of Jaquelyn pretending to be seduced when they both knew that she was the ultimate seducer. "Yes, our councils are all foreplay. We've known that for years. You like more foreplay than I do usually, which is the story I hear from almost all the women I work with. Rarely is it the man who wants more, although that does happen, sometimes even with us."

"When?" Jaquelyn challenged him with her innocent smile. He laughed.

"I've been talking about 'dying into our Third' for a while, even though you don't like that image particularly."

"I'm not crazy about it, but I get it more clearly now with the ovum-sperm image. It really is a good exercise. I can't wait to try it with a group of couples."

"Let's do it ourselves first," Jack suggested.

"I knew you'd say that. You have a one-track mind." He laughed again and they were quiet for a while working with the image of conception. Jack finally broke the silence.

"Since the ovum is like a spaceship, the man is having a close encounter of the goddess kind. He's being abducted, willingly. Of course, he has no idea of what's in store for him."

"Nor does the spaceship, really."

"True, but presumably as the primary vehicle she knows something about the journey ahead. The poor sperm certainly doesn't."

"Poor sperm." Jaquelyn crooned. "Oh, the pooooor baby sperm. He's been allowed to enter the goddess and taken on the most exciting journey possible. I can't be too sorry for him."

"Indeed, nor can I. While we were quiet just now I began to enter the ovum."

"And what did you see."

"That I was going to be ecstatically annihilated," Jack said, this time with a smile. "That's as far as I got in the meditation. We need to pick up the journey from there."

"In bed, right?"

"Of course. The fact is we don't really know what we're creating when we fuse. Whatever it is, expanding Third consciousness must be part of the harvest—whether we think of it as a galactic journey or annihilation or just great lovemaking. When we make love that way, evolution is being served."

"It's called Jack and Jaquelyn's fucking service. We're doing it all for the good of the world."

"You have a way of putting everything in perspective."

A few minutes later they proceeded to support evolution with full abandon—Richard's rebirthing included.

26 ✒ Spiritual Tumescence

As 2009 drew to a close, J&J focused more on how intimacy shed light on the evolving connection between the physical and spirit worlds. Obviously, an unbridled imagination is a necessary ally in such explorations. Without exuberant innovation evolution loses a primary impetus, now that human consciousness is to play a central role in shaping the future.

It's New Year's Eve and J&J are at home at the Blue House, enjoying the passage alone, as was their preference on such occasions. They had decided to celebrate the transition in part by taking a walk along the Cane Road, during which their conversation took on a reflective tone befitting the occasion. When they returned home it was almost dark, so they moved right into council.

Jack poured a little wine into a small glass for their celebration. His dedication honored the many gifts and challenges of intimacy: "Our sexual merging is so complex because we have wildly different aesthetics about the world, which is what makes our Third so rich. We're like two musicians who come from different cultures learning to make music together. I'd like to begin with what you said on our walk about overcoming obstacles."

"Remind me."

"The moment that touched me the most was when you said you were ready to move past your long-held insecurities about your writing skills, feeling beautiful enough and all the rest. 'I can let them all go,' you said."

"Yes," Jaquelyn remembered "I trust you and the relationship can keep me from getting too big for my britches, so I don't need to carry the old insecurities any more, at least for that reason."

"Here's to that major step! Once again I drink this fermented harvest of grapes as the blood of the goddess. When her—your—blood runs in my veins our erotic union can take place even more completely."

"When a man drinks his woman's blood, it flows to his cock. So a path to tumescence is vampirism!"

"Right on." Jack said with a laugh. "Maybe that's one reason why vampire stories are so popular now. If a man embraces wine in his intimate sacrament as the blood of the goddess, then, when he enters his woman, the blood that is throbbing in his phallus is *her blood.*"

"Sounds good to me!" Jaquelyn said with a big smile.

"It's a blessing—and another one is how the Beatles' mantra continues to reverberate in me. When we commit to live by, '*all there is, is love,*' spiritual hell simply becomes the absence of love. Defining hell that way might be a powerful ally in shaping evolution. Eventually, there will be no need to create terrifying concepts of hell to help people become more conscious."

"Now that I think about it love has been part of biological evolution for a long time. Women generate a lot of oxytocin when they give birth, which binds them deeply with the newborn. Basically women fall in love with their babies—at least they have that capability. The biology supports what the mother has to do for the baby to survive. For you, the oxytocin is relationship itself, with all its passions, thoughts, ideas and feelings. Your oxytocin has all those mental complexities, while mine just makes me want to eat the baby up. There's not too much mentation in that!"

"Since babies grow up, both kinds of oxytocin are needed," Jack observed playfully . . . "The blue moon is full now. Shall we go out for just a moment and be with that form of the goddess?"

They slid open the French doors of the bedroom and stepped onto the wooden porch, taking the wine with them. The moon hung just above the long stand of trees along the gulch to the east—yes the famous gulch! Thin wisps of clouds passed over the bright lunar surface. Jack draped his arm around Jaquelyn's shoulders to guard her from the evening chill, although the air still remembered the day's balminess. The glass was in Jack's other hand, which he slowly raised until the wine was in their line of sight with the moon. He let the moonlight pass through the wine to purify it for what was to come. When they came back into the bedroom and sat down, he reached for the package of Viagra he had placed near the Third's pillow.

"Ah, the blue stiffener!" Jaquelyn said with a smile.

"Since you've named it, you get to create this part of the ceremony," Jack said and handed her the pill.

His invitation surprised Jaquelyn but she didn't miss a beat. With the pill in her hand they locked eyes in a way that allows souls to meet. In the next moment they both knew exactly what she was going to do. He took another sip of the wine as she slid forward in the rocker and opened her blue house robe, exposing her genitals. She inserted the pill in her vagina ceremonially until it rested near the G-spot. The Viagra felt a little strange at first, but the way it disappeared into the moist mystery of the goddess had the feeling of an ancient ritual.

Jack looked at her with a mixture of awe and desire: "The spirit world seems so present tonight, dancing in the moonlight. I wonder if the beings in that world are as challenged as humans are right now."

"I don't think the beings on the other side have all the answers," Jaquelyn responded. "How could they? I imagine the majority of spirits that appear to people now were embodied during the last historical period and so are dominated by patriarchal ideas and attitudes just as we are."

Jack saw the logic in her observation. "Then the other world must be shaped by judgment and power stuff too. Still, some spirits can be allies and guides."

"And some spirits are drawn to sexy women just like dolphins are."

"Right! I suspect the worlds are much more mutually related than most of us realize."

"That was common knowledge in the goddess era," Jaquelyn observed. "Life and death were both seen as part of the goddess's domain."

"Yes, and I imagine that understanding was largely instinctive in the same way animals are instinctive. That innate wisdom about death has been profoundly diluted during the past five thousand years."

"Perhaps the spirit world seems closer now because 'they' are perplexed too and want to close the gap."

"That history may dominate both sides of the veil is not a happy thought," Jack added.

"That's why the goddess is waking up now after being submerged brutally for so long. She hears us calling. The mother in her hears us calling for help and guidance."

"That reminds me of a chant we used to sing at Ojai:

She's been waitin,' waitin'
She's been waitin' so long
She's been waitin' for her children to remember to return."

Jaquelyn remembered the chant too. "Yes, the kind of relationship we have can serve as the oxytocin for the awakening goddess. If we can entice her with the magical fusion we're discovering, she will fall in love with the world again and help us all co-create evolution."

"That fusion *is* the goddess manifesting in physical form. She is the wisdom of the body—particularly the woman's body—that has been largely denied in the patriarchal era because of fear. We touch that wisdom through the blessings of our lovemaking."

"When we make love my whole neurological system transcends its usual level of activity and reaches a state of aliveness that feels new—I could say evolutionary. I hope that happens for many people, each in their unique way. The physical world and the spirit world are both stuck. We need to work together."

"Evolution is brutal." Jack spoke the words slowly. "The survival of the fittest remains a harsh reality and maybe now the fittest are becoming—"

"—those who can love beyond what humans have known of love before. 'Love to save your life.' That's our new motto."

"Love to save our *collective* life," Jack added.

"I'm feeling aroused and I'm feeling the pill in me too. I planted it like a seed for merging."

"Then this Viagra will surely go beyond the simple effects of increased blood flow. There's magic in the air!"

When she removed the Viagra seductively a moment later, it was warm and moist but still intact. Jack swallowed it with the last sip of wine.

Having drank the goddess's blood and consecrated the phallic stiffener Jaquelyn was ready to invite the divine feminine to join them. "Our council reminds me of Ron Elgas' prediction that the goddess was going to arise on one of the Hawaiian Islands in the near future. It was so preposterous when I heard it years ago that I didn't take it seriously."

"Maybe that's why we're here and why so many visionary people are showing up in our little town," Jack suggested. "After all, our Third is a mixture of the emerging divine feminine and her awakening male lover. It's a strong consciousness already but now we seem to be envisioning a bigger picture in which the Third creates a pathway into the spirit world."

"Is that pathway the state in which the man comes to know spiritual tumescence?"

"You've nailed it again in your inimitable way! Yes, my challenge is to enter you with every energy center wide open—including the crown."

"Spiritual tumescence creates the consciousness we need to stay awake through the crossing," Jaquelyn said, tapping the wisdom of her woman's body.

"And allows us to leave sexual signposts to light the path between the worlds."

"So spiritual tumescence is all about being able to make love through the crossing. I want more women to know about all this. Do you think I'm unrealistic to want to write the kind of book I've been imagining?" It was Jaquelyn's innocent voice asking the question.

"Absolutely not! When you're satiated with all the books you're reading and can put them aside, the goddess will be there for you. She will be your muse."

"That would be such a delight, just to sit down and have the words flow."

"It will happen," Jack answered confidently. "We are on a path of serving the divine feminine. When we make love we are being her disciples. You have taught me that my cock is not mine, my body is not mine, and you certainly are not mine. You have shown me the wisdom of your body and helped me to see that it is holy. You will be able to describe all of that in your writing. The energy that floods our lovemaking is sacred. Lovemaking has become our holy land."

"If more people knew that kind of holy land, they wouldn't have to fight over *the* Holy Land. They could find their own intimate sacred land and celebrate it as part of nature's mystery!"

"Right on! When I ask what it's like to interact with the spirit world, the answer comes back loud and clear: 'You're going to find out when you make love.' That's because, in our own personal way, we're integrating the two worlds when we make love. We have been creating our own intimate spirit world in Third consciousness for a long time. Now we're joining with many others to create a new awareness that is—"

"—exactly the opposite of what fundamental religion teaches," Jaquelyn had to finish his sentence in that way. "True heaven exists in this collective Third consciousness. That's where the divine lives."

"Yes, and each time we make love we're moving towards the spirit world together leaving sign-posts along the way. When we actually make the crossing, hopefully we will recognize these markers. We trust they will light our way."

"You know that in *Conjugal Love* Emanuel Swedenborg says angels are the fusion of a man and a woman in the spirit world."

"That's great confirmation . . . By the way, you'll be glad to hear that all these insights are expanding my tumescence. So, as you desire, my mind is learning to be in service to my cock."

Jaquelyn's face lit up. "Far out! Council as foreplay!"

With that Jack reached out from where he was sitting on his back-jack and touched her calf. "We speak glibly of eternal love but I see in this moment that it simply means that we can—we will—keep on learning how to make love through and beyond the veil."

"What a blessing!"

Jack continued to caress Jaquelyn's calf gently, moving slowly around the lovely shape of her leg like a bee exploring a cluster of exotic flowers. "My fingers are inviting your cells to awaken into goddessness."

"OK, so let's make love."

"Not yet. I suspect you have other ideas you want to talk about."

"Well, I am always searching for the writer's voice," Jaquelyn admitted.

"OK, I invite you to move into the voice of the one who is going to actually sit down and do the writing. Can you imagine yourself doing that?"

"No, that's exactly my problem."

Undaunted, Jack continued. "Let's take the erotic energy that's building, including my touching you, and drop into meditation with the intention of finding your writer's voice."

They were quiet for several minutes until Jaquelyn broke the silence. "My Amazon queen wants to penetrate you energetically. While we were meditating, I saw you as a woman. Then I actually penetrated you and felt what that would be like."

"I would love that. For the man to allow the woman to truly enter him celebrates the demise of the patriarchy."

"Yes," Jaquelyn replied, "and in order for me to do that, I need to imagine I have an energetic cock . We have to go all the way."

"OK, how are we going to play that out?"

"First I want you to penetrate me physically and ignite any part of my Amazon queen that is still resisting becoming the goddess-lover."

Jack nodded. "OK, first I'll penetrate you in that way and then we'll arrive at a certain stage in the love-making when it's time for you to enter me."

"It might be when the Kundalini starts to rise," Jaquelyn suggested. "That moment is usually pretty overwhelming for me, but this time I'm going to direct the rising into you as if the serpent was a Kundalini phallus."

"Then I can begin to know what a woman experiences."

"Right."

"And then we can become an androgynous angel," Jack was enjoying the plan thoroughly.

"Right."

He fell silent, anticipating their love-making, until an unfamiliar sensation passed through his body leaving a question in its wake: "Do you have any fear right now?" he asked.

Jaquelyn lived the question for a moment, creating one of those iconic moments of rapport for them both. "No," was all she said finally in a soft voice that was unequivocally authentic.

"Good. I'm not aware of any either. I feel we'll be going through a doorway when we make love tonight," Jack said in a quiet voice. "That's why I asked the question. I felt the import of what lies ahead."

"We've been headed for this level of fusion for a long time—*Flesh and Spirit* had a whole chapter called *Interpenetration*. But we haven't described the ceremony in such detail until now." Jaquelyn continued to look at him carefully, partly because of his question and partly because there was a glow around his upper body that seemed to have a life of its own. "Are you OK?" she asked.

"Yes, I just saw you, I mean *her*."

"I felt the goddess with me for a moment just now. My brain actually just went through a shift. You must have picked that up. There's a light around you."

"There *is* a shift going on," Jack affirmed. "The Amazon queen has been struggling these past few weeks, pondering the question, 'dare I trust you?' My answer is that I intend to 'die into you.' That's the only way I can describe it. I intend to encounter the other world through our lovemaking. I penetrate you in the physical world and then, when you enter me, we will go through a doorway. I just set the intention in the meditation that the muse, the voice of the writer in each of us, will be born out of this lovemaking. We will conceive."

"So our books will serve others in the way we hope."

"Yes. Then I wondered if I should climax physically in order for that to happen. I wondered if I needed the full physical surrender of an orgasm and I got back, 'No, you're not going to come.'"

"You will have a new kind of spirit come instead," Jaquelyn envisioned.

"The ejaculation is to be on another level. I enter you, then you enter me and then we'll be introduced to a new kind of climax."

"How about something to nibble on—not anything sweet. Maybe a cheese and cracker. Is that too much trouble?"

"Not at all," Jack shifted focus without missing a beat. "One cheese and cracker coming up."

"Two cheese and crackers and a pear or a banana." (laughter)

Jack dutifully returned with four crackers, two small bananas peeled and two dried apricots. They both ate one cracker. "Eating the cheese and crackers brings in the natural world," Jack commented, "grain, cows, fermentation—all those natural processes."

"A lot of lacto-bacillus. Can we have some banana now?"

"Yes, some now and some afterwards. In the kitchen I was told that the bananas are an important part of the ceremony. So I'm going to watch you eat part of yours while you watch me."

"OK," Jaquelyn agreed, "and I want you to let the lattices of your mind dissolve, so that all the usual structures disappear, even the commitment to non-thinking."

Jack watched her take the peeled banana, a small apple variety from their land, and slowly put one end in her mouth. The association was immediate. Then he surrendered to her instructions and went to a place in his body beyond mind.

A few minutes later, when he shifted again into more ordinary consciousness, Jaquelyn greeted him as if he had been gone on a vision quest. "I could tell you what I saw, but first you have to say how your mind handled the challenge I gave you."

"As I let go," Jack responded, "I had the image of crystals hanging in a lattice free of gravity. The crystals were all moving and gently touching each other, changing my brain waves."

"Into something like Brownian motion."

"Yes, and then I remembered to call in the muse."

"Meanwhile I was imagining your cock fully aroused doing Kegels inside of me," Jaquelyn reported. "With its slight bend you touch

310

me where I have more feeling than any other place in my vagina . . . Do we eat more banana now?"

Jack nodded and after finishing the banana Jaquelyn began to eat her second cracker slowly. "Do you have any insight about this cracker as part of the ceremony?" she asked.

"It's about grounding, so we can stay conscious as we begin to make love. What we're doing requires a deep level of trust. The queen has been the queen for thousands of years. The goddess-lover is new, so it takes a huge leap of faith for her to fully surrender. I want to bring that into my loins as I eat this cracker. I just had a glimpse of the moment in our lovemaking when you will enter me. The feeling was expansive."

"You've already started to surrender."

"Yes—and the cracker will nourish my tumescence. You're merging with the goddess. She's known how to celebrate sexuality before, but never with the love she feels now."

"You asked me if I was scared," Jaquelyn said with a touch of awe. "I may have some fear of the unknown. Where we're headed is so huge."

"Let's embrace the fear and transform it into desire," Jack said in a quiet voice. "The expansion of desire is endless."

"Shall we go to bed and have our apricots later, or shall we eat them now?" the goddess asked.

The lover was up to making the big decision. "We should go to bed and then have the apricots."

Although it was difficult for J&J to remember details afterwards, the ceremony of interpenetration lived up to its expectations. The goddess fulfilled her desire to enter her lover in a way that initiated him into further mysteries of the divine feminine. The subsequent climax they reached together created a bright marker on the path between the worlds. As they held each other in gratitude before falling asleep, they both knew they had been given a glimpse of the mystery of that ultimate journey.

27 ❧ A Playful Reconciliation

As J&J became clearer about their path, they became more playful. This was particulaly true of Jaquelyn who by now was letting her love flourish unimpeded a good deal of the time. Playfulness can be a powerful force for healing. Let me share a brief example of what I mean— one that further shifted J&J's relationship to the god of the Old Testament.

As you have already heard, Jaquelyn invited Jack to sit in for Jehovah—the name for the New Testament god that was familiar during her childhood—so he could be initiated sexually by the goddess. In this story J&J entered the mists of the Old Testament and focused on the primal god Yahweh, as the Hebrews named him. Of course, Yahweh and Jehovah are names for the same god, but the sense of the *divine father* of the Judaic-Christian tradition evolved somewhat with time and so Jaquelyn decided that a second initiation was required.

Jaquelyn's anger about Yahweh was real and personal. He was not simply a made-up creation of the early Hebrew patriarchy for her, even though that was what she ostensibly believed. Rather, she spoke of him at times as a real, almost embodied, patriarch who at various times was 'terrified of the feminine,' 'a jealous male jerk,' 'a vengeful beast,' and a variety of other epitaphs. Historically, Yahweh's primary adversary had been the great goddess—and that made him Jaquelyn's arch-enemy number one. Under that banner she took the shadowy patriarchal tendencies in all the men she had known (including her father and Jack, of course) and rolled them into this ancient male sky-god.

Jack handled this deeply personal "vendetta" (one of Jaquelyn's favorite words) pretty well, although at times he found it necessary to remind her she was anthropomorphizing a historical spiritual projection to which she responded, "Of course, but his destructive qualities exist in abundance in the men of the world and are abhorrent to the goddess." Jack couldn't disagree but he knew that as long as Yahweh was seen as enemy number one, progress along the path of evolutionary relationship would be difficult. Fortunately, Jaquelyn had also come to the wisdom that the goddess was all women—actually all of nature's females—which inevitably led to her imagining Jack as any and all of the men who are their lovers. Over time, holding this expanding vision shifted her perspective about Yahweh enough to invite Jack to play a delightful game with her during one of their councils . . . It's a cool December day in 2009; Jaquelyn is speaking:

"Now that you've had some practice being some of the men that love the goddess and we know Yahweh was obviously a collective male projection, you could move into playing him in a conversation with the goddess."

"As a reconciliation?"

"Yes, Yahweh is afraid of women, doesn't know how to make love, and is angry, murderous and extremely jealous."

After a pause, Jack responded. "I'm trying to move into that role and I realize I'm not consciously angry at women."

"You have to take on all men's fear and anger. You have to be a very porous actor, like Meryl Streep. Wouldn't you playing all men and I playing all women make a great scene in an animated film?" (laughter)

"You and I are an animated film already. We're a 'toon,' as they say in the business."

Seeing themselves as a movie inspired Jaquelyn. "I'm going to play the role of the great mother goddess and I'm talking to you,

Yahweh. The first thing I want to tell you is that men can't do without women. They simply cannot do without them." She repeated the words with passion. "Women can't do without men either, but they function a little better alone than most men do because they embody the creative mystery. Heterosexual men have to be with a woman to feel fully alive."

"And how do you know that, mother goddess?"

"I grew up with many brothers and watched them carefully. Then I was with many men intimately and noticed how they also couldn't do without women. I saw how their need for women made them fearful and then angry. Men need to learn the ways of love. The challenge now is to get them off their fearful and murderous ways and interested in learning the ways of love."

"Are there going to be lessons?" Yahweh (alias Jack) asked.

"Oh, yes, but they first need to release their preoccupation with power and become interested in the mysteries of love."

"And how am I to let go my need for power and my obsession with suppressing women?"

The great mother goddess responded immediately. "You have to be able to see sex as part of loving in order to really understand what sex can be. You haven't experienced that kind of sexuality yet."

"Are there going to be lessons?" Yahweh repeated. 'He' was having a good time.

"Yes."

"That will enable men to experience the magic of which you speak?"

"Yes!"

"Have you experienced this magic?"

"No," the great goddess admitted. "I need a male who is ready and willing to have that experience with me . . . but I know of it."

"So you're inviting me to discover a new world with you because you need a partner in order to do that. In exchange I have to fully acknowledge you."

"Yes, it's a mutual need but I'm choosing you and *I'm a goddess,* so, if you can't do the job or don't want to do it, then I'll find someone else. So there!"

Jack laughed in character. "So you're a fickle goddess."

"No, no. I'm just telling you what will happen if you can't—"

"—Why are you telling me what will happen if I say, no, when I'm clearly open and ready to say yes? I'm just asking a few questions about the curriculum. After all, this is a big move for me, a move that has been many thousands of years in the making."

"What got me off on this?" The voice was more Jaquelyn's now.

"I have no idea, but what you are proposing is a joint venture that will lead to a birth, a christening and a consummation. It's the birth of the male into true manhood through his initiation as lover. It will eventually lead to a consummation of a new marriage between the mother goddess and Yahweh. Meanwhile, the mother goddess in you will become more fully realized as the lover-goddess."

"Yes, she has known the essence of sexuality forever but she's had sex only with brothers—like Isis did with Osiris—or with temporary lovers, as the queens did with their kings-for-a-year."

"And warriors too. The goddess practitioners made love with warriors too," Jack reminded her. "Now—finally—you will be making love with your lover and possibly your magus, your shaman, as well. Do you still want to make love with kings and warriors, or just lovers and shaman?"

"I want it all Baby!"

"That can be arranged!"

Jack played out a seducible Yahweh for obvious reasons—and they did indeed go on to have a magical time that evening consummating the mythical marriage. Jaquelyn's anger towards Yahweh, never quite reached the same biting intensity after that.

28 ✺ Nature's Gifts to Intimacy

It's time once again to pick up the thread that describes the strong connection between the culture of the Islands and J&J's path of awakening. Jack had become quite involved with the Youth Center in Honoka'a that served many of the local families with a full after-school program for kids, ten to eighteen. In addition J&J widened their circle of friends in the community as people began to see them as *kupuna*—elders—who had something intriguing to share about relationship. In return, the local community and culture offered many gifts. A great example is how exposure to hula began to directly influence J&J's experience of Third consciousness. The next story describes the way in which the beauty of these traditional Hawaiian dances and chants awakened new aspects of their connection to the divine feminine. The time is a day in November when one of the Islands' favorite musicians, Keali'i Reichel, gave a gala performance in Honoka'a's picturesque People's Theater.

J&J came home from the concert flying high. The theater had been completely full—a rare occurrence—and Keali'i had everyone in the palm of his hand or, better said, in the complex folds of his heart. But it was the hula performed by the small band of women dancers accompanying the musicians that really captured J&J's attention. Jack kept shaking his head in wonder, as if he were watching the traditional dance for the first time. He couldn't find the words to describe his reactions until they sat down late in the evening to have a council, accompanied by a shared glass of wine.

"I learned something tonight."

"Was it the music?" Jaquelyn wondered.

"It was the whole day, as well as the concert. We honored the *keiki*—the children—in the afternoon at the Youth Center when Keali'i came by to talk with the kids about the power of music to build *ohana*—the sense of extended family. Most of his songs celebrate what these Islands mean to the people who have lived here for generations. The music makes it clear that Hawaii is where the goddess is unabashedly venerated, certainly more than in any other place I've ever been."

"I agree."

"When you think of places we've lived or visited often," Jack continued, "New York, Oklahoma, Marysville, the San Fernando Valley, Haifa, even Ojai and Taos, none come closer to supporting the presence of the goddess as do these Islands. That may be the major reason why we're here. Before we started to steward this land years back, Hawaii was not the place I imagined living out our life together!"

"Yes, you probably will end your life here. If I die first, you'll stay, whereas, if you die first, I wouldn't be able to take care of the place. It takes a lot of your time to steward the land and support the community as you do."

"I'm not too worried about leaving you here alone because I trust we're being offered the possibility of going out together in one way or another. We've been learning to 'die' in each other's arms for a while now."

"I've told you my fantasy," Jaquelyn responded, picking up the thread. "There will be a time when our lovemaking is so intense that we won't come out of it."

"Yes, a few of my more powerful orgasms felt like they took me to the edge. I've had the feeling I could go out in the middle of one of those."

"Oh my!"

"It was just a blink," Jack assured her.

"Probably the longer you go without coming, the more likely you'd have that reaction when you finally do."

"Can you actually imagine us making the journey at the end of a long night of . . . ? Our lovemaking is so . . . You start singing and then . . ." He couldn't finish any of the sentences.

"The waves come from deep in me, from my anus it seems," Jaquelyn shared. "It feels like I'm instinctively programming you to do exactly what I desire you to do when we make love. Does that make sense to you?"

"Absolutely"

"If I knew where this guiding force comes from, it would all seem calculating, like I was controlling you. But I don't know its origin." She threw her arms up in the air to acknowledge the mystery of what she was describing.

"That was a great gesture—unlike any you've made before. I loved it."

"Maybe the hula inspired me. You were talking about the sensual and erotic, and even maternal qualities of the dancers. They all had a sense of their own beauty, without any self-consciousness about being heavy. Some of them were quite abundant, as you would say. Did you imagine embracing all that flesh at any point during the concert?"

"It would be a memorable experience," Jack acknowledged with a smile. "My reactions honored those women as part of the circle of all women. They were definitely manifesting goddess energy. I'm curious what will happen if we take the hula energy into our relationship, since it arises mostly from the traditional Hawaiian love of nature. We're less familiar with that part of the goddess-spectrum, although I suspect we come close to it during our lovemaking when we go beyond the personal and celebrate the goddess's flesh."

Jack's observation triggered an association for Jaquelyn. "I don't know why but that reminds me of something I was reading of Ibn Arabi's today. He says men *love* women and women *yearn* for men. I wonder if that yearning is what makes women so magnetic. Maybe men are drawn to women's yearning for them. I haven't heard anyone say that before. Have you?"

"No," Jack acknowledged, "but let me check it out. (long pause) "Yes, there's a lot of truth to the distinction. Men yearn and women love, of course, but I agree that yearning generally describes women's way of loving more closely than men's."

"Is that just the nature of the beast?"

"Yes, in part because the patriarchy systematically tried to block men from yearning for women. Women were allowed to yearn but suppressing them limited the yearning. Now, as women become empowered, their yearning for men could very well expand and even become an evolutionary force. Yearning is a call for completion and in the world of intimacy sets love in motion. Women's yearning also supports the social coherence needed for cultures to survive. As we leave the patriarchy, yearning could be a part of the expanding love-consciousness that will be realized by men and women—together."

Jaquelyn's curiosity had been whetted. "The deeper question is whether the differences in yearning between men and women are genetic and hard-wired. We need to know more about that if we are going to evolve consciously. Do you remember what I came to in the bathtub the other night about evolution? I felt we have been guided along our relationship path in the past, like initiates, but now we needed to take on more of a proactive role."

Jack nodded. "The evolution taking place now is clearly a co-creation with the *powers-that-be* or nature or the collective Third—however we want to name it. For us the path to co-creation is through our personal Third. Sometimes, that can feel like being guided, because co-creation is beyond personal will. I don't even know what personal will is anymore."

"Clarify how nature fits into all of this."

"At the heart of it, nature is relationship manifest and the ultimate model of interdependence. The thrust of this new era is to take that model into intimate relationships. In particular, now the magical way in which women and men celebrate nature through hula has appeared along our path."

"Yes, hula is about flowing ocean waves and the trade winds and tropical trees," Jaquelyn mused, "all of which I can feel in my body too, although I have less flesh than some of those women. The dancers were so sensual. You can feel how much they love their bodies—as well as food. They love life."

"That love of life is the heart of the dance. Hula is also the moving manifestation of Hawaiian mythology—particularly those stories that celebrate the complexities of love and the nurturing beauty of the Islands. Watching the hula gave us a glimpse of what it was like during the goddess era. I became aware that you are a descendent of all that woman-ness."

"Did you see something in the feminine that you hadn't seen or let in before?"

"Yes," Jack acknowledged, "some of my less developed erotic sensibilities were awakened. By the second time the dancers came on stage I was ready to celebrate nature more fully with them. It was almost like making love with them."

"Keali'i's voice vibration and his eroticism are part of that too. Let's face it, honey, we're just sex fiends—which reminds me of something I read recently: The biological purpose of kissing is for the man to give his bacteria or any infection he has to the woman, so she can build up anti-bodies and transfer those to the baby. Couples that don't kiss are not providing their baby with the healthiest environment."

"So we recommend that parents kiss rather than vaccinate their kids."

"It's much healthier," Jaquelyn exclaimed. (laughter) "I want to get back to the difference between the yearnings of men and women in relationship."

"When we say women are more innately relational, that doesn't do justice to what is actually true. In fact, the statement is questionable in some cases—such as ours. The notion of 'yearning' is more useful. A woman yearns for the connection because it means survival for her child and herself, and so for the species. While conventional wisdom says a man's cock yearns to penetrate, a woman's vagina is not the only part of her that yearns—when she is allowed to be free. Then her whole body, her whole being, can be like a receptive vagina. Most men don't bring that kind of yearning into their whole body the way a woman does until he really matures as a lover."

Jaquelyn liked what she was hearing. "A younger woman yearns because her body knows that relationship is necessary for procreation and biological survival. After menopause, that shifts and she has the opportunity to embrace sexuality as a way that is increasingly spiritual. A man on the path of relationship develops in a parallel way. To procreate he has to be sexually active and readily aroused but, as he matures into being a lover of his goddess, his cock becomes more of a major transmitter of love. I call yours my 'magic wand.'"

Jack looked at her silently for a moment. "My yearning is strong right now. It's hard for a man to yearn. It doesn't seem manly because of his patriarchal imprinting. In the patriarchy masculine yearning is often associated with the part of his mind that sets goals."

"Yes, feminine yearning is different and happens in waves. My yearning is like a pulsing flow that goes through my whole body. It is more sensual and feeling oriented without necessarily setting specific intentions or goals. Women's yearning can be so sensual."

"Hawaii helps expand the sensuality," Jack added. "Our sensuality has grown substantially since we've been living here . . . How about a sip of wine?" He held the half-filled glass between them, remembering their new understanding. "This glass of wine is—"

"—a feminine vessel suggesting menstruation and communion with the goddess."

"When I drink her blood, I acknowledge her increasing presence in our lives and in the world."

"The goddess began as the entire natural world," Jaquelyn continued, "but we are not calling in that ancient mother goddess now. We want to honor her—and then invite in a more evolved form of the divine feminine in which spirituality and sexuality are more integrated. I feel that is inherent in the woman's body. The man has to develop his feminine side extensively to achieve the same degree of integration. Maybe he struggles because he's not bathed in estrogen his whole life, and maybe evolution will eventually decrease the differences between creatures dominated by such diverse hormones as estrogen and testosterone. We might be in a cycle where the gap is going to close slowly—that is, men will make a little more estrogen and women a bit more testosterone."

"What I saw as you were talking," Jack responded, "is that the rebalancing will take place in the *relationships* between men and women. When couples have access to Third consciousness, I suspect their bodies will become more balanced hormonally."

"What you just described is exactly how I feel when we make love. In that state estrogen and testosterone merge in a beautiful work of hormonal art. Talking about all this inspires me to look again at the steps needed to move from the patriarchal state, in which the masculine is fearful and jealous and needs to control the feminine, into the kind of balanced culture that we and many others are talking about. What are the actual steps?"

"That's the sixty-four thousand dollar question! One major step is for there to be a co-arising of Eros in all our bodies and minds. There has to be something unusually powerful that wakes people up, not necessarily the particular erotic flavor that you and I enjoy but the awakening can't be primarily mental. The awakening has to occur in the body as well."

"Yes, and this awakening has to do with spirit and sexuality being allowed to celebrate their natural union in bed together," Jaquelyn reiterated.

"As that's happening, another big step in the transition is for people to see their gods and goddesses of the past in the context of collective cultural stories, not an absolute reality. History has evolved to a large extent through the lens of religion—and it's been a mixed bag. On one side have been the achievements in art, music, literature, architecture and science, and on the other the terrors of tyranny, war and the subjugation of women. I trust we're awakening finally from believing these devastating shadows are inevitably part of the human condition."

"We're moving out of civilization as we've known it! The words sound strange."

"Into a more overtly relational culture," Jack continued, "in which men and women take new risks. The big risk for men is loving their women beyond fear, beyond restraint. All that will happen as a harvest of the spiritual-sexual integration—flesh and spirit. That's been our bumper sticker for a long time."

"That's exactly the kind of loving so many women want right now."

Jack nodded. "Yes and the challenge for a man is to love in that way even though he doesn't really understand the mystery of woman. He has to learn to love that which he does not know. He has to love in the face of fear. We need what Buddhists call the 'don't-know mind" but in an erotic context. That traditional practice is good training for what needs to happen now in relationship. Thinking one knows is an obstacle to bringing in the new paradigm. You and I are blessed with insights that keep us going as long as we meet each new situation without the need to know."

"And there has to be enough dying out of the old to create space to explore the new," Jaquelyn added, "particularly regarding the coming together of sexuality and spirituality. We are offering a path that winds its way from birth to death, from the beginnings of relational life to the crossing, a path that involves lovemaking as a practice . . . We could do an experiment about the crossing right now."

"I just saw the Goddess smiling and suggesting we be careful what we call in. If the practice of lovemaking is going to be our way of making the crossing, then every time we start making love, it might be wise to prepare to leave the plane."

"That's our reality now! The expansion of love and trust that's required to implement that kind of practice is huge."

"I know that almost every generation feels they are in the throes of major evolution," Jack continued, "but it really does seem that way now. We're evolving from a world in which the basic elements are called creatures, people, individuals—a lion, a cockroach, a human—into a world in which we are more likely to think in terms of relational entities. We're being shown that the Thirds of all kinds of relationships will become the basic elements, the 'atoms,' of the new cultural body."

"Yes, including our relationships with roaches," Jaquelyn added with a grin. "They look at us and wiggle their thingies. They're trying to figure out what we're going to do with them. 'Is that jerk going to slam a glass over me and throw me outside again?'"

"We may be well-known in the cockroach world: 'Hey, you guys, come to the Blue House if you want a real trip. It's a little scary, but it turns out OK in the end. This thing comes down over you that you can see through but you can't escape from. Then this other thing comes sliding under you like a thin carpet. So you crawl around in a frenzy. That's followed by a brief journey that leads to your prison coming apart and the next thing you know you're flying through the air and land on the grass. What a trip!'" (lots of laughter)

Jaquelyn had something more to say about the don't-know practice. "When you love like an explorer, without the need to know, then intimacy leads to real growth that eventually becomes evolutionary. We're bathed in the potential for change now. What I'm curious about is how the whole culture gets erotized. Is it similar to what's happening to us?"

"For that to happen, enough people have to experience sexuality without all the associations humans have developed over the past five thousand years. Meanwhile, change may continue to be a battle in the trenches between what is dying and what wants to be born."

"Yet I feel the growing power of change in the absurdity of the resistance. Would you say the expanding interest in sacred plants is part of this inevitable movement?"

"Absolutely!" Jack declared. "Without a deeper relationship with the plant world, evolution will be at best slower. The ceremonial use of that aspect of nature is another powerful evolutionary force, just as Terrence McKenna used to say and many have preached for years."

"And women meeting together is also part of it, right?" Jaquelyn wanted to check-in about their old debate.

"Yes! Since the goddess is all women, when women meet, she will be present!"

"Basically, the challenge in the sexual arena is to let people know that it's OK to be ecstatically involved in love-making because that is one of the main ways for spirit to manifest."

The simple clarity of Jaquelyn's perspective once again touched Jack deeply. "I'm so grateful for the gig we've been given—and mostly for you! When we screw up, we screw up. We do our best to clean up our mess and we learn. The level of training we're in is a blessing."

"There is no assignment I can imagine wanting more," Jaquelyn agreed.

"We need to finish these books because there will be further tasks."

"Yes, I've been thinking about our mission in Israel. That work will continue in various ways. It's a stroke of brilliance for the people we know there to plan a day when hundreds of circles—mostly made up of women—will meet all over the country. The idea of flooding a small country with women's energy is right on. The U.S. is too large for that but Israel is a contained enough space for all those women to be visible and make a difference. That kind of event would begin to satisfy my desire for women to have their day."

"Yes, opportunities are arising. I agree that the women's circles are a way to go, along with training couples and singles who are inspired to continue the Inbar work by developing the presence of a cultural Third . . . Are you ready for some soup?"

"I am ready for Jack's special soup-stew that tasted so delicious yesterday."

They dined late on a unique, thick soup of red cabbage, onions, carrots, a few okra and chilies, all from the garden, augmented by potatoes and celery. It was a hearty meal, which was followed by a newly created instant dessert—an apple Newton covered with ice cream. It was an appropriate finale for the special day in Honoka'a.

29 ❧ Sexuality and the Big Bang

In their commitment to provide insights and practices for the era of Eros J&J didn't limit their attention to the transformation of traditional myths and scripture. Science was also fair game for creating new metaphors and understandings of the mysteries of intimacy. In the spring of 2010 Jaquelyn found herself absorbed in Richard Friedman's book about the Big Bang and its implications for human spirituality. When she first told Jack about the book, he remembered listening with excitement to Brian Swimme's heartful offering of the Big Bang as a universal creation myth many years before. In the councils that followed they explored the connection between the Big Bang story and the current evolution of intimacy. I'll give you a taste of one of these dialogs in which Jaquelyn makes the connection starting with intimacy:

"I know in my goddess body what we need to do to take our intimacy deeper. As I've said many times before, I want you to be hard and still not rush me into bed before our council is truly finished. But most of all I want us to be able to hold absolute stillness while you're inside me fully aroused."

"I hear you, but that doesn't mean I can do it all the time. I may need you to cut me some slack when the energy gets so strong I can't resist you anymore."

"That's exactly when I want us to be still," Jaquelyn countered.

"I want you hard and crazy in love with me with no holding back, no fears—all that in complete stillness. Is that too much to ask?" Her voice had the tone of ageless wisdom combined with innocence that he had grown to treasure.

"Of course it's too much but that doesn't matter. I say, yes to it all. We've been headed in that direction for a long time."

"Stillness is the key. Since we've been talking about the Big Bang lately, I've been trying to understand how it might be related to sexuality. I feel intuitively that, if we can be totally still in lovemaking that we can approach the energy of that original creative moment. When you start moving or touching me vigorously, I get caught up in body sensations and we lose the path to that extraordinary mystery. I know this all sounds wild, but—"

"—I get it," Jack reassured her. "In fact, since you first started talking about the Big Bang, I've also been playing with a way to connect the origin of the universe with relationship—and I had a startling image of what was inside that small mass of high density material fifteen billion years ago. I saw a three-dimensional yin/yang-like symbol, consisting of two S-shaped entities nestled together in a tiny sphere. When I looked more closely, I could see that they were like twins *in utero*—say a male and a female—heads to thighs with their legs bent back at the knees. I took that to suggest that inside the incredibly dense matter lived the potential of all of nature's intimate erotic connections, including human's love for the divine and for the earth itself. These gestating creatures held each other for eons in an embrace that kept the mass together and then . . . and then . . ." He paused, searching for words to describe the original moment of creation.

"Yes?"

". . . and then they couldn't hide their curiosity any longer. They couldn't resist wanting to discover what it would be like for their one-ness to become two-ness—perhaps so in turn they could experience how two-ness becomes one-ness again."

"So they blew up their one-ness." Jaquelyn added.

"They exploded into what became the universe and it has taken fifteen billion years so far for their curiosity to be satisfied."

"So the Big Bang was a sort of reverse orgasm of one becoming two."

"That might be as good a description for relationists as I've heard," Jack declared. "The original orgasm that started the universe was the mitosis or fission of *the one*. Paraphrasing Joe Campbell at the end of his life: 'The ultimate mystery in life is that of *the one* becoming two and then *the two* becoming *one* again.'"

"So without the original split, we would not be able to know the kind of coming together we're experiencing now."

"Without fission, there can't be fusion."

Jaquelyn was already on to the next step. "So the completion of the Big Bang has to be a fusion of everything in the universe back into a mass the size of a large pea."

"Yes—metaphorically, of course," Jack agreed. "Perhaps all the focus on 2012—just two years from now—means that will be the time when consciousness is headed back towards the state of the Big Bang. Many of us sense this *Great Turning* but don't know what's going to happen. Some are fearful of any change and are clinging to the familiar past. Some are not convinced that human consciousness has anything to do with evolution. Some share the vision of co-creating evolution but are fearful that a life-affirming perspective will not prevail. Many people live with an abundance of fear. Now survival of the fittest also involves acts of immense faith. We and many others have faith that Eros must become a dominant force in shaping evolution."

"Eros is creating the turning!" Jaquelyn's voice was joyous.

"Yes, and obviously fear is still very present—perhaps even more so than ever before. But, as the experiment continues and we make the journey back to wholeness, the fear will ease and Eros will expand. Our particular task is to erotize the journey back home."

"Awesome thoughts. We know now that the more conscious we are when we make love, the more of this mystery we can embrace. For us, returning to the Big Bang means the ultimate lovemaking. I think we're farther along on the physical-passion part than we are on the staying conscious part."

Jack nodded. "We're playing in the outskirts of the fire-zone now and it's getting hotter all the time. And now you're challenging me to stay conscious in complete erotic stillness!"

"Your mind needs to connect with your cock and heart in a new way, so there's no part of you that's left out. That might sound like crazy-in-love, although the more I love you, the saner I feel. The love grounds my outrageousness, so I can explore everything without losing my mind. If we can stay conscious and whole in this way, then how we think of death will change too. We're being shown that, as we approach a more fused state of awareness, life and death become inseparable. It's hard to put it into words, but each being *is* everything and is also *in* everything. That experience changes our sense of identity completely."

"Our fusion has so many layers. If we were to touch now . . ." He reached out his hand which Jaquelyn took gently in hers. They remained perfectly still for a few minutes.

"That was startling," Jaquelyn broke the silence. "Our hands were totally fused just like when we're making love."

"That helped me to see something more clearly. When we're together like this the desire for physical intimacy is enormous. But stillness balances that force, which is one reason you're so drawn to the embrace meditation now. In that position there's an impetus to remain still and conscious, no matter what. The urge for greater consciousness has finally become as strong in me as the urge to manifest love physically. They dance with each other, so I can explore desire more deeply and not lose my way."

Jaquelyn laughed. "It's a wild game right now and will continue to be right through 2012—and beyond. The return to wholeness defines an entirely different era."

"Ultimately, as we approach the Big Bang *as a state of consciousness*, our individual energies will become mixed with the energies of every other being in ways we can't even imagine now."

"That's already happening for some people!"

"Yes," Jack agreed, "and in ways that go beyond the familiar spiritual teachings about interdependence. In the new era, interdependence will stare us all in the face, literally, and—"

"—I just resisted the temptation to tell you that I really like the shorts you're wearing," Jaquelyn interrupted, "because I thought you would see it as a seductive invitation. That is one of those comments I spring on you and then say I'm not ready to go to bed yet. I caught myself."

"And you still shared it, so let's see how I would have responded. Hmmm . . . I would have handled it—"

"—Look! It's beautiful. The shorts show your cock more than any other pants. I bought those pants for you."

"—akido-like by moving the energy into tumescence," Jack completed his sentence. "The Big Bang means infinite tumescence after all."

"Ho! I'll go for that! The goddess will love that!" (laughter)

"For us, the return to the Big Bang is like a grand tantric event in which interdependence is increasingly tangible. The climactic event could be a moment of fusion that many people share."

"Did you know that before this moment?" Jaquelyn couldn't quite believe what they were saying.

"We've hinted at it but there's knowing and *knowing*," Jack answered. "Knowing is a spiral." They locked eyes again for several minutes which left them both in awe. "Just acknowledging what my body is capable of feeling fills me with gratitude," he added.

"We're doing an erotic duet. While we're seducing each other, our desire grows and re-shapes our thoughts and feelings. All that is part of foreplay." They were quiet for a moment and then Jaquelyn spoke again. "All the tsunami warnings this morning give me an idea. Let's also be open to simultaneous tsunamis of consciousness and physical passion too. If we explore a new aspect of Third consciousness, our bodies have to go along, and if our bodies celebrate some new sexual awakening, our Third will witness it all. The ultimate Eros happens in total stillness. All evening I've been practicing being in that stillness with you—at a distance—even when we've been talking. Your lips were on mine; your tongue was making love with mine; your arms were around me; your cock was in me, and your Kegels were pulsating. Then your cock went through all my layers of moist sweetness until you reached my center and I spread out into the goddess that I am. My union with you is timeless now—and began in that dense mass at the beginning of physical reality. We're practicing our ability to hold this energy for as long as we can. Do this practice with me now."

Jaquelyn had a ready student. He nodded immediately, shifted into a meditation position and they went on a journey of desire in Eros-time . . . As soon as she opened her eyes, he opened his. They had traveled together.

"We were using visualization and active imagination to make love," Jaquelyn said in a quiet voice. "You touched that thickening that defines my G-spot and then you encountered my cervix. I was getting so turned on that I wanted to spread and spread. Spreading makes me feel all our boundaries are disappearing. What were you feeling?"

"I traveled the return cycle to the Big Bang as a journey in consciousness, starting with the *Great Turning*. As the universe becomes more intimate, I actually felt how everything will be in relationship to everything else more tangibly. . . Right now it feels like I'm devouring you."

"I think I'll force feed you tonight," Jaquelyn said with a seductive smile

"What?"

"Force feed you."

"Sounds wild!" Jack matched her smile. "During the meditation my hands were on my thighs in the old biblical position of testifying. That reminded me that for us the return to the Big Bang is about moving away from traditional scriptures. Our personal life together has become our testament and the source of teachings that many people get when they attend their church or temple or mosque. Since our story is uniquely our testament, as it will be for others on the relationship path, there are no avatars for us, and no single generally accepted story. But there will be the sharing of stories and a collective understanding of relationship as a spiritual path. The barriers will keep falling as Eros ripples out in all directions, just like you describe your surrender in lovemaking."

Jaquelyn nodded. "Are you including surrendering your buttocks too?" She glanced out of the bedroom window that faced east. "The moon is playing peek-a-boo with the clouds. The night is full of light."

"Let's raise the blinds so we can see the moon," Jack suggested. While Jaquelyn put on a new filmy chemise he arranged the blinds and bed pillows to fit the scene they had been imagining all evening. "OK, the moonlight is there, the candles are there and you are here," he said.

"And you?" Jaquelyn asked. "Are you here—or there? Which world are you in?"

"I'm right here, having a wonderful thought. We can make love for a long time, maybe as long as fifteen billion years."

"Sounds good to me."

"I'm going to look at you continuously tonight," Jack affirmed. "Closing my eyes can easily lead to unconsciousness when the energy is this hot."

"If we look at each other as we begin to fuse, then we can stay the wild horses at least for a while longer."

"Still there are no guarantees! When you put on your new top just now, one lovely breast was completely in view. I don't know if you intended to do that. Now, they're both partially hidden and radiating a sublime invitation."

"They emanate the energy of toti-potential fertility," Jaquelyn explained innocently.

"When my fingers touch your breasts, I feel every cell is welcoming them."

"That's called divine magnetism. Hey, how come you still have your shirt on? Take it off, take it off, cried the girls from the rear," Jaquelyn laughed and opened her chemise completely.

"OK, don't forget, we're still continuing our council about the return to the Big Bang," Jack reminded himself out loud as he took off his clothes. They fell silent again, now in ongoing erotic meditation. "I'm touching your body with the intention of awakening you as a musical instrument of love," Jack said finally. "The image isn't new but the feelings are stronger now." He looked deeply at her body in the candlelight.

"I can feel you disappearing when you look at me that way," the goddess said.

". . . OK, I'm back."

"Do you want to be really tested?" The goddess asked.

"Yes."

"OK, lie down—here, all the way down in the bed so there's room for me." Jaquelyn pulled him towards the foot of the bed so he could stretch out. Then she arranged the blanket so only his feet were covered, slipped off her top and straddled him so her genitals were right over his mouth. The force-feeding was about to take place. "OK, Baby, you're going to get it!"

"Promises, promises. I'm right here. I'm right here," Jack repeated to maintain his courage. Jaquelyn let her labia descend slowly until they touched his waiting mouth. He greeted them with a darting tongue. She shuddered and let out a groan of pleasure. His tongue and whole mouth became a hungry entity, independent of his mind. Mouth and labia kissed passionately until the moment was celebrated with goddess songs. As joyous as the music was, after a while Jaquelyn realized her legs were going to sleep.

"I'm still right here," Jack said in a hoarse whisper, as Jaquelyn climbed off of him and lay back in her usual position on the bed.

Jack arranged himself along side of Jaquelyn with one arm underneath her neck and the other free to roam. "I could feel myself entering you just now. My whole body was following my tongue and my lips. I was deep inside you. Did I pass the test?"

"Yes, so far, but we're just getting started," Jaquelyn said in her classically seductive, yet innocent way. They looked at each other with trespasso intensity, eyes now only inches apart while the erotic flow was celebrated in silence for several minutes.

"I can feel our mitochondria exchanging energy." Jack explained finally. "In this state the mitochondria of the man and the woman create the mitochondria of a new Third being."

Jaquelyn nodded. "Your flesh is magic," she responded, as he began to stroke her breasts gently. They continued to talk sporadically as the lovemaking deepened.

"Tumescence extremis," Jack said in a half whisper as Jaquelyn continued to display her magic with his cobra. "I'm still conscious," he added reassuringly a breathless moment later.

Soon all the elements came together in a dance of nature that the lovers dedicated to the *Great Turning*. They shared that thought silently, before the tsunamis of passion and consciousness came together and, merging, the lovers were carried homewards.

30 ❧ How Do Sons Become Lovers?

Although embracing J&J's vision of evolution might be a stretch for some, you will not be surprised to hear that the particular way our intrepid warriors see this time of great change is strongly aligned with their mission to expand Third consciousness. J&J combine sweeping views of history (which I must admit at times run the risk of being simplistic) with contemporary understanding of relationship and family dynamics. To this mix they add their unique proclivity for seeing the world through an intimate erotic lens. A good example is how they framed the transition from the goddess era to the patriarchy using an apocryphal story of a queen in the former time falling in love with her "king for a year"—a shepherd. That version of the evolutionary story led to describing the patriarchy as a five-thousand year period of adolescent male development that unfolded concurrently with the often violent submergence of women and the divine feminine in general.

Looking at these past five thousand years in terms of intimate relationship, as unusual as that may seem, is quite important now because humans are in fact making a transition into an era in which Eros will eventually flourish. It is time for everyone to learn how to use an intimate lens to view both the past and the evolutionary future. To those of us who steward Third consciousness, the deepening and expansion of intimacy are essential ingredients of the *Great Turning*.

Alternatively, J&J also talked of the patriarchy as the period of the "son" trying to become a man worthy of the identity, *lover of the goddess*. Since this perspective describes the transition out of the patriarchy in tangible relational terms, I want to share a sons and lovers story with you now. J&J's idea is simple: Every man, at least those born into any of the Abrahamic cultures, has a son in his inner council—that is, his psychic makeup—yearning to be a man who has overcome his fear of the divine feminine, whether he is conscious of it or not. Some men have traveled a great distance along this path while others are still battling through the rough terrain at the journey's beginning. This means that most men are in an internal Oedipal triangle with themselves (as well as with the father figures in their lives), battling a stern father who might speak to them as a jealous Yahweh or a wrathful Allah or some other more tangible external authority, such as leader, teacher, priest or boss. Usually, the greater the man's proclivity for religion, the more intense the battle. No wonder so many women and an increasing number of men are discovering rebellious, angry, insecure sons hiding under the cover of paternalistic Abrahamic patriarchs. Despite the mystical power of revelation that is also a part of the Abrahamic tradition, the day-to-day effect of all these inner and outer conflicts tends to limit seeing intimate relationship as a spiritual path, particularly for fundamentalists.

Then there are the endless battles among male "father-gods" that have manifested in the ongoing holy wars that have so bloodied history during the patriarchal era. These horrific results of a competitive reading of the first commandment ('My *god is the one true god, so your god is a false god*') have been devastating enough in human lives. But the battle between all our current father gods and the primal mother goddess out of which they all emerged is also pernicious, not only because of the violence it has generated against women, but also because the struggle continues intensely inside both the male and female human psyches to this day. Just as Yahweh evolved to battle the great mother goddess in the first part of the Hebrew era, men continue to rebel against their internalizations of the divine feminine in a variety of (mostly unconscious) ways. In other words, the story of the queen and the shepherd is still going on for many men. So what is needed is nothing less than a wide-spread evolutionary commitment among men and women to work out these primal gender issues along the spiritual path of intimate relationship.

J&J take on this assignment directly for which I am grateful. The consequences in terms of their relationship's dynamics have not always been pretty, particularly in the earlier years, but their willingness to persevere is admirable. More currently these bumps in the road (as Jack optimistically calls them) are sometimes triggered by seemingly minor personal events that can be traced to the major evolutionary issues lying under the surface. My next story will give you an example. Let's pick up J&J as Jack is about to dedicate an evening council. A small plate of fruit, two chocolates and a half glass of wine sit by the Third's pillow.

"I light this candle in honor of authenticity. Our integrity has been deepening but if a relationship is going to fully embrace Third consciousness, the couple has to journey *'out beyond all knowing of right-doing and wrong-doing,'* to paraphrase my favorite Rumi poem. Even though they are challenging and humbling, the bumps along our road provide opportunities for learning. Our interaction today did, in fact, create a shift."

"We need to talk about that," Jaquelyn responded. "When I wanted to come in with you this afternoon to make sure Charles saw the rash on your back, you hesitated. You didn't actually say anything but what I heard was, 'I'm not going to be treated like a son or a baby. You don't have to come with me to tell my dermatologist what to do.'"

"You're right! My inner son got activated in that moment. If you had been in an erotic mood and said to the nurse, 'I'm the keeper of his lover's body so I get to come,' I would have had a totally different reaction."

"That's exactly what I did say!"

"Yes, but not until five minutes later when we were sitting in the exam room waiting for Charles," Jack argued, "not when we were standing in the hall when you first asked to come in. My son came out then because of the tone of your voice. The nurse also resisted your request because that's their policy and I got caught between the two of you. It was an awkward moment. Looking back, it's clear that the universe produced that interaction so I could see a part of my son that was still unconscious. Whether you meant it that way or not, I heard a mother telling her teen-age boy, 'I need to be with you and Charles to be sure you ask him the right questions.'"

"Yes, because you can't see the rash on your back! You still don't know what those bumps look like."

"It has nothing to do with whether I've seen them or not." Jack argued. "Charles will treat any important defects on my back."

"Not true."

"That's because you care about aesthetics as well as medicine, since I'm your lover."

"I want to bring his attention to the rash," Jaquelyn persisted, "because I don't think he takes enough notice of cosmetic matters."

"So you are in judgment of Charles and telling me I need a consult from another doctor." They both started laughing at the absurdity of the dialog. "Anyway, in that moment the tone of your voice triggered my son. We're beyond right- and wrong-doing here, remember? This banal interaction can serve us. Lately, I've been looking at the remnants of my 'son' so I can grow him up to be your mature lover. That's my primary intention now. Of course, when I choose to be the son *consciously*, we can both enjoy the dance."

"Like when I cut your hair and take care of your cuts and bruises."

"Yes but for the son to be fully conscious requires healing of all the oedipal stuff—including the years of dancing in our triangle with Richard. When enough men have done their oedipal work, evolution can move onward."

"Leaving the patriarchy behind," Jaquelyn added with a smile.

"Exactly," Jack took a deep breath. "In this moment I call for the total demise of the patriarchal era for us. I commit my still emerging man-ness to join my love for you."

"Ho! The man's unconscious attachments to the mother keep the goddess and her lover from truly seeing and knowing each other. Although the transition from son to lover begins early in life, the process obviously continues right into elderhood. Vestiges of the son are hard to eliminate."

"Yes and it helps," Jack added, "if the woman can let go her attachment and possessiveness as well. You possessed me for a flash there in Charles' office."

"But you *are my baby*." (laughter)

"In years past, when my son was present unconsciously, I suspect I was engulfed by the great mother at some point during our lovemaking. When the son goes unconscious, he pulls the man in with him and they both burn in the confusion of the oedipal fire. The unconscious son blocks the deepening of love."

"It's an oedipal death rather than an oedipal victory."

"Exactly," Jack affirmed, delighted they were on the same page. "Once the man has individuated his son—and, of course, the woman has done the same with her daughter—then intimacy can expand dramatically. When the lover of the goddess reaches that level, his woman actually experiences her divinity. He doesn't need to say much."

"I do feel my goddessness in your love. But what about my daughter? You love that part of me. I don't want to get rid of her."

"I do love her. Getting rid of the daughter or son is not the goal. Individuation means becoming conscious of those underlying patterns and transforming rather than eliminating them. Your daughter is pretty individuated already. The only part that isn't is the descendent of the young rebel who told your father to take his Christianity and stuff it. The residual unconsciousness of that rebel shows up in the Amazon queen and in your still lingering, mostly negative, attachment to Christianity."

"I did get married the first time just to have sex in wedlock," Jaquelyn remembered, "so even at the midst of my rebellion I played the game."

"Obviously, the residual of the Christian imprint is much more subtle now, because your sexuality is so pervasive. The rebellious daughter and her mother the rebel queen are wild and ready for anything. The Christian mind imprint doesn't stand a chance. We can make love like teen-agers at times when the daughter is up. Now your sexual wisdom shines through everyone in your inner council, so even the Christian remnants can't hide when we're really aroused. So, yes, you're well on your way to individuating the daughter and there are only a few Christian shards left to clean up."

"I think my rebel is less benign in other parts of my life, like when I dash off an email in anger and have to spend hours later cleaning up the mess."

"Yes, that's the queen and her anger mostly about the patriarchy. You do need to take care of that. However, clearing our relationship of the patriarchy is mostly about the son growing up. It seems to me that sons are more in the way than daughters because the sons have been hiding behind patriarchal disguise. There are lots of mature women around, daughters and all, who are ready to boogie with a grown up man. As I integrate the son, I can be more wildly sexual and affectionate simultaneously. The passion has been there since the beginning and grows stronger all the time. As our love expands, it balances the passion and helps us to stay conscious even under the spell of our sexuality."

"I'm not sure I understand what you're talking about. The love and passion are all together for me."

"Yes, that's because all members of your inner council share a common sexual awareness and wisdom," Jack responded. "For me—and many men—affection and passion are not so seamless. Because of the patriarchal imprint, we have to learn to bring those fundamental streams together. The state of love inherently supports being conscious, while passion inevitably tempts us into unconsciousness. When they are both present and integrated, the passion is more conscious and the couple can explore radically new erotic territory."

"All that seems complicated," Jaquelyn confessed. "It all happens naturally for me. I don't think about it like you do."

"When we're making love, I don't think about it either. It's when we're in council that my curiosity about the process arises. My job is to understand how it works so I can share what we learn with others."

"I'm glad that's your assignment and not mine, but tell me more about the affection you feel. It sounds like you're able to witness our lovemaking even when we're deeply in it. Is that the result of the affection?"

"Yes!" Jack said enthusiastically. "Love allows for more witnessing. Passion is not as conducive to self-witnessing by its very nature. So the more conscious we are, the wilder the territory we can explore. That's why our lovemaking gets more wondrous all the time."

Jaquelyn could feel he was moving towards lovemaking—and she wasn't finished with the conversation. "Can we dedicate some of our energy to Chelsey and all the women in the family?"

"I would love to do that . . . Here's to Chelsey—and all our daughters. May they realize all the powerful magnetism of their woman-ness and still know by experience that men are more than iron filings."

Jaquelyn laughed. "You're cute tonight. The poet-lover is alive and well."

"And here's to the sons too—Bruce, Eric and Richard . . . I remember the way Bruce used to look at me, years ago, when I would talk about you and me. He'd give me a sly smile and say 'You'll never be able to handle her power; she's too much for any man.'"

"He may have been projecting."

"Yes," Jack agreed, "but his attitude got me in touch with how long and arduous the path of growing up the son can be."

"As I said before, a natural early marker in the transition from son to lover is when the young man becomes more interested in sex and procreativity than protection and nourishment. Those changes have to take place in the body too. All of him has to be involved, not just his mind."

"Yes, and then he begins the journey of developing his worldly king and warrior, which can take quite a while. But the lover needs even greater maturity. Eventually, transcending mother-love doesn't mean rebelling against it or detouring around it either. To be a lover he has to fully embrace his relationship to mother in his sexual body. That means full oedipal clarity—not a common state of consciousness."

"Freud questioned whether that was possible," Jaquelyn interjected.

"We think it is, but I didn't have a real glimpse of the Eros world beyond mother until I met you. Growing up I rebelled against my mother attachment by taking out non-Jewish girls almost exclusively and being drawn to daughters. I acted out the oedipal drama without much awareness. When we met I still had the perspective of a man attached to his mother, although I would have argued vehemently if you had told me so at the time. I gradually began to come out of my attachment as the group ended and we started our relationship. It was only then that I began to see the world beyond mother, where the man can become the lover of the goddess. You know that old expression, 'playing in the fields of the lord.' Well, you and I are playing in the fields of the goddess now. That's Rumi's field. To get there the man has to know the solid ground of mother under his feet. Then mother-stuff doesn't shape his behavior unconsciously—and his lover and his magus capabilities can flower . . .Do you remember when my mother came to me in meditation after she died to tell me she approved of you?"

"She knew you had a woman that would bring out the full man in you."

"Yes, it was as if she knew that I would finally work through all the early identities of my life: good student, competent intellect, good father, successful professional, etc.—and finally see myself as lover."

"But didn't you always love a lot of people?" Jaquelyn wondered.

"Yes, but now my *identity* is being your lover."

"Well, then get to it! Surrender finally and be a man who can love without any patriarchal imprint. You know what that means, don't you?"

"That I will love all women, eventually," Jack responded. "You could become any woman you choose and I would become her lover." He looked at her with what can only be described as awe. "It's a miracle, Sweetheart."

"I know. It's because you smell so good—much better than you used to. I smell sweetness because of the love. There's nothing more manly than a full surrender to love . . . I just thought about Bruce again and wondered if he and I are still attached to each other in a subtle way. I have to admit that I lean on the way Bruce loves me. He never has to say anything; I just feel and know it. He would die for me. He loves me that much."

"How do you lean on his love?"

"It somehow makes up for the rejection I feel from Richard sometimes," Jaquelyn responded. "It's so hard for Richard to acknowledge any love, so Bruce balances him, literally. But I don't want to do anything that would hold Bruce—or Richard—back. So let me know if you see me holding on unconsciously."

"Just posing the question will help. Bruce seems so strong and capable, so the first place to look is in yourself. Are you using Bruce's love to hold yourself or us back in any way?"

"I never looked at that before, so I don't know if using Bruce to balance Richard is a problem."

"No, that seems alright to me," Jack responded. "Obviously, there are more challenges with some children than with others, so balancing them all seems OK. The only situation that would hold us back—and Bruce as well—would be if you rely on him for love in a way that's outside our relationship. Is there some escape hatch marked 'Bruce' that would allow you to deal with the pain of feeling separated from me in some way? Can you imagine a situation in which you would use the way Bruce loves you to compensate for some lack in our relationship?"

"It's hard to imagine such a situation but it's possible. When you act like the Lone Ranger and I feel left out, I could imagine thinking that Bruce would never do that. I don't think I've ever had that thought, but I can imagine having it."

"Subtleties are important as we go deeper. I pledge to love you in a way that will never tempt either of us to use our children to compensate for a lack in our relationship. That's the biggest gift I can give Bruce or any of our children."

Jaquelyn was silent for a moment. "I wonder if it was my sexuality that Bruce was talking about when he saw me as so powerful. I was working on my chapter about Christianity today, trying to get at why men were so scared of women's sexuality that they had to suppress and control it violently. I had an insight that the goddess force in evolution, whatever it is, has both a biological streak and a wanton streak. The biological streak has to do with reproduction occurring, which is life-affirming and not at all malicious."

"And how about the wanton streak? Was that present during the goddess era?"

"It must have been there to arise later because there was no reason for it then. Maybe wantonness came out later as women became suppressed and had only a few healthy ways of expressing their innate passionate sexuality. The goddess was not going to tolerate total repression so she used her powers to seduce men with irresistible magnetism."

"Which made men feel justified in controlling erotic femininity even further," Jack added. "That's one of patriarchy's many vicious circles."

The conversation had whetted their appetites in various ways, so they began by eating a strawberry from the garden, which triggered a natural wave of sensuality. "Let's eat the dried apricots next," Jaquelyn suggested. "They are a gift from nature. I have such fun sitting here in the bedroom, like I did today, working on my book and looking out at the ocean and watching you in the garden."

"What a blessing! Let's eat these last apricots and then we can have the chocolates in bed," Jack suggested. They ate the dried fruit in a ceremonial way. "Now it's time for the last sip of wine. Drinking the last of her blood means we are her full devotees in this moment."

Their devotion unfolded further after they ended the council and held each other in an embrace meditation. Jack let the images of Chelsey and then all women, known and unknown, become a part of his love for Jaquelyn. She celebrated that expansion in her body. All the women they imagined danced with goddess devotion until their collective power transported the lovers' bodies beyond imagery into the fullness of Rumi's Field. In that landscape of love there was no need for words.

31 ❧ Love or Die!

As the spring of 2010 headed towards summer, J&J found themselves talking more and more about the connection between deep sexual communion and death. Jack's insights often arose by plowing the fertile ground between physics, metaphysics and relationship dynamics. In contrast Jaquelyn's wisdom increasingly arrived through a kind of direct transmission from what seemed to be the divine feminine. That often took Jack's breath away.

For example, they were talking about the Big Bang again one evening, using Jaquelyn's image of the "orgasm of creation." A quarter-filled glass of red wine rested on the floor between them. Jack is speaking.

"The question still remains about what created that incredible high density mass that became the Big Bang. There's always another question. It's worth noting how the pace of evolution has a lot to do with how intensely people live deep spiritual questions. The old ones responsible for what we know as the Abrahamic bibles were courageous in their own way. Considering the level of consciousness then, how they dealt with fear was quite sophisticated—up to a point. But as the patriarchy began to evolve, the fears of the mainstream male leaders apparently became overwhelming and they stopped asking the deeper questions, consolidated their bibles and proclaimed that scripture provided timeless answers to life's deepest mysteries. That may have been OK for a while but, from our present perspective, the situation is no longer tolerable. Facing fear with fixed scripture does not support *living* the deepest questions. Instead a certain level of fear becomes encoded in the culture's spiritual life. The Abrahamic cultures, all with bibles fixed in time, are at a point now where that level of fear clearly leads to increasingly destructive behavior. It's time to live the great questions again and create a new vision."

"The basic fears are those of death and man's fear of woman," Jaquelyn continued the thread, "which the Hebrews tied together neatly in the Garden of Eden story. The patriarchal era was born out of that bundling of fears. Now thousands of years later, we can see that the three traditional bibles no longer realistically ease our anxiety about death and most men are still afraid of women to varying degrees, whether consciously or not."

"Fortunately the wisdom of the early sages also lay in recording enough of the stories and myths to reveal the limitations of the conclusions they drew from them. That has allowed us to reconstruct the stories as part of a bridge to a new mythology. I hope we show at least as much wisdom as we evolve and document our story."

"We are offering a whole new way of facing the fear of death through an erotic path of awakening. Preparing for the crossing erotically has clearly become our approach now."

"Yes, our intimacy is creating a 'goddess stairway,'" Jack went on. "Each time we make love, we create another step and leave a marker—the *illuminata* we've called them. The stairway connects the physical and spirit worlds, and seems like a spiral to me with one end centered in this life and the other in that part of existence we call death. With each step along the spiral we're learning more about how we can make the crossing consciously and together."

"There's only a sip of wine left," Jaquelyn announced. "Shall we finish it off now?"

Jack nodded and allowed the sirah to touch his lips gently. Then he handed her the glass and she drank the last few drops. "Being aware that we're drinking the blood of the goddess makes me think again of the time when the queen and her circle of priestesses drank the blood of the king ceremonially at the end of his one-year reign."

346

"Don't forget the blood-drinking part of that story has never been authenticated and might be what the Hebrew scribes created to justify the aggressive policies of the emerging patriarchy. We don't really know."

Jack nodded. "In any event our version of the old myth offers a transition into the present. The chosen man had to love and be loved by the queen if he was to live more than a year, so the challenge to love or die was at least mythologically literal during the end of the goddess era. When this practice was eradicated by the patriarchy, it went underground for millennia and now is emerging again in a more sophisticated way as a powerful erotic teaching along the path of relationship. The contemporary empowered woman says, 'Love me or die'—die in the sense of not living a fully awakened and loving life with her. The woman then adds more playfully and seductively, 'Love me *and* die,' since, if you do become my lover, you will be putting an end to the illusion that you're a separate individual with a well-defined identity. That's a very different kind of death."

"That's brilliant honey! Love me and/or die says it all. I love it. That's the battle cry of the goddess now! You've been talking about 'dying into the Third' for a long time."

"Until we bring love into the field of death, we haven't really been tested and so we don't really know what love is. That's an old teaching, of course and, by the way, also the moral of the Kali-Siva story."

"I'm so grateful to be shown this path." Jaquelyn's voice was soft and loving. "My fear of losing our kind of erotic love is stronger now than my fear of death."

"What an incredible statement."

"I've always felt that way."

"That's the essence of the woman's innate gift," Jack responded with a touch of wonder. "It begins with the love for her child—a love that has faced death at least since the beginning of human evolution. Rather than feeling put down by her power or competitive, as in the past, a man on the lover's path is challenged to match her love as a way of confronting his own fear of death more *directly* rather than through scriptural dogma. Meeting that challenge requires a new kind of male courage because being so vulnerable goes against the patriarchal image of what it means to be a man."

"Being a lover is terrifying!"

"When a man enters a woman he loves in that way—whether he knows it or not—he's actually returning to his source and so completing the cycle of life."

"Yes," Jaquelyn affirmed, "to return to the womb as lover takes the courage to return to the source of life."

"I want to be that lover tonight in a way that allows us to fulfill the dream of the ancient goddess."

"Sounds good to me! I trust that the core of our union is magnetic enough to face our remaining fears."

"The unknown calls us," Jack went on, "and we've come to trust the call because of the wondrous harvest of Eros, each time we say, 'yes.' As the goddess emerges in the woman, she shows the man the new landscape of her mystery—and his mission is to explore the unknown terrain with her. Those are the new vistas that keep arising during our lovemaking. As more couples do this practice, each in their own way, women's collective consciousness will expand, the new lover-goddess will manifest and the patriarchal era will recede."

"That's our evolutionary vision, but first, men have to acknowledge and forgive women's power."

"Yes, acknowledgment and forgiveness are parts of the practice. I finally get that now. I also see that the courage I need to be your lover tonight means being fully in the writer's voice without any of my usual insecurities. The doubt about being the writer is really the doubt about being the lover."

"Knowing our relationship," Jaquelyn challenged him, "it's hard for me to see how you can have any lover's doubt."

"I suppose it's still the residual imprint of the patriarchy in me, just as you find the footprints of Christianity along your goddess-path . . . You look so beautiful tonight. I love your hair that way."

"I got tired of my frizzy hair today, so I tied it back like an old-fashioned high school girl of the 1950s. That's when I came into my real sexual power, just from having pretty legs, and looking people right in the eye, I guess."

They pulled down the covers and settled into an embrace meditation. Soon the goddess was singing, this time of the pain of longing for her lover and the joy of finding him finally after waiting eons. They made love for a long time, long enough to work up an appetite for some dark chocolate and vanilla-Swiss-almond Haagen-Dazs which they devoured with relish.

"I had a full body orgasm," Jaquelyn reported over the Haagen-Dazs. "Your whole body was coming too—energetically. In patriarchal times the woman said, 'If you don't love me, I'll die.' Now, as we transition into the era of Eros, she says, 'If you don't love me, you'll die.' That's it! That's the evolutionary answer to the patriarchy. For thousands of years, men have been making woman live by the first version. Now the second version can and will be spoken."

"If I couldn't touch you and make love with you, it would be like a death in many ways," Jack acknowledged. "I accept that."

Jaquelyn watched him turn out the small lamp on the dresser and open the window a little. "You're so sexy," she said in a voice that translated directly into, "I want more." He got the message.

They moved into an embrace meditation immediately and in a few moments she reached for his cock. "You don't want me to feel neglected, do you?" she teased. The goddess spread her legs and took hold of him. He slipped easily into the scissors position and let her have her way. When she stroked her vulva with his again erect phallus, she let out a groan of pure joy. There was no pain about the long dark winter of the patriarchy in her songs this time. She sang with the gentle passion of reconciliation. "Love or die is the mantra that connects us to the old story," Jaquelyn said in the timeless voice of woman just before they fell asleep.

32 ❧ Intimacy as a Lifeline

As you know so well by now, J&J saw their councils and lovemaking as ceremonial practices along the path of relationship—and there were other kinds of rituals that occasionally played an important role as well.

Around the time of their move to Hawaii, one such sacrament entered their lives through a close friend's passionate interest in the shamanic practices of the indigenous Peruvian culture. J&J participated in a series of challenging traditional ayahuasca/chacuna ceremonies she arranged which, in turn, led to semi-annual adventures of a more contemporary nature led by their friend and an experienced shaman with Peruvian roots. J&J participated in a number of these two-day journeys over a period of several years. The shaman utilized a wide range of substances—all legal—including various combinations of the traditional ayahuasca vine and other plants (but not chacuna). These second generation medicines avoided purging and yet were quite effective, particularly in the exploration of deeply hidden shadows.

For the most part these journeys were warmly shared experiences for the small on-going group involved (a novel feature of this particular shaman's approach to ceremony) during which J&J often played the role of relationship elders. Their friend set the field with meditation and guided imagery before the shaman offered his teachings and intuitively provided each person the substance he felt they needed at that particular time. The ceremony extended into the night with spontaneous interactions occurring among most of the participants. J&J usually ended up receiving visitors in their corner of the meeting room, particularly those who wanted to talk about initiating or deepening their intimate relationships.

In late August of 2010 J&J traveled to the mainland to visit Chelsey and her family in Phoenix, after which they flew to California to attend one of these shamanic ceremonies. For this particular occasion Jaquelyn decided to use the more familiar cannabis as her medicine while Jack was given a new substance that took him to a place he had never been before—the twilight of his life. He felt ancient, and walked and talked like a man in his nineties on the rim of death. During the journey he was possessed with a range of fears and insecurities, even needing help from others to move around the room. As long as he was in physical contact with Jaquelyn he was basically OK, but even then, he saw shadows everywhere. Fortunately, the darkness of his journey was somewhat balanced by a simultaneous—and dramatic—sense of the evolution of consciousness that he envisioned would reach critical proportions by 2012. Although shaken for days after the experience, Jack worked hard to use the teachings to enlighten his relationship with Jaquelyn and, in particular, their exploration of the crossing yoga practices.

We catch up with J&J shortly after they returned home from California in early September, a few weeks after the ceremony. As usual we find them in the middle of a council. Jaquelyn is speaking.

"Since we have been back, I've been thinking about what you said about being so vulnerable after the ceremony. You explained it in terms of letting go parts of yourself, but my understanding of something like that happens through my body, so I still don't get it."

"In this moment my letting go is best described as the death of the patriarchy in me," Jack explained. "We've seen how the deepening of our erotic life is moving us along the path to fusion. At the same time, our personalities are so different, that we face aesthetic challenges in maintaining a cohesive merged entity. We handle that by living in Third consciousness more of the time, which is why our personal selves feel like they're disappearing. That is also the state we need to be in as we approach the crossing."

"That's your experience. My aesthetic sense is not being violated. The merging is a joyous experience for me and I appreciate it fully. I hear you saying that it's stressful for you."

Jack felt a touch of frustration. "You asked me what I had to let go of and I was in the middle of explaining when you assumed that I was feeling upset about our merging—which is not the case at all. We're not communicating very well. I've noticed that we've been struggling trying to connect with each other for several days now."

"You mean since we got back?" Jaquelyn asked.

"It actually started during the ceremony with Bernardo, so my extreme vulnerability during the journey may be part of it. We're in an ongoing process of consciously dying and being reborn every time we make love—at least that's the way I see it right now. It's different for you. During the ceremony I had the feeling that I could have died—literally—were it not for our physical connection. I went to places from which I felt I would never have returned had you not been with me, touching me. In a way I gave you my life-line, which is directly contrary to the patriarchal way for men. Women know that state of consciousness because they hold their children's life-line for years. During the ceremony I entered the state of consciousness of a needy elder at the end of life. You took care of me like a mother."

"I understand. You were and still are having feelings that transcend patriarchal masculinity."

"That's what the man has to go through on our path," Jack emphasized.

"You have to know what it is to be fully dependent, which means really facing the dark side of the patriarchy. So many men are afraid of exactly what you're going through, which is sharing the power to control your life with a woman."

"Yes, you have an innate gift for merging and living in relational consciousness. I, and almost every other man I know, have to work hard to get there. That includes taking the risk of 'getting ahead of the medicine,' as they say in the shamanic world."

"Ah, tell me more," Jaquelyn asked.

"The stakes are high. It's like the famous Baal Shem story about his early training. He's in the forest with another novitiate and they find a magic parchment in a clearing. The Baal Shem says we're not ready to read those esoteric secrets but the other guy can't resist, so the Baal Shem hides in the trees while his friend starts reading the old teachings. Suddenly a huge burst of fire strikes the friend and consumes him."

"I get it, but how are we getting ahead of the medicine?"

"We're being shown a new kind of relational alchemy with love-making as the core practice," Jack explained. "We're merging more now, as if we're making love all the time. When we're fully attentive to our connection, we're relatively safe, but we are still new at this—at least I am. So I risk burning up if we lose our connection in any significant way. The being I'm looking at with awe—your wondrous fuzzy head and lovely body and craziness and brilliance—all of that is my life-line now. When a man loves a woman as I love you, he's saying that who she is, the particular way she manifests the goddess's magic, is exactly what he needs to be fully alive and healthy. That was literally what I went through during the ceremony. I went right to the edge of life, hanging on to you. You saw my deepest fears, as well as my trust and confidence in our connection."

"We're in this together all the way," Jaquelyn affirmed.

"Ho! That's putting it mildly. We're *becoming* together is more accurate."

"It's funny you talk about life-lines. I've been clinging to you lately, wanting to be near you. Your body is like a magnet for me. I can smell our intimacy all the time now."

"What you call `smell' is so important since it relates to our animal nature," Jack observed.

"It's more like sensing with your nose, not really smelling."

"Yes, it's like what Castaneda called *seeing*, which he always wrote out in italics. You're *seeing* what's happening through the olfactory metaphor. Scent is the most primitive of the senses and touches our deepest memories. The word 'smell' startles people as well. Smelling is the way you read the field. You've been doing that since the early days of our relationship."

"Definitely," Jaquelyn agreed. "It's like a spiritual sense for me. That's what makes it jazzy."

"What also makes it jazzy are the intimate implications of the word smell. When you say to someone, I see you or I'm aware of you, it doesn't have the same impact as saying, I *smell* you. The magic arises from using intimate physical terms to describe the spiritual world."

"The magic is part of the goddess's spiritual scent."

"Which enlivens Third consciousness," Jack continued her thought, "and the goddess needs the Third to manifest."

"Yes, the goddess expresses herself through Third consciousness and embodies that energy.

"Sometimes I see relational consciousness as a network that moves in an undulating kind of way, with awareness flowing through it—like an immense neurological field. We are part of the grid in different ways at different times. In effect, the Third increasingly provides us a matrix for life."

"It's like an expansive aura in a way," Jaquelyn added.

"I just had a flash about why I lost my old wedding ring. I hadn't really thought about it until this moment."

"Remind me how it got lost."

"I don't really know," Jack explained. "I just looked down at my finger during a meeting and it was gone. I have no idea how or where I lost it. I wore those two interlocking simple gold bands for thirty-five years! They represented our becoming interwoven and inseparable. We've finally achieved that state, so my ring had served its purpose and disappeared. Now interweaving is moving into merging, so we need a new ring for the next cycle."

"Which needs to be a symbol of fusion," Jaquelyn continued his thought. "How about one like mine with the man and the woman in an embrace meditation?"

"Amazing. I had the same image just a few seconds ago."

"I have the earrings you gave me with the same design. I love them but they weigh my ears down. We could weld the two figures in the earring to a solid band."

"Let's do it!" Jack exclaimed. "We've been talking about intimacy as an ongoing death and rebirth process for a long time. Maybe we're actually ready now to enter a new marriage that will manifest the practice. You have a continuously evolving lover!"

"Life is moving so fast now."

"Yes and my behavior is more erratic lately, which is disarming."

"Stern and less affectionate is how I would describe it," Jaquelyn added. "When I feel the gruffness I get mad at you sometimes. But I know I'll get over it, as long as you don't hound me to find out why I'm mad. You'd save a lot of our energy if you'd let me get over my reactions on my own sometimes."

"You're right about the gruffness and I do need to give you more space sometimes."

"Maybe you don't realize that I am also growing and changing every time we make love. That's been going on for months and months. I'm being transformed too."

"How could I not be aware of that?"Jack responded. "Two very different people with radically different cultural backgrounds are merging. We're becoming an entity. Our Third is juicy. That's why we've been useful to others at times. Every time we make love we leave spiritual flesh inside the other."

"That's a good way to describe the merging."

"The path of the man is simple. He learns to love the manifestations of the goddess in his woman as she becomes increasingly empowered. At some point in the journey he may be attracted to other women, but once he takes on being the lover of the goddess that no longer happens, not so much through restraint but because he discovers *his Beloved is already all women*. If the man is not ready to love her as all women, his ability to reflect her divinity is diffused and their relationship plateaus. They get stuck or she may even decide to look elsewhere. But, if the man faces his fear and is present for all of her, including the wild and destructive parts, she can see herself in the wholeness of his love and come into more and more of her goddessness."

Jaquelyn nodded and continued their shared thought. "Making the more challenging aspects of the goddess bad or sinful, creating categories of good and evil, is when the trouble starts. This may be hard for many men to understand at first because they don't think they have the power to deal directly with the divine in their woman. They have given that power away to the gods of traditional religion."

"Yes," Jack agreed, "and so they may even call what we advocate blasphemous. Discovering the divinity in another is obviously a risky experiment. More of us need to take that risk."

"The earth is over-run with notions of the divine, most of them off the mark. *She* is missing from virtually all of them. It's obvious that the feminine brings life into this world. That has to be at the core of any path to the divine."

"Yes and for a while we explored the notion of a divine couple. But, if I had to give a new definition of what goddess-god really is at this evolutionary time, the one that comes the closest to what we're learning is, simply, *she-he is an experiment.*"

"That provides a good context for devoted spiritual scientists," Jaquelyn affirmed.

"That definition removes the externalized divine as an object of our focus and puts the emphasis on the evolutionary process. From that perspective, people can more clearly witness how they've created their divine figures in the past."

"The conclusion seems clear to me. We can do much better than we've been doing! We have to do better."

Jack wanted further insight. "So back to my grumpiness. I suspect it has to do with the friction in our merging—and we are really merging. That's not just a metaphor. The way we love each other allows for the very different histories and aesthetics to magically share a growing state of common consciousness . . . Your foot is like an electric socket. Do you feel it?"

A moment before, while Jack had been talking, Jaquelyn had moved her foot so that her toes rested on his leg."Yes, of course I feel that. After all the words, the main thing is that you are a man and I am a woman."

"That boils it down to essentials!"

They fell silent for a moment shifting the focus to where their bodies were touching. The erotic door opened quickly, particularly for Jaquelyn. "I can feel you inside me right now, filling me."

The silence that followed invited Jack to cross the threshold. "Your words shifted my consciousness to my body and I became aware of my genitals. Now the tumescent process begins. The way our bodies prepare to make love is like a dance. The music is created by your fingers playing on my tumescent keyboard. As your lover, I provide you with an instrument on which you can play tumescent tunes."

"That lead to goddess songs."

"*Tumescent tunes and goddess songs.* Now there's a subtitle!" (laughter)

"That's got to be at least a chapter title," Jaquelyn added with a smile. "Anyway, even though you've been gruff, I still feel your love underneath the crust in a way that I never have before. The flow is steady now."

Jaquelyn's words took him home in a flash. "You're my lover and my life. A person who has tasted the end of life arose out of the recent ceremony with Bernardo. When we make love now we're going to be moving in and out of the veil, literally. It feels as if our love is expanding beyond life itself."

"It seems like I've been in that state for quite a while. What you're describing feels familiar to me."

"I hear you. *She's been waiting, waiting* . . . Part of the art of being a lover that I'm learning from you is the ability to be in stillness without a trace of passivity. You've wanted that for a long time. Now that I'm also learning how to live in the veil between the worlds, I see that stillness is part of a radical change in our sense of time. Time in the veil is different and stillness is what makes it so. I suspect there is an absence of any predisposed movement in the veil. It's more like one is perpetually on the edge of movement."

"That is just how our lovemaking feels when we're fully interpenetrating and not moving," Jaquelyn added enthusiastically. "That place is where the goddess reigns. We're both creative in our own ways but it's the combination that really serves the world."

"What an exquisite opportunity I have been given. There's this unfathomable energy manifest in a beautiful body complete with swells and breasts and the holiest of holies. I get to make love with all of it

and feel it change like the ocean or a multicolored forest in the fall
. . . And then as we fuse, we get closer to glimpsing *the experiment*."

"Yes, to glimpsing the *nature* of the experiment, or to the *possibilities* of the experiment or even to the *outcome* of the experiment."

"That all began with dense matter the size of a pea—or an orange or whatever they're saying now—and has finally reached an evolutionary state in which co-creation of the future is actually possible."

Just then all the lights wavered, dimmed noticeably . . . and stayed subdued.

"I like it better this way," Jaquelyn purred, "as long as they don't go out. You seem so precious and delicious to me in this moment. I want to absorb you and it's a little easier to do that in the dimmer light when your features are less distinct."

"I wonder what it will be like for you to make love with a man who is exploring veil consciousness."

"That sounds a little like work. I just want to melt into you and totally merge."

"You're embodying a powerful energy right now," Jack observed, "maybe more powerful than I've ever felt before. I'm honored that you let me see this part of you."

"Does it have a smell for you?"

"Yes, the smell of tumescence. Tumescence is a major part of what we talk about now—which raises a good question. What's a woman's tumescence?"

"Secreting juices and nipples becoming taut and the awakening of her flesh—and a lot more," Jaquelyn answered immediately.

"I'm touching you already sitting way over here. We can image our lovemaking so strongly now."

"Tangibly! I'm spreading wide and bringing you home. My Kundalini is awakening. Wow, I'm an easy lay tonight, Baby."

He laughed. "You an easy lay? You're an absolute inferno of passion, and we're still sitting three feet apart."

"Oh my dearest. It's been a loooong time." Jaquelyn's voice dropped to a whisper.

"The queen has waited for eons. Tonight feels like a culmination of the new marriage, a—what's the word that describes what you do after you get married? The word begins with a 'c.'"

"Celebrate?" Jaquelyn offered.

"It's a word for making love. What's the word?"

"Coitus?" (laughter)

"There's a word," Jack repeated. "We must be losing it. The word means acknowledging the marriage, recognizing it, grounding it."

"Forget the word and tell me exactly what you're feeling."

"Our new marriage is a ceremony of merging, even fusion now. When love becomes the fabric of life consciously, there's a quantum leap. You have been teaching me how to love in a way that brings you into goddessness. Then the ceremony in California brought me to my knees and showed me the ways in which you are my life-line. When a man on the path says, 'I die for your love,' those words become increasingly literal. And so a *Lover* is created, with a capital L that, in turn, allows the woman to release her full power."

Jaquelyn's face lit up. "I'm not aware of holding anything back but as soon as I discover more of the goddess, you'll be the first to know."

Jack got up on his knees and put his forehead on the carpet in front of her. "Are you alright," Jaquelyn asked.

"I'm bowing to what's emerging in our new marriage. Then I need to feel your whole body."

"Promises, promises."

"I want to feel the fullness of your power and passion."

"Be careful what you ask for, Darling." She wasn't kidding.

"I'm respectful—"

"I know."

"—and I'm here," he assured her. "Your face in this light is amazing. You look very young."

"I am young is some ways. Your tumescence is flowing. You're pumping it out."

"You're adorable. The power of your magnetism is extraordinary."

"It is simply my love for you," she said truthfully.

"What you emanate is the essence of embodied love—*consummation!*" Jack shouted the word. "That's the word we couldn't recall. We are going to consummate our merging in a new marriage tonight."

"Yes, as a celebration of the goddess's magnetic love."

Still on his knees, he lifted up his body to meet hers as she leaned forward in the rocker. Their faces were close now. They held that position for as long as they could withstand the pull of Eros. The embrace was gentle at first, largely in respect for its power and what they knew lay ahead.

"Your whole body is like a hot cock," the bride said.

"Exactly," the groom agreed.

Jack let the now familiar image of himself as a Siva shrine fill his inner screen, until it dissolved into the undulating grid of luminous color that had become the transition into full merging. Jaquelyn suggested they move to the bed, where they slowly prepared to be consumed by the fusion of love.

33 ✍ Songs of Evolution

When J&J awoke early the next morning and moved into an embrace meditation, they knew something had shifted. Remembering the dance with the word "consummation" they turned the story around and asked, "exactly what was the marriage we consummated last night?" As darkness eased into dawn, the simple clarity of early morning consciousness answered their question by offering a vision of a future event. Jack is speaking.

"I'm going to reach eighty a year from now and it will be your turn in January of 2012."

"Yes, if I can get my hair in shape, I'll look so good everybody will think you're a dirty old man."

"They think that already," Jack responded with a grin. "I'm remembering the council we called in California when we hit seventy. We had more than forty people in the circle. It was a great event."

"Do you want to have another circle next year?"

"After last night and this morning, I'm thinking about something more elaborate, like a gathering that might go on for a few days."

"We could make it a several day affair for friends and family," Jaquelyn suggested. "I bet a lot of people would come if we give them enough time to plan for it."

"We could have it here but traveling and finding places to stay would make it expensive."

"We could do it at the Ojai Foundation. That would take care of the accommodations and be a lot more accessible."

"Wow, what an idea!" Jack exclaimed. "It touches me that you thought of Ojai."

"Well it would be a healing all around, since the Foundation was your mistress for all those years, and it's a beautiful place to hold a big gathering."

"Let's do it!! I'm working at the pool today, so let's talk more about it tonight."

Restructuring the Honokaa Pool locker room roof in preparation for installing a new solar system turned out to be a strenuous job. Jack was challenged physically at first, but he gradually got into the flow and, as usual, enjoyed working with his regular co-volunteers, Joe, an engineer, and Greg, J&J's new resident caretaker. Greg had taken over the job a few months before, after Seppe and his family left. When Jack returned home, tired and with aching muscles, he nevertheless had enough energy left to suggest they have a council and make love. Jaquelyn readily accepted, eager to hold him in her arms again after missing him all day. Although the evening light was fading faster now that the Fall Equinox had passed, they started the council while reflections from the sunset still colored the meadow and garden with the familiar soft pinkish glow.

After lighting the candle, Jack began. "Greg began our lunch break by telling me that I had changed while we were away in California. 'What's going on,' he asked as we got out of his truck."

"Did you ask him to comment on the shift?"

"Yes, but all I could get out of him was that I seemed a bit more stressed out now."

"Not quite as flowing?" Jaquelyn asked.

"Yes, but he also said there seemed to be a shift in consciousness as well. Greg said he hadn't seen such a significant change take place in someone as stable as me in so short a time. His reflection was helpful, since it confirmed the changes that we've been discussing. So I told him about the ceremony and how my identity fragmented and blew away in the wind like those delicate dandelion seed pods. That was the image that came up for me. As I'm telling you the story now, I realize I'm being put back together after that dissolution, but in a new way. What was the name we used to give to being in two states of consciousness at the same time, way back at the Center for Healing Arts?"

"You mean *biplanar* consciousness?"

"Yes, that's the term," Jack recalled. "We were exploring that concept thirty years ago! We really didn't know what we were talking about then, but that's literally what seems to be happening now—finally. It's like I'm being re . . . re—"

"—programmed."

"Yes, that's a perfect word for it. The software is changing. I'm reforming a new identity around two centers of consciousness: One is located in the veil between the worlds and the other is planted in our familiar life as elders and devotees of evolutionary relationship. This broader base of awareness can embrace the crossing more fully and invite the divine to enter our life more directly."

"As the oneness created by two mature lovers." Jaquelyn extended the thought. "That has become our divinity."

"Yes, that's the core of it. Other couples may describe it differently, but in the new culture, each couple will find a community of couples—and singles too—with whom they can share deeply enough for there to be cohesion and mutual support of everyone's unique path. Communities of couples and singles will find ways to gather regularly, just like participants in the *Flesh and Spirit* intensives often want to continue meeting monthly in 'circles of lovers.' The flow of cultural life will be more cohesive through intimacy." Jack took a long drink of water to cool down. "As soon as something new arises, like biplanar consciousness just did, I bring it to the primary test—will it make me a more conscious lover of the goddess?"

"Besides being the right measure, asking that question helps us avoid falling into codependence and attachment."

Jack nodded. "I trust our Eros is strong enough for me to be in both veil and elderhood consciousness at the same time. To be able to enter you that way has got to expand our lovership, so it would seem biplanar awareness will pass the test."

"Actually, I think you're already entering me that way. That's one reason why I've been coming continuously lately. The goddess songs celebrate what you pour into me, which is already on various levels of consciousness. Making love with you is like being intimate with a variety of men."

"Thank you for that vote of confidence . . . And, speaking of variety, while I was doing mundane work today, I kept tuning into you, which led finally to taking on the identity of your 'workman husband.' You were home in our trailer with your curly hair. I was still working at my advanced age because we needed the money, like a lot of elders in town do now. I was feeling good about stretching into a less-familiar male consciousness, shared by so many men. I've worked hard all my life, but today was one of those days that had a different—"

"—flavor," Jaquelyn finished his thought once again.

"Yes, and perhaps learning to make love in both worlds could be useful to a broader group of people, whatever words we use to talk about it."

"We need to find the right words."

"OK, I'll be specific," Jack responded. "The cock that enters you tonight will be partly on the edge of the spirit world—in the veil—and partly very much in the physical world of my elder's body, which knows the ocean and the garden."

"You're a phallic hybrid, living in Third consciousness." (laughter)

"In many ways you seem to be already in that state, waiting to welcome me. But you don't actually know where you are until I show up."

"I have more fluid boundaries than you," Jaquelyn elaborated. "I'm not sure where I am."

"Yes, it's our ongoing story. You go some place and I track you so we can be together and make love. When we connect, I tell you where I think we are and then we explore the landscape together. Before long your curiosity entices you to explore further. The goddess is alive with creating herself. Since she represents the creative principle in you, you're perpetually re-creating yourself. 'Goddess' is not a fixed entity, and we get to share the more erotic aspects of her embodiment—lucky us!"

"An ideal assignment."

"When we make love you embody her fully," Jack affirmed. "That's why your songs are so powerful—awesome actually. And now I can enter you consciously as flesh and spirit— simultaneously! With what intentions would the goddess like to receive her lover tonight?"

"With the desire to dedicate our lovemaking to the needs of humanity—and all creatures—just as she has always done. By the way, your new wedding ring will be a symbol of what we are talking about."

"Having male and female figures intertwined on the ring will be the perfect manifestation of our new marriage. What happened with the rings is perfect."

"Yes," Jaquelyn agreed, "and, if the jewelers do it right, the ring will look like a single band even though the figures are distinct. That will represent exactly what we're celebrating. We're a fusion about to happen. The ring will be a glimpse of the state just before we disappear into a unified consciousness. That image will be on your finger forever."

"I just saw what we can do for our joint 80th birthday celebration next year! It's so obvious. I don't know why we didn't see it this morning when the idea of a gathering arose. We can celebrate our new elder marriage by renewing our vows! We'll invite our family and all our close friends and colleagues to celebrate the kind of intimate relationship that leads to the goddess singing her new evolutionary songs!"

"It seems to me that the goddess songs are becoming a celebration of the passage to the other side. I had no idea that could be part of sexuality! The fusion is so joyous that the preparation feels like a celebration."

"Songs of the crossing!" Jack said the words exuberantly. "Your songs are the bridge between the worlds. What we've been envisioning is actually happening!"

"Isn't that the way it's supposed to be?"

"You betcha! And tonight my cock is going to be literally made of interwoven flesh and spirit."

"I always take you in that way," Jaquelyn reminded him.

"You keep on saying that."

"But I love being made more aware of it."

"And when I enter you the fusion feels familiar?"

"Oh, yeah!"

"Of course," Jack exclaimed. "It's because you're already in goddess consciousness. I've tracked you there . . . It was a treat to be a carpenter today with you as my woman. The essence of our sexy spirit was so apparent."

"Did you feel me with you when you drove off this morning?"

"Yes, I saw you wave to Greg in the truck as we were pulling away. I waved back but I don't know if you saw me. The younger buddy was picking up his older buddy to go to work and the wife was waving goodbye. You knew the story we were about to play out. You had a good day just being you, and also being the woman in the story of my day."

Jaquelyn grinned. "I sent you huge batches of love when you drove out and Greg got caught in the action. Did you feel all that?"

"Yes! That's why the day unfolded the way it did. You actually created the scenario and we all ended up living it out."

"The rain is coming down now, softly. Do you hear it? She's blessing us again. I would love to put biplanar awareness to the ultimate test and see what your spirit cock can really do."

"Ah, the goddess is a sexual pragmatist," Jack said with a laugh.

"Of course, but let's slow down and meditate first. Let's imagine your spirit cock entering my yoni."

"And shall we call the other cock the 'earth cock'?"

"I'm still focused on the spirit cock and yoni," Jaquelyn replied. "I don't want to let the other cock enter my consciousness just now."

"Is there some reason for that?"

"Maybe the goddess is just spiritually horny. I want to feel your spirit cock separately. I like it all."

"Well, if you like it all," Jack persisted, "I'm peddling a new offering. If it please the goddess, imagine having the play of two becoming one—cocks that is. I'm offering the two cocks becoming one in you."

"That will happen when we actually make love."

"But now we're going to have a meditation in which we imagine that, right?"

"Yes, and we begin with the spirit cock and spirit yoni,: Jaquelyn reiterated. "Are you ready?"

Jack surrendered and the meditation took him deep. Finally he broke the silence. "I feel so tender right now. I'm not sure why. I see the process of our aging as simultaneous and inseparable from the expansion of Eros in our lives. We're taking the familiar attitudes about age and sexuality and—"

"—turning them upside down."

"The trust needed to do what we're doing takes my breath away."

"That trust is what it takes to co-create Third consciousness as our natural state of awareness," Jaquelyn responded firmly. "And that will finally put an end to narcissism. As love itself evolves, many more people will be drawn to explore sexuality as a frontier of their relationship rather than remaining in familiar fearful patterns. We never dreamed it could be like this ourselves. How can we expect people to believe what we're saying unless they experience it directly? What's the best way to transmit what it's like through our writing?"

"By avoiding saying 'be like us' and rather write in the spirit of 'we invite you to read this story and see what happens to you.' If our words can transmit the experience, then readers will either recognize they're already on the path or our story will inspire them to explore Eros in their own unique way."

"Our constant erotic flux from merging to differentiating and back to merging is like fantastic jazz."

"Yes," Jack agreed, "and I see now that my image of the two phalluses was not the right one to hold in our meditation or during lovemaking for that matter. It's too much of a phallic focus. As you suggested, the union of lingam and yoni in each of the two worlds is the image needed at this level of lovemaking."

"Yes, and for this kind of lovemaking you need to transform the actual substance of your engorgement into another more fluid kind of tumescence that actually pulsates and . . ." Jaquelyn paused, a touch of color rising in her face. The concrete image of a pulsating phallus had arisen before and now it had reappeared during the meditation. Sharing it, she felt vulnerable for a moment.

Jack was delighted. "I love it! Don't be shy. Keep on going. The lingam pulsates and . . ."

". . . Kegels." Jaquelyn found the word. "The pulsation leads to spontaneous Kegels."

"When we were meditating I saw myself entering you. I could feel the energy radiating from your vaginal wall. Then, you said, 'imagine that our mitochondria are doing a line dance together,' which immediately shifted my image into explicit cellular interactions. Dancing together, our mitochondria became cohesive, as if new, relational mitochondria were being created. I wondered once again if the Third was actually being realized 'in the flesh' through our lovemaking. It appears we are literally creating a new being by joining together flesh and spirit."

"That's pretty far out. Even though we're in the world in so many ways, we're also like the shaman meditating in a cave in the mountains who impacts a specific group of people who, in turn, impact other people."

"We wouldn't be where we are now were it not for those shaman of bygone years," Jack added. "Now it's time for us to leave our cave and do the gathering in Ojai."

"I had a strong image today while I was writing. I saw myself with a small group of women discussing the emerging nature of the goddess. All plant and animal life and the solid essence of the earth itself are parts of the great mother goddess. That's what men have feared throughout the patriarchy, particularly in the beginning. But now we're entering another era in which she's transforming from the mother goddess into the lover goddess—the relationship goddess. She's coming into women now, not as sovereign, but as an older sister or a loving friend to inspire us and to help heal the places in ourselves where we are afraid or unconscious. She's coming into men now as well to encourage them to make love with their women as goddesses and to carry that vision in the image-making part of their psyches. Artists can portray all this in many different ways, through music and writing—and lovemaking. I saw all that as I was writing today and realized I am learning to allow that goddess energy to come into me. I've been calling it *goddess nature*, which includes its emotional and spiritual and physical dimensions."

Jaquelyn's openness and passion activated a wave of physical sensation that started in her calves and moved up through her genitals into her heart. "The goddess is hungry for flesh," she said giving the word "flesh" an almost animalistic sound. He matched her ardor in a flash by moving onto his knees in front of the rocker. She spread her legs a little and let her robe drop away, leaving her upper thighs covered only slightly by her white chemise. How she managed to do that so quickly and gracefully always impressed him. The goddess's magic also lies in the details, he thought. Jaquelyn leaned forward a little so they arrived at the gateway to a kiss simultaneously, like two dancers who have practiced forever and now are ready for the ultimate *pas-de-deux*.

Jack approached Jaquelyn's mouth slowly and then, quite consciously, stopped a few inches away for what seemed like forever to her. They acknowledged the attraction with a silent smile of gratitude. Then her smile turned eloquently seductive: *if we don't touch immediately I will surely perish.* Slowly, Jack closed the charged distance between them, letting his lips just lightly brush hers. She groaned with delight. He resisted the urge to devour and brushed her now parted lips once again. By this time Jaquelyn was through playing that game. Her arms surrounded his shoulders and head in a single sweeping gesture that pulled him to her waiting mouth, now fully open. He matched her as they came together, creating their own intimate *little bang*, with serpentine tongues wildly dancing along with hungry lips.

The kiss lasted fully five minutes, after which they were both satisfied as if they had made love—for, indeed, they had. At the same time they felt the longing for the interpenetration they knew would follow. They talked a while longer, mostly in gratitude for the blessings of awakened bodies abandoned to love, and then moved to the bed.

They were not disappointed. The goddess sang with joy to be seen so fully, which took them further into the veil between the worlds. The songs that evening also honored the centuries of her impatience with men's—and women's—denial of her existence. Her disciples gratefully celebrated the opportunity to finally fulfill her vision of intimacy, dreamed so long ago.

34 ❧ Dawn of the "Erossic" Era

And so an event was conceived that had a fourteen month gestation period. Although the initial vision was to gather a large group of friends and family to celebrate J&J's 80ᵗʰ birthdays and a renewal of their marriage vows, it soon became clear that the broader purpose of the gathering was to celebrate the evolution of relationship itself. By the fall of 2010 the vision had matured enough to send out an invitation to a hundred close friends, colleagues and family:

> We are delighted to invite you to join with us in a *"Celebration of Relationship"* in October, 2011 . . . Just a week ago Jack turned 80 and Jaquelyn will join him in four months. As the two of us sat in council about how to celebrate this milestone with family, friends and cohorts, the idea of renewing our marriage vows kept arising. We saw a very different kind of wedding—one that celebrated elderhood, the last cycle of life, the journey through the veil and, most important, a ceremony focused on the emerging new vision of relationship rather than on us individually. We are both involved with writing about the coming era of Eros, in which we see larger numbers of people embracing relationship as a spiritual path. A core experience on this journey is the

movement of the divine from a focus on external images of gods and goddesses into the relational fabric of life itself. For us personally this transition is a culmination of our decades of work with the practices of council and *Flesh & Spirit* that we have been blessed to explore more deeply, particularly during these past few years living on the Big Island. We see the expansion of intimacy in all kinds of relationships as an integral part of the consciousness evolution occurring now, the "*Great Turning*" as Joanna Macy calls it. We have been working with Joanna's vision in our own intimate way.

This kind of celebration needs extended time to unfold— in the spirit of a Greek wedding— so we are grateful that the Ojai Foundation has offered to host the event next October in the days just before Halloween. We both recognize that having the event on the land will (among many other blessings) be an acknowledgment of the Foundation's strong influence on our personal relationship. For us, gathering in Ojai honors how the interaction of community life and intimate relationship can be at different times challenging and mutually supportive.

During the days together we envision councils with a variety of relationship themes, opportunities for couples to experience some of the *Flesh & Spirit* practices, women's and men's councils, morning dream-sharing, councils for people who want to honor previous relationships or look forward to new ones, and a stone people's lodge for those who want to pray in that traditional way. Sunday will culminate in "the wedding"—perhaps not only for the two of us, but for other couples present who are inspired to renew their vows. However it unfolds, we trust the time together will celebrate the emergence of "Third consciousness" as a direct spirit-filled experience of two equally empowered partners uniting on the path of intimacy . . .

The letter went on to give logistical particulars and was signed, "*Love, J&J*."

Naturally, sending out this message "stirred the cauldron" for J&J, just as happened in the old days whenever they were planning one of their *Flesh & Spirit* trainings. Although they had traveled the path for a long time, their commitment to "go public" meant they would have to articulate their vision of intimacy more fully. In particular— since Jaquelyn was fully engrossed in what it meant to be a vessel for the emerging evolutionary lover-goddess— one of the many questions that continued to consume her contemplative and writing times was the very different ways that men and women love each other. As usual, it was the personal version of that question that most captured her attention: *I want Jack to love me the way I love him, with that all-inclusive embodied passion and lack of self-involvement that seems so hard for most men. Is that an unreasonable request—and, if it is, so what!* Despite years of dialog about this issue and the obvious conventional wisdom that everyone loves differently—and also despite Jack's steady growth as an exuberant lover— the bar was set quite high now so the question demanded attention. Jaquelyn appreciated his efforts, but they still had the flavor of efforts and that suggested he still hadn't fully understood her call for a deeper and more "woman-like" love.

So a few days after the invitation went out by email, Jaquelyn asked for a council to address her concerns. The hour was late so they agreed to suspend their usual pattern and not make love that evening. Ojai was still almost a year away but they felt they needed to be further along the path if the celebration was to realize its full intentions.

Jaquelyn lit the candle in honor of the Ojai gathering and then posed a question. "What is 'realization' along our path and how far down that road do we need to have traveled to serve the people who gather at Ojai."

"I wonder if we dare to even talk about realization," Jack responded.

"Yes, to say the word is a little scary," Jaquelyn acknowledged. "What does it mean to you?"

"As has been noted by so many for so long, man's desire for women is inseparable from his desire for connection with spirit. In the past the patriarchal impulse has done its best to separate these two desires by creating and sustaining religions that, in part, create a wall between them. You and I— and many others— have been exploring the possibility of satisfying man's hunger for woman directly, not detouring around the challenge through an abstract god that is fearful of her. The path of realization for us means that we are ready to take this direct road, not as a reward in some far off heaven, but as an evolutionary reality in the here and now. We believe our councils and love-making can provide direct encounters with what people have called spirit or the divine. That's *our* faith. For us, all of the paradises and the dark places are part of human consciousness in the here and now— including the flesh! To be simplistic about it, along our path men's liberation depends profoundly on his relationship with the divine feminine in his Beloved. In the patriarchal era that's open uncharted ground for most men— and most women for that matter."

"That's a dream of empowerment the patriarchy can't offer," Jaquelyn added, "because the Eros vision needs full gender equality to exist at all. For me, the path of realization has to do with the divine feminine manifesting in me— particularly in my body. As this happens, I see the path more clearly. The woman teaches the man to love her at the divine level she has learned to love him with her whole body— *with her flesh*. Most men have to learn to love in that way almost from scratch. To start the journey we can ask these men, 'Why would you continue to suffer a path of evolution and a notion of the divine that is focused on the fear of women?'"

Jack picked up her thread without missing a beat. "And then we could ask, 'Why not walk a path on which the shared practices are directly life-affirming, rather than trying to transcend a punitive biblical story that starts out with original sin— that is, with a sweeping negative judgment of the human condition?' We no longer need a god to remind us incessantly that humans are capable of sinning. We see that conclusively every day. Let's put the energy where it's needed. What the old shaman called the *Large Body*—the totality of all sentient life and the earth itself— is suffering with a serious auto-immune illness called religious fundamentalism. The key to healing this condition so evolution can move forward more rapidly is embracing the divine feminine in a new and tangible way. This has been our path. Each time we make love you are surprised. In fact, what the goddess often sings about is her wonder."

"I can't believe what happens, time after time."

"Part of the wonder is you looking into the mirror of our love and seeing who you are becoming. I have the honor of helping to manifest the emerging goddess, despite your lingering doubts. We're practicing what you've preached for years— winging it and trusting our Third."

"And now we have a new ring and almost a year to plan the celebration of our marriage renewal at Ojai," Jaquelyn added gratefully.

"Whatever else it may be, the new marriage means a commitment to practice the crossing yoga together. With our new capacity to explore the veil, we can shift our consciousness anywhere between the present moment and preparing to make the crossing. Most of the time it's the familiar elder who inhabits my psyche, but the part of me newly grounded in the veil, is quite present at times, particularly when we make love and when I'm deeply listening to you."

"I see the man-of-the-veil sometimes, mostly when you're quiet."

"He speaks fewer words than the elder," Jack agreed, "and so he's more mysterious. In order for the man to become the lover of the goddess, he has to have a touch of mystery himself."

"But what is most mysterious of all is Third consciousness, even though it is becoming more accessible to us all the time. There are so many mysteries. Since you're using the word a lot lately, tell me again what 'veil' really means."

"The veil is like the indefinable edge between the light and dark parts of the moon. I'm using it metaphorically to describe that time at the end of life when we're actively preparing to make the crossing. Our growing intention is to die making love, but whether that happens literally or not, our experience of the veil should, at the very least, be erotic."

"We could commit to make love when one or both of us start to cross," Jaquelyn mused.

"That would be remarkable! As we move towards veil consciousness during lovemaking my mind opens to the deepest insights of the lover."

"How about your mind also being soft, like a vulva."

"You want me to celebrate my love for you in every way," Jack said with a big grin, "literally with every image and every breath."

"Of course! That's like showing your peacock feathers. Males in nature go to great lengths to attract the females. They even offer themselves as food for the females and progeny."

"I'm delighted to show my peacock feathers but I don't think 'feathers' does justice to what you want." (laughter)

"You're right," Jaquelyn agreed. "Tumescent feathers don't quite turn me on . . . But in the spirit of radical honesty I need to say that you've seemed distracted lately and busy. I've been feeling neglected. Maybe that's what you're calling living in the veil but to me you have been a little distant. I've had flashes of irritation."

"Yes, it's been a busy time with clients and in the community here but mostly it's about my getting used to the new consciousness that arose from the ceremony in California."

"I'm glad to hear it's mainly an adjustment."

"Mostly to having one foot in the veil," Jack explained.

"Do you want a graduation diploma when you're done?"

Jack flowed through her edge with barely any notice. "The process is ongoing, although there will be a critical mass of veil awareness sooner or later. Of course, on our path the process of realization never ends."

"Maybe not until your identity comes into alignment with who you really are," Jaquelyn proposed, "which also has to involve the flesh. Sensitivity to the body is part of what makes our path so alive! It helps me to hear that you are going through something. Then I know we will come together again in a way that is magical. Now tell me one more time how what you went through during the ceremony in California affects *us*."

"During the ceremony my journey into the veil left me feeling our relationship is inseparable from the life force itself. As a result, the way you love me with the innate wisdom of the divine feminine has become my conscious standard for love in a deeper and more expanded way than before. It's not primarily that I love the way you love me—although I do! I know in the past you were afraid that was my main attraction. Rather your goddess inspired love has become my model, purging whatever patriarchal attitudes about love remain in me. The man matures out of the old patriarchal models into seeing the divine feminine embodied in the way his woman loves him. That becomes his teacher and inspiration. Then the goddess becomes more real as she manifests in his Beloved and they both take the next step towards full lovership."

"I think I understand the distinction," Jaquelyn responded, "but I'm not sure that you do, at least at times. On the other hand, I also love the ways in which you *do* love me. You're learning and growing all the time as a lover. I know I set the standard for the kind of love that involves the flesh. Actually, it's been that way since the beginning."

"To see the divine feminine as the way you love me is to acknowledge the extraordinary presence filling you now. To actually identify the goddess as the full range and power of women's love is another way to describe relationship as a path to the divine."

"Yes, it is woman's natural potential to have her heart and sexuality—and her crown—all open and flowing in an integrated state. Men have more trouble with that integration, mostly because of the long-standing patriarchal attitudes about sexuality."

Jack nodded. "But I trust that eventually both of us will be entering a state of love that includes the body in which we can face our fears of death because we are living together in Third consciousness. That's certainly the state in which we want to make the crossing. By believing in the traditional external parent-like images of divinity, people are somewhat shielded from fear—including the fear of death— but then they're not motivated to experience the level of love *in their bodies* that can overcome that fear. As long as the divine is out there— however loving, jealous or judgmental it may be— I suspect it's harder to feel what we're feeling and do what we're doing."

"Seeing men and women as equally divine is obviously necessary for that level of trust," Jaquelyn continued the thought. "Besides the desire to pass on ownership of land to their sons and all the other justifications for male dominance and polygamy, I believe the early Hebrew leaders weren't ready to see the importance of men being monogamous because they couldn't comprehend the idea of loving all women in one Beloved."

"And so without benefit of the unbounded vulnerability in loving a woman that way, western men have practiced humility mostly through the notion of being humble before god. Hubris is an almost universally accepted spiritual danger. But when relationship becomes the path, humility is practiced— primarily in Third consciousness— through the dynamics of relationship itself, not in comparison to something external and all-powerful."

"Seeing the Third as a path to the divine and in particular the link to the divine feminine may appear to many as a big risk, to say the least. For millennia a lot of people have accepted the scriptural manifestations and descriptions of divinity, while there are relatively few of us exploring the way of Third consciousness. There will be those at Ojai who will question the reality of Third consciousness at first."

"Yes," Jack acknowledged, "and to build trust requires being committed to the practices of mutual reflection, like council and radical honesty— and from knowing the ultimate inseparability of love and sexuality. Every obstacle along the path has to be processed with great perseverance. For example, it's been very humbling for me to deal with the remnants of defensiveness in me, but the integrity of Third consciousness is at stake."

"The emerging goddess wants us to evoke her in many ways so she can experience everything. She's using us to learn about humanity. I feel she's teaching us and we're manifesting her at the same time . . . I have more questions, but I want you to hold me now. Let's get ready for bed and then move into an embrace meditation while we continue talking."

Jack readily agreed and a few minutes later Jaquelyn posed her new question. "Does what we call the mystery have shadows? The patriarchal gods certainly do."

Jack was silent for a moment. "I suppose the shadow of Eros is loveless chaos. Undoubtedly there are many who believe that without traditional religion that state of darkness would prevail."

"And ironically it's religion that has ended up creating and supporting so many loveless shadows!"

"Yes, but we can't offer any guarantees. As we've been saying, evolution itself is an experiment, and the universe will undoubtedly remain a mystery even as we understand more about it."

"And I still see that mystery as feminine, like the old images of the great mother," Jaquelyn responded. "Does the mystery have a masculine part too?"

"Those adjectives have less meaning for me now. I'm fine thinking of the mystery as the divine feminine because I'm in love with you and naming the divine that way serves you and me and the needs of evolution. The mystery doesn't have much to do with gender for me anymore. As we evolve into the *erossic* era—I've been thinking we need a new word like that to suggest the inseparability of love and sexuality— I believe that gender will gradually lose the kind of importance it's had in our patriarchal lives."

"*Erossic*. I like it! Erossic feels broader than *erotic* and the sound of it does suggest the inseparability of love and sexuality. Speaking of which, I want to hear more about how my love has become the inspiration for the way you love me."

Jack paused a moment. What else could he say? "There have been a few occasions when I've been astounded by the love I feel from you. It's as if you're showing me how a goddess loves. All I can say is that those wondrous moments set the standard for loving."

"Meaning that if you could trust my love even more, you'd be willing to expand yours as well?"

"The feeling I'm trying to convey is qualitative rather than measured in terms of more or less. I trust your love and I feel your love as an invitation for me to expand mine. When we make love, we both invite the other. We both say, 'let's see how far we can go.' The answer is usually quite far."

Jaquelyn still wasn't satisfied. "Let's go back to the related question I've been asking you forever— what is it that makes women so desirable? I feel the answer has to do with the way woman's flesh invites touching and even becomes the very source of man's desire. She has many other magnetic qualities, of course, but her flesh holds the most magic and the hidden secrets of erossic love. We're beginning to practice that magic. Do you understand what I'm saying?"

"Yes, you describe it beautifully."

"Thousands of years ago, this same magnetic quality of women was also what made men of unusual consciousness— but fearful— get together and create a sky god, a phantom spirit deity made up of their male thought-forms. Ironically, their fear of the feminine that permeates scripture confirms that they really knew women embody the secrets of life . . . Are you going to sleep?"

"No, I'm thinking about what you're saying," Jack responded in a drowsy voice.

"I thought I heard heavy breathing."

"I might have drifted."

"*Drifting along with the tumbling tumble weed . . .*" Jaquelyn sang the old tune softly. Jack held her lightly and began to stroke her hip. She stayed on topic.

"I'm still trying to figure out what is so fearful about women that would cause men to castrate themselves or go off to monasteries to have a celibate relationship with a male spirit? Why don't men understand that the women they suppress will never be able to love them in a way that would directly satisfy their spiritual longings?"

Jack was getting sleepy and didn't know how to answer her question any more clearly than he had done many times before. "You're looking for a simple answer, and there isn't one. The deep power of woman's sexuality is beyond description."

"So love can free us from the fear that has shaped the world for so long?" Jaquelyn's voice sounded angelic to him.

"That's what our life is about, and the lives of countless other people, however they describe it. When we make love and you sing you're in goddess consciousness."

"Yes, I'm actually embodying the goddess!" They had spoken of it so many times but in that moment Jaquelyn accepted what was happening in a new way. As always, he marveled at her paradoxical mixture of assuredness and innocence.

"Your way of singing is unique and magical," Jack spoke softly as he began stroking her thigh gently. "The energy in your body *is* the flow of love, just as you say. It's life affirming just to touch you, magically and mysteriously life-affirming—and there's no simple answer to your question."

They held each other quietly for a few moments until he fell asleep. She listened to him breathe in the darkness, her mind still full of questions, until she too succumbed to tiredness.

35 ✒ Ode to the Mighty Mitochondrion

Like a dry wine refreshes the pallet between main courses at a banquet, we need a short and playful piece at this point as we approach the end of our journey. The next brief story picks up on J&J's playful speculations about how their mitochondria might "dance" together when they make love. Let me first set the context.

As you know, Jaquelyn's involvement with the autism community had diminished steadily since J&J's move to the Big Island. However, her natural medical curiosity and, most important, the need for Chelsey's continued treatment, kept her in touch with recent research and biomedical protocols primarily via Internet correspondence with former colleagues. One promising example of this was the discovery of the importance of mitochondrial health in the treatment of toxicity and pathology in general, and autism in particular. As a consequence of the excitement around these discoveries, mitochondria became a frequent topic in J&J's councils to the extent that Jack decided to write a poem to honor the primal role of these tiny DNA producers in moving evolution forward. A greater focus on these remarkable components of almost all animal cells could very well be a major focus of the coming revolution in medicine.

The poem's images and words are a good example of J&J's attempts to integrate erotic intimacy and physiology, in this case micro-biology. I'll begin with the poem and then pick up J&J's conversation as it unfolded when Jack first read the ode to her.

Holding each other sharing dreams one morning long ago
You felt our Third as a tangible entity
Surrounding us in a mantle of new consciousness.
We honored the moment by calling our cuddling
The *embrace meditation*

Daily now heart to heart our rhythms find a common beat
Our bodies awaken, then forget their boundaries
And, if we manage to lie still long enough
Wrapped around each other, we disappear the illusions of
Individuality

In this state our Third becomes a healer, a modern shaman
In relational mode, ready to make the connection
To those we're called to serve even at a distance.
When healing is intimate even vast oceans can
Be spanned by strong intentions

One regular recipient, of course, is Chelsey
Now in the torrent of her teens, almost a woman
A devoted disciple of the goddess
Still in a body housing toxic tenants with
Mitochondrial mishaps

The mitochondrion's fertile folds cease their magic
When looted by mercury and other irreverent intrusions
Creating a cascade of suffering
That leaves the host weaker and mourning the loss of a
Primal source of energy

Yes, soiling of our sentient nest is poisoning our mitochondria
The special children but one stream in the deluge of diseases

Eroding the roots of human evolution.
The mitochondrion's mortality would surely sweep
Us all to obscurity

So the cry goes out to revive the ailing mitochondria
Find their favorite foods and magic medicines
To recharge their batteries
So they in turn can jump-start brains bruised and weary from
Searching for healthier lives

What links the Third and the mitochondrion's mission
That can empower love to span the seas to revive
The charismatic Chelsey as she sleeps
Innocently without an inkling's insight
To her true identity?

Long ago the goddess upped the pace of evolution
By joining simple cells with eukaryotic elders
Knowing that a billion years later
We would need flesh sexier than bacteria
To celebrate her beauty

We were only a remote twinkle in the goddess's eye
When she created the mighty mitochondrion
The original *Little Engine that Could*
And what it 'could` gave cells a vision of
Evolutionary life

Soon the cells started families and the families created clans
And the clans went tribal until finally evolution
Achieved her primal heart's intention
In the ultimately mixed blessing of
The multi-organ human

The link was relationship, for the mitochondria made
Possible beings that yearn to love and finally discover

They could co-create their wholeness together.
Thus our Third magically manifested
As a gift of the goddess

We can stem the suffering and more by joining
Mitochondrial alchemy with awakening Thirds
To start a revolution in healing
And create a new medicine to replace the old
Allopathic alliance

For when we hold each other now, merging moves beyond
Our wildest imagination, embracing light and dark
Man and woman, oppressed and dominant, death and life.
We awaken from the ills of individuality
With the healing heart of love!

"That's wonderful Sweetheart!," Jaquelyn exclaimed shaking
her head. "I don't know where you get some of those phrases. It's a
mystery to me and turns me on too. You're too much."

"As you would say, I'm not too much—just enough for you."

"You better believe it, Baby! So I have a question. What do
you think is really happening with our mitochondria when we're
making love?"

"The poem just touches on that," Jack responded, "so let's see
what comes up now . . . Give me a moment." He took a breath and
they were both silent for a while. When he spoke again, Jack's voice
took on a distinct erossic tone. "Let's start with a simple image. When
I'm inside you and certain connections begin to be made, the cells
on the outside of my cock and those on your vaginal wall begin to
intermingle—literally."

"They vibrate together."

"And as a result the mitochondria get involved in a resonating dance. In effect our mitochondria become aware of each other
and so the DNA they produce become relational. In this sense
mitochondria can be the bridge between intimacy and physiology.

Imagine that! Maybe this is one reason why we've been feeling our lovemaking has an evolutionary quality. It's subtle— and magical."

"What we do know is that the mitochondria are the beginning of self-aware life on earth," Jaquelyn responded. "They awakened the possibility of complex life being created by the coming together of two to create a new being— a new one. How else does our erossic energy affect them?"

"Without a doubt, our mitochondria hear your songs of love."

"My singing nourishes the mitochondria!"

"Indeed it does," Jack exclaimed and leapt into speculation. "As the songs build, perhaps the first layer of cells actually begin to merge and the mitochondria involved bond among themselves, creating an enhanced field that embodies our love-making. Maybe this is a way our resonating mitochondria become the source of DNA for our expanding Third. Maybe we're effectively 'fleshing out' Third consciousness when we make love. The longer we stay on the edge, the more relational awareness we manifest."

"Imagine that!" Jaquelyn said with a teasing smile. "I've been reading about medicines that are being developed to detoxify or eliminate mitochondria that are weak due to toxins and illness. How do we accomplish that on our path Dr. Zimmerman?"

Jack didn't miss a beat. "Our approach is not allopathic. Love-making awakens our mitochondria, stimulates them, detoxifies them and literally brings any that are moribund back to life. Many people's mitochondria are ailing because they're not bathed sufficiently in a field of love. That kind of medicine is powerful, like when we are inside each other."

"How do we bottle that?"

"As do others on our path— through our relationship, our writing, our healing meditations and, most of all, through our lovemaking. Every time we make love now, we add to the pool of erossic endorphins!"

"That's how lovemaking increases endorphins!" Jaquelyn shouted joyfully. "You remember! There are five things that increase endorphins— dark chocolate, acupuncture, making love, massage— and there's one more."

"We do them all except acupuncture!"

"Exercise! That's the other one."

"We get plenty of that just making love."

"Promises, promises!" Jaquelyn's familiar response left them both laughing.

36 ✍ The Celebration of Relationship at Ojai

By the summer of 2011 the focus of the Ojai gathering had fully expanded to include the evolution of intimacy in relationships generally, not only between lovers but also in relationships with community and the natural world.

Those attending the gathering included all the Ojai elders, many long-term Board members, several current staff, most of the Flesh and Spirit Trainers, core members of the council facilitators community, many close friends, key professional associates and, of course, family. Including partners, twenty-one family members spread over three generations attended the celebration, some of whom had never been to the Foundation before. On one of the days leading up to the Sunday wedding, J&J invited the family group to step into the center of the large circle and form a visible genealogical tree. Children and grandchildren from their early twenties through nearly sixty playfully arranged themselves on the beautiful wooden floor of the large circular Council House which had been a dream of the Community's since the late 1990's. Now this 'tent of meaning' was an exquisitely realized structure with hay-bale adobe walls, and a fluted living-sod roof whose internal beams and lines spoke profoundly of sacred geometry. The Council House's large French doors and high windows offer stunning views of the mountains of the Sespe wilderness to the north.

More than sixty gathered for the beginning of the celebration on the Thursday before Halloween, some arrived a day later and a few more joined the group just for the wedding on Sunday. The final affirmations of love after the ceremony were sounded by a chorus of a hundred voices. The weather was late October perfection with warm, clear days, cool evenings and rosy blessings from the mountains at sunset.

Imagine the pale greens of Southern California's mountains with large inland oaks, chaparral and sage in the foothills and valleys. Picture a ridge dotted with adobe and canvas yurts for retreatants, a large outdoor eating area and mature landscaping with a wilderness flavor. Recall that J&J had lived on the land for a while some eighteen years before and keep in mind how strongly the Foundation had influenced their lives since its conception in 1979.

The gathering also celebrated the evolutionary *Great Turning* we have spoken of often in sharing J&J's story. For this storyteller the gathering marked a leap in the recognition of Third consciousness in a world that will eventually acknowledge deep gratitude that this human capacity for relational consciousness finally has begun to blossom. As an un-embodied but extremely present witness, I felt abundant appreciation for the fervent honoring of the *Erossic Era* (as J&J like to call it now) that took place at Ojai in the fall of 2011— a whole year before the critical mass of evolutionary awareness presumably will flower more fully in 2012.

As the final chapter of our big story, I offer a brief chronicle of J&J's wedding, including their vows of eternal marriage plus a sample of the many other voices that were heard at the ceremony. Needless to say, I was very active throughout the gathering and particularly at the marriage ceremony where I was represented in the form of a simple orange meditation pillow.

Before the wedding the women met in the Council House to support Jaquelyn, dance and talk about the divine feminine, while the men gathered near the Foundation's ancestor shrine to support Jack and council about the ceremony of marriage renewal. The slow beating of two drums started the groups walking towards the "Teaching Tree," a four-hundred year-old mountain live-oak whose branches had already seen many weddings, gatherings with teachers, ceremonies and community meetings. In the embrace of its large limbs, some of which literally leaned on the ground for support, the men and women formed two moving circles that intersected each other to form a sacred *mandorla*. To the sound of the drums and a pan-flute, the men and women made silent eye-contact as they circled past each other, subtle smiles on some faces, joyous grins on others. When the mandorla had been formed, J&J joined hands and stepped into the gracefully shaped area, now strewn with flowers. They bowed to each other, arranged their meditation cushions for council and opened, as usual, by resonating with their Third, represented by a burnt-orange safu. A cordless microphone became their talking piece.

Jack: "When I was with the men, someone asked if there would be rings in the ceremony. I explained that we already had our rings and told them the brief story of their creation. Then I passed my ring around to all the men for an informal council in which they shared their love and gave me advice, including, 'you can still get out of this!' (laughter) By the time the ring came back to me, I felt totally affirmed in the knowing that I will always love you and will always be with you. When we were celebrating my 80th birthday last month, I imagined this moment with loved ones. I saw us take each other's hand, turn and face the end of life anew, as if we had just been reborn out of the sweat lodge. My first pledge is to love you in ways that we haven't yet discovered. Every time we council or make love or take a walk or have a difficulty to get through or help one other with our writing, our relationship deepens. What used to be primarily celebrated in the world of physical intimacy is expanding into other realms. Our mantra has always been, 'Can we live our whole life as if we were making love in the magic of Third consciousness?' The Third is not physically manifest in the usual sense but when we make love in Third consciousness, we actually embody it! Our love-making—all lovemaking—can be a contribution to the *All-that-Is*, as well as an ever-expanding sharing of joy for the lovers."

Jaquelyn: (After a long pause) "You are a hard act to follow but

I've been trying for 38 years and I've learned a lot from you. I feel so blessed by these four days. When we envisioned the gathering, I had no real idea of what it would turn out to be. I imagined meeting with some friends and family to celebrate our 80th birthdays and renew our vows. It's been all that and much more . . . It's been a cauldron of love. I am amazed to see someone whose hair has turned from black to snow white since I saw them last and still feel all the love between us. The many connections I've had these few days have been wondrous. Yes, I do feel we will be together eternally. Actually, I have felt that since the first time—the second time—I made love with you. The first time didn't last long enough, but you're a fast learner. (lots of laughter) I have felt the love ever since I laid the Jesus transference on you, which you've lived up to and gone beyond. It is all wondrous and I do feel we are riding an evolutionary wave that is moving fast now and is essential for the planet. I feel honored to be on the path with you, my Beloved."

Jack: "The reason I was a fast learner is that my body was inside the body of the goddess and so was being taught more about Eros in that moment than I had ever known before. When I touch you, I'm exploring the body of woman-ness. It's not just Jaquelyn's beautiful body. Your flesh takes on the vibrancy of the evolution of woman that is upon us now. The wisdom in your body is magnified by a compelling innocence that comes from your open honest sharing. Our councils are a core of our practice and so illuminating for me. I go on for a while and then in two sentences you take it all in and move the conversation to the next level. I describe the new terrain and then, once again, you take us further. One of the main harvests of this process is that you become more familiar with whom you truly are. The goddess is coming into you, into our relationship, and I'm learning to be her lover. She's telling us there's a possibility we can live the rest of our life—and beyond—on this path of deepening love. This ceremony is a prayer for that to come to pass and also that we be fully in Third consciousness when we make the crossing. We're beginning to move along the spiral between the worlds now. Each time we make love, we move a little further along that magical path. Each lovemaking is less centered in the physical world and more in that larger reality that embraces life and death. We are entering this larger world together. Our lovemaking is the bridge, as are our councils and our walks along the Cane Road. I pray that our writing will also be part of that bridge."

Jaquelyn: "I feel all of that every time we make love. Now we've also learned how to make love to support others. I used to feel sad for those who yearn for deep love and wished everyone could feel their unique version of what we have been shown. Now I know that's starting to happen. Our lovemaking is more wondrous all the time and you get more wondrous all the time. I love you with all my heart, and I always will, eternally."

Jack: "Eternally, yes, that's our prayer, which means that love will slowly change our sense of time. Being your lover has become my identity for the rest of this physical life, and beyond. When I look at you in council and feel your radiance, my love knows every cell of your being. Since I've awakened to love through the magic your body teaches me, I assume it will also teach me how to embrace the crossing. Sometimes we talk as if we're going to make the crossing in the embrace meditation or while making love or doing one of our other crossing yoga practices. These practices continue to take our breath away . . . As we embody the Third more, it becomes something tangible that others can actually feel. People relate primarily to our Third now, as Jack and Jaquelyn disappear into Third consciousness."

Jaquelyn: "We were way ahead of our time almost fifteen years ago when we wrote, *Flesh and Spirit: The Mystery of Intimate Relationship*. It's still a mystery and will remain so, but I do feel that flesh and spirit are coming together for us and many others in unique ways. Five thousand years ago, women were seen as divine—all women, not only the queens that were representing the great mother goddess. When it came time evolutionarily for men to start showing their power in religion and politics, the first thing they did was create dogma that separated those magical elements in woman that are inseparable—her spirituality and her sexuality. When I started studying the goddess religions and realized that flesh and spirit hadn't always been so falsely polarized, I went on a vendetta, which you suffered for quite a while, since the patriarchy was all your fault after all.

(laughter) But now I feel that flesh and spirit are re-uniting. They have to or we're done for. Otherwise patriarchies will continue to dominate our world, conquer and destroy even themselves in order to be 'victorious.' That has to change—and it is changing. I'm glad to be a part of the transformation."

Jack: (very slowly) "I will love you in ways I cannot imagine . . . I will love you out of time . . . Your beauty is indescribable . . . We are in an embrace meditation at this moment. We are making love with the blessings of all our dear ones, in this moment. There is a field being created by all of us, in this moment. The field is a part of the *Turning* that is happening all over the world at this time."

They held hands again, touched the Third's pillow and kissed gently. Effusive affirmations acknowledged their embrace.

Then, not knowing how many would respond, J&J invited individuals and couples of all persuasions to step into the mandorla to renew their vows or share a moment of realization with those gathered. To everyone's ongoing surprise seventeen couples arose one by one to take their place in the intersection of circles. Some had been together for decades, some were more recently married, and a few were heading towards a new marriage in mid-life. Each spoke of their connection with J&J and the ceremony in a unique way, and many made eloquent pledges of transformative love to each other. After the ceremony, one woman who had been deeply moved by the wedding ceremony described her experience:

"Jack and Jaquelyn are transcending the veil between the worlds and grounding the consciousness of sacred presence right here in our bodies. And so they become more youthful instead of aging. We all stepped into eternity during the ceremony. Our gathering has been beyond time. We are saying, 'yes' to an eternal presence in our relationships."

Finally, after seventeen couples renewed their vows, an old and dear friend arose and entered the mandorla alone to speak of an inner relationship she had nourished for many years.

"Martin and I are standing in front of the goddess who has called us. She is asking, 'Martin, will you commit to love itself?' Sacha, she asks me, 'will you commit to love itself, whatever it brings, whatever it takes to feel your deep connection as eternal?' And Martin says, 'I will commit to love itself.' And then from a pool of love I have not known before, I answer, 'I will commit to love itself.'"

She sat down to a profound silence that allowed the wild creatures of the land and the winged ones to offer their blessings. Intimate relationship had reached even into the heart of apparent aloneness and filled it with love. When she had finished and no one else came forward, Mark, another old friend experienced in the world of international relations, took the microphone spontaneously:

"How and where will what happened here go out into the world with you? Imagine our circle facing outward and say to yourself, 'I'm taking this love, I'm taking this joy, I'm taking this beauty out into the world.' Imagine where you are taking it!"

Then J&J stood again to call the gathering into a final affirmation. Those who had witnessed the long ceremony took each other's hands and formed a huge circle under the tree. Holding on to Jaquelyn with one hand and the microphone in the other, Jack found a few words with which to close the celebration:

"What starts with two people in love, then becomes many people in love, as we have seen today. When the love grows, the Thirds begin to come together and become the invisible presence we have been talking about these past few days. As someone said yesterday, the gathering Thirds become *everything*. On the evolutionary path of relationship 'the everything' includes darkness as well as light. Nothing and no one can be excluded. This circle is devoted to intimacy growing among different cultures, among differing peoples, between men and women according to their erotic persuasion, and between people and the earth. In other words, *Intimacy is a global affair*. We affirm that intimacy can grow where it has not existed before and between people that have long histories of mutual distrust. We are entering a new era of intimacy we have not known before."

Affirmations, dancing and spontaneous celebrations brought the ceremony to a close. A joyous feast followed. Such gatherings are an essential part of the evolving nature of intimacy!

Epilogue

*A*s I put down the story-teller's wand for now, the fear and despair shaping the world seem no less ominous and intense than when we began our story. Does the ongoing tide of violence mark the end game of the patriarchal era—the bloody breaking of long-held attachments that usually accompanies major historical transitions? Will the forces of change that are also very apparent and growing be powerful enough to turn the tide? When evidence of the *Great Turning* becomes visible in the midst of turmoil, it shows up brightly in contrast with the darkness . . . Hope springs eternal.

So once again I turn to J&J's story itself to answer the questions posed at the outset of our journey—the foremost of which is, *can a path of relationship be defined clearly enough for the deepening of intimacy to become a decisive evolutionary force in shaping the future?*

The sample size is small but I remain convinced that J&J—and a surprising number of other committed couples—are forging a trail through the thickets of resistance and fear that are the legacy of the patriarchal era. Since the Ojai celebration, J&J continue to move along their path—at times even at an accelerated pace. As mysterious as it remains, the awakening of Jaquelyn's "goddess-flesh" provides ongoing blessings in their daily life together. Jack is beginning to experience his own version of this transcendent experience in his own body, primarily through their lovemaking and councils. Despite some lingering unconsciousness, Jack has burned through a lot of his patriarchal self-involvement, as he has shifted his basic male perspective from the "king-warrior" to the "shaman-lover."

The emerging goddess in Jaquelyn and Jack's capacity to recognize, welcome and encourage her empowerment are real and co-arising, not only in the fire of their lovemaking—where it is unmistakable—but also in the way they share Third consciousness with their family, circle of friends, cohorts and community. Their work in Israel and Africa may have been a little ahead of the medicine, but the harvest of these efforts continues to be promising.

The way in which J&J's intimacy has become virtually inseparable from their growing relationship to nature is also encouraging, as it contributes to the reversal of the long-standing trend of the Abrahamic religions to objectify and so to violate the natural world. J&J clearly experience nature in its elemental and timeless form, not only when they make love but also increasingly in how they live their daily lives.

As you have heard, it's been a challenging journey. Nature had to wash them off "the road they traveled" and take them to the edge of life to further reveal the power of love. With time they are becoming clearer that the divine feminine inherent in the natural world and potentially in the evolving bodies of humans—particularly women—are the same presence. That mostly lost ancient teaching is now being remembered in many contemporary ways—particularly in the lives of intimates on the path of relationship and in the hearts of those who know "earth as lover."

Although there are analogies, J&J's journey continues to have little to do with traditional paths of enlightenment or realization. The only aspects of Jack and Jaquelyn individually that are in any sense unusual might be the devotion and attention with which they have nourished their relationship over the years. As I said at the outset, it is what they have touched together in their relationship that needed to be shared—most important the qualities of the divine that can arise from deep intimacy in the daily fabric of life. Experiencing the divine in this way has been the primary harvest of their hard work and service over the years. If evolution is to involve Third consciousness in the way I am convinced it must and will, then J&J's story ultimately will be just one of many that describe possibilities along the path of relationship. One of my deepest intentions is to support a human culture in which the sharing of relationship stories becomes a primary practice for both couples and singles exploring deep intimacy.

That's why I called J&J's story *an* adventure in evolutionary intimacy. We hope others will be inspired to share their stories in the spirit of empowering a new mythology of relationship. If evolution is to be a co-created phenomenon among humans and the "powers-that-be," it follows that the context for the process has to be something shared by all peoples more or less independently of their cultural, racial, religious and economic backgrounds. Clearly intimate relationships—with nature and among people—are obvious candidates to provide fertile and universal ground for the *evolutionary spring* that so many yearn for now. Touching the divine in this way is an experience that eventually can be shared in groups that develop appropriate practices (that is already happening) and eventually expand to the interactions among groups and communities."

Finally, we should ask once again, how do we describe the powers-that-be that emerge along the path of relationship? Although a certain mystery remains inherent in the question itself, after hearing J&J's story, we can offer a partial answer. At this stage of what is possible in intimacy, the powers-that-be have to do with the presence of love in the bodies and psyches of intimates traveling the path. We have growing evidence now of what some have envisioned and a few have known for a long time: *a tangible experience of the divine can be created by two humans in love.* How transformative and ultimately evolutionary such experiences will be remains to be seen, but I can't imagine a more powerful evolutionary force. So I suggest lovers continue to live these questions, along with all the others they will encounter as we pass the story-teller's wand around the circle—hopefully around many circles. I trust that those on the path eventually will share what they have been learning with groups of practitioners of all kinds, and so seed a new vision of intimacy in the mainstream culture.

Thank you for listening—and sharing your adventures with others!

Made in the USA
San Bernardino, CA
03 February 2018